CW01675014

# Cultural Atlas of the
# VIKING WORLD

*Editor and Project Manager*
Susan Kennedy
*Art Editor* Chris Munday
*Design* Adrian Hodgkins
*Picture Editor* Linda Proud
*Picture Manager* Jo Rapley
*Cartographic Manager* Olive Pearson
*Cartographic Editors* Sarah Phibbs,
Pauline Morrow
*Cartographer* Richard Watts
*Editorial Assistant* Marian Dreier
*Proofreader* Lin Thomas
*Index* Barbara James
*Production* Clive Sparling
*Typesetting* Brian Blackmore

AN ANDROMEDA BOOK
Copyright © 1994 Andromeda
Oxford Limited

Planned and produced by
Andromeda Oxford Limited
9-15 The Vineyard, Abingdon
Oxfordshire, England OX14 3PX

Published by Time-Life Books,
Amsterdam 1994

All rights reserved. No part of this book may be reproduced or utilized in any form or by any means, electronic or mechanical, including photocopying, recording, or by any information storage and retrieval systems, without the prior permission in writing of the publisher and copyright holder.

TIME-LIFE is a trademark
of Time Warner Inc., U.S.A.

ISBN 0 7054 0870 1

Origination by Eray Scan, Singapore

Printed in Spain by
Fournier Artes Gráficas, S.A., Vitoria

10 9 8 7 6 5 4 3 2 1

# Cultural Atlas of the VIKING WORLD

Colleen Batey, Helen Clarke, R. I. Page, Neil S. Price

edited by
James Graham-Campbell

TIME LIFE BOOKS

# CONTENTS



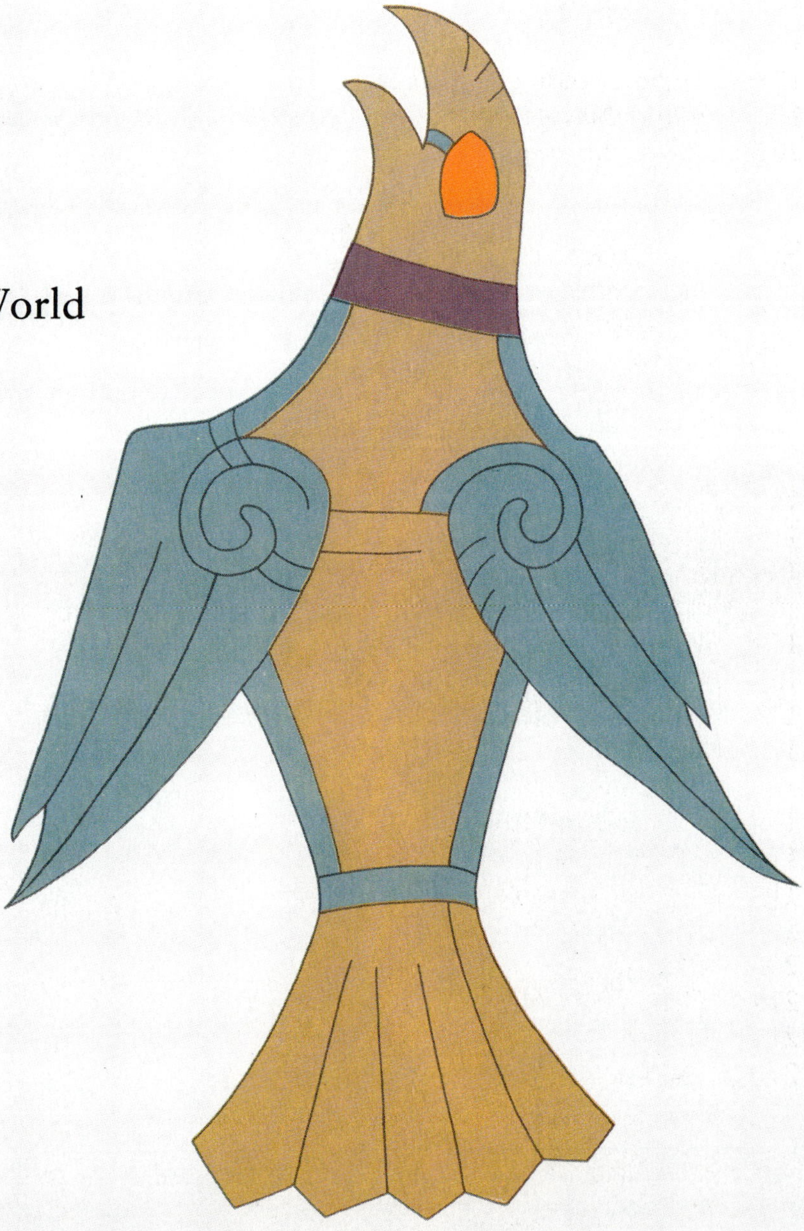

## Special Features



## Site Features



## List of Maps

# CHRONOLOGICAL TABLE

| | 700 | 800 | 850 | 900 |
|---|---|---|---|---|
| **SCANDINAVIA** | 790s Viking raids in western Europe begin | 800s Godfred, king of Denmark, in conflict with Charlemagne; builds second stage of the Danevirke and settles merchants from Reric at Hedeby<br>810 Murder of Godfred<br>c.825 Danish coinage begins in Hedeby<br>820s Ansgar's first missionary journeys to Denmark and to Birka in Sweden (829–31)<br>834 Oseberg ship burial, Norway | 850s Kings Horik the Older and the Younger permit Ansgar to build churches at Hedeby and Ribe; he revisits Birka<br>c.870–c.940 Harald Finehair, king of Norway<br>880s Harald Finehair attempts to unite Norway<br>c.890 Battle of Hafrsfjord, Norway | 948 Bishops appointed to Hedeby, Ribe and Århus, Denmark<br>c.934–60 Hakon the Good, king of Norway; attempts to convert his country |

*Picture-stone, Gotland, 8th–9th century*

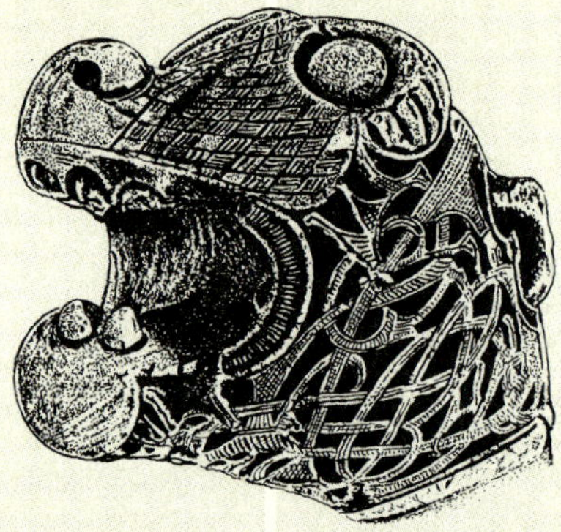

*Animal-head post, Oseberg ship-burial, c.800–850*

*Bed plank from Gokstad, c.900*

| | 700 | 800 | 850 | 900 |
|---|---|---|---|---|
| **BRITAIN AND IRELAND** | 793 Viking raid on Lindisfarne monastery<br>790s First Viking raids on Scotland and Ireland | 830s Renewed Viking raids on England<br>839 First wintering of Vikings in Ireland<br>841 Viking *longphort* established at Dublin | 850 First wintering of Vikings in England<br>860s Intensive Viking activity in England<br>866 The Great Army lands in East Anglia<br>867 Danish capture of York<br>870 Vikings kill Edmund, king of East Anglia, later St Edmund<br>c.870 Establishment of the Earldom of Orkney<br>871–99 Alfred the Great, king of Wessex<br>873–4 Viking winter camp at Repton, Derbyshire<br>876–9 Vikings settle permanently in England<br>878 Battle of Edington and Treaty of Wedmore; the partition of England | 902 Vikings expelled from Dublin<br>902–54 Anglo-Saxon recovery of the Danelaw<br>c.917 Refoundation of Viking Dublin<br>937 Battle of *Brunanburh*, England |
| **CONTINENTAL EUROPE** | 799 Viking raids begin on Frankia | 800 Coronation of the Emperor Charlemagne<br>814 Death of Charlemagne and succession of Louis the Pious<br>830s Viking raids on Frankia increase<br>834–7 Annual raids on Dorestad<br>840s First Viking winter camps established in Frankia<br>844 Viking raid on Spain<br>845 Sack of Hamburg and Paris<br>First *Danegeld* paid by the Franks | 856–7 Paris sacked by the Vikings<br>859–62 Viking expedition to Spain and into the western Mediterranean<br>861 Vikings again sack Paris<br>862 Charles the Bald builds fortified bridges to block rivers in Frankia against the Vikings<br>c.862 Rörik/Ryurik, ruler of Novgorod<br>866 Viking raid on Spain<br>c.882 Novgorod and Kiev united<br>885–6 Siege of Paris | 911 Foundation of Normandy by the Viking chieftain Rollo<br>912 Viking raiders on the Caspian Sea<br>914 Viking conquest of Brittany<br>926–33 Expansion of Normandy<br>930s Vikings expelled from Brittany |
| **NORTH ATLANTIC** | | c.800 Irish hermits in the Faeroe Islands and Iceland | c.860 Norse settlement in the Faeroe Islands<br>c.870–c.930 Norse settlement of Iceland | 930 Foundation of the Icelandic Althing |

| 950 | 1000 | 1050 | 1100 |
|---|---|---|---|
| 958/9 Gorm the Old, king of Denmark is buried at Jelling<br>958–987 Harald Bluetooth, king of Denmark<br>c.960 Harald Bluetooth converted to Christianity<br>c.964–1000 Olaf Tryggvason, king of Norway<br>968 Refortification of the Danevirke<br>c.970 Foundation of Sigtuna, Sweden<br>970/1 Mammen chamber grave, Denmark<br>c.980 Construction of the Danish circular fortresses and Ravning Enge bridge<br>c.987–1014 Svein Forkbeard, king of Denmark<br>c.995–1021/2 Olof Skötkonung, king of Sweden, converted to Christianity; establishment of bishopric at Skara<br>995 Olaf Tryggvason unites Norway | c.1000 Battle of Svöld and death of Olaf Tryggvason<br>1019–35 Cnut the Great, king of Denmark<br>1027 First stone church at Roskilde, Denmark<br>1028 Cnut encourages uprising against Olaf Haraldsson, king of Norway<br>1030 Battle of Stiklestad and death of Olaf Haraldsson, later St Olaf<br>1035–47 Magnus the Good, king of Norway<br>1042–47 Magnus unites Norway and Denmark | 1047–66 Harald Hardradi, king of Norway<br>1047–74 Svein Estridsson, king of Denmark<br>1066 Harald Hardradi invades England, defeated and killed<br>Destruction of Hedeby by the Slavs<br>1066–93 Olaf Kyrre, king of Norway<br>1070 Adam of Bremen's description of pagan temple at Uppsala<br>c.1070 Urnes stave church built, Norway<br>1086 Death of Cnut, king of Denmark, later St Cnut (1100)<br>1096–1103 Eric Ejegod, king of Denmark | 1103 Archbishopric at Lund for all Scandinavia |
| 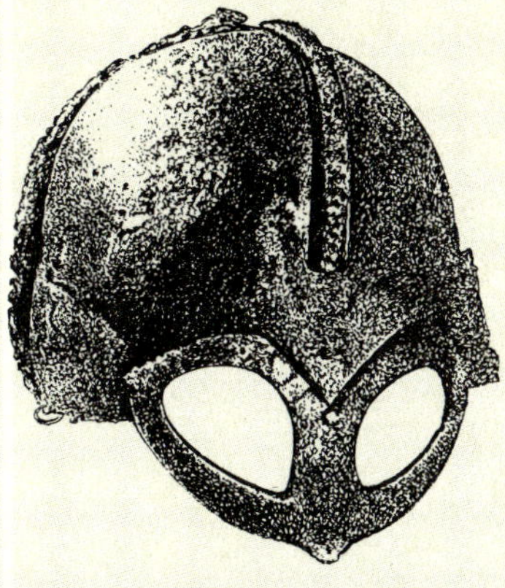<br>*Gjermundbu helmet, 10th century* | 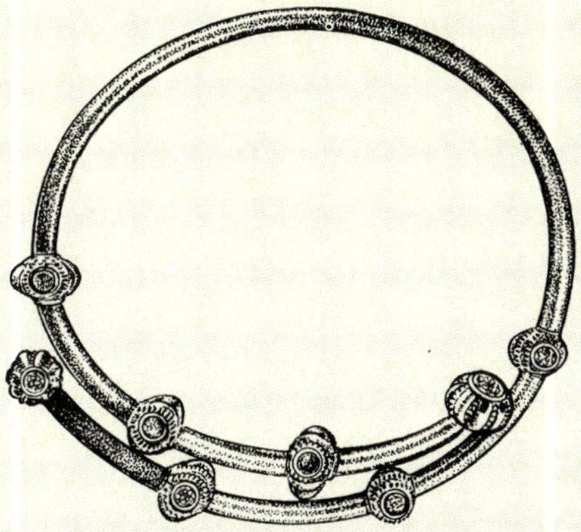<br>*Silver neck-ring, Gnezdovo hoard, 10th century* | 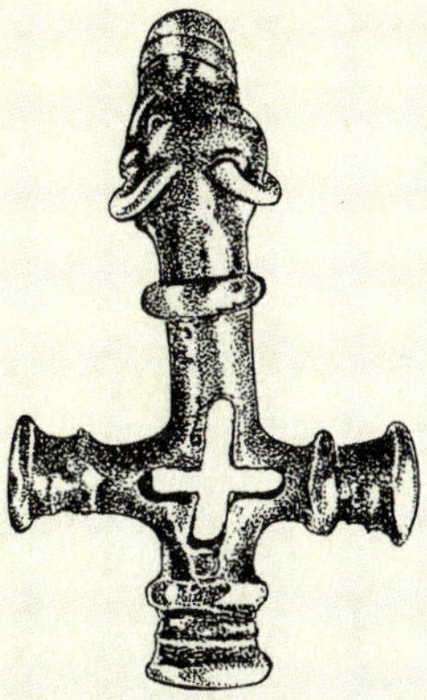<br>*Pendant cross, Iceland 10th–11th century* | <br>*Gunhild cross, walrus ivory, c.1150* |
| 954 Eric Bloodax expelled from York and killed at the battle of Stainmore<br>980 Renewed Danish attacks on England<br>Battle of Tara, Ireland<br>c.985–1014 Sigurd the Stout, earl of Orkney<br>991 Battle of Maldon, England | 1002 Æthelred orders massacre of the Danes in England<br>1014 Danish conquest of England by Svein Forkbeard<br>Battle of Clontarf, Ireland<br>1014–65 Thorfinn the Mighty, earl of Orkney<br>1016–35 Cnut the Great, king of England<br>1042 Death of Hardacnut, king of England<br>c.1050 Bishopric established in Orkney | 1066 Harald Hardradi, king of Norway, killed at the battle of Stamford Bridge, England<br>1066 Battle of Hastings: the Norman conquest of England<br>1066–87 William I, king of England<br>1069 Danish fleet attempts to conquer England<br>1079 Battle of Skyhill won by Godfred Crovan, king of Man<br>1085 Danish invasion of England prepared, but abandoned | 1103 Magnus Barelegs, king of Norway, killed during an expedition to Ireland<br>1117 Magnus, patron saint of Orkney, murdered on Egilsay |
| 980–1015 Vladimir, prince of Kiev<br>980s Conversion of Russia<br>Foundation of the Varangian guard | 1015–54 Jaroslav, prince of Kiev<br>c.1040 Ingvar's expedition to the east | 1066 Norman invasion of England<br>1091 Norman conquest of Sicily<br>1096–99 The first crusade | |
| c.985 Eric the Red settles in Greenland | c.1000 Iceland converted to Christianity<br>Thjodhild's church built at Brattahlid<br>Voyages to Vinland in North America | 1056 Creation of the first bishopric in Iceland, at Skálholt<br>1067–1148 Ari Thorgilsson, historian of Iceland | 1106 Hólar becomes second bishopric in Iceland<br>c.1125 Bishopric in Greenland, at Gardar |

# PREFACE

The Viking Age was filled with drama both in the Scandinavian homelands and in the countries overseas where the Vikings raided, traded and settled by force. However, many of the lasting changes that it brought about were the result of peaceful endeavors and gradual developments. This book is about peoples and places: a cultural atlas of a widespread northern world, centered on Denmark, Norway and Sweden, but reaching westward across the Atlantic Ocean, eastward to the shore of both the Black and the Caspian Seas, and southward into the Mediterranean. The Viking world can be seen as a network of the sea crossings and river routes that were traveled by the ships that have come to symbolize the Viking Age.

The Viking raids on western Europe began at the end of the 8th century AD when these pagan pirates fell upon undefended monasteries, settlements and trading centers for loot and tribute. The Viking Age proper had lasted scarcely three centuries before the Scandinavians had ceased to export violence to the west, even if the 12th century saw them conquering and crusading in the Slav and Baltic countries to impose Christianity there by force. It was the conversion of the Scandinavian countries to Christianity, accompanied by the establishment of a literate culture, that represents one of the major transformations of the Viking Age – a transition that involved several false-starts and piecemeal progression during the 9th to 11th centuries.

The Viking Age was also the period that saw the formation of the three European nation-states of Denmark, Norway and Sweden, as a result of processes of internal consolidation that had already commenced before the beginning of the Viking Age. Indeed, political problems at home, with enforced exile for rival claimants and dispossessed leaders, may have had as much to do with the fact of Scandinavian expansion as any threat of famine or land-shortage in the homelands – or any of the other explanations offered for this remarkable phenomenon. However, we shall never fully understand this aspect of the Viking Age, for there is very little written evidence about most of Scandinavia from before 1200, though archaeology is throwing light on state fortifications and other monuments that reflect the growing centralization of power in this period.

Scandinavia also experienced growing economic sophistication during the Viking Age, on the back of the wealth created by means of raiding and trading. One of the most obvious impacts of this process was the foundation of towns as centers for trade and manufacture. Recent archaeological work has revealed how this process was already underway, in Denmark at any rate, before the beginning of the Viking Age proper.

Though the study of contemporary sources, such as the works of Anglo-Saxon, Frankish and Arabic writers – and the runic inscriptions of Scandinavia – throws much light on the Viking Age, as can also the famous saga literature written down in the 13th and 14th centuries, it is to archaeology that we must turn to fill out our picture of life during the Viking Age. Recent decades have witnessed much increased excavation throughout the Viking world. This book has thus been written, for the most part, by archaeologists to highlight many of the most recent discoveries, particularly through the special features that complement the main text.

This Cultural Atlas is the creation of Susan Kennedy and her team at Andromeda, listed on page 2, given life by myself, but substance by a team of four authors. Chapters 1–5 that set the Scandinavian scene, both before and during the Viking Age, were written by Dr Helen Clarke, my former colleague in Medieval Archaeology at University College London, whilst Professor Ray Page, of Corpus Christi College, Cambridge, has given us the benefit of his particular expertise in contributing Chapter 6 on Scandinavian "Learning and Religion". Chapters 7 and 10, on the Vikings in western and eastern Europe, are the work of Neil Price, who studied the archaeology of the Vikings in London and York, before embarking on a fieldwork career in Sweden; Chapters 8 and 9 on the Scandinavian involvement in the Celtic west of Britain and Ireland, and the Norse expansion across the North Atlantic, were written by Dr Colleen Batey, of Glasgow Museums, who has specialized in excavating and studying the Vikings in Caithness and Orkney. The final chapter, on "The Later Viking Age and After" makes use of contributions from both of these authors. Amongst others who have helped with the production of this book, we are particularly grateful to Professor Sean McGrail, of the University of Oxford, for advice on Viking ships and for writing the feature on pp. 180–81. The features on pp. 42–43, 64–65, 90–91, 94–95, 98–99, 138–39 and 158–59 are my own responsibility, as well as the captions to the illustrations in the main text.

To end on an explanatory note: it is not possible to be completely consistent in quoting Viking name forms and words. Where there is a recognized modern form of a personal name, we have used it: e.g. Eric Bloodax. Where there is not we have tried to simplify the original form by removing inflexional endings, accent marks or diacritics and replacing unusual letter forms by more common ones: e.g. instead of the Old Norse ð and þ we have used the modern English equivalents *d*, *th*. So *Haraldr Harðráði* appears as Harald Hardradi, *Sigvatr þórðarson* as Sigvat Thordarson (Old Norse words quoted being commonly in *italic*). If there is a standard modern form of a place-name we have used it. Otherwise we have used as far as possible the local or recorded form.

*James Graham-Campbell*

PART ONE

# THE ORIGINS OF THE VIKINGS

# THE LAND, CLIMATE AND PEOPLE

The people known to us today as Vikings had their homelands in the three countries that together make up modern Scandinavia: Norway, Sweden and Denmark. Together they cover a vast area, stretching from North Cape (Nordkapp) far into the Arctic Circle at a latitude of 71° southward to the border between Denmark and Germany, at about 55° latitude. The total landmass is nearly 790,000 square kilometers. Not surprisingly, there is great diversity in landscape and climate within this enormous area. The flora and fauna, the economic base and even the character of the inhabitants vary from district to district; this is true today, and the differences must have been even more pronounced in earlier periods before the advent of modern technology and communications.

In Norway and Sweden, which together form the Scandinavian peninsula, the underlying rock is pre-Cambrian granite, overlain in the west and north by rather more recent folded and tilted rocks forming a chain of high mountains, and in the south mainly by limestone and chalk. During the period of glaciation, or ice ages, from about 1,500,000 to 13,000 years ago, massive glaciers moved southward from the Arctic regions to cover much of the northern hemisphere. At their maximum extent they reached as far as central Europe, but over the millennia their range fluctuated. Nevertheless, during all this time they covered much of the Scandinavian peninsula. As they advanced in

*Left* Northern winters are long and severe so that snow can lie for months in inland valleys and passes. It is hardly surprising that skis originated in Scandinavia in prehistoric times to maintain communications under such conditions, whilst sledges and skates are known to have been used during the Viking Age.

capital city
other important city
mountain summit (height in meters)
international boundary
meters
2000
1000
500
200
0 sea level
200
scale 1 : 7 700 000
0
200 km
0
150 mi
4°
12°
20°
28°
36°
70°
66°
62°
58°
54°
North Cape
ARCTIC OCEAN
NORWEGIAN SEA
NORTH SEA
WHITE SEA
Arctic Circle
Tromsø
Senja
Vesterålen
Hinnøy
Lofoten
Narvik
Kebnekaise 2111
KJOLEN MOUNTAINS
Torne
L Inari
Tuloma
Murmansk
Kola
RUSSIA
L Pyaozero
L Topozero
Kem
Kemi
Lule
Hornavan
Luleå
Oulu
L Oulu
Ume
L Vygozero
Pielinen
L Segozero
Gulf of Bothnia
Vaasa
Trondheim
Storsjön
SWEDEN
Sundsvall
FINLAND
Lake Onega
Jostedalsbreen
Glittertind 2470
NORWAY
Sogne Fjord
Hardanger Fjord
Bergen
Glåma
Mjøsa
Klar
Siljan
Dal
Gävle
Näsi
Päijänne
Tampere
Saimaa
Lake Ladoga
Turku
Åland
Helsinki
St Petersburg
Gulf of Finland
Drammen
Oslo
Stavanger
Mälaren
Örebro
Stockholm
Tallinn
RUSSIA
ESTONIA
Lake Peipus
Kristiansand
Skagerrak
Vänern
Vättern
Linköping
Saaremaa
Göta
Göteborg
Jönköping
Gotland
Lim Fjord
Ålborg
Kattegat
Riga
LATVIA
Jutland
Århus
W Dvina
Öland
DENMARK
Helsingborg
Karlskrona
Copenhagen
Roskilde
Odense
Malmö
Fyn
Sjælland
BALTIC SEA
LITHUANIA
Neman
Lolland
Bornholm
Vilnius
Kaliningrad
RUSSIA
Kiel
Rügen
Gdansk
Minsk
Hamburg
BELARUS
NETHERLANDS
Elbe
Vistula
Oder
GERMANY
Berlin
POLAND
Warsaw
UKRAINE

the coldest eras they flattened and smoothed out the land, and in places their weight forced it down to hundreds of meters below its original level. When they retreated during warmer phases the melting ice dropped deposits of gravels and stones that had been picked up and carried along on their advances south, and left behind moraine ridges (eskers). Thus, much of the peninsula is covered by infertile, gravelly soils poorly suited to agriculture or even forestry. The southern parts of Sweden (the modern provinces of Skåne and southern Halland) and Denmark were covered by glaciers only when they reached their maximum extent during the coldest periods, and they have fewer glacial deposits and more fertile soils with limestone and chalk overlain by clay, as well as the glacial gravels.

When the glaciers melted the land beneath was relieved of the great pressure that the weight of the ice had placed upon it, and it began to revert to its original level. This "eustatic change" or "land elevation" has been a continuing process ever since the end of the last ice age some 13,000 years ago, and is still going on, quite rapidly in the north, less so farther south. In the interior of the northern Scandinavian peninsula the land is still rising at a rate of roughly 1 meter per century. In the central regions of Norway and Sweden the change is less pronounced but the rise is some 50 centimeters over a hundred years. There is hardly any change in the height of the land in southern Scandinavia where the impact of the glaciers was not so strongly felt.

With the melting of the glaciers at the end of the last ice age the sea level also rose, its increasing height being most noticeable in southern Scandinavia where the eustatic change was less pronounced. For example, about 8000 BC Denmark was part of a single landmass that straddled the present countries of Britain, Denmark and southern Sweden. It did not acquire its present shape until several millennia later when the land between western Jutland and England was flooded by rising sea water to form the North Sea, and the straits between the Danish islands and the Øresund, the sound between Sjælland (Zealand) and Skåne (Scania), were formed.

As the glaciers melted people moved into Scandinavia to settle on the new land, traveling slowly northward as the ice retreated. Denmark, free from ice by about 13,000 BC, was occupied first, but areas farther north were not available for settlement until some millennia later. However, by about 8000 BC most of Scandinavia was open for settlement. These first settlers were probably the ancestors of those living in the region during the Viking Age (the three centuries from about AD 800).

Scandinavia has seldom been subjected to fresh waves of immigrant peoples, though it has always been open to new cultural influences from the European mainland. The exchange has not been all one way. Before and during the Viking Age there was movement of people and cultural influences from eastern Sweden into southwest Finland and around the Baltic coast (present-day Estonia, Latvia and Lithuania). In the 5th and 6th centuries AD there were population movements from the western seaboard of Denmark and (to a lesser extent) Norway to eastern England, and in the Viking Age itself migrations from western Scandinavia led to the setting up of new communities in the North Atlantic: the Faeroes, Iceland, Greenland and even America. As late as the 19th century, mass

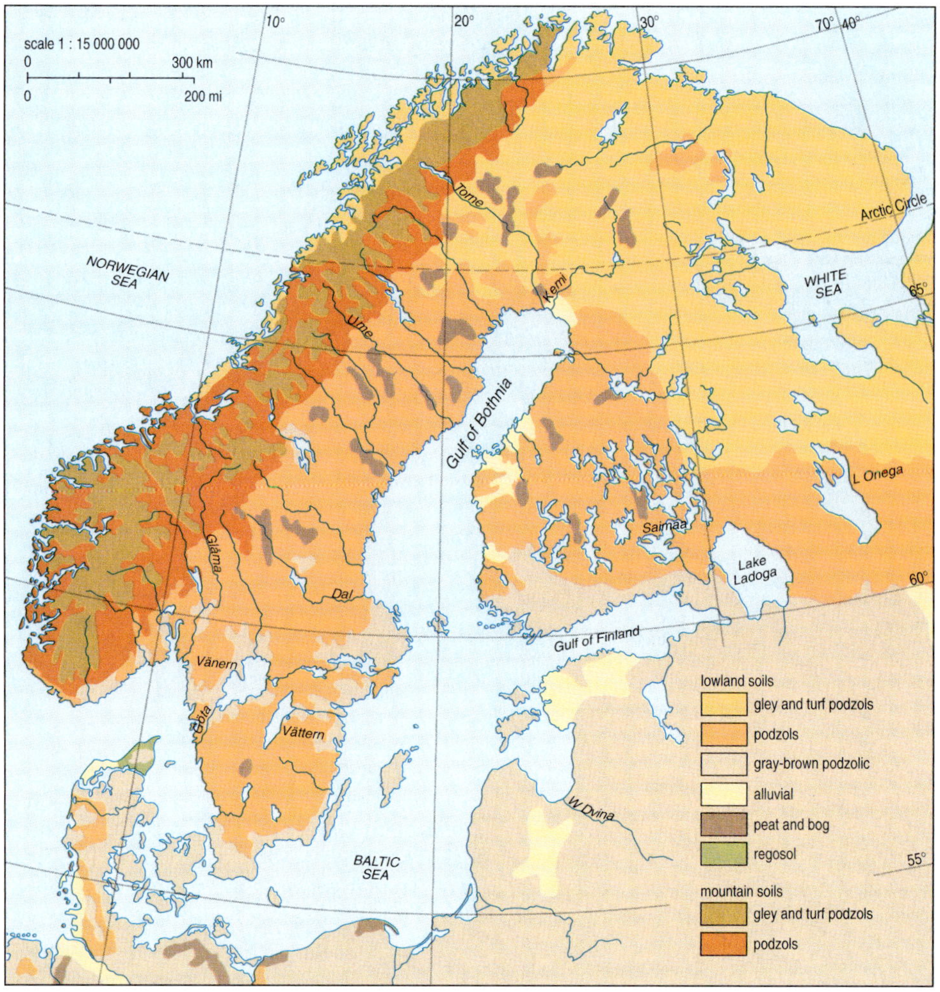

migrations led to the transplanting of Scandinavian culture to communities in the Midwest of the United States and in Canada.

Even today the Scandinavian landmass supports a population of little more than 17 million people. The highest density of population is in Denmark, by far the smallest of the three countries, where about 5 million people live in an area of something over 414,000 square kilometers. Norway, about eight times as large as Denmark, has only about 4 million inhabitants, and Sweden, more than ten times the size of Denmark, has a population of about 8 million. In the Viking Age the distribution was much the same, although there were many fewer people; they lived mainly in the southern parts of Scandinavia with an increasingly sparse and scattered settlement pattern toward the north. The Arctic and sub-Arctic regions of Norway and Sweden were, then as now, populated by the Lapps (or Saami), ethnically different from the Scandinavian peoples farther south. The Lapps kept their own essentially Stone Age culture and traditions until recent times and their natural and closest contacts were with their Lappish kinsmen in Finland and Russia rather than with their alien southern neighbors.

## Norway

Norway is distinguished by its immensely long coastline – more than 20,000 kilometers in all – which is heavily indented by long narrow fjords (flooded glacial valleys) stretching for many miles inland between steep and towering mountains. Numerous islands lie off the coast. The country's predominantly mountainous terrain has always made land travel difficult, and throughout the centuries of human

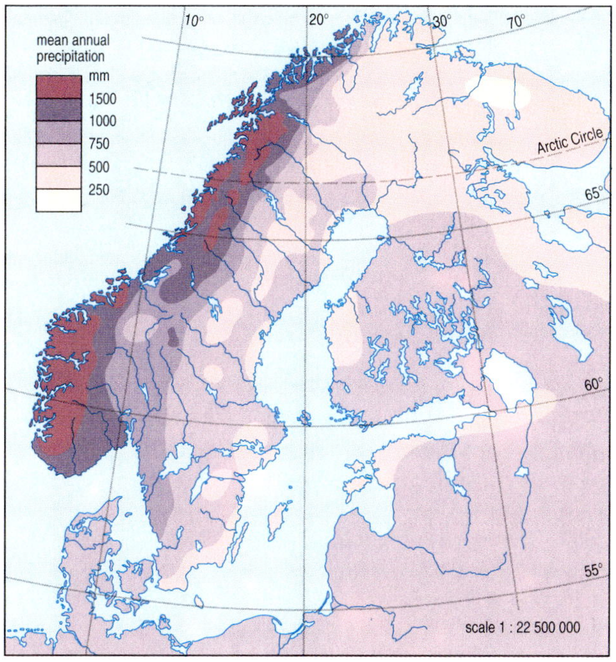


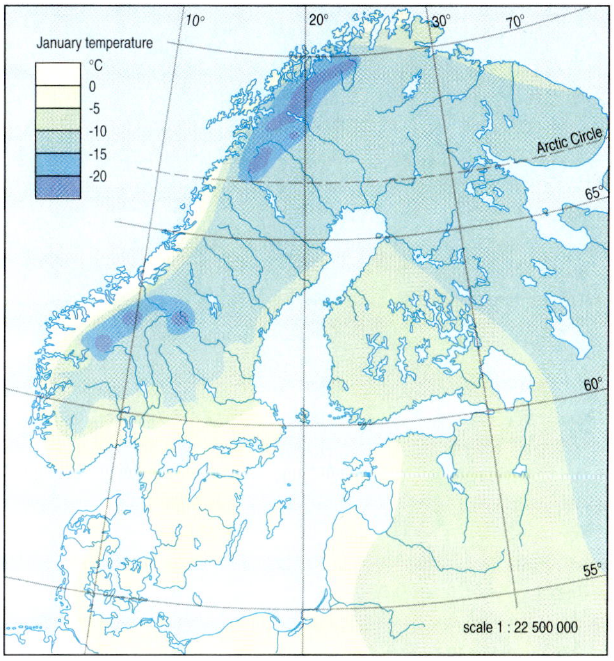


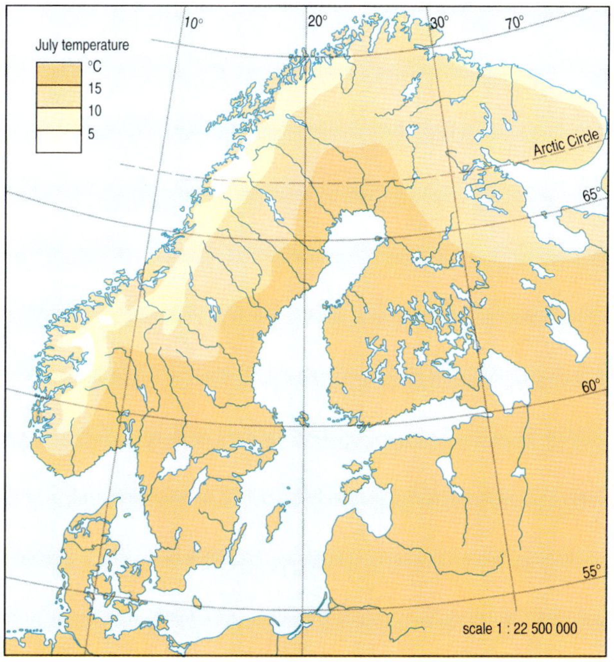


**Climate and soils of Scandinavia**
For their latitude, the countries of Scandinavia enjoy a surprisingly mild climate – the result of the moderating influence of the warm waters of the Gulf Stream, which are blown toward Scandinavia by westerly winds. Along the west coast of Norway, the mountains force the warm air to rise and drop its moisture (*right, top*). Farther east is much drier, and much of the precipitation falls in the form of snow. Influenced by the sea, the west coast has comparatively mild winters and cool summers (*right, center and bottom*); in the east, where continental influences are stronger, temperatures are more extreme with long, cold winters and short, warm summers. The mountain climates of Norway and Sweden are also harsh. The soils of the region (*left*) are generally podzolic – acidic, heavily leached and poor in quality; heavier gley and peaty soils are found in waterlogged areas.

*Below* Norway's mountainous west coast is cleft by fjords that were carved by glaciers: Sogne fjord is the largest of them all. These dramatic sea-valleys provide sheltered pockets of land for farming, whilst their usually calm waters mean that otherwise isolated settlements are readily linked by boat.

occupation communications have largely relied on the sea. Settlements were concentrated on habitable land around the fjords, and many small communities grew up in isolation from each other, each with their own traditions and culture. A sturdy independence has always characterized the fjord dwellers.

In the northern interior of Norway, winters are long and severe with temperatures well below freezing point; thick snow lies on the ground for many months of the year. Along the coast the climate is far less rigorous, with the Gulf Stream keeping harbors as far north as Narvik free from ice throughout the winter. The climate therefore also encouraged coastal settlement, with fishing and whaling being the main means of livelihood. Livestock (housed indoors during winter) can be kept in the climatic conditions of coastal western and northern Norway, and cattle, sheep, goats and horses were and are bred for meat, milk, cheese and transportation. Though relatively mild temperatures along the coast allow the cultivation of fruit trees and some other crops where soil conditions allow, crop-raising has never been of very great account in the country as a whole and even today only about 3 per cent of the land is devoted to arable farming, mainly in the south and east.

Fish from the rich coastal fishing-grounds of the North Atlantic and Arctic oceans has remained a staple of the Norwegian diet up to the present day, supplemented in earlier times with seabirds, found in abundance along the coast, and their eggs. Up to the end of the Middle Ages dried fish was the country's most important export commodity. Sea mammals such as seals and walrus were trapped for their skins, and, in the case of walrus, ivory.

Norway is not heavily forested, as much of it lies at heights above the tree-line, but what woodland there is consists of coniferous forest of fir, pine and spruce. Deciduous trees such as oak, ash and beech grow in the south interspersed with conifers, and probably never formed a very dominant feature of the vegetation. The far north is covered by tundra – a bleak, open terrain of permanently frozen ground, supporting little vegetation, with taiga (coniferous forest), a little farther south. Reindeer, elk and bear, together with smaller fur-bearing animals such as Arctic fox, marten, lynx and squirrel, are found in these northern regions, and all have been hunted through the ages for food, as well as for their fur or antlers. In the Viking Age these raw materials were traded in exchange for luxuries obtainable only from the more southerly and industrially advanced countries of mainland Europe.

### Sweden

Sweden has a total length of about 1,500 kilometers from north to south. Along its eastern border it shares the mountainous terrain of Norway but most of the country is less than 500 meters above sea level with low, undulating countryside, clothed in coniferous forest, being the norm. There are numerous freshwater lakes and many navigable rivers, which have served as arteries for waterborne traffic over the centuries. An open landscape of tundra is found in the far north.

The lowest and flattest land lies in three distinct areas in central and southern Sweden: around Lake Vänern in the west where there is the fertile plain of Västergötland and the river valley of the Göta; in the east centered on the great lakes of Hjälmaren and Mälaren and bounded to the south by the plain of

*Above* The coniferous forests of Norway and Sweden provide the natural habitat for fur-bearing animals that were hunted for their winter coats. Furs were traded by Viking merchants to the east and west in return for other luxury goods, such as silks and wine.

**Vegetation of Scandinavia** *(top right)*
Deciduous forest is the natural vegetation of much of Denmark and southern Sweden, gradually giving way to mixed woodlands. Unbroken coniferous forest (taiga) covers nearly all the rest of the region. Tundra – a treeless vegetation of grasses and lowgrowing shrubs – is found in the permafrost areas of the far north and in mountainous areas above the treeline and below the permanent snowline.

*Right* Inland lakes and waterways were important for communication during the Viking Age in Sweden, whether by boat in summer or over the ice in winter: Lake Siljan, shown here, lies in Dalarna, an important area for iron extraction.

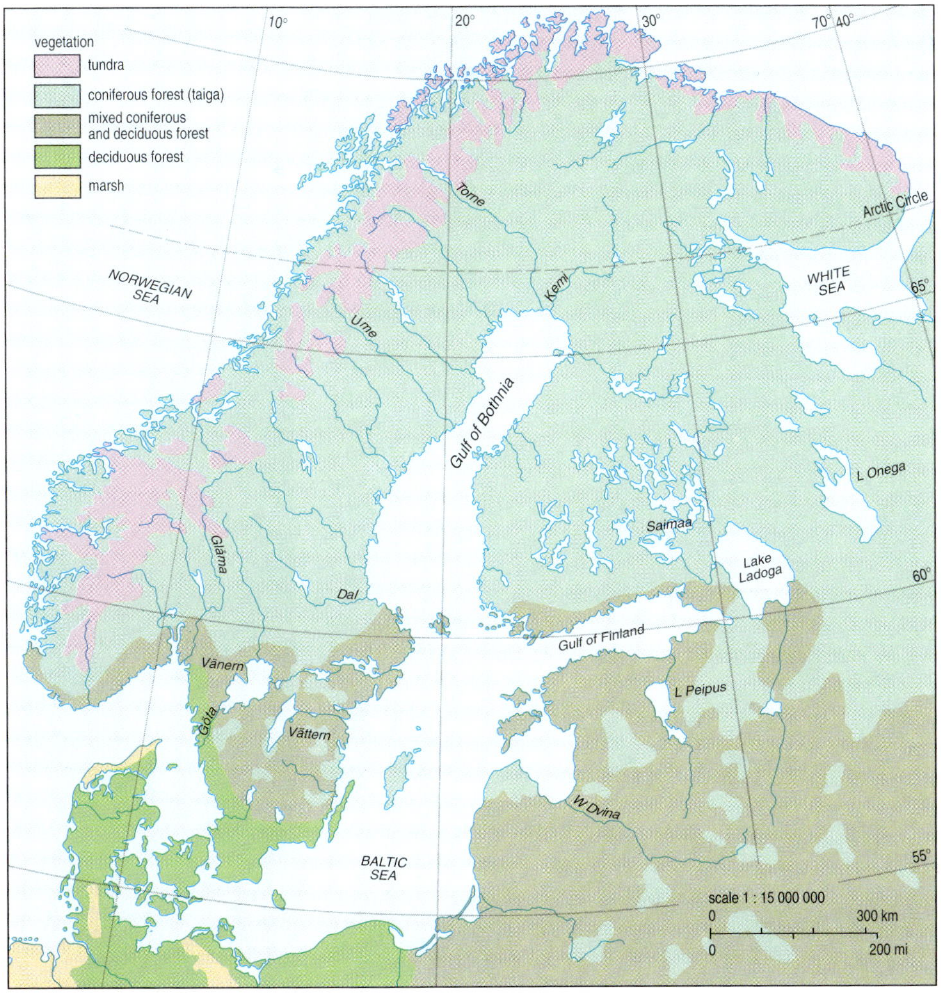


Östergötland and to the north by Dalälven; and in the south where the flat lands of Skåne and Halland have many of the characteristics of neighboring Denmark. These areas, which naturally support deciduous woodland mainly of oak, birch and beech, are the fertile, crop-growing regions of Sweden.

Until the 17th century, Skåne was virtually cut off from the land to the north by the dense woodlands of Småland. Until this time it was actually part of the kingdom of Denmark, and its contacts and influences derived from the south and west, the continental mainland. The plain of Västergötland was surrounded by forest, except on the west where it was connected with the coast through the valley of the Göta, and its contacts were largely westerly, with Denmark and Norway and to the North Sea and beyond. The Mälaren region formed another distinct unit with contacts mainly eastward and southeast across the Baltic and northward along the moraine ridges that penetrated into the forests of the north and carried some land transport. This has always been the richest area of Sweden and it was here that the Swedish state began to emerge as a consolidated power in the centuries just before the Viking Age.

Finally, the two Baltic islands of Öland and Gotland differ from the rest of the country in their maritime situation and their geological makeup. Both are limestone formations with shallow but fertile soils, temperate climates and good potential for both pastoral farming and crop-raising. Gotland lies almost as close to the lands of the eastern and southern Baltic as to Sweden itself, and its strategic position in the middle of the Baltic Sea led to it acquiring control of trade routes over the centuries, and the consequent

accumulation of wealth. In the Viking Age and into the Middle Ages it was virtually independent of the Swedish mainland.

Sweden's environment afforded the same natural resources as Norway's. Wild animals in the north were trapped for meat and fur; seabirds and fish (but fewer sea mammals) were caught along the coasts; its forests and woodlands provided softwoods and hardwoods for building and many other purposes. Sweden also has abundant sources of iron ore which were exploited in ever increasing amounts up to recent times; copper was first mined in the Middle Ages. Though by no means densely populated, Sweden has always been able to support a greater population than has its Norwegian neighbor.

### Denmark

Denmark belongs to the same geological formation as southern Sweden and the flat lands bordering the south coast of the Baltic Sea. It is low-lying – its highest point is only 173 meters above sea level – with a long coastline in comparison to its landmass, which is made up of the Jutland peninsula and hundreds of large and small islands. Today, Denmark has wide expanses of arable fields and very little tree cover. This landscape is, however, mainly a product of the past 200 years, during which time bogs have been drained, heaths reclaimed, and woodlands cut down to make way for farmland. Until the end of the Middle Ages much of Denmark was covered with deciduous trees. Water-meadows, marshes and bogs flanked its numerous streams and surrounded the lakes, most of which have long since been drained.

Denmark's climate is more temperate and equable than the rest of Scandinavia, and this is reflected in its flora and fauna; it lacks the fur-bearing mammals that brought wealth to its more northerly neighbors in earlier periods. Agriculture has long provided its economic base; arable crops could be grown on its drier soils and livestock reared on the lush grass of its water-meadows. Fish and wildfowl came from the sea and from inland watercourses.

Like Norway and Sweden, Denmark is divided into a number of regions. The largest of these is the Jutland peninsula, physically connected to the European mainland. Throughout history, cultural innovations from northwest Europe reached Jutland first, and from there were disseminated to the rest of the country, and then to Norway and Sweden, often after a considerable lapse of time. In most periods it has been the richest part of Denmark; it was not by chance that Jutland became the main center of royal power when Denmark finally emerged as a unified state in the 10th century.

The Danish islands, particularly the largest, Fyn and Sjælland, have distinct characters. In earlier periods, they had their own systems of chieftainship. The easternmost parts of Denmark had closer cultural contacts with the peoples around the Baltic Sea than with those of northwest Europe, and many Slavic

*Left* The Jutland peninsula connects lowlying Denmark to the European mainland: its western beaches, unlike Norway's mainly sheltered coastline, are exposed to the full force of the sea, but this was not a deterrent to Viking Age sailors, whether raiders or merchants.

*Above* The landscape of central Finland is characterized by coniferous forest and innumerable lakes. Whilst Finland is the most easterly of the Nordic countries and its people are not of Scandinavian stock, its western and southern coasts came under the influence of Sweden and Gotland during the Viking Age.

*Overleaf* The Lofoten islands lie toward the northern end of Norway's Atlantic seaboard; despite their northerly situation, they are kept mild and damp by the Gulf Stream, and have been inhabited by fishing communities from early times. Norway's island-shielded and fjord-indented west coast provided a searoute from the south and thus gave rise to the country's name, the "North-way".

traits – for example, in pottery types and methods of shipbuilding – are evident there in Viking times. The island of Bornholm is different yet again, more akin to the Swedish islands of Gotland and Öland than to Denmark proper. It lies far out in the south Baltic Sea, some 140 kilometers east of the east coast of Sjælland where Copenhagen, Denmark's modern capital, lies. It is thus something of an anomaly in an otherwise fairly tight-knit country. However, it lies only 30 kilometers off the coast of Skåne, which – with Halland – was a Danish possession until the 17th century. Unlike those two provinces, Bornholm remained politically affiliated to Denmark, if never entirely culturally so.

### Finland

Finland, on the other side of the Gulf of Bothnia from Sweden, was not a Viking homeland. Its people are not of Scandinavian stock: the Finnish language, belonging to the Finno-Ugrian group of languages, is closely associated with Estonian, spoken on the south coast of the Gulf of Finland, and is more distantly related to Hungarian and Turkish. However, southwest Finland was strongly influenced by Sweden particularly in the Viking Age. Many Viking traits such as art styles, types of jewelry and weapons can be traced here from the 9th century onward, and for this reason Finland is considered here as a Viking country.

Geologically, Finland is very similar to central and northern Sweden, though it has no mountain ranges. It was heavily glaciated during the ice ages, and most of the land is covered with gravelly soil that is ill-suited to agriculture. In the far north there is open tundra, and farther south coniferous forest interspersed with innumerable lakes characterizes the landscape. The Finnish landmass is somewhat larger than Norway, about 363,000 square kilometers. The Arctic and sub-Arctic north is still occupied by Lapps belonging to the same cultural group as those of northern Norway, Sweden and Russia, but most of the Finnish population, which today numbers about 5 million, live along the western and southern coasts. This area was both visited by and partly occupied by Swedish Vikings, and it is mainly there that the archaeological remains of Viking Age settlement are to be found. Finland subsequently became part of the medieval kingdom of Sweden and remained a Swedish possession until the 19th century.

# SCANDINAVIA BEFORE THE VIKINGS

*Left* Ceremonial flint ax-heads form a votive offering at Hagelbjerggård, Sjælland, Denmark, reflecting the important role played by the stone ax in Neolithic society – over and above its fundamental use as a work tool for land clearance.

*Right* The stone-lined entrance to a large "passage-grave" mound at Gillhög, Skåne, Sweden: passage graves were used by Neolithic farming communities for depositing bones from skeletons that had previously been exposed.

*Right* The Bronze Age rock carvings of Scandinavia, such as this group from Bohuslän in western Sweden, provide mysterious testimony to cult activity. They portray men, animals, ships, weapons and various symbols, the most common of which are the "cup-marks" – shallow, round hollows chiseled out of the rock face, either in groups by themselves, or in association with other carvings.

The first Scandinavians were an itinerant people, gaining their livelihood from hunting, fishing and gathering wild plants for food. Their settlements were temporary encampments, mainly situated along the coasts, on the banks of rivers, and on the shores of lakes to take advantage of their food resources – fish, shellfish, marine mammals and seabirds, and the animals that roamed the countryside nearby. They moved their camps in pursuit of game, and so left few remains apart from their tools and weapons, made from flint and other stone, and a few burials of individuals who were interred beside the encampments. This migratory and widely scattered type of existence continued for about 4,000 years and is known to archaeologists as the Mesolithic or Middle Stone Age.

### The Neolithic revolution

A very great change took place about 4000 BC in southern Scandinavia, when the growing of crops and raising of cattle began to supersede hunting as the main means of support. This change ushered in the next great age of prehistory, the Neolithic or New Stone Age, which lasted for over 2,000 years. The new method of subsistence came to Scandinavia from the south and may have been introduced by bands of immigrants from continental Europe. It is unlikely, though, that there was largescale immigration, and the native population remained the same as the hunters of the previous period.

Once agriculture was adopted, the form of settlement changed. People occupied their homes for longer periods, cultivating the adjacent land that had been reclaimed from the primeval forest. But even these settlements would not have been occupied for very many years, for the surrounding fields would soon have become unproductive from over-use and the lack of fertilization, and the inhabitants would then have moved to a new site where more new land could be cleared and crop-raising begin anew. These semi-permanent settlements remained small, consisting only of a few buildings to house not much more than a family group, and they were scattered sparsely throughout the countryside, taking the form of isolated farmsteads rather than villages. Nevertheless, the burial customs of these early farming peoples show that they had some idea of communal identity. They were buried in large and elaborate grave-monuments built above ground from enormous stones, known as megaliths (as a consequence of which these structures are termed megalithic tombs). They consisted of a huge central chamber tall enough for someone to stand erect, and a passage leading from it. The whole was covered by a mound of earth encircled by a ring of smaller, upright stones around the edge. Remains of pottery vessels found within and around the entrance to these tombs, which accommodated many individual corpses, indicate that the burial of a body was accompanied by elaborate rituals involving feasting, and perhaps sacrifice, demanding the participation of the inhabitants over a wide area, for whom the communal tomb provided a focus. Society as we understand it today was starting to evolve.

These early farming communities are best known from southern Scandinavia (Denmark, south Sweden and southeast Norway). Not only was the climate milder here, but they came earliest into contact with the new cultural and technological impulses spreading northward from the European mainland. In the forests and tundra farther north, hunting, fishing and food-gathering remained the primary means of livelihood, and changes in economy and culture took place much more slowly. Nevertheless, some tools and weapons found in the north are of southern origin and show that there were contacts between the two regions.

Neolithic farmers used more diverse tools and weapons than did their hunting forebears, but these were still made of locally occurring natural materials. Flint and other stones were shaped into ax-heads, which were fastened to wooden handles and used to fell trees to clear the land. Sharp flint flakes were fashioned into the cutting-edges of sickles for harvesting crops. Arrow-heads used in hunting were also made of flint. As time went on the shapes of some of the implements, particularly weapons, evolved into highly elaborate forms that must have demanded great skill in their manufacture. Battle-axes of polished stone and daggers of flint attest to the sophistication that could be achieved by the craftsmen who worked in these apparently intractable materials. It was not until the end of the Neolithic Age, in the second millennium BC, that stone and flint began to be replaced by bronze for some simple weapons such as flat axes and daggers. This change marked the transition to the Bronze Age.

## The Bronze Age

Bronze is an alloy of copper and tin. Both these metals had to be imported into Scandinavia from central and western Europe in the prehistoric period. The use of bronze must have marked a pronounced change in the economy of early Scandinavia, drawing it into a wider network of cultural contacts and making it more open to influences from outside.

The Bronze Age began in Denmark about 1800 BC and lasted for over a thousand years. Its culture penetrated the northern parts of the Scandinavian peninsula much more slowly, though discoveries of bronze objects of uniform type throughout Scandinavia show that there were contacts between north and south, as there had been in earlier periods. In the Bronze Age these contacts were apparently fostered by trade: raw materials, perhaps mainly hides and furs, were exchanged for copper and tin to make bronze locally, or for manufactured bronze weapons such as swords and axes which were imported from central Europe and the British Isles.

Most of our information for the Bronze Age in Scandinavia comes from burials or from the hoards of objects in bronze and precious metals that were buried or deposited, probably as religious votive offerings, in bogs, swamps, rivers and lakes. Many graves have been excavated from this period. Individuals were buried under mounds of earth (barrows) or piles of stone (cairns). Some of the mounds in Denmark and southern Sweden were huge, still standing today up to 3 or 4 meters in height, and were situated on high ground so that they dominated the landscape for miles around. Cremation, with the burnt bones placed in pottery vessels beneath the mounds, was common in the later centuries of the Bronze Age but in earlier phases inhumation (burial of the unburnt body) was predominant. These graves have much to tell us.

Denmark is particularly rich in the remains of Bronze Age inhumation graves. In some, the hollowed-out trunks of oak trees were used as coffins to enclose the corpse, which was buried fully clothed and accompanied by possessions including items of personal hygiene such as razors and tweezers. In some cases, damp soil conditions have preserved the woolen garments of the deceased, and from these we have learned that men wore belted tunics covered by cloaks, and simple headgear. Women wore two-piece costumes and their hair was covered by an elaborate net or bonnet. Thus we get a vivid glimpse of how some of the people who lived in Scandinavia in these distant times must have looked.

Remarkably little is known about settlement sites in the Bronze Age, but what little evidence there is suggests that the people at this time were basically farmers who lived in long, rectangular farmhouses with a cattle byre or barn at one end. Some farmsteads were grouped together into small villages. Pottery vessels, commonly used for storage and for preparing food, were probably made by the women on the farmsteads for their own use. At first farming implements continued to be made of stone and flint, with bronze being reserved for weapons or decorative objects of status or display. By the end of the Bronze Age, however – toward the middle of the first millennium BC – bronze was being used for all implements including the blades of sickles used for harvesting crops.

Many of these bronze tools were probably made by local craftsmen–farmers, but there must also have been specialist metalworkers to make the more elaborate objects that are most often found as votive offerings in bogs. They include trumpetlike musical instruments known as lurs, which consisted of a tube, mouthpiece and flat "bell"; pictures of lurs found on Swedish rock carvings suggest they were used at ritual ceremonies. Intricately decorated helmets, shields, bronze and gold bowls and female jewelry have also been found, indicating that the Bronze Age was a period of great wealth over much of southern Scandinavia. Bronze Age society seems to have been dominated by a rich and powerful chieftain class. Splendid grave-goods of both bronze and gold concentrated in a few male graves suggest that the men interred there belonged to a ruling class, and the presence of a single very large farm in a village of otherwise smaller dwellings may also indicate some form of internal hierarchy. It has also been suggested that the votive deposits of the Bronze Age were manifestations of chieftainship: the rich and powerful placated the local god or spirit who inhabited the place with a splendid offering and at the same time secured their position over their rivals with a display of conspicuous waste.

## The Iron Age: the roots of the Viking Age

About the middle of the first millennium BC a further technological revolution took place, when iron replaced bronze as the material for most tools and weapons. The idea of using iron was, like the use of bronze, introduced from central Europe, but the metal itself did not need to be imported. Abundant sources of iron ore lay close at hand and easily obtainable on the beds of the lakes in central and southern Norway and Sweden and in Denmark. Known as bog-ore or lake-ore, these deposits could be raked up very simply without having to be mined. The ore itself is not of high quality and contains many impurities, but the Scandinavians soon learned to extract serviceable iron from it by smelting it in simple furnaces. At first the tools and weapons made by the early Iron Age blacksmiths were few and simple, but the skills and repertoire of the Scandinavian craftsmen increased over the centuries until their products were on a par with any made elsewhere in Europe.

The Iron Age in Scandinavia lasted for about 1,500 years, and has been divided by archaeologists into a number of distinct chronological phases. The Early Iron Age (also called the Celtic Iron Age or the pre-Roman Iron Age) spans the first 500 years of the period. The Roman Iron Age denotes the time when the Roman empire dominated the European mainland (from the 1st to the 4th century AD) and influenced Scandinavian culture, even though Scandinavia itself never formed part of the empire. The 5th and 6th centuries are known as the Migration Period (referring to the mass migrations of peoples from east to west across Europe); in Denmark this period is also called

*Above* An oak coffin has preserved the fully-clothed body of a young woman (about 18–20 years old), from the Early Bronze Age, at Egtved, Jutland, Denmark. She was wearing a string skirt and a shirt with elbow-length sleeves. Her body had been placed on a cowhide and covered by a blanket before the coffin was closed.

the Early Germanic Iron Age. The 7th and early 8th centuries are variously known as the Vendel Period (in Sweden), the Merovingian Period (in Norway), or the Late Germanic Iron Age (in Denmark). Then follows the Viking Age, the beginning of which is usually placed about 800. The end roughly coincides with the adoption of Christianity into Scandinavia – during the second half of the 10th century in Denmark, somewhat later in Norway and Sweden.

### The Early Iron Age (5th–1st centuries BC)

The first five centuries of the Iron Age in Scandinavia remain comparatively obscure, for very few settlements are known from this period. Farming must still have been the economic mainstay, but evidence of a deterioration in climate since the last centuries of the Bronze Age suggests that productivity may have declined. Grøntoft, a rural settlement in western Jutland dating from about 200 BC, throws some light on these early Iron Age farmers, who must have lived in buildings very similar to those of their Bronze Age predecessors, grouped in villages surrounded by fences. Grøntoft probably housed about 50 people and about 60 cattle, but it is difficult to know whether this was an average-sized community for the time.

There are, however, signs that rural settlements were increasing in number and size toward the end of the Early Iron Age. Once again, the evidence comes mainly from Denmark where a number of settlement sites occupied during this period have recently been extensively excavated. Hodde, Jutland, is typical of the 1st-century BC rural settlements found in that area and has many traits that are present in Danish villages right up to the beginning of the Viking Age. At its greatest extent Hodde consisted of 27 farmsteads, each composed of a longhouse with dwelling and cattle-byre under the same roof and a couple of smaller subsidiary buildings, perhaps barns or workshops. Each building-complex was surrounded by a fence, and the entire village was enclosed by a common fence pierced by gateways affording direct access from each farmstead to its fields. There was an open area (a "village green" or "village square") in the center of the settlement. One of the farmsteads was much larger than its companions and may have housed the village chieftain, his family and retainers. Blacksmithing, pottery making, weaving and spinning were common activities, but the basis of village life was cattle breeding and crop-raising, following the traditions of the Bronze Age, but on a larger scale.

*Below* A reconstruction of an Early Iron Age farm, comprising a typical three-aisled longhouse, together with its subsidiary buildings, standing within a fenced enclosure. The farm is to be seen at the Historical Archaeological Experimental Center at Lejre, outside Copenhagen.

# Bog Sacrifice

We can today only guess at the reasons why in Scandinavia from the Neolithic period onwards right through the pre-Viking period the bodies of humans and animals, as well as a variety of artifacts including weapons and even warships, were thrown into bogs, lakes and streams. But we can be fairly certain that they were placed there as votive offerings or sacrifices to the gods. From the number of depositions that have been recovered, often in the course of draining land for farming, it is clear that the practice was very widespread. The different nature of the objects jettisoned suggests that the offerings were made, perhaps accompanied by ritual prayers, to obtain a particular end – such as an abundant harvest, or fertility in men, women and animals, or success in battle.

The earliest depositions, made in the Neolithic period, consisted mainly of stone and flint weapons. In the Bronze Age more elaborate sacrifices were made. Collections of personal and household objects such as cauldrons were deposited, possibly to commemorate the passing of a great or powerful individual. Bronze weapons, particularly swords, were also sacrificed. Very often the blades had first been bent back on themselves or otherwise damaged, and it is argued that this was done to represent a ritual "killing" of an enemy. Animals, particularly horses, were also slaughtered as part of the ritual. Human sacrifice seems to have become widespread in the 1st century BC: most of our evidence for this practice comes from Denmark where the bodies of the men and women killed in this way have been preserved in the acid soils of peat bogs. The Roman Iron Age and the Migration Period saw a return to predominantly weapon sacrifices.

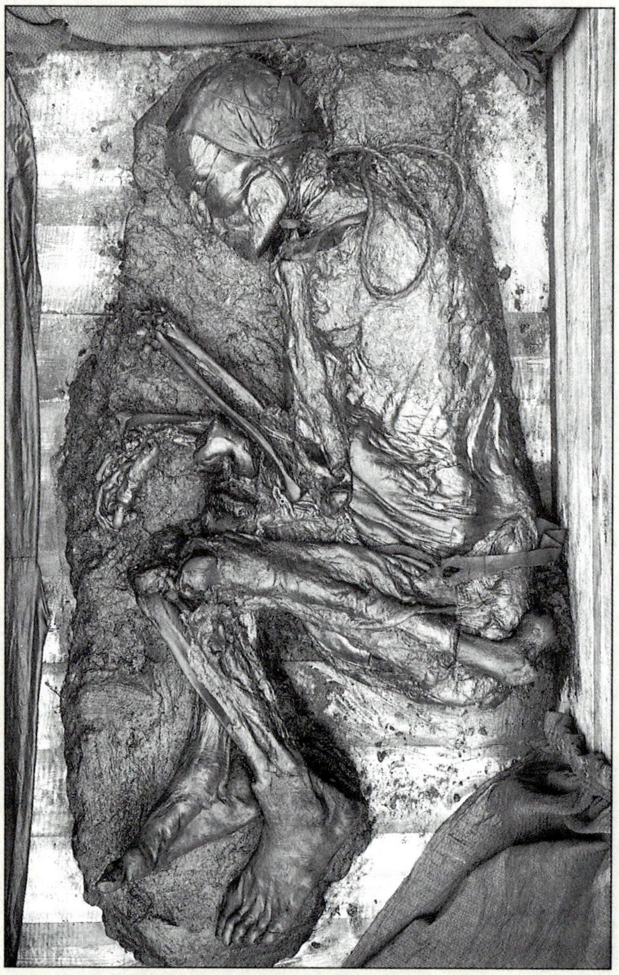

*Above* Bronze objects, from about 500 BC, found at Hassle, Närke province, Sweden, must once have belonged to a Bronze Age chieftain of that area. The bronze cauldron, which contained all the other finds, was made in Greece; the ribbed cylindrical buckets, the swords (which had been bent) and the roundels (originally from a chariot) were manufactured in northern Italy or the Alps.

*Top left* Tollund Man, now displayed in the Silkeborg Museum, Denmark, was hanged by a hide rope before being submerged in a bog. He had eaten what may have been a sacrificial meal of gruel, and was clothed only in a leather cap laced around his chin, and a leather girdle. He had a day's growth of stubble on his chin.

*Left* The Nydam ship, which dates from the 4th century AD. Built of oak, it is almost 23 meters long, and is the precursor of the great ships of the Viking Age. It was found in a bog in Denmark together with two smaller boats and a large number of iron weapons.

Other sites in Jutland show that alongside such villages there were also smaller agricultural settlements with only two or three farms, but we do not know why there were such great variations in the scale of settlement in the Danish countryside.

The practice of making votive offerings and sacrifices in bogs and lakes continued throughout the Iron Age. By far the greater number of the recovered offerings are of weapons, pottery or metal vessels containing food, and animals, but a number of spectacular discoveries of human sacrifices have been made in the peat bogs of Jutland. These "Bog People" – many of them displayed in fantastic states of preservation in Danish museums – enable us to reconstruct with amazing accuracy the physique and appearance of some of the people who lived in the farming settlements of Early Iron Age Scandinavia.

Most of these bodies have been found accidentally by people digging peat in the bogs of Jutland, though some have also been found in similar situations on the Danish islands and elsewhere in northwest Europe. We know them to be sacrificial victims because their feet and hands are bound and in some cases a noose has been fixed around their necks; some have also had their throats cut. The acidity of the peat soils has preserved their skin and hair, and even the contents of their stomachs, in such a remarkable state of preservation that we are able to discover such details as how they dressed their hair or even what they ate. We know, for instance, that Grauballe man (so called because he was found in a peat bog at Grauballe, near Silkeborg, Jutland) had eaten a final meal of porridge containing mainly barley, oats and emmer wheat with some weed seeds shortly before he had his throat cut sometime in the 1st century BC.

**The Roman Iron Age (1st–4th centuries AD)**

Though the deposition of sacrifices in wetlands continued throughout the Roman Iron Age, some marked changes in the nature of the offerings can be observed. Most of the objects belonging to this period are weapons of war and – particularly in south Scandinavia – are of Roman origin. It seems safe to assume that they were booty taken in battle and were thrown into lake, bog or stream as a thank-offering for victory in war. These depositions may, therefore, be taken as indication that there were numerous skirmishes at this time between the Scandinavians and their neighbors to the south who, though not part of the Roman empire, were allies of the Romans and armed with Roman weapons. Some Scandinavians may also have left their homelands to serve as mercenaries in the Roman armies, returning home after their tour of duty with valuable and luxurious items of Roman workmanship. Many of these objects eventually found their way into graves, symbols perhaps of the adventurous life and high status of the individuals buried there.

Not all the products of the Roman empire came to Scandinavia through these means. Throughout the four centuries of the Roman era in mainland Europe there was undoubtedly peaceful contact between the Scandinavian peoples and the Romanized areas to the south. Some of the more splendid items such as glass, bronze and precious-metal drinking-vessels that have been recovered may have arrived in Scandinavia through the exchange of gifts between chieftain families on either side of the border, but other more everyday objects no doubt arrived through trade. They are found in Norway, Denmark and central and southern Sweden, but in the later part of the period are most common on the island of Gotland, occupying a position in the middle of the Baltic Sea. The distribution of the finds shows the routes along which the trading commodities traveled from southern and central Europe: along the rivers Elbe and Rhine and then up the western seaboard to Denmark and Norway, or along the Oder and Vistula to the Baltic coast, Gotland and central Sweden. Jewelry, pottery and coins (*denarii*) all attest to this trade. They had an important influence on the subsequent development of native Scandinavian artifacts and art styles.

It is difficult to be sure what Scandinavian products were exchanged for the more long-lasting Roman objects, but furs from the north no doubt played an important role. Agricultural products, particularly grain and cattle hides, were also in demand by the Roman legions and probably made up the bulk of the goods sent south. There is evidence to suggest that agricultural activities increased in Scandinavia during these centuries and it is more than possible that this was in response to a widening market. The villages of Denmark multiplied in number, size and complexity, and in Norway farming for the first time became an important aspect of the economy. New land was settled and cleared for crop-raising and stock-breeding, and there is evidence of livestock being kept among some of the small, scattered fishing communities north of the Arctic Circle.

It is in the centuries of the Roman Iron Age that we can first trace the beginnings of the social and political organization in Scandinavia that finally led to the formation of kingdoms some hundreds of years later, and it is reasonable to suppose that trade and cultural contacts with the Roman empire played their part in these developments. The best evidence for incipient political centralization comes from Denmark where a class of warriors with wealth deriving both from control over trade and possession of land, and perhaps also with religious responsibilities, emerged as chieftains over distinct regions of the country.

A center from which one of these chieftains may have operated has recently been investigated at Gudme near the east coast of the island of Fyn, Denmark. A settlement was established there in the 1st century BC and expanded in wealth and size over the following centuries. It was at its most prosperous in the late Roman Iron Age (the 3rd and 4th centuries AD), though it continued in occupation at least until the end of the 6th century. Excavations have shown that the settlement was made up of longhouses of the usual rural type, but objects discovered within and around it are radically different from those usually found in farming settlements of this date. Gold fittings from weapons, gold rings, and chopped-up pieces of gold and silver show that this was not just an agricultural center, and Gudme's exceptional character is underlined by the discovery of small figurines stamped into gold foil, normally associated with cult centers in the later Migration Period. Gudme's name itself has religious connotations: it means "the home of god".

A contemporary site lies at Lundeborg on the coast, some 5 kilometers away. Investigations have shown that this was not a permanently inhabited settlement, but was seasonally occupied, probably in spring and summer, and was a trading and manufacturing center where luxury goods were imported, jewelry was made and ships were repaired. It consequently appears

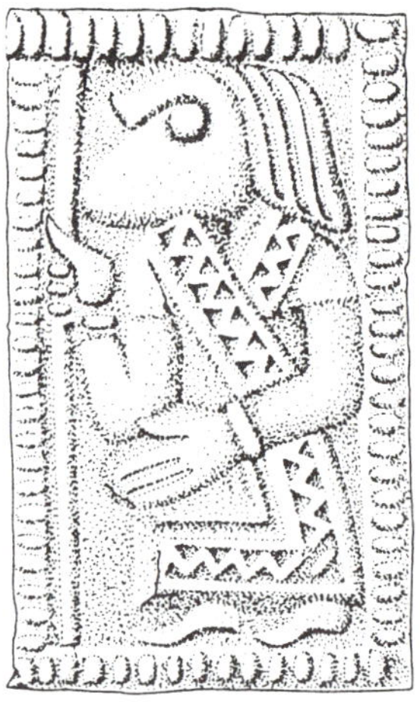

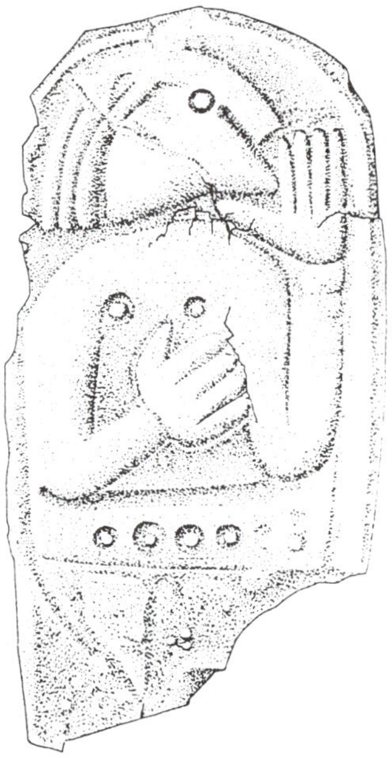

*Above* One of the most enigmatic features of Scandinavian archaeology from the Migration Period to the Viking Age is a series of gold foil figurines that are interpreted as votive offerings. About 2,300 of these tiny plaques come from the settlement site of Sorte Mulde, on the island of Bornholm – a remarkable discovery. One of those shown here is of a man in a long cloak carrying a staff, whilst the other has his hand raised in greeting – or might he be swearing an oath?

*Above left* This Migration Period "bracteate" from Sweden was clearly a prestige ornament – and may have been intended as a protective amulet. Bracteates are pendants in the form of single-sided gold disks, originally imitating Roman medallions with the emperor's bust. The design was gradually transformed into Scandinavian styles, including the proliferation of the concentric borders, as seen here.

to have served both as a market or fair and as the place where visitors (many of them possibly pilgrims) would disembark for Gudme.

Dankirke, near the west coast of Jutland, seems to have served a similar function to Gudme, and may have been the power base of a chieftain who controlled the region of southern Jutland. Other sites of similar type must have existed in Denmark and the Scandinavian peninsula during the Roman Iron Age, but they are as yet undiscovered, though their Migration Period equivalents are known.

### The Migration Period (5th–6th centuries)

The 5th century was a period of great turmoil on the European mainland as the Roman empire broke up, to be replaced later by new political groupings such as the Frankish kingdom (modern France and the Low Countries) and the Visigothic kingdom of the Iberian peninsula. This process was initiated by the mass movement of peoples east-west across Europe, but the great migrations affected Scandinavia only slightly. Some people set sail from western and southern Denmark to settle in eastern England; a few others may have migrated westward to northern England from southwest Norway. But, in contrast to what was happening in most of northwestern Europe, the Migration Period in Scandinavia appears generally to have been one of stability and prosperity, with thriving agriculture and trade.

In Norway, the agricultural expansion that had begun in the previous period continued. Many settlements have been excavated in the southwest of the country and seem to represent isolated farmsteads devoted to stock-breeding, with some crops being grown in neighboring small fields. The rectangular longhouses, built of stone, sheltered both people and cattle. A typical farm consists of one longhouse with several smaller outbuildings, all surrounded by a stone wall and with stonewalled droveways for cattle. Similar farms are found on Öland and Gotland where

**Iron Age settlement in Scandinavia** Unlike mainland Europe, the centuries before the Viking Age in Scandinavia were ones of stability, during which agriculture and rural settlement expanded steadily. Pagan rituals such as the deposition of votive offerings and human sacrifice were widespread until the introduction of Christianity in the Viking Age. Though the connection between religion and trade still needs investigation, it is clear from the archaeological evidence that religious centers began to be established in the Migration and Vendel Periods, and these were often associated with trading outlets: the religious settlement of Gudme had close connections with Lundeborg only a few kilometers away and Helgö, central Sweden, was both a religious and commercial site. Evidence from some excavated pre-Viking sites, such as Borg on Lofoten, Hovgården in central Sweden and Högom, farther north, shows them to have been high-status sites, possibly chieftains' residences.

*Inset top right* This 6th-century bronze plaque is one of a set of four discovered on a settlement site at Torslunda, on the Baltic island of Öland. They were made for use as dies to impress bronze sheets for the ornamentation of helmets similar to those found at Vendel and Valsgärde. This example depicts two warriors taking part in a ritual dance. One wears a horned helmet ending in beaked heads and the other is clad in a wolf-head mask. The scene may be connected with the cult of Odin.

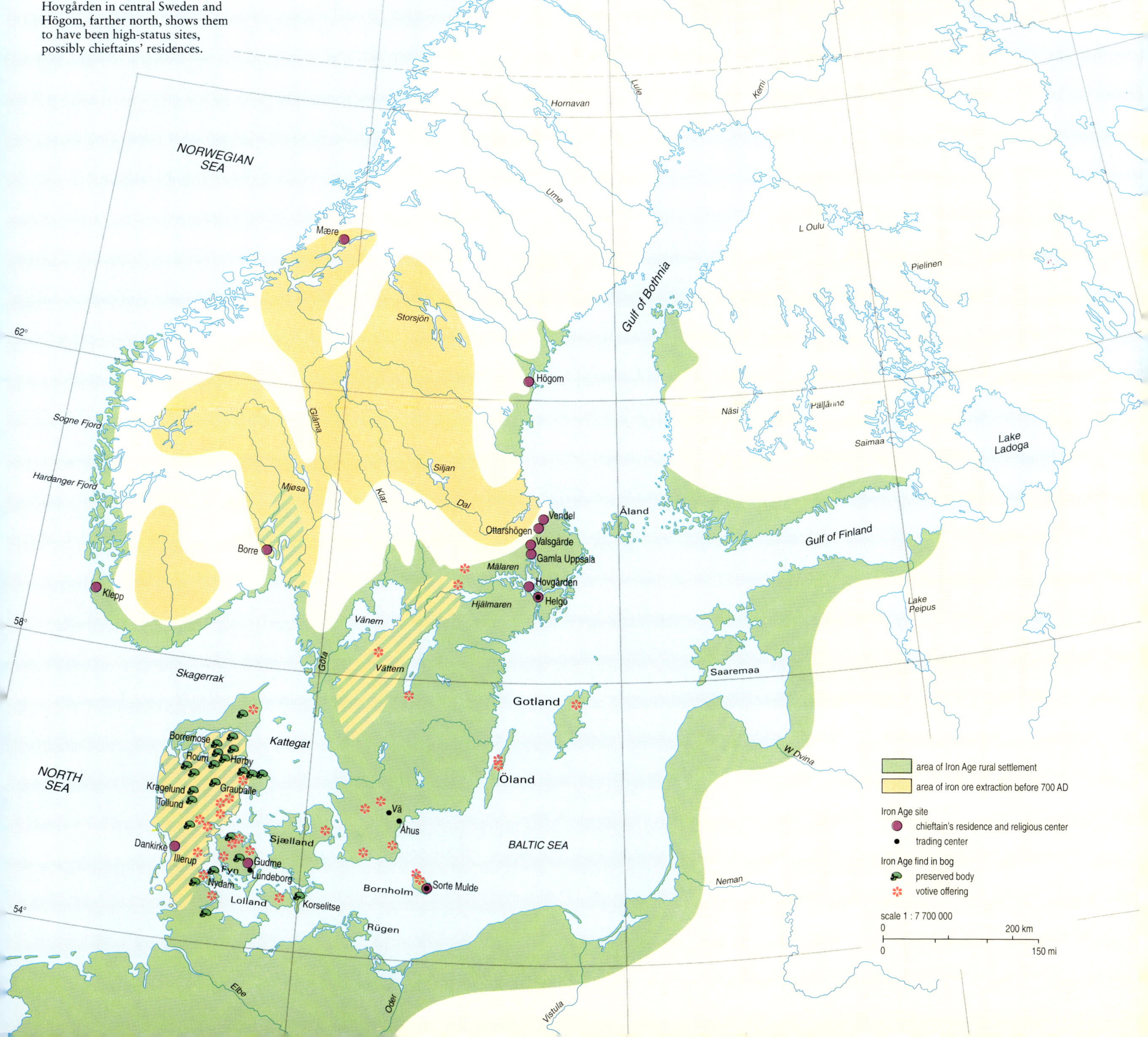

# Eketorp

*Below* Excavations revealed the full extent of Eketorp II. Both the encircling wall and the buildings were built of limestone bedrock. It is because the foundations were so well preserved that the fullscale reconstruction of the site could be made.

Eketorp, one of 16 definitely identified ring-forts on the island of Öland off the coast of Sweden, is the only one to have been completely excavated. It was first built about 300 AD, and for the first 100 years of its existence was sporadically occupied. The remains from this period are known as Eketorp I. In about 400, a much larger area was surrounded by a stone wall and filled with 53 buildings. This site is known as Eketorp II. Though described as a fortification, it was essentially an agricultural village. Between 150 and 200 inhabitants lived there in some 12 farmsteads and raised sheep, cattle, pigs and horses. These were kept indoors in winter, but in summer would have been pastured in the surrounding countryside, where crops of barley, wheat, rye and oats were grown. This diet was supplemented by hunting and fishing, and the occupants also made simple bronze objects and forged iron tools and weapons. Eketorp II was abandoned about 700. It was reoccupied in the late Viking Age in about 1000, but on a much smaller scale; this is known as Eketorp III.

*Above* The interior of a cattle shed in the "living museum" that has been reconstructed on the actual site of Eketorp II. As well as cows, pigs, sheep and hens are kept and roam at will in and out of the buildings.

*Right* Visitors to Eketorp are able to gain an impression of what life was like inside a defended Iron Age village before the Viking Age. The entire outer wall has been rebuilt, and can be seen in the background. Each of the farmsteads consisted of a dwelling-house, cattleshed and outbuildings. In some of the reconstructed buildings visitors can see pots being made and iron and bronze being worked.

*Right* The circular wall of Eketorp II was pierced by three gateways; it enclosed an area of about 5,000 square meters. The 53 buildings were arranged around the periphery wall, and in a block in the center. A single well served all the inhabitants.

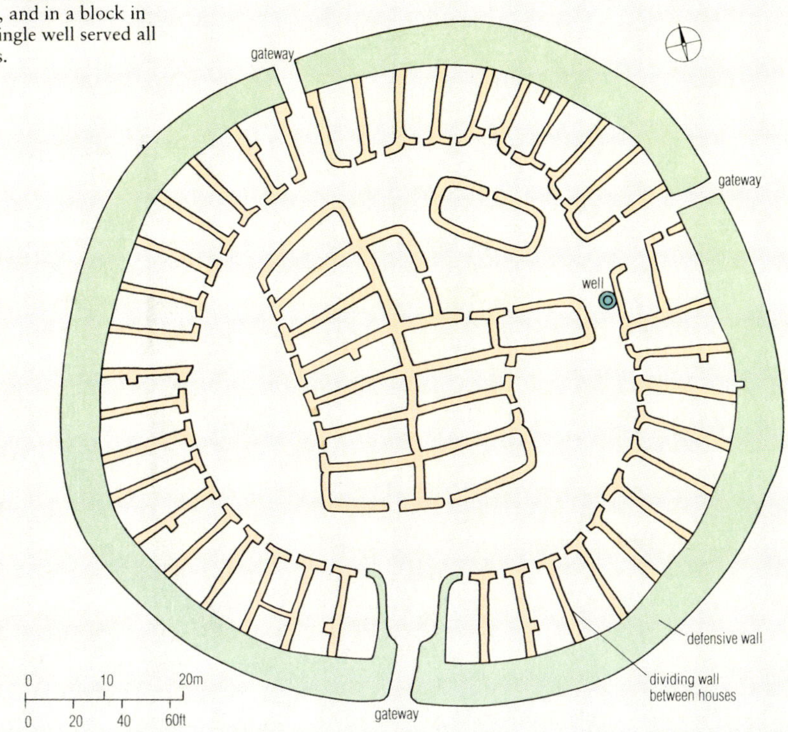

the same kind of husbandry was practiced. The scattered distribution of these farmsteads differentiates them from the village settlements of Denmark, which continued to grow in extent.

Commerce and crafts flourished in the Migration Period. These activities appear usually to have been combined at a single site, as at Helgö on Lake Mälaren, central Sweden. Here exotic imports such as gold coins (*solidi*) from the eastern Roman empire and a figurine of Buddha originating from northern India have been found alongside the molds and crucibles that were used to cast native bronze jewelry. Some gold-foil figurines similar to those found at Gudme have also been discovered at Helgö and suggest that it, too, may have been the site of religious observances. These gold-foil figurines – tiny plaques of thin gold stamped with male or female figures – were votive offerings, and have been found at many other places, but the greatest known concentration is at Sorte Mulde on the island of Bornholm in the southern Baltic, where an astonishing 2,300 were discovered during excavations in 1986 and 1987 alone. Sorte Mulde must have been the center of the chiefdom of Bornholm, which controlled the waterborne trade of the southern Baltic. It was the center of craft production on the island and appears also to have been the island's religious focus.

Sites such as Gudme, Helgö and Sorte Mulde suggest that the rites associated with religious belief were becoming concentrated in specific sites during the Migration Period. The deposition of votive offerings in bogs, lakes and rivers, the main manifestation of the religion of earlier periods, stopped sometime in the 6th century. After about AD 500, sacrifices were usually in the form of human beings, and precious objects such as the gold-foil figurines and gold bracteates (coin-like pendants) were buried on dry land, most often in the vicinity of an important chieftain's residence. This fundamental change in practice must signify a very deep change in ideas of religion and society, and it has been argued that the regional chieftains had a role both as religious and as political leaders, acting in some way as intermediaries between the gods and the people.

The Migration Period in most of Scandinavia was a time of religious, political and social change taking place within a background of increasing prosperity: agriculture became more productive and trade expanded. In contrast to mainland Europe, it must have been a time of peace. And yet, some 1,500 defensible forts were being built at more or less the same time. Most of them are unexcavated and difficult to date precisely, but the first phase of the fort of Eketorp on Öland, for example, has been securely dated to the 4th and 5th centuries, and other investigated examples indicate occupation at roughly the same date. The building of forts is usually attributed to times of unrest, but most modern scholars believe that the forts of Migration Period Scandinavia were built for entirely different reasons. They probably represent centers of a well-organized society in which the regional centers of power were demarcated and clearly visible to the surrounding populations.

**The Vendel Period (7th–8th centuries)**

The last phase of the Iron Age before the advent of Viking culture takes its name from a site in central Sweden whose rich burials indicate the presence of a royal dynasty in the years immediately preceding the

# Helgö

Excavations on Helgö, an island off Ekerö in Lake Mälaren, have shown it to have been an important trading and manufacturing site in the centuries immediately before the Viking Age. It seems in particular to have been a center for the production of the bronze jewelry popular in the Migration and Vendel Periods, for many thousands of molds used for the casting of brooches and other decorative objects have been found in the buildings that make up the site. Iron ore was brought there from farther north in Sweden to be worked into tools, weapons and objects of everyday household use.

An abundance of exotic and rich finds have been found on the site, but the reasons for this have long been puzzled over since in many other respects Helgö seems to have been a perfectly ordinary agricultural settlement: the buildings on the site are of the type found on Iron Age farms elsewhere in central Sweden, and the grave-goods in the cemeteries that surround the site are not particularly rich. Part of Helgö's importance may lie in its having been a cult center for the pagan religion. This view is supported by the presence of gold-foil figurines similar to those found at other religious sites, such as Gudme in Denmark. It is probably not insignificant, either, that Helgö's name means Holy Island.

*Below* The site on Helgö consists of several groups of buildings – shown here as rectangles – standing on artificially constructed terraces on a north-facing slope of the island. Each terrace supported a number of long, rectangular wooden buildings, some of which were dwellings and some workshops. Not all the building groups were occupied simultaneously – perhaps only two were in use at any one time – for though the settlement was occupied for some 400 years, the total population could never have been great. The hillfort and most of the cemeteries that surround the habitation site date from before the settlement.

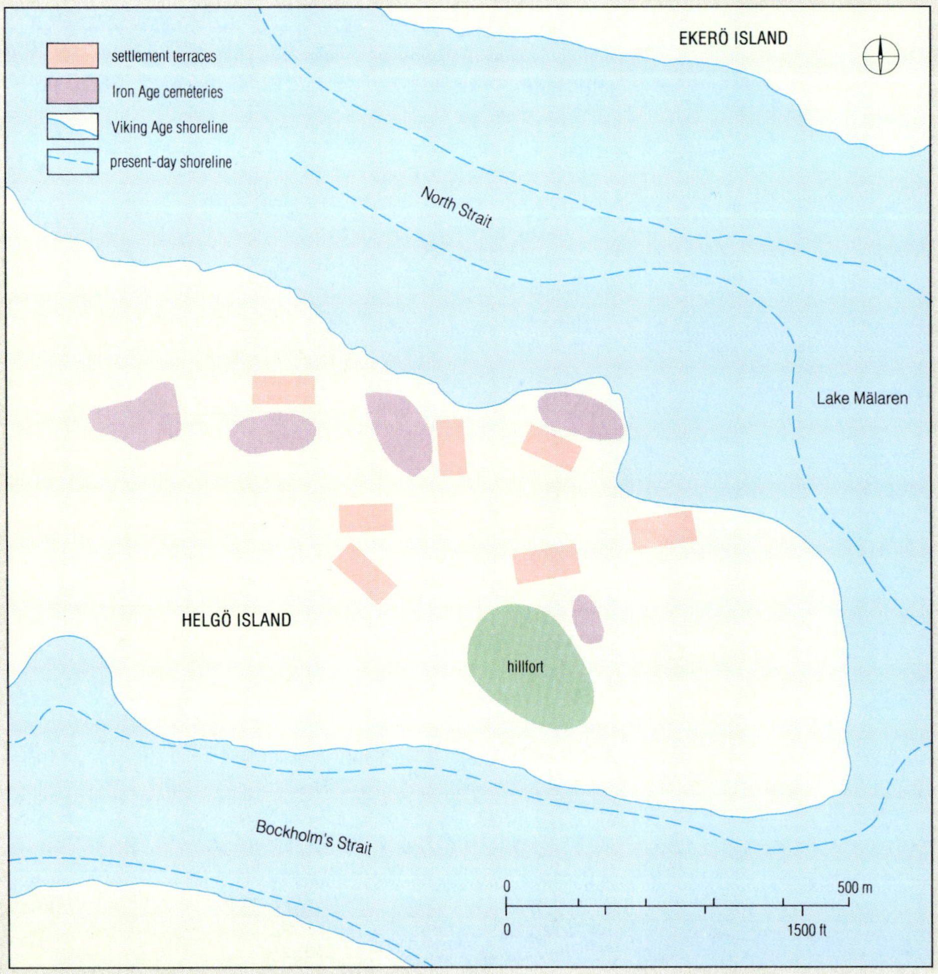

*Left* The amazing wealth generated by the inhabitants of Helgö is illustrated by this hoard of 47 Roman gold coins, minted in both the eastern and the western empire in the 5th and 6th centuries. There may originally have been even more, for the arm-ring was probably made from gold derived from melting down coins. It is unclear how and why they reached this remote island in central Sweden. A possible explanation is that Helgö was the focus for an extensive trade in commodities such as furs from the far north, greatly in demand in the lands around the Mediterranean.

*Right* This decorated head from a bishop's crozier was found in excavations at Helgö. It is of cast bronze, richly ornamented with inlays of glass and enamel, and has a man's head gripped between the jaws of a wild beast. All these features indicate Celtic workmanship, and it may have been made in western Britain or Ireland during the 8th century. As with the other objects of remote origin found at Helgö, its presence there remains a mystery. It has been suggested that missionaries may have visited the island before Christianity was formally established in that part of Sweden.

*Left* This bronze statuette of Buddha sitting on a lotus throne, only 8.4 centimeters high, is evidence of Helgö's extraordinarily far-flung connections. It was made somewhere in north India in the 6th or 7th century AD, and probably arrived at Helgö during the latest phase of its settlement in the Viking Age, possibly in the baggage of a traveler who had returned along the rivers of Russia from the east. It seems to have been regarded as an amulet: when it was discovered, a narrow leather thong was tied around the neck and one arm.

# Royal Burials of the Vendel Period

The center of the region of Uppland dominated by the Svear was at Gamla Uppsala, some 10 kilometers north of the modern town of Uppsala. Here are the three great burial mounds, standing up to 20 meters high, that are attributed to the Svears' 6th-century kings. They were excavated in the 19th century and found to contain cremation burials with rich grave-goods such as garnet-encrusted gold jewelry dating from the early Vendel Period. The place retained its importance into the Viking Age, serving both as a royal center and as the center of the "official" pagan religion of the time. The association of royalty and religion was always close, and the king himself was probably the high priest. Vendel and Valsgärde, north of Gamla Uppsala, are also thought to have been important centers from about 600 to the end of the Viking Age. Cemeteries have been found and excavated at both. In the 7th-century burials, the bodies were placed within boats, and the mounds covering the burials were quite low, in contrast to those at Gamla Uppsala. From the quality of the grave-goods it is clear that the people interred here were of extremely high status – powerful chieftains, if not actually kings.

*Above left* This mid 19th-century lithograph of Gamla Uppsala shows the three "mounds of the kings" with the 12th-century church in the background. The view is taken from the southwest, and is little changed today. According to tradition, the east mound is the burial site of King Egil, the central mound that of King Aun, and the west mound of King Adils – all members of the Yngling dynasty mentioned in the 13th-century history of the kings of Norway, *Heimskringla*.

*Left* The cemetery at Valsgärde. The burial mounds, dating from the Vendel Period to the end of the Viking Age, can be seen on the ridge behind the modern house. The earliest burials contained the richest grave-goods. The deceased were laid in boats – suggesting they were making a journey – and were supplied with food and cooking equipment. They were often accompanied by horses and hunting dogs.

*Top* An iron helmet, with bronze decoration, found in a 7th-century boat burial at Vendel: it has a spectacle-shaped guard for the eyes and nose. Some Viking helmets – which did not have horns – would have been of a similar type to this. The burials at Vendel and Valsgärde are noted for their magnificent armor. This warrior was buried with a shield, two swords and other weapons, all of the highest quality and finely decorated.

*Above* Many of the finds in the Vendel cemetery were elaborately decorated with stylized patterns of interlaced animals, from which the Vendel style is named. It can be seen on this drawing of the central boss of a circular shield that was found in a boat burial at Vendel. The boss is of iron plated with bronze; the shield itself would have been made of leather-covered wood and has rotted away.

Viking Age. Centers of regional power had begun to emerge in Scandinavia, particularly Denmark, during the earlier phases of the Iron Age, and the political entities of the Vendel Period should be regarded therefore as merely the culmination of what had gone before, and not as innovations. Their importance lies in the fact that they provided a basis for what was to come: the emergence of kingdoms proper in the Viking Age and the true crystallization of the kingdoms of Sweden, Norway and Denmark at the beginning of the Middle Ages.

The cemetery of Vendel in the province of Uppland stands on the east bank of the river Fyris, which flows southward to Lake Mälaren. The rulers of the Svear, a people or tribe mentioned by Latin writers of the Roman period as being the dominant force in the Baltic, and who gave their name to the later country of Sweden, were buried in this cemetery. Their bodies were placed in boats with their personal equipment arranged about them as a sign of their rank. A similar cemetery has been found at Valsgärde, a little farther south on the same bank of the Fyris, and 27 kilometers beyond, nearer to the Fyris's outflow into Lake Mälaren, stands Gamla Uppsala, the religious center of the Svear, with its great burial mounds.

The opulent grave-goods – highly decorated armor, horse trappings, glass drinking vessels and cooking equipment, including cauldrons – and the profligate use of boats in the burials at Vendel and Valsgärde may be taken as evidence for the conspicuous creation and consumption of wealth by a family or families who controlled the lands and population over a large area. They are the best examples we have of a royal center at this time. The wealth and power of the Svear probably resulted from their control of the trade that flowed up and down the river Fyris, carrying furs and iron from the north to centers in the south. Most burials of this date in the same area contain poor-quality grave-goods, and we may consequently assume that the great bulk of the population living on rural settlements enjoyed nowhere like the same standard of living or luxuries as the occupants of the Vendel and Valsgärde cemeteries.

The growth of strong central authorities in Scandinavia during the Vendel Period led to other developments, notably the establishment of market and craftworking centers. Some of these – Ribe, Denmark, for example – later developed into Viking Age towns, but others, such as Åhus in Skåne, Sweden, flourished mainly in the 8th century and were later abandoned. Largescale engineering works were also undertaken at this time. The Danevirke, a great defense work across the foot of the Jutland peninsula, was begun before 737. It must have been a formidable obstacle, consisting of an earth rampart about 10 meters wide revetted with timber, with a ditch (the digging of which probably provided the earth for the rampart) in front. The whole barrier extended southwest for about 7 kilometers from the western end of the Schlei fjord. The digging of the Kanhave canal on the island of Samsø, in about 726, was equally impressive. A passage about 1 kilometer long and 11 meters wide was cut through a narrow isthmus in the north of the island and deepened to allow shallow-draft ships to pass. Its sloping sides were revetted with timber, and all in all the work required considerable technical skill as well as the availability of a large labor force. All these achievements paved the way for the later developments of the Viking Age.

# PART TWO

# VIKING AGE SCANDINAVIA

# SOCIETY, KINGSHIP AND WARFARE

## The Vikings

For historians, the Viking Age conventionally begins with the first recorded raid by a Norwegian fleet on the undefended monastery of Lindisfarne, an island off the coast of northeast England, in 793 and ends in the 11th century after the conversion of all the Scandinavian countries to Christianity. For archaeologists, who look to material evidence for signs of cultural change rather than historical events to usher in new periods in human history, the dates are somewhat different. Cultural change can result from many factors and manifest itself in different ways. Internal changes can produce a new social organization, with new centers of power and social hierarchies; these may derive from external influences such as what is happening in adjacent lands, from invasions from outside, or from increased knowledge of the outside world as a result of enlarging spheres of exchange and trade.

It is very obvious that such changes were taking place in Scandinavia during the 8th century, very largely as a result of contacts with the Christian continental mainland. There, highly organized kingdoms with their roots in Roman civilization were growing more powerful and attempting to expand. They were casting their eyes toward the lands of the pagan northerners whose countries were the source of commodities much sought after in the Christian south: furs, walrus ivory, amber, for instance. The fact that the north was pagan was also a challenge to the Christian church, and attempts at conversion went hand in hand with political and commercial interests. Thus, Scandinavia found itself more and more open to influences from the continent. We can see evidence of this, for instance, in changes in the art-styles that decorated the jewelry and other ornamental objects manufactured and used by the Scandinavians at that time. Imported goods from the south also show that Scandinavia was becoming more closely involved with its continental neighbors. Pottery and glass from the Rhineland is found in increasing amounts, particularly in Jutland, and coins (a form of exchange quite alien to the Scandinavians) began to circulate in small quantities, and were even minted there for a short time.

It is to things such as these that archaeologists turn when defining a period of cultural change such as they believed occurred in 8th-century Scandinavia. Thus, the beginning of the Viking Age can clearly be seen in the move away from the lifestyle of the Vendel Period toward a different style – a different culture – in the second half of the 8th century. The raid on Lindisfarne in 793 is thus the outward manifestation of a process that had been going on throughout the previous 50 years – the bringing of Scandinavia into Europe.

For about 50 years after the initial attack on Lindisfarne the Vikings raided with ever-increasing frequency along the coasts of the British Isles and the western seaboard of mainland Europe, swooping down on defenseless monasteries where there were rich pickings in the form of church plate and other fine objects. We can get some idea of what the Vikings seized from the highly decorated metalwork that has been found in some graves in Scandinavia. This early phase seems to have been one of pure piracy: these raiders, who came mainly from Norway and Denmark, had discovered the ease with which they could rob the rich sites of western Europe, and their lightning attacks were aided by their fast and seaworthy ships.

In the second half of the 9th century, a new pattern emerged – the Vikings turned from piracy to colonization. Their ships now carried groups of settlers with their domestic equipment and other supplies to new homes in the Orkneys and Shetlands, Iceland and Greenland, and later even as far away as North America. It was mainly the Norwegians who traveled in this direction. The Danes turned their attention to the more populated countries of England and France, first of all sending fighting expeditions and then settling there. The Swedes mainly looked eastwards; their journeys took them to southwest Finland, to the southern and eastern Baltic, and then across Russia to Byzantium (Constantinople;

*Left* This enameled mount from a bronze bowl is of characteristic Irish workmanship, though found in a pagan Viking grave at Myklebostad in western Norway. Such fine metalwork was amongst the loot taken back to Scandinavia by the first Viking raiders who attacked monasteries and other sites in the British Isles and western Europe.

*Page 36* Without the clinker-built sailing ship there could have been no Viking Age. Sea trials of full-sized reconstructions of Viking ships have demonstrated their maneuverability, which gave them the ability to carry out surprise attacks.

*Above* The Viking raiders and armies would never have achieved their successes without first-rate weaponry. This Norwegian array of 9th and 10th-century iron swords, spear-heads and axblades, together with a unique helmet from the chieftain's grave at Gjermundbu, Norway, is displayed on one of the 64 wooden shields found in the Gokstad ship-burial.

modern-day Istanbul) and to the Caspian Sea and as far as Baghdad. A smaller number of people from Västergötland in central Sweden, with access to the west, also traveled to the British Isles.

All these people are commonly referred to today as Vikings. The derivation of the name is obscure. It is very rarely mentioned in contemporary sources, and when it is it refers to men who had gone "a-viking", that is, who had left their homes and land to take up piracy in preference to normal farming pursuits. "Vik" means creek or inlet in Scandinavian languages, and it may be that the term "a-viking" derives from the places from which the pirates set sail, or refers to the sheltered waters in which they hid before swooping down on their prey. It is possible, too, that "vik" refers to the trading places on the European mainland and in the British Isles visited by the Vikings, many of which were known as "wic" (meaning trading settlement) – for example Hamwic near modern Southampton, England and Quentovic in northern France. In the 8th century there was tremendous commercial growth in northern Europe, and the wealth of these towns would have made them attractive targets for piracy and colonization. Perhaps the Vikings were originally the people who visited these sites, either as pirates or peaceful traders. To contemporary writers in Europe the people from Scandinavia were not known as Vikings. They called them Norsemen or Northmen, and it is from this that the term Norse derives, now often used interchangeably with Viking. Whatever its derivation, Viking was never used of the Scandinavians

as a whole, and only came into common usage with the rise of the Scandinavian nationalist movements in the 19th century. At this period, the Vikings began to be depicted in the horned helmets that are inextricably associated with their popular image today, but have no basis whatsoever in historical fact.

At the beginning of the Viking period Danes, Norwegians and Swedes all spoke roughly the same language known to themselves and to outsiders as the "Danish tongue" (but referred to by linguists today as Old Norse). Belonging to the Germanic branch of languages that were spoken around the North Sea, it shared common roots with Anglo-Saxon and Old High German, but had diverged from them sufficiently to be thought of by contemporaries as a separate language. During the course of the Viking Age more distinct, phonetic variations developed in the different regions of Scandinavia. These dialects formed the basis of modern Danish, Icelandic, Norwegian and Swedish, but could be understood by all Scandinavians (as is still true of their modern derivatives).

Anthropological examination of the skeletons recovered from inhumation burials indicates that the Vikings were on average a little smaller than the modern Scandinavian population. It is clear that some people, we may assume from the upper ranks of society, were taller, sturdier and generally more healthy than the rest, whose skeletons show obvious deformations from the effects of malnutrition and heavy labor. Infant mortality was higher than today and life expectancy shorter, though it was not unusual for individuals to live to between 40 and 50. Greater longevity was rare. The most common diseases, reflected in the skeletal remains, were rheumatism and arthritis, but there is little sign of the dental caries that so plague people in modern societies, no doubt due to the Vikings' sugarfree diet.

Even when the Viking raids were at their height, most of the population must have remained peaceably at home to tend their flocks and herds, grow a few crops or work as craftsmen. Why so many chose to leave Scandinavia at this time to take part in seasonal raiding expeditions or settle overseas remains something of a mystery, but over-population in the homelands, lack of cultivable land, and conflicts between different warring factions have all been put forward as reasons. Probably all these factors played a part in the great Viking emigrations of the 9th and 10th centuries.

### The social hierarchy

The evidence obtained from archaeology – especially burials, with striking contrasts between the grave-goods of the wealthy and the poor – rune-stone inscriptions and scanty references in the written sources all suggest that Viking society was highly stratified. Within each territorial unit there was a strict hierarchy with a chieftain or king at the top and an aristocracy to support

*Above* A picture-stone from Gotland depicts seamen manning the sail in the stern of a ship. They are protected by a row of overlapping shields tied to its side. The men who went "a-viking" perhaps looked like this.

*Right* A silver coin of the Danish king, Svein Forkbeard (d. 1014), minted c.995. This is one of the earliest Scandinavian coins to have been struck bearing a king's name and with a symbolic royal portrait on the front; they imitate Anglo-Saxon originals, with a cross on the reverse.

*Above* A bucket made of yew with brass hoops found in the Oseberg burial. It had been placed inside another bucket, which itself lay in a barrel in the prow of the ship. Buckets of this type were imported.

him and provide fighting forces when necessary. Below were the lesser landowners – the farmers and merchants who made up a class of free men (and also served as the pool of fighting men), and on the bottom layer of all were the slaves.

Before the Viking Age, power was already becoming concentrated among a handful of dynastic families who controlled the wealth of an area. The local ruler was also military leader, religious head, administrator and peacekeeper within the area he controlled. Wealth was mainly in the form of landholdings, the produce from that land, and taxes paid in kind by the people who worked and tenanted it, but as society developed and power became centralized in the hands of a single ruling family, royal income was also derived from towns in the form of market tolls and customs dues. Representatives of the king, who wielded great power on their own behalf, as well as his, were stationed in the towns and elsewhere around his lands.

One of the clearest ways in which a king could proclaim his power was by minting coins. The fact that coins were minted at Ribe and Hedeby in Denmark for brief periods in the 8th and 9th centuries, though a monetary system did not become firmly established in Scandinavia until the 11th century, gives strong grounds for supposing that there was royal control over these two early Viking towns. It is particularly significant that Olof Skötkonung (c. 995–1021/2), recognized as the first king to control the whole of central Sweden, was the first to strike coins at the town of Sigtuna, which he founded, from about 995 onwards. Coins were first minted in Norway at about the same time, by Olaf Tryggvason (c. 964–1000). As the countries became more united and the kings more powerful in the 11th century, the issuing of coins became commonplace.

Though royal power was hereditary, a smooth succession from father to son was by no means assured – any male member of the family might enforce his right to succeed. This often resulted in family quarrels. Dynastic feuding was particularly strong among the sons and grandsons of Harald Finehair (reigned c. 870–c. 940), the first recognized king of Norway. Sometimes potential claimants spent considerable periods in exile, accumulating wealth in campaigns abroad, in order to recruit an army and return home to attempt to secure the succession by force. Compromises were sometimes reached whereby two kings could rule simultaneously, or the country was divided into regions, each with its own royal overlord, as frequently happened in Norway in the 10th century.

The kings and their queens were buried in great style, their bodies interred beneath great burial mounds sometimes more than 20 meters wide at ground level. Some of these graves have been excavated to reveal grave-goods of enormous magnificence. Some of the most spectacular finds have been made in southeast Norway, most notably at Oseberg and Gokstad on the Oslo fjord. Excavations undertaken at Oseberg at the beginning of the 20th century showed that a young woman, thought to have been a queen, had been buried there in 834. It is possible to be so precise because tree-ring dating shows that the timber used to build her burial chamber came from trees felled in the fall of that year. Her body had been placed inside a magnificently carved ship together with all the splendid accoutrements of her daily life: beds, bedding, and all manner of household equipment. Other items she would have used in life were also included; for example, sledges for transport in winter and a wagon for summer journeys. Beside her in the burial-chamber was the body of an older woman, possibly a servant or slave.

Just a little to the north of Oseberg, lies the largest concentration of great mounds in Scandinavia at Borre, traditionally associated with the Viking Age royal house of Norway. When one of the mounds was destroyed by gravel digging some 150 years ago, the remains of a ship were recorded and some magnificent objects dating from about 900 retrieved. Several great mounds have been investigated in Denmark. At Jelling, central Jutland, a site associated with the 10th-century kings of Denmark, two mounds have been excavated. The wooden chamber in one has been dated by tree-ring analysis to 958/9, and probably contained the burial of King Gorm, the last great pagan ruler of Denmark, who was later reinterred in the adjacent church by his son Harald Bluetooth, who was a Christian. Striking grave-goods, indicative of great wealth and rank, have been found in a 10th-century burial chamber in a mound at Mammen, in Jutland. Tree-ring dating of the corner posts of the grave chamber that enclosed the body and its equipment (including embroidered clothing and the famous Mammen ax) shows that the trees used to make them were felled in 970/1; the burial must have taken place shortly afterwards.

# The Oseberg Ship Burial

The Oseberg mound beside the Oslo fjord in southeast Norway, excavated in 1904, was found to contain the most richly furnished burial known from the Viking Age. It belonged to a woman who had been buried with a companion in 834: we can be sure of that because recent tree-ring dating has shown that the oaks used to construct her burial-chamber were felled that year. Though her jewelry had been robbed, the quantity and quality of the surviving artifacts found with her was extraordinary.

The burial-chamber was set behind the mast of an elegant ship, perhaps providing transport for the deceased. Also included were a wagon, four sledges and 12 or more horses; the idea of making a long journey is reinforced by the provision of a tent and food, including an ox and a bucket of apples. There were five beds, storage chests, oil lamps, a chair, a tapestry wall-hanging, assorted kitchen and eating utensils, and farming tools. In the chamber itself, among various personal items, were the remains of looms and a set of tablets for weaving a braid that had been left unfinished. The sumptious nature of the Oseberg grave-goods reveals the standing of the woman whose family was able to dispose of so much wealth in her honor – clearly she must have been someone of the very highest status, possibly a queen.

*Above* Vessels and other utensils of wood have rarely survived from the Viking Age. This selection from amongst the Oseberg grave-goods includes two brass-bound buckets from Ireland, the larger with enameled mounts for its handle. These are in the form of human figures in Buddha-like posture.

*Top right* Excavation of the Oseberg ship in 1904 was directed by Professor Gabriel Gustafson, seen here standing in front of its elegantly decorated stern: the burial-chamber has already been removed. The trench in which the ship was placed was lined with blue clay, and this kept it and its contents moist, preserving them from decay. However, the weight of the mound had crushed the timbers into many pieces. These have since been carefully reconstructed.

*Left* The four-wheeled Oseberg wagon is far from being an everyday cart, though these were certainly used for ordinary transportation, but is richly carved in a manner befitting a ceremonial vehicle. Human heads terminate the cradle that supports its detachable body. This is decorated on the front with a scene of a man surrounded by snakes, who some identify as the legendary hero Gunnar, thrown to his death in a snake-pit.

*Above* A narrow tapestry frieze was found in fragments in the Oseberg burial-chamber. It was woven in colored wools in a variety of techniques. This scene shows a procession of armed figures, both male and female, on foot and on horseback, accompanied by horse-drawn wagons. This remarkable survival is a dramatic reminder of how little is now known of the colorful hangings that would have decorated the walls of the rich in the Viking Age.

*Top* A reconstruction of a bed that was placed in the prow of the Oseberg ship. Its head-planks are carved into animal heads, which were originally painted. Four other beds, including the one the dead woman was lying on, were found, as well as bedding stuffed with feathers and down. Beds did not form part of normal household furnishings. The Oseberg beds are easily dismantled, and may have been used when traveling.

## The lower ranks of society

Beneath the royal and aristocratic class were the free men, a highly diverse group covering all ranks from the king's close retainers to servants, that formed the largest class in Viking Age Scandinavia. Most were farmers. They had the right to own and bear weapons and to attend and speak at the Thing, an assembly of all the free men in a particular region that took place regularly (at least once a year, sometimes more frequently) to make laws, settle disputes about land and adjudicate in crimes of violence and theft. Decisions were taken by casting lots. A number of Thing sites are known (the most famous is at Thingvellir in Iceland), usually consisting of a flat, low mound surrounded by a shallow ditch. *Thing* is a frequent element in Scandinavian place-names, indicating the presence of such a meeting place, and similar evidence from Scotland and elsewhere in the western Viking world shows that the Vikings carried this form of government to their overseas settlements. In Scandinavia, however, as royal power increased, the king was able to use his authority to overrule or manipulate the decisions of the Thing.

Wealth, in the form of land, was the chief determinant of the relative status and importance of the free men. Some owned immense estates that were leased out and worked by tenants. The farmsteads or manors that stood at the centers of some of these great estates are still visible today, usually marked by huge burial mounds. Toward the end of the Viking Age many of the richest landowners erected monuments that carried runic inscriptions glorifying themselves and their families.

The lowliest class in society were the slaves, about whom we know little, though references in written sources make it clear that they played an essential role in the economy. They are difficult to pin down through the archaeological record. Graves with few or no grave-goods may be those of slaves, but it is doubtful whether they were even allowed the dignity of being buried in a cemetery. A dead slave had no worth, and was probably disposed of without ceremony. Some double graves contain a richly furnished body and one with no possessions, and these may be the burials of a master or mistress and a slave slain as a human sacrifice. A description of a Viking funeral on the river Volga in the 10th century, left us by Ibn Fadlan, an Arab merchant, describes such an event:

*What they do is this...if he (the deceased) is rich, they gather together his wealth and divide it into three – one part for his family, one part to provide clothes for him, and a third part for* nabidh *which they drink on the day that the slave woman is killed and burned together with her master...When a chief has died his family asks his slave women and slaves, "Who will die with him?" Then one of them says "I will." When she has said this there is no backing out...most of those who agree are women slaves..."*

The indigenous slave force was supplemented from time to time by captives acquired in raids abroad. Some were brought back to the homelands as forced labor, others were shipped on to be sold in the slave markets of the east, for slaves were an important commodity in the Vikings' trade with the Abbasid caliphate of Baghdad, sold in exchange for large quantities of silver.

## The emergence of the Scandinavian kingdoms

The development of Denmark, Norway and Sweden into unified countries each under a single ruler took place during the Viking Age. The process is not well documented, the written account being limited to scattered references in contemporary continental histories. The *Royal Frankish Annals* occasionally mention Danish kings in the 8th and 9th centuries, and more information is given by Rimbert's *Life of Ansgar* written at the end of the 9th century. The latest continental source for Viking Age Scandinavia is Adam of Bremen's *History of the Archbishops of Hamburg-Bremen*, which was written at the end of the 11th century and based on eyewitness descriptions given him by informants. As all these works were written by Christian clerics about pagan lands we have to assume some prejudice on their part, but they seem on the whole to be fairly realistic contemporary accounts. They give us the names of places, and of people, some of whom can be confirmed by the later Icelandic sagas. The Icelandic sagas also provide a historical source, but were written mainly in the 13th century – that is, nearly two centuries after the end of the Viking Age – and so must be treated with caution. Nevertheless, from these and from material evidence such as the construction of great monuments and engineering works that obviously had royal direction behind them, it is clear that all three countries had emerged as separate powers by the end of the 11th century at the latest.

Most is known about Denmark, where it is possible to discover the first indications of centralized royal power in the foundation of the town of Ribe, the digging of the Kanhave canal and the building of the Danevirke, all perhaps instigated by King Agantyr, known to us from the biography of St Willibrord, bishop of Utrecht, who visited the "wild Danish people" in the early 8th century. Somewhat later, in 808, King Godfred is mentioned in the *Royal Frankish Annals* in connection with the building of the second stage of the Danevirke, and he is also said to have settled merchants in the early Viking town of Hedeby (then in Denmark, now in Germany). Other kings are mentioned in the 9th century, including the joint kings Horik the Older and Horik the Younger, who allowed the German missionary Ansgar to build churches in Hedeby and Ribe in the 850s.

No kings are known by name for the next hundred years. In the mid 10th century a new dynasty, founded by King Gorm, arose with its center at Jelling in central Jutland. Gorm, about whom little is known, was succeeded by his son Harald Bluetooth in 958/9. He set up a great rune-stone in the churchyard at Jelling that proudly proclaimed he had acquired for himself all Denmark and Norway and made the Danes Christian. During his reign Harald defended his realm by a chain of fortresses (sometimes referred to as the royal fortresses of Denmark) and initiated other great engineering works such as the bridge at Ravning Enge on the road to Jelling. He was deposed by his son Svein Forkbeard (d. 1014) about 987, who later conquered England in 1013. Svein was the first of a line of kings to rule both Denmark and England until 1042, and also control south Norway.

**Norwegian unification**

With its long and indented coastline and high mountains which made communications in the interior extremely difficult, Norway was a difficult country to bring under the rule of one man. At the beginning of the Viking Age numerous chiefdoms were dotted around the Norwegian coast, from the Lofoten islands in the far north down to Vestfold and Østfold around the Oslo fjord. Fiercely independent, each was unwilling to submit to outside overlordship, and conflict rather than cooperation was the norm. Excavation of an 8th- to 9th-century homestead at Borg in the Lofoten islands allows us a glimpse of the life led by some of these early Norwegian chieftains. It must have been occupied by a family whose wealth and position were derived mainly from the rich fishing grounds of the area. However, finds of glass and pottery from the Rhineland show that Borg was no ordinary fishing community, but a place occupied by a family of great status with contacts with the outside world: the home of one of the lords of the North.

The move to bring these independent chiefdoms together into a single realm was a bloody and protracted undertaking that took 200 years to complete. The rich burials inside the great mounds of Oseberg and Borre attest to the presence of a ruling dynasty in southeast Norway in the 8th and 9th centuries, and we know from references in poetry and the sagas that Borre was a center of kingship in the Viking Age. The first king to achieve any sort of unification was Harald Finehair, who brought together Vestfold and the southwest of Norway in the 880s and in so doing seems to have alienated many of the people. This may have been the reason why so many emigrated to the Scottish islands and Iceland at the end of the 9th century. The north of Norway remained out of this union and was independently ruled by a family of earls based at Lade near Trondheim in Trøndelag, who must have achieved overlordship of the other chieftains there. The following centuries saw constant conflict between north and south, with the Danish kings at times playing a prominent part in the south. Sometimes the earls of Trøndelag supported the southern ruler, sometimes they did not, and the sagas tell of many battles and internecine quarrels.

At the end of the 10th century Olaf Tryggvason, great grandson of Harald Finehair, returning to Norway from exile abroad (where he had taken part in Viking attacks in England), used Trøndelag as a base from which to consolidate his control over the whole of the west coast. But after his death (in a sea battle at Svöld about the year 1000 fighting against the allied strength of Olof Skötkonung of Sweden and Svein Forkbeard of Denmark) the country was once again fragmented and for the next 15 years rule was divided between the Trøndelag earls in the north and Danish and Swedish kings in the south. The introduction of Christianity was an important factor in the unification of Norway. Olaf Tryggvason, converted during his exile in England, attempted to impose the new religion (and was instrumental in its introduction into Iceland) but there was a resurgence of pagan belief after his death, and it was left to his successor Olaf Haraldsson (1015–30) to win its general acceptance. After his death in the battle of Stiklestad in 1030 he was proclaimed a saint as St Olaf of Norway. More years of tumult were to follow, but by the end of the 11th century Norway was a substantially united and Christian country.

**Developments in Sweden and Finland**

It is not clear whether Sweden was ever united under a single ruler in the Viking Age. Most of the evidence for an incipient royal dynasty comes from the previous period – from the great burial mounds of the Svear in Uppland at Vendel, Valsgärde and Gamla Uppsala, which was famous as a center of pagan worship in the Viking Age. Similar great mounds with high-status grave-goods are known at Hovgården on Adelsö, an island in Lake Mälaren where there are also the remains of a later medieval royal castle. For the Viking Age itself, though, there is scant information. Kings are mentioned

*Above* Excavations in Borg on Vestvågøy, an island in Lofoten, have revealed the remains of an early Viking Age chieftain's house, over 80 meters long; it is situated on the low hill in the left foreground of this aerial view. Its owners possessed gold objects as well as pottery and glass from western Europe, reflecting their high social standing. However, most of the finds are of a domestic nature, farming and fishing being the basis of the family's livelihood.

from time to time; for example, we know from Rimbert's *Life of Ansgar* that King Bjorn welcomed the missionary to the town of Birka on the island of Björkö in Lake Mälaren in the 820s, after he had visited Hedeby and Ribe in Denmark. But it is not until the late 10th century that we know of a king whose rule reached beyond the land of the Svear. This is King Olof Skötkonung who extended his authority across the whole of central Sweden from the east to the west coast. It seems clear that, as in Denmark and Norway, Christianity played a significant part in the unification of Sweden. Olof was a Christian, and founded the first Swedish bishopric at Skara in Östergötland. It was, however, left to his successors to complete the country's conversion to the new faith in the later 11th century.

Finland remained pagan even longer, until the 12th century. Though "kings" are mentioned in later written sources, the areas dominated by Swedish Vikings – the southwest coast and the Åland islands – were probably ruled by a number of petty chieftains. Finland was in no sense united until well after the Viking Age.

## Fortifications

The dynastic quarrels and armed struggles that accompanied the process of state formation must have made the Viking Age a time of great uncertainty and unrest. Towns were becoming more prosperous, and needed stronger defenses against pirate attacks. By the end of the 10th century the Vikings had become skilled in the construction of town ramparts. Before that time fortifications in Scandinavia were built mainly to define and protect boundaries or to provide places of refuge for the population in times of trouble.

The most striking example of a linear defense work was the Danevirke, the name given to the series of ramparts built at slightly different times that together form a chain about 30 kilometers long across the southern neck of Jutland. In 808 the Danish king Godfred extended the original earth rampart, begun over 75 years earlier. The *Royal Frankish Annals* claim that he built a line of defense from the Baltic to the North Sea, but in fact his extensions stopped well short of the coast in the same extensive tract of boggy

# Gotland

In the Viking Age, the Baltic island of Gotland (a province of Sweden since the Middle Ages) was virtually an independent state. Its limestone soils provided fertile land for farming, and it was to a large extent self-sufficient, though raw materials for manufacturing – iron ore, fine-grained stone for making whetstones, glass cullet for beads, amber and silver – had all to be imported from outside. Its culture differed markedly in a number of respects from that of the Swedish mainland; for example, picture-stones – limestone slabs carved with mythological scenes and depictions of ships and warriors – are unknown outside Gotland. The jewelry that was made on the island to be worn by women was also different in type from the rest of Scandinavia. It was often of very high quality and – together with the immense quantities of silver found in hoards concealed in the Viking Age – provides evidence of the island's great wealth. Yet we are not entirely sure how this was acquired. Though its position in the middle of the Baltic Sea placed Gotland at the center of trade routes in the later medieval period, there is little to suggest that it had far-flung trading connections in the Viking Age. Its closest contacts seem to have been with the neighboring island of Öland to the west and the coastal areas of the southeast Baltic. It has been suggested that the Gotland islanders became rich through piracy, by preying on the merchant ships that plied the Baltic Sea routes. If so, they were truly the marauding Vikings of popular legend.

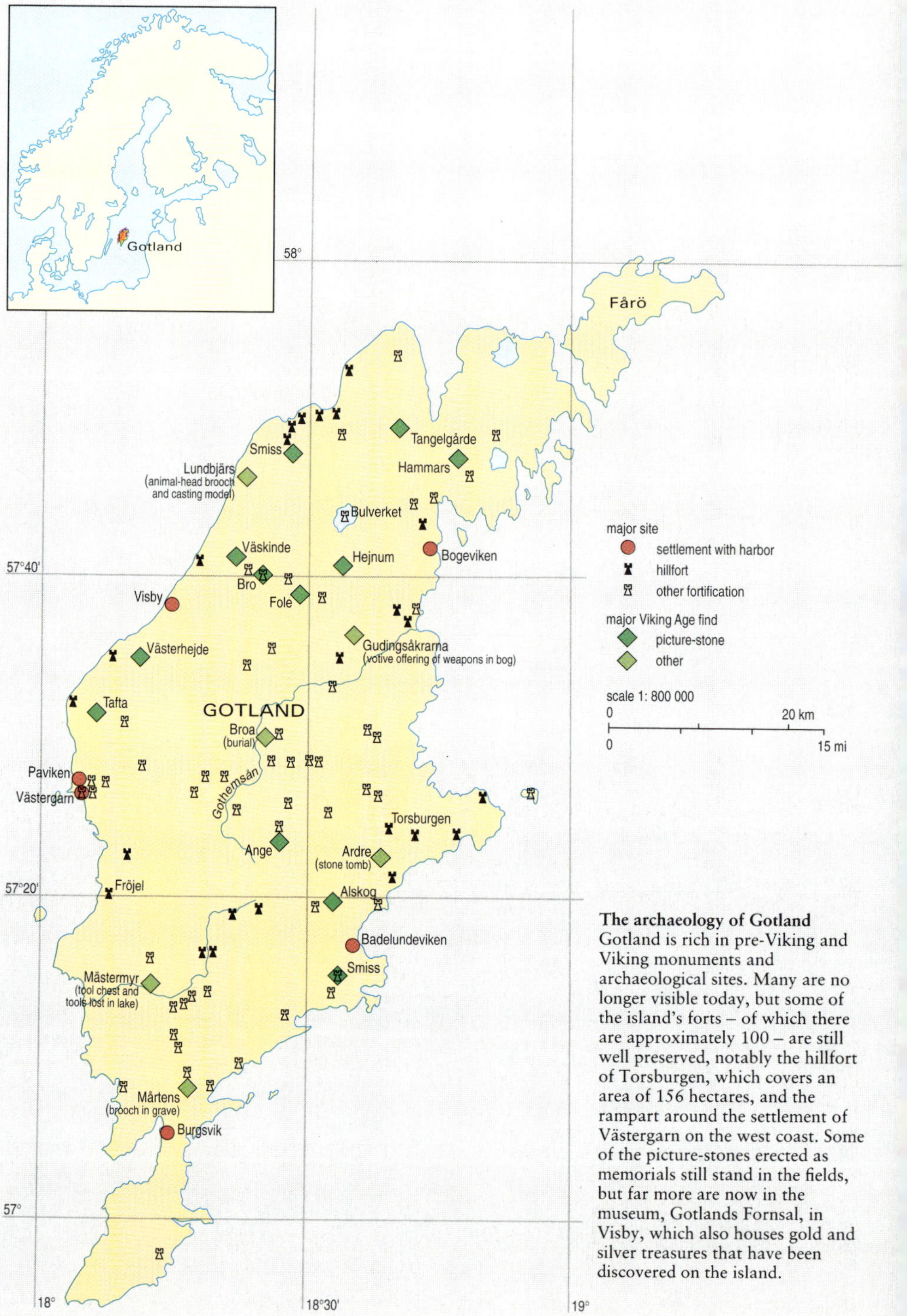


**The archaeology of Gotland** Gotland is rich in pre-Viking and Viking monuments and archaeological sites. Many are no longer visible today, but some of the island's forts – of which there are approximately 100 – are still well preserved, notably the hillfort of Torsburgen, which covers an area of 156 hectares, and the rampart around the settlement of Västergarn on the west coast. Some of the picture-stones erected as memorials still stand in the fields, but far more are now in the museum, Gotlands Fornsal, in Visby, which also houses gold and silver treasures that have been discovered on the island.

*Below* This drum-shaped brooch would have been worn by a woman of Gotland as an ornament in the middle of her chest. It is characteristic of the high-quality jewelry produced by Gotland's native craftsmen in the Viking Age. The brooch is of bronze embellished with gold and silver, the gold foils carrying human and animal ornament in filigree work and granulation, and the silver having plant decoration in the Ringerike style. Brooches of this type are unique to Gotland, and emphasize its cultural distinction from the rest of Scandinavia.

*Below* About 700 Viking Age hoards of silver coins (mainly Arabic, English and German) and jewelry have been found on Gotland. They represent the accumulated wealth of the islanders, perhaps acquired through piracy. This hoard, weighing more than 10 kilograms, was placed in a bronze bowl and buried about 1140 beneath the floor of a farmhouse at Burge. It consists of around 3,000 German coins, arm-rings and other jewelry made on Gotland itself. More than half its weight is made up of silver bars, many of them from Russia.

*Left* The small market center of Paviken, reconstructed here, lay beside a sheltered lagoon on the west coast of Gotland, which was otherwise badly provided with good natural harbors. Here the raw materials to support crafts such as bead-making and ironworking were imported, and ships were built and repaired.

*Right* The people of Gotland first began to erect memorials in the form of carved picture-stones in the 5th century, and did so throughout the Viking Age. Stone sculpture was hardly practiced anywhere else in Scandinavia before the 10th century. The vivid scenes they depict provide us with evidence about such things as styles of dress, armor and the way ships were rigged. The example shown here is from Tangelgårde in the north of Gotland.

land where the original rampart had ended. Godfred's wall was only broken by the Army Road (*hærvejen*), a prehistoric track or droveway, also known as the Ox Road, that ran the length of the Jutland peninsula and passed through a well-defended gateway in the rampart.

Some 160 years later the final Viking Age phase of the Danevirke was completed by King Harald Bluetooth. He joined the first two walls to the newly erected defense around the town of Hedeby at its eastern end by building an immensely strong earth rampart up to 13 meters wide, faced with turf and surmounted by a timber palisade. In all these early stages of building the Danevirke was made entirely of earth and timber; it was not until the 12th century that more durable materials such as stone and brick were used. Nevertheless, the Danevirke proved an enduring monument and so spectacularly successful in its purpose of defense that it was refortified during the Prussian–Danish war of 1864, and was even defended with anti-tank barriers in World War II.

Also predating the great period of fortification in the 10th century are the hillforts: almost 1,000 of them in Sweden alone, where they crown the tops of rocky hillocks in the broken landscape and are particularly numerous in the Mälaren area. It is not easy to date these monuments, which consist of rough walls made of huge granite boulders, from the archaeological evidence; there are no written sources to give us a guide, and at least some of them may be earlier than the Viking Age. Many of them, however, contain occupation remains from the Viking as well as earlier periods, and were clearly used, or reused, by the Vikings for communal defense.

Some of these Swedish hillforts, such as Stenbyborg on the island of Adelsö in Lake Mälaren, where there are also large burial mounds from the pre-Viking period, have associations with royal power; others, such as Gåseborg in Järfälla near Stockholm, may have served both as refuges and as religious cult centers. A particularly spectacular example is the fort of Runsa on a peninsula that juts out into the northern part of Lake Mälaren. It has an inner and outer rampart, the latter running along what was the lakeside in the Viking Age, and the inner enclosing the remains of buildings. This fort may have been occupied sporadically for fairly long periods of time, but it must also have served as a temporary refuge for the surrounding rural population. A burial ground close by contains an important burial marked by upright stones (some up to 2 meters high) arranged in the shape of a ship. It is surrounded by other less spectacular burials, and has been taken to suggest that Runsa may have had some cult significance.

The town of Birka, on the island of Björkö in Lake Mälaren, was already a flourishing center in the 9th century. The hillfort (*Borg*) close to its southern edge must have served as a strongpoint and refuge until the town was surrounded by defensive walls in the 10th century. The Birka fort consists of a rampart of earth and stone encircling the landward side of a hill whose western edge is naturally defended by a steep rocky cliff against the lake. The fort (*Hochburg*) overlooking the town of Hedeby in Viking Age Denmark (now in Germany) would have served a similar purpose. The fort crowns an outcrop of diluvial clay to the north of the town, but because the countryside is generally so flat, this type of monument is rare in Denmark.

The island of Gotland has about 100 forts, again

not all of Viking Age date. The largest is at Torsburgen near the east coast. Its great limestone wall stretches for 2 kilometers around the crest of a steep slope, standing up to 7 meters high and 24 meters wide in places, making it one of the most spectacular archaeological monuments in the whole of Sweden. Excavations have shown that it originated in the 4th century AD but was then reused in the early 10th century. Another defensive site on Gotland of considerable interest, though not a hillfort, is Bulverket in Lake Tingstäde Träsk in the north of the island. Standing in shallow water at the edge of the lake, it consists of a series of cellular wooden platforms built together to form the four sides of a square, each 170 meters long. They originally supported buildings. The central square is open, and the whole structure is surrounded by a palisade of closely set, heavy wooden stakes. This site is remarkably well preserved because of its waterlogged situation, and is unique in Scandinavia. The methods used in its construction are reminiscent of building techniques practiced by the Slavic peoples of the southern and eastern Baltic, and it may originally have been built by immigrants to Gotland. Its purpose is not entirely clear, but the place-name "Tingstäde" suggests that it was part of a Thing site in the Viking Age, when it was built and occupied, and therefore not used exclusively as a defensive structure.

The long narrow island of Öland has 16 pre-Viking forts, of which at least two, Ismanstorp and Eketorp, were also in use in the Viking Age. Both consist of a circular enclosing wall of limestone with the remains of buildings inside. Ismanstorp is 127 meters in diameter; its wall survives to a height of 2.5 meters and it is broken by as many as nine entrances. This number suggests that it cannot have been a very secure fortification; nevertheless, it seems to have been used as a refuge at the time of its construction and later in the Viking Age itself.

The Iron Age fort of Eketorp, abandoned as a permanent settlement about AD 700 except for sporadic use as a refuge, was reoccupied about the year 1000 when the earlier stone buildings were rebuilt in wood and the stone wall supplemented by an outer defense. In contrast to Ismanstorp, Eketorp's wall was pierced by only three entrances and it gives the impression of having been a much more formidable fortification, perhaps serving as the headquarters of a garrison charged with defending the south part of the island against seaborne attack. The finds from its latest phase show that it was also a trading center of considerable wealth and significance. Despite its trading activities, it did not develop into a fortified Viking Age town. These were provided with defenses of quite a different nature.

### Town defenses

Before the 10th century Viking towns were undefended unless, as at Hedeby and Birka, they had a hillfort some little distance away. The fact that the towns had been open settlements until then tells us that life must have been fairly peaceful in the 8th and 9th centuries, allowing urban activities to be carried on without threat from outside. Conditions had clearly changed in the 10th century, which witnessed a great campaign of wall-building. Hedeby, for example, gained the great rampart that connected it with the outer defenses of the Danevirke and is still visible today, standing up to 10 meters high in places. However, it began as a fairly small earth bank no more than 3 meters high, which was crowned by a timber palisade, and it reached its subsequent dimensions through repeated rebuildings and refurbishments. When it attained its final height it probably no longer needed a palisade to make it defensible, and in this respect it seems to have differed from other town walls. Its semicircular shape, though, is extremely characteristic of the encircling defenses of Viking Age towns.

Hedeby had grown up along the shores of an inlet, Haddeby Noor. The main objective of the defenses was to protect the town from the land. The semicircular rampart therefore enclosed the area in which the settlement lay, with its two ends running down to the waters of the Noor, but the whole of the shore lay open to raids from the sea. This danger was counteracted to some extent by the construction of an underwater palisade to protect the eastern approaches to the harbor.

A similar arrangement can be seen at Birka, but the town wall here is much slighter than that at Hedeby and must surely always have needed the added protection of a palisade. It is also very likely that the wall at Birka was never completed; only the northern part is visible today, and the long stretch that would

*Above* The Danevirke – a system of linear earthworks, built at various times, that cut across the base of the Jutland peninsula – formed the southern boundary of Denmark during the Viking Age; it also protected the developing town of Hedeby. Each of its various earthen ramparts carried a timber palisade and was fronted by a ditch, with cross-border traffic confined to a single gateway. It was thus a substantial fortification.

*Overleaf* The Danish Viking fortress of Fyrkat in northeast Jutland is one of a number built during the reign of Harald Bluetooth in the late 10th century.

## Viking Age Scandinavia

During the Viking Age, Denmark and southern and central Sweden supported small agricultural villages with a mixed farming economy. In Norway, scattered farming and fishing settlements extended up the Atlantic coast and along the fjord valleys. The first Scandinavian towns were founded at the beginning of the Viking Age as trading and manufacturing centers. More towns were founded in the 10th century; other settlements were seasonal market centers where goods were manufactured for local consumption. Hillforts served as defensive sites, but towns were not defended with ramparts until the 10th century.

have connected it to the fort (*Borg*) was possibly never built. The surviving length of wall describes a gentle curve, suggesting that it was intended to enclose a roughly semicircular area with the north end of the rampart continuing as far as the Lake Mälaren shore. The harbor was defended by a curving line of stakes and blockading timbers.

It is impossible to tell whether similar harbor defenses were built at Århus in Jutland, a town founded in the 10th century and surrounded by a substantial earth and timber rampart right from the beginning, since the modern harbor has wiped out all trace of a Viking Age predecessor. The shape of Århus's defenses, however, conforms closely to those of Hedeby and Birka, as does the semicircular rampart that defended Västergarn on the island of Gotland. Excavations have shown that this was also built in the 10th century. Finally, recently discovered urban fortifications at Ribe in Denmark suggest that this town, too, was surrounded by a semicircular defensive system in the 10th century. Excavations have exposed the remains of a ditch 1 meter deep and 8 meters wide, with some vestigial traces of an associated earth bank, and the short stretches of the ditch that have been traced follow a curving line.

The consistency of the town defenses of Denmark, Sweden and Gotland in the 10th century is intriguing. Their layout is so very similar that one is tempted to think that they are all part of a common plan. But this is unlikely to have been the case. They are more likely to represent spontaneous responses to the need for prosperous trading centers to defend themselves from attack by land or water, whether by Viking pirates or by Slav raiders, such as those who were to destroy Hedeby in 1066.

### A common defense plan

A group of sites in Denmark do, however, very definitely display a common plan. The so-called royal fortresses of Denmark were all built in the second half of the 10th century, occupied for a very short period and then abandoned, never to be reoccupied. Three of the forts (Aggersborg and Fyrkat in Jutland and Trelleborg on Sjælland) have been excavated and their plans and buildings can be reconstructed in detail. The fourth (Nonnebakken) lies beneath the present town of Odense on Fyn and almost all traces of it have long since disappeared. A fifth has recently been discovered at a site on the south coast of Skåne, also called Trelleborg. Its discovery was no great surprise; the coincidence of its name had always suggested to scholars that a fort similar to that of Trelleborg in Denmark might once have been built here. All the forts were exactly circular in plan although differing in diameter. The interior was surrounded by an earth and timber rampart with an external ditch, and divided into quarters by streets which crossed at right angles at the exact center of the circle. Long buildings with curved sides were positioned within each quarter. The similarity of the forts' plans, the precision with which they were laid out and the skill with which they were built single them out from all other Viking Age fortifications, strongly suggesting that they were built to the specifications of a single person.

The purpose for which these remarkable forts were built has been a matter of controversy ever since Trelleborg in Denmark (the first to be located) was excavated in the 1940s. The original suggestion was that the forts were built as garrisons and assembly points for the army that invaded England under Svein Forkbeard in the early 11th century. However, the tree-ring dating of timbers from the forts have since shown that they were built about 980 when Harald Bluetooth, Svein's father and predecessor, was king of Denmark. Excavation has shown that they were in existence for only a very short period, probably no more than 20 years at the most and perhaps much less than that. Moreover, had they been designed to house warriors who attacked England from the sea, they would have been situated close to the coast beside the harbors where the fleets would have assembled. The forts, however, lie adjacent to land rather than water routes, with only Aggersborg on the Limfjord standing beside a navigable fairway. They are all located in the north and east of the country, and look toward the Baltic rather than the North Sea.

Their role in the 11th-century conquest of England may therefore be discounted. All the evidence points to Harald Bluetooth as being the individual who commissioned them, probably to impose and maintain order in the kingdom that he had recently consolidated and converted to Christianity. They were undoubtedly strongholds and probably garrisoned, but their inhabitants did not restrict themselves to warlike activities. Living within their ramparts were gold- and silversmiths, and blacksmiths. Some of the buildings were used as barns and stables.

The most likely explanation, therefore, is that the Danish forts were centers of royal power from which armed forces could quickly be dispatched to control the surrounding countryside and uphold the authority of the king. They would collect tribute and taxes in kind from the rural population, and the forts both served as treasuries where the king's accumulated wealth could be kept safe and housed workshops where it could be converted into precious ornaments for himself and his court.

### Warfare and weapons

The right to carry weapons in the Viking Age was enjoyed by all free men. They were expected to assemble when called upon to do so by their king or overlord. In some areas, notably central Sweden, local people would also be required to man and arm ships. For this purpose, the land was split up into units containing a certain number of farms, each of which, when required to do so, had to provide a fully equipped ship.

The Vikings generally fought on foot. The fact that horses were buried with some rich Vikings suggests that there were some mounted warriors, but this was certainly not usual. The Viking warships were used mainly to transport armies to the scene of land battles; maritime engagements were less common, though some are mentioned in written sources. The best known of these is the battle of Svöld about 1000.

Accounts in English and Frankish sources of the land battles fought by the Vikings in western Europe attest to the strength and skill of their fighting forces. The Vikings struck terror into their opponents and carried fire and sword throughout northwestern Europe. The weapons that wreaked such havoc were the sword, the spear and the battle ax. Short fighting knives and bows and arrows were also used. Depictions in contemporary carvings, such as the memorial picture-stones found on Gotland, give us some idea of how these warriors looked fully armed for battle. We can learn much more from graves in the Scandinavian

*Right* Practical and beautiful: four Viking Age swords from Sweden, richly ornamented with inlaid decoration on their hilts, including animal ornament on the third from the left. These were single-handed weapons with double-edged blades, the finest of which were pattern-welded (like the one on the far left) by Frankish smiths in the Rhineland; their grips were finished with wood, which has perished in the ground.

countries and elsewhere, many of which contain the weapons and armor of the fighting men who were buried in them.

The sword was the finest of all the weapons, highly prized for its fighting strength and as a status symbol; the higher the rank of the warrior, the more magnificent would be his sword. Often the hilt would be richly decorated, but though an elaborate hilt denoted a powerful owner, it was the blade that was the most important part of the weapon, for it was on this that the life of its owner depended. The double-edged blades, between 70 and 80 centimeters long, were light and flexible, strong and sharp. Some of them were imported from the Frankish empire but their hilts were made and mounted in Scandinavia and they were often ornamented in the art styles favored by the Vikings. The most famous of the Frankish swordsmiths' workshops was that of Ulfberht, whose name is inlaid on many blades.

Blades of native Scandinavian workmanship were not inferior to the more exotic imported examples. They were also made in a method known as pattern-welding whereby long strips of iron of slightly different composition were welded together to form a core, and a cutting edge of a harder and sharper steel was welded to the sides. Then the blade was polished and a longitudinal groove (known as a fuller) ground out along the whole length. The purpose of the fuller was to lighten the blade without reducing its strength and to increase its flexibility. After a thousand years in the earth, most of the sword blades that have been recovered are now badly corroded but some of them still display beautiful patterns on their surfaces.

Swords were carried in scabbards made of strips of wood covered in leather and lined with fleece; the lanolin from the wool would have served to preserve the blade from tarnishing and rust. The most splendid swords were kept in magnificent scabbards decorated with bronze or gilt mounts around the mouth and at the tip (the chape). Scabbard mounts have been found in many graves, though the organic materials of the scabbard itself have usually disappeared.

The double-edged swords were used to slash at the enemy, no doubt inflicting terrible wounds. The mutilated bones of skeletons unearthed at Hedeby and elsewhere give some idea of the sort of injuries caused. Short, single-edged fighting knives were designed for thrusting at the opponent when engaged in close combat, and the Viking warriors sometimes carried both sword and knife. The most efficient thrusting weapon of all was the spear with its slender, tapering iron blade up to 50 centimeters long attached to a wooden shaft by means of a socket. Some spears, like the finest quality swords, must have been weapons of status. Their blades were pattern-welded with sharp cutting-edges and point, and the sockets were inlaid with silver or bronze. Most of the spears that have been found in graves, however, are simpler and undecorated – but nevertheless very efficient.

Though the battle ax is popularly associated with the Vikings, on the whole it seems to have been less favored as a weapon than the sword and spear. Fewer have been found, and those mostly in western Scandinavia. They were made in a quite simple way: a sharp cutting-edge was welded onto a shaped block of iron, and the butt end was then slotted over a wooden

*Below* Ax-blades and spear-heads from the river Thames at London are grim reminders of the return of Viking armies to England during the reign of Æthelred II (979–1016). Any ax could always have been used as a weapon, but those shown here, with their elongated "bearded blades", were developed specifically for use in battle by Scandinavian warriors.

*Above* Not all axes were merely functional. This ceremonial ax has inlaid silver decoration on both faces of its blade. It was buried in a high-status chamber-grave, constructed c. 970, at Mammen in Jutland, and may well have been made in a royal workshop of King Harald Bluetooth. Its high-quality ornament has given its name to the Mammen style of Viking art.

handle and wedged tight. Most battle axes were undecorated and are indistinguishable from working axes; their attribution as battle axes results from the fact that they have been found in graves with other weapons. A few examples are much more splendid and must have been made for ceremony or display. The finest by far is the ax from the royal or aristocratic burial at Mammen, Jutland. This is inlaid with silver in the elaborate patterns that give their name to the Mammen art style, and it is difficult to imagine it ever being used in battle; it was probably a symbol of wealth, status and power.

Bows and arrows were also used in warfare, but were probably most commonly used in hunting. Iron arrow-heads in various different shapes survive in large numbers, though their wooden shafts have nearly always disappeared. Wooden bows are rarer, as – being made of wood – they have usually decomposed entirely in normal soil conditions, but a complete one has been found in waterlogged ground at Hedeby. It is 192 centimeters long and made of yew, a strong, supple wood that was used to make bows throughout the Middle Ages.

The Vikings defended themselves in battle by carrying circular shields that gave protection to the body from shoulder to thigh. They were made of wood, often lime, and were sometimes covered in leather with the rim strengthened by an iron band. The shields might then be decorated with metal mounts and symbols and were sometimes brightly painted. An iron boss in the center protected the carrying hand. Little of the wood from the shields has been preserved, but it is possible to calculate their size from the metal fittings that have survived. The shields found in the Gokstad ship burial, which were painted black and yellow, are 1 meter in diameter, and it is reasonable to assume that this was the normal size.

Another means of protection was provided by the helmet and body armor worn by at least some Vikings. However, such items are found so rarely in graves or other archaeological sites that it seems unlikely that they were ever commonly worn and were probably the prerogative of the highest ranks of society. The only helmet to have been preserved from the Viking Age was found in a grave at Gjermundbu in Norway. Clearly a very great man was buried here, for as well as a helmet he had a coat of chain mail and a fine sword with a hilt inlaid with silver and copper. Both helmet and mail coat were in a fragmentary condition when discovered, but the helmet has been reconstructed and is now in the Oldsaksamling Museum, Oslo. The iron helmet is dome-shaped with a central crest and a sort of visor to protect the nose and cheek-bones. Some chain mail hung from the back to protect the neck. The rest of the chain mail was probably in the form of a short tunic worn over a padded or leather jerkin to provide extra protection.

Other helmets are known only from pictorial representations. The helmets of the warriors depicted on the Gotlandic picture-stones are invariably conical in shape and have a nose guard. A little figure from Sigtuna in Sweden, carved in elk antler, also wears a conical helmet with a nose guard, which is decorated with a ring-and-dot motif. It is impossible to tell whether these helmets were made of iron like the Gjermundbu example; they may have been of a less sturdy material such as leather. However, we do know that none of them carried horns.

Equipment such as this probably belonged to the rich and powerful among the Viking forces, or to the professional fighting men who made up the private armies or bodyguards of kings and lords, particularly in Norway. The splendid swords with decorated hilts and Frankish blades, the helmets and chain mail tunics, would have been quite unknown to the vast mass of fighting men, farmers and fishermen who were pressed into service at times of trouble to fulfill their duties to their overlord. These men would have been simply armed, probably carrying only their working ax to serve as a battle weapon.

# Royal Fortresses of Denmark

The 10th-century fortresses of Denmark are one of the clearest evidences we have of a centralized power structure in Denmark in the late Viking Age. Five such fortresses are now known: Trelleborg on the island of Sjælland, Nonnebakken on Fyn, Fyrkat and Aggersborg in Jutland, and (only discovered in the late 1980s) Trelleborg in Skåne. Most of our information about the fortresses comes from Trelleborg in Sjælland and Fyrkat, which have both been extensively excavated. The forts are precisely regular in plan. The circular earth and timber rampart is pierced by four equidistant entrances, and the axial streets divide the interior into four segments, or quadrants. At Trelleborg and Fyrkat each of these quadrants was filled with four long buildings arranged in a square: at Aggersborg there seem to have been 12 buildings in each. At Trelleborg, a further 15 buildings were laid out concentrically to the rampart, but outside it, in an outer defended area. All the buildings were of oak, and the streets were surfaced with timber.

Construction of the forts must have taken considerable planning and engineering skill. To build the fort at Fyrkat, for example, the site had first to be leveled and extended, and 10,000 cubic meters of turf and earth were shifted to construct the rampart. The plans of the forts are so similar that they can only have been the work of a single organizing authority, presumably the king's, and given the regularity of the layout, it is not surprising that they were at first thought to have had a purely military function: the buildings, it was argued, must have served as barracks, perhaps for the army assembled by Svein Forkbeard to invade England at the beginning of the 11th century.

This view is no longer accepted. Excavation of the buildings at Fyrkat showed that some were used as dwellings, others as workshops where blacksmiths and jewelers worked. Women and children were found to have been buried in the cemetery just beyond the rampart. Moreover tree-ring dating indicated that the timber used in the buildings at Trelleborg came from trees felled about 980 – in the reign of Harald Bluetooth. Those at Fyrkat give similar results, and the buildings show no sign of having been repaired, suggesting that they cannot have been in use for more than 20 or 30 years. If, as is now supposed, the fortresses were used as centers of royal administration where taxes were collected, and as strongpoints for controlling the local population, their short life and rapid abandonment suggest that political changes at the end of the century rendered them unnecessary.

*Left* Aerial view of Trelleborg, Sjælland, from the west. It stands at the tip of a low peninsula that was surrounded by marshy ground in the Viking Age. The precisely circular earth rampart with its four entrances can be clearly seen, and in the foreground there is a slighter rampart enclosing an outer area. The postholes of the buildings have been marked in concrete, showing their curved shape, and a full-scale reconstruction of one of the houses appears in the foreground.

*Right* This reconstruction of one of the buildings at Fyrkat was erected next to the site in the 1980s. The long walls are bowshaped, and as a result the roof is also curved. Outer posts slope up to support the top of the walls. On the Trelleborg reconstruction, the posts are upright and form part of a verandah or gallery round the building, but evidence from the excavations at Fyrkat and reinterpretation of the archaeological remains at Trelleborg show that the Fyrkat reconstruction must be correct. The interior of the house is divided into three rooms – a large hall in the center and a smaller room at each end.

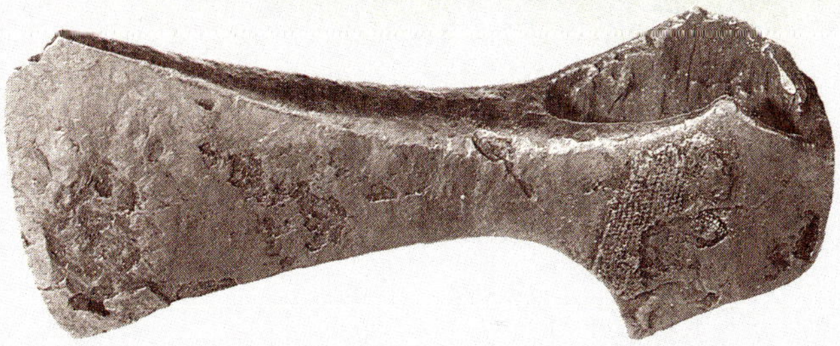

*Left* The head of a battle-ax from a grave at Fyrkat. Battle-axes were particularly favored by the Vikings of Norway and Denmark, and they became the symbol of Norse ferocity to the people of western Europe who suffered their attacks.

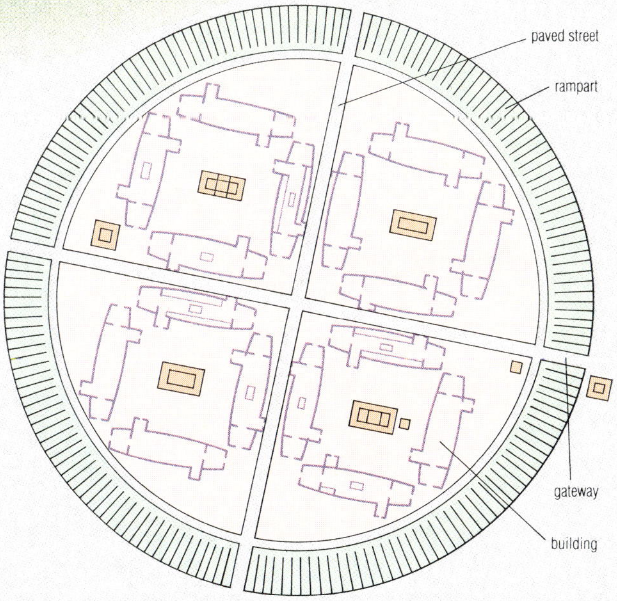

*Top* This reconstruction gives an artist's impression of the royal fortress at Fyrkat based on the findings of the excavations. The outer face of the rampart was lined with heavy tongued-and-grooved timbers to prevent attackers from scaling it. One of the four quadrants has not been excavated.

*Above* The regularity of Fyrkat's plan – with four long buildings symmetrically placed within each quadrant, streets crossing at right angles, and an exactly circular perimeter – gives the fortress a distinctly military appearance, but recent investigations have shown that it was not merely a barracks. The buildings were used as dwellings, workshops, stores and stables.

# DAILY LIFE

**Rural communities**

Most Vikings were farmers. Even those who went on raiding parties to western Europe or sailed east or west as merchants generally returned home to the farm, bringing their loot or profits with them. Since agriculture was of such importance, it is strange that we know comparatively little about it. The best evidence comes from Denmark, which had the largest area of cultivable land. Many farming villages have been excavated there in recent years, and several rural settlements are also known from central Sweden, where crop farming was also important. In Norway it was limited to the south, and virtually nothing is known about the farms.

The most important cereals grown on Viking Age farms in Scandinavia were barley, rye and oats, with a little wheat also being cultivated in Denmark. Although wheaten bread has been found in some of the graves at Birka, central Sweden, there is no positive evidence to show that wheat was grown in the vicinity of the town, and it may have been imported as a luxury foodstuff. Peas, beans, root vegetables and cabbage were also commonly grown crops.

*Above* A selection of iron tools used by Viking Age farmers, found in Norway. Sickle blades (center), needed for harvesting, are those most commonly found, in both male and female graves; other tools, such as scythe blades (top) and plow shares (right) are more generally restricted to male burials. As well as hay, foliage was an important source of winter fodder for cattle, and special broad-bladed "leaf-knives" are known (bottom), but these are less commonly found in graves.

*Left* A massive drift of sand covered this field at Lindholm Høje in northern Jutland sometime during the 11th century. When this was removed, the field was revealed exactly as it had been before the fatal storm, even down to the footprints and wheel tracks across the broad parallel beds that are separated by narrow furrows. It is not known what crop was being grown here.

Archaeological investigation in Denmark has yielded evidence of some of the fields where crops were grown, as well as some of the farming methods used. At Ribe simple scratchings have been found on the ground surface beneath the Viking Age town. These show that an ard was used to break up the soil preparatory to sowing. The ard is a primitive wooden plow that merely cuts a groove through the earth and does not turn it; it was in common use until the late Viking Age when a heavier plow with an iron-shod share was introduced. A rare find was made at Lindholm Høje in north Jutland in the 1950s, when archaeologists removed the thick layer of blown sand that had submerged the site, bringing occupation to an end in the 11th century, and discovered beneath it a fossilized Viking Age field with its long, slightly curving furrows still intact from its last plowing.

Other agricultural tools must have been very common on all rural settlements, but have not survived in very great numbers. Cereals and hay were harvested with iron sickles, and vegetation was cut for fodder with a special implement known as a leaf knife. Wooden pitchforks and spades have been found, and flails and sieves for threshing and sifting the grain would also have been made of wood. Barrels and baskets were used for storage, and hay grown for fodder may have been transported from the fields in carts.

Denmark's Viking Age villages were surrounded by arable fields, but they were also well placed for access to pasture. The rearing of animals was just as important as crop growing, and indeed cattle farming was probably the predominant activity in many villages. Pigs and sheep were also raised. On the Scandinavian peninsula pastoralism was even more important, and transhumance (seasonal migration) was practiced in the upland areas (as it still is today in some places). Flocks and herds would be driven up to the higher pastures in the summer when grazing was good and brought down to the valley farms in the fall. Cattle would be kept under cover during the hard winters and stall-fed with the hay grown on the valley pastures in the summer and cut and stored as fodder for this purpose.

The best-known of Denmark's excavated farming villages are at Sædding and Vorbasse in central Jutland. Though not identical in plan or layout, these and others share a number of features in common. They consisted of about six or seven individual farms, each of which contained about eight or nine buildings of various size, enclosed within a fenced compound. The largest building was the dwelling house, which had a cattle byre at one end with stalls for up to 50 animals. The outbuildings included barns and smithies and a scattering of sunken-floored huts that may have housed the farm slaves or laborers. There was usually a wood-lined well within the compound. Each farm would have been occupied by a single family, and all give the impression of having been very prosperous between the 8th and the 10th centuries. At Sædding the buildings within their fenced enclosures lie around a central open space that was never built on and must have served as a communal "village green"; at Vorbasse the farms were laid out along a village street, four to the north and three to the south, each with a gateway in the fenced enclosure giving on to the central track. This difference in the overall layout suggests that the two settlements may have had dissimilar social functions.

These settlements do not lie beneath the villages of today, but are found a short distance away. During the 300 years of the Viking Age they did not occupy a permanent site, but shifted to a new location a few hundred meters away every generation or so. The position of Denmark's farming villages only became fixed with the coming of Christianity when a stone church was built as the community's focal point. This was at a time when population was increasing, and there was a shift toward greater arable farming. The villages founded then have remained on the same site – usually one that was close to the best land for growing crops – until the present day.

At one time it was thought that the Viking Age farms of central Sweden were isolated from their neighbors, as they are today, and perhaps lay beneath today's farms – in other words, it was suggested that the same farm sites had been continuously occupied for over 1,000 years. However, excavations of Viking Age villages at Pollista and Sanda in the Mälaren district have made it clear that this was not the case, assuming that they are typical. Though much smaller than the villages of Denmark, each contained several farmsteads with a dwelling and outbuildings, which are reminiscent of the Danish groupings. The villages in the Mälaren valley seem to have moved from time to time, as they did in Denmark, and are therefore unlikely to have been located where the present farms now stand.

The agricultural communities of Viking Age Norway remain elusive. Many farms from the pre-Viking period have been discovered in the southwest of the country, but the Viking Age itself is hardly represented. The reason for this may be that here the farms were indeed isolated and scattered, and so are difficult to find today. One of the few Viking Age farms to have been excavated in Norway is the 9th- and 10th-century settlement of Ytre Moa at the inland end of the Sogne fjord. It is not a village of Danish type, but a single isolated farmstead consisting of several small roughly square buildings, each used for a different purpose; for example, dwelling, storehouse or cattle shed. The shapes of the buildings and the methods of their construction also differ from their Danish counterparts. All the Ytre Moa buildings are no more than a few meters square, with thick walls of stone and turf with wooden paneling on the internal faces. The difficulty of locating Viking Age sites in the Norwegian countryside means that much more work is needed to be done before the agriculture of that country can be fully understood.

In some parts of Scandinavia – particularly along the coasts of Norway – fishing played an even more important role than agriculture in the Viking Age economy. Many fishing implements have been found showing that nets, lines and harpoons were all used. Seal and walrus were also caught in the northern waters. Ivory from the tusks of walrus was highly prized throughout Europe at this time; it was only in the 13th century that it began to be replaced by elephant ivory in large quantities, and the trade declined. Walrus hides were cut into strips and twisted to make rope.

Lakes and rivers supplied freshwater fish. Salmon were especially abundant in Finland, and regular fishing expeditions were made to the north in the spawning season when the rivers teemed with fish. That fish and shellfish featured prominently in the Viking Age diet is evident from the large numbers of fish bones and shells that have been recovered from household refuse heaps in the towns. At Birka, for example, fish would have been caught in Lake Mälaren and the rivers that flowed into it, but it is also clear that they were transported considerable distances from the sea, probably having been salted in barrels to preserve them.

## Houses

The Vikings of Scandinavia mostly built in wood, though stone and turf were also used in some areas, particularly Norway. Nothing remains of the houses themselves above ground level, and we have therefore to rely on the interpretation and reconstruction of archaeological evidence, recovered through excavation, to give us a picture of the buildings in which the Vikings lived. For example, the traces of postholes in the ground (distinguishable from the surrounding soil by differences of color and texture) allow archaeologists to estimate the length and arrangement of a timber-framed building.

The basic shape of the buildings was the same

*Left* Iron fish-hook and barbed fish-spear, with a stone net-sinker, from Norway. This fish-spear was found near a waterfall and may have been used for salmon fishing.

*Above* A river in central Sweden. Coastal and freshwater fishing contributed greatly to diet in Viking Age Scandinavia, and there was even some trade in fish products.

throughout Scandinavia: rectangular, sometimes with curving walls, and of variable length. Buildings excavated at Sædding in Denmark are nearly 50 meters long; at Borg in Lofoten, Norway, one even reached a length of 83 meters. The width, however, was seldom more than 5 meters, and was dictated by the dimensions of the crosstimbers used to carry the roof. These were supported on two rows of posts that ran the length of the building and divided it longitudinally into three sections consisting of a central nave and two rather narrower side aisles. Sometimes, though, the posts were set back into the walls, and these then carried the ends of the roof rafters. This latter arrangement provided an uninterrupted internal space, and was the norm by the end of the Viking Age. Aristocratic halls would have most likely resembled these rural buildings, except that they would have been larger and more richly furnished – the very great length of the house at Borg suggests that it was a chieftain's dwelling. No royal halls, with the possible exception of one at Lejre and those in the 10th-century royal forts of Denmark, have been excavated.

In Denmark the deciduous woodlands provided oaks to build the framework of the houses and hazels and willows for weaving the wickerwork panels that filled the spaces between the upright posts of the walls. These were then covered with a mixture of clay and dung to make them draft- and weather-proof. This type of infill is known as wattle-and-daub. The buildings in the royal forts had solid timber walls but these have not yet been discovered on any farming settlements; they used very large quantities of oak and would probably have been beyond the resources of the average farmer.

Few oaks are found in Sweden and Norway, except in the far south and so softwoods (conifers) were used for building. These provided the long straight horizontal timbers that were piled one on top of another and

# Life in the Home

Much of what we know about domestic life in Viking Age Scandinavia comes from the household possessions that were included as grave-goods in burials. Often, though, these are found in the graves of wealthy individuals, and it is likely that most ordinary households – especially those in the countryside – contained few possessions. What people had they made themselves, from their clothes, toys and cooking utensils to their own houses. Only iron implements and items such as combs, brooches and necklaces were provided by itinerant craftsmen or bought in the towns in exchange for farm produce. Imported luxuries such as spices, wine, and silks were mostly enjoyed by the cosmopolitan urban populations.

It is clear that men and women had distinct roles in the household. The men worked in the fields and on the farm, fished and hunted for game, while the women prepared the food (including grinding the grain for flour, baking and dairying), spun the wool from the farm's sheep and worked at the loom or with the needle. In wealthier households, servants and slaves would have carried out many of the most menial tasks. The men would often be away from home for long periods as sailors, warriors or traders, leaving the women to guard the house and to supervise the work of the household.

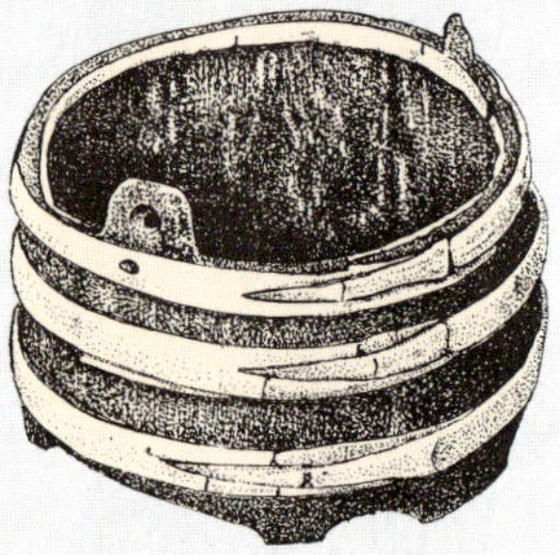

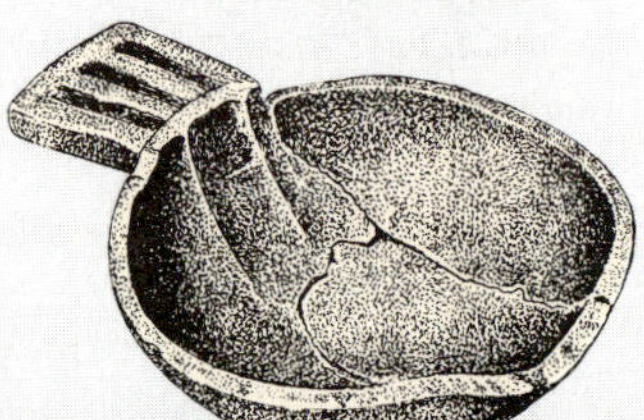

*Above and right* The iron cauldron and griddle (top) were part of the household equipment of a Norwegian family. Gruel, stews and boiled meat and fish would have been prepared in the cauldron, and the griddle was probably used for making flat, unleavened bread over the fire. Wood was more common than iron for household vessels, and would probably have been carved and shaped by the men of the household. The small bucket (center) is made of staves of ash bound together with osier hoops, and the bowl (bottom) of elm. Its handle is pierced so that it could be hung up when not in use.

*Left* This interior of a Viking Age house, based on one excavated at Hedeby, has been reconstructed at Moesgård Museum, Århus, Denmark. The long open hearth is the focus of the room: a source of heat and light, and the only means of cooking. An iron cauldron is suspended from the ceiling on a chain; a soapstone bowl and a wooden bowl and ladle stand beside the fire. The furniture is very sparse – just a stool covered by a sheepskin on the raised earthen bench against one wall. Most people slept on the ground. The two looms leaning against the walls would have been in daily use by the women. The larger loom with its stone loomweights to tauten the warp (*bottom left*) was used for weaving woolen cloth; the smaller loom produced narrower bands of finer wool, or perhaps linen (flax was grown in southern Scandinavia). The bone pins (*bottom right*) were used for adjusting the thread during weaving. Finished products would have been smoothed by rubbing them on a whalebone board with a glass smoother (*below*).

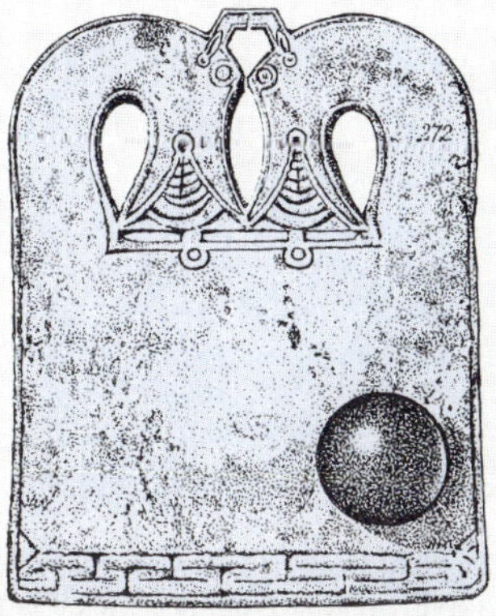

*Left* This full-size reconstruction of a Viking Age town house from Hedeby stands at Moesgård Museum in Denmark. It measures 12 by 5 meters and has wattle-and-daub walls in a timber framework, with the weight of the thatched roof supported by external buttresses. This Hedeby house, built about 870, had a central living room, between two other rooms, one of which contained a baking-oven.

*Below* This blockhouse construction of horizontal logs with lapped corners is just one of the many different methods of building in wood that were utilized in Viking Age Scandinavia.

notched together at the corners to form firm joints. The length of each building was dependent on the length of tree trunks available, and so these houses were often made up of a series of independent rooms joined end to end to form a single blockhouse. Sometimes, however, a farm consisted of a scattering of small buildings, each with its own function. The lowest timbers of the walls usually rested on a row of stones that formed a sill and this prevented the logs from rotting as they lay on the damp ground. The sill might also support a timber floor, which raised in this way provided some form of insulation and was protected from decay. These sill stones are often all the evidence that remains of the buildings in a rural settlement.

One end of the dwelling houses was used as a barn for storing crops or partitioned into stalls for cattle. Living under the same roof as their animals provided a source of heat for the inhabitants; a rather noisome form of central heating. It also ensured that their beasts would be safe from rustlers, as cattle were wealth. The living quarters of the house had a hearth in the middle of the floor to provide heat, light and cooking facilities. There were no chimneys and the smoke from the hearth escaped through gaps in the roof, which was covered with thatch, turf or wooden shingles depending on the availability of local materials. Benches ran along the walls. They were usually an integral part of the structure, consisting of flattened banks of earth reinforced at the front with wickerwork. There was little other furniture, and the benches acted both as beds and as seating accommodation during the day. Simple crafts such as spinning, weaving and basket-making were carried on at the benches, but some farms had separate buildings for particular activities. A forge has been found at Sædding, for example, and many farmsteads must have had similar provision for making and repairing essential tools. The sunken-floored huts that are a feature of Danish Viking Age villages may also have been used as workshops for weaving, primitive potting and so on.

Buildings in towns did not need space for crop-storage or cattle, so they were shorter than those of the countryside. The best evidence we have of town houses comes from Hedeby where waterlogged conditions have preserved the foundations and lower parts of the walls of wooden buildings and even a complete gable of one house, about 5 meters high. The Hedeby houses were rectangular, about 12 meters long and 5 meters wide. The walls were made of upright posts infilled with wattle-and-daub and they were buttressed on the exterior by sloping posts. There were three rooms; the largest, central room contained the hearth and the smaller rooms, one at each end, provided storage space and working areas for the merchants and craftsmen of the town who occupied these houses.

One of the Hedeby houses contains an oven in one of the small rooms, but ovens were not common in Scandinavia in the Viking Age, and the provision of a separate kitchen is unusual. Most of the light inside the houses came from the fire in the central room, possibly supplemented by oil lamps, but a couple of tiny windows would have let in a little daylight. Wood-fronted earth benches were set along the walls close to the hearth; the floors were of beaten earth. The solid wooden doors to the houses could be locked.

# Leisure

Gambling games with dice have been played since antiquity, and it is clear that the Vikings were no exception in finding relaxation and excitement in this way – the dice found in Viking Age graves are often large and oblong. Gaming-boards have also been found, including a double-sided one from the Gokstad ship-burial in Norway, as well as numerous gaming pieces for playing games that combined luck and skill: some were positional games, similar to nine-men's-morris or three-in-a-row, but games of pursuit similar to fox-and-geese were also played. A particular type of war-game played throughout Scandinavia during the Viking Age was known as *hnefatafl*. It appears from the many references to it in the Icelandic sagas to have been a game calling for real skill, but even so it did not survive the advance of chess, which superseded it in the early Middle Ages: the chessmen, carved from walrus ivory and of Scandinavian origin, found on the Isle of Lewis in the Hebrides, belong to the 12th century, at the end of the Norse period. The rules of *hnefatafl* are not recorded, but finds of playing pieces and knowledge of later games indicate that it was played between two players who had unequal forces and different objectives – a king with a small army was attacked by a larger army that tried to drive the king into a corner.

Feasts provided indoor entertainment for the better-off and were occasions not only for drinking and general excess, but also for listening to recitations of poems and stories by professional skalds, as well as for music and dance. We know little of the latter, however. Musical instruments have only rarely been found because they were made of wood and other perishable materials, but we know that the lyre or harp were played, as were simple flutes and pan-pipes and a form of fiddle.

Outdoor activities included contests of strength and skill. The importance of training with weapons led naturally to competition in fencing, spear-throwing and shooting with bow and arrow. Ball-games were played for pleasure, and were also enjoyed by spectators. Horse-fighting, too, was popular with audiences – contests in which specially selected stallions would be goaded on to fight with each other by the sight and smell of tethered mares. The sport is often referred to in Icelandic stories, since it frequently gave rise to quarrels and fights between contending owners. Clearly, though, relaxation could also be sought in private, in such solitary pursuits as playing a flute or whittling a stick.

Children had their toys and some of those that survive, such as wooden weapons and toy boats, show them engaged in imitative play. For adults, there was often no sharp line to be drawn between leisure and doing things in earnest – animals were hunted both for food and for sport, though the nobility had, as always, more time for the latter, and falconry was a pursuit reserved to the aristocracy. We know from the sagas that "swimming and board-play" were sports to be taught to a young *jarl*, or earl.

*Right* Playing-pieces were made of many materials and in all shapes and sizes, both flat bottomed and with pegs, for use on different types of board. Sets of pieces, including "kings" have been found in Viking Age graves. These various examples in glass, bone and stone were excavated from the Swedish town of Lund.

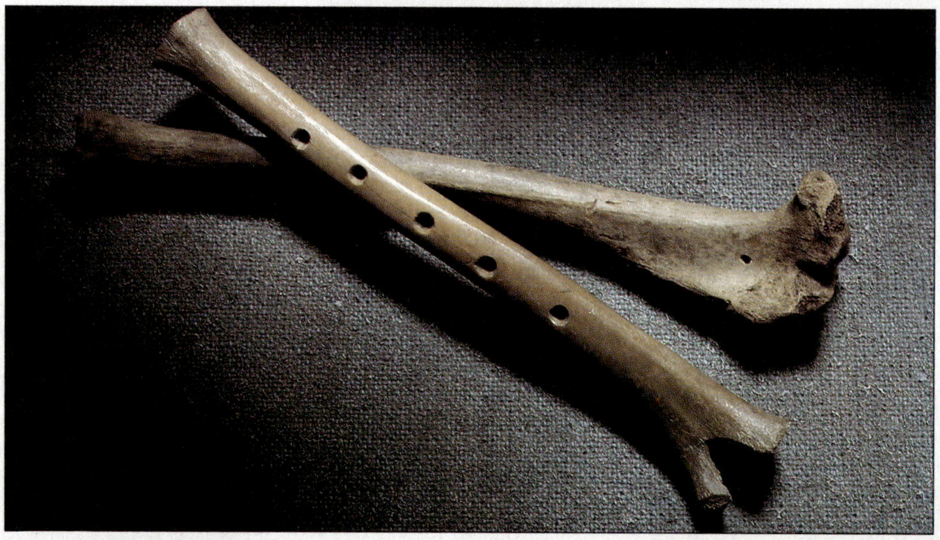

*Below* Among the few musical instruments to have survived from the Viking Age are end-blown flutes, such as this one from Sigtuna in Sweden. They are similar to the modern recorder and were made from the long bones of animals or birds, with varying numbers of finger-holes.

*Left* Falconry was the sport of noblemen. It may be portrayed on this 10th-century cross-shaft, an Anglo-Scandinavian carving from Sockburn in Co. Durham – though this horseman carrying a bird on his wrist, beneath a snake, has also been interpreted as a depiction of the pagan god Odin.

*Top right* This 11th-century Swedish rune-stone shows two men playing "at board" (*at tafli*): the game may be nine-men's-morris, which was widely played in the Viking Age, or *hnefatafl*. The wooden *hnefatafl* board (*right*) was found on a native Irish settlement at Ballinderry, Co. Westmeath. It has a marked center and corners, and 7 x 7 peg-holes; the style of decoration suggests that it could well have been made in 10th-century Dublin. The number of playing spaces on the *hnefatafl* board varied, though it was always uneven – the Gokstad board has 15 x 15, as has another from 10th-century York.

*Below* Horse-fighting as a Viking Age spectator sport may have had its origins in earlier horse cults. These fighting horses depicted on a stone from Häggeby in Uppland, Sweden, carved in the Migration Period, have clearly had horns attached to their heads. They are being urged on by armed men.

## Domestic life

The house was the center of Viking life. Here people found warmth, food and shelter. Here they worked at their everyday tasks and relaxed by playing board games, making music and listening to poets telling stories about the gods and the exploits of past heroes. Life was carried on around the long central hearth. The brushwood fire rarely went out, but when required to be relit, it was done by striking flint against steel. Meat and fish made up most of the diet. Domesticated animals (cattle, sheep, pigs, goats and poultry) were supplemented with game and wild fowl. Both meat and fish were smoked, dried or salted in the summer and fall to ensure adequate provisions for the long winter months. The meat was mostly cooked by boiling in coarse, hand-made pottery or soapstone bowls embedded in the embers of the fire, or in an iron cauldron suspended over the flames by an iron chain. Iron hooks were used to fish the meat out of the boiling liquid. Occasionally a particularly tender joint might be roasted on a spit.

Bread was made from barley, rye and pulses, and (less commonly) wheat. Flour was handmilled on circular grindstones or querns. These have survived in quantity and, particularly in south Scandinavia, were often made of lava stone imported from the Rhineland in Germany. The bread was unleavened and would have been baked over the fire on a flat iron or stone plate to make a thickish pancake or griddle cake. Vegetables were grown in the adjacent fields and berries and other fruits gathered in the forests, or even imported; the discovery of plum stones in rubbish pits in Hedeby suggests they were brought there from central Europe, for instance. Cheese was made from cows', sheep and goats' milk, mainly perhaps as a way of using the surplus. Meals were washed down with large quantities of ale, made with barley, and mead, made of fermented honey and water. *Bjórr*, possibly a strong liquor made from fermented fruit juice, was also drunk.

Drinking cups would have been of wood or pottery; drinking horns were also used. Imported glass vessels would have been used only by the upper strata of society. Platters, bowls, spoons and ladles were made of wood, and have mostly vanished, either through decay or because broken wooden objects would have been thrown in the fire as a convenient source of fuel. Some examples, however, have been preserved in waterlogged ground. Most have the appearance of being hand-carved, probably by members of the household, but some vessels were lathe-turned, suggesting that specialized woodworkers may also have produced goods for the home.

From the grave-goods found in royal and aristocratic burial mounds we may deduce that many aristocratic halls were furnished with tables, settles or chairs, and possibly even beds: a chair and beds, for example, were buried with the 9th-century queen interred at Oseberg in Norway. Fragments of a woven tapestry, used as a wall-hanging, were also found. However, ordinary people had few such possessions, making do with stools and chests in which valuables (such as jewelry, silver and clothing) were kept under lock and key. Wrapped in blankets or skins, they slept not in beds but on the fixed benches: the closer to the hearth, the higher your rank in the household.

Occupying a place against the wall in most houses would have been the upright warp-weighted loom for weaving the woolen cloth used by the household and also for making the sails of Viking ships. Being made of wood, no complete Viking Age loom survives. However, there are many examples of the baked clay or stone weights that held the vertical threads (the warp) tight. Tablet-weaving was also done on small rectangular frames of wood or antler to produce intricately patterned bands, braid and ribbons to decorate clothing. Cutting shears for the cloth and the combs used to card the wool before spinning were of iron; the whorls that weighed down the wooden spindle were of stone, pottery or occasionally amber. Needles and pins were of iron or bone and were often carried by the women in small cylindrical containers suspended from their brooches. Small glass bun-shaped objects found in women's graves may have been used to smooth seams, and it has also been suggested that carved whalebone plaques, nearly always found in wealthy female burials, were used as boards for smoothing or pleating cloth.

Spinning, weaving and sewing must have almost constantly occupied the women. The discovery of gaming-pieces made of bone, antler, glass or amber show that the men had more time for relaxing. Board games were much played, including a war-game known as *hnefatafl*. Wooden animals, boats, swords and spinning tops have been found in many places, showing that children had simple toys.

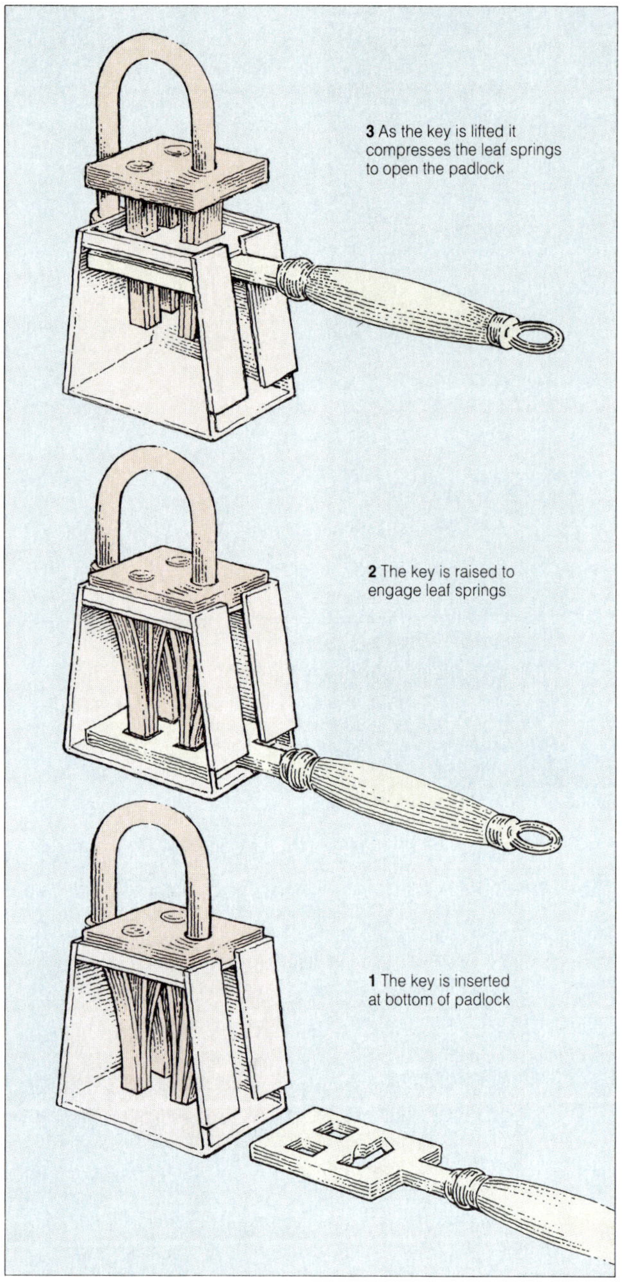


*Left* Cut-away drawing of a box padlock with T-shaped slot to show how it was used with a distinctive form of sliding key that worked by compressing a system of leaf springs to open the lock. Such locks and keys are common in 11th- and 12th-century Scandinavia, and from there they also reached England, Iceland and Greenland.

# Costume

The social distinctions that are evident in so many aspects of Viking Age life were reflected in the kind of dress worn by individual men and women: the style and cut of the garments themselves, the materials used and the quality of the brooches or pins that fastened them made a clear statement about the wealth and status of the wearer. Dress accessories, being made of metal, have been recovered in large numbers from excavated Viking Age cemeteries and settlements, but textile remains are much harder to come by. We can learn a little from the cloth impressions left, as part of the manufacturing process, on the back of cast bronze brooches, but the best evidence we have comes from some bundles of cast-off clothing found preserved in the mud of Hedeby harbor; they had been used as packing material or perhaps for tarring ships. They provided a rare source of information about the different types and qualities of cloth in the Viking Age, and the methods of tailoring. Fashions changed slowly in this period so we can be reasonably confident that the styles reconstructed from this discovery are representative of the Viking Age as a whole.

*Above* Bronze brooches and pins were worn on the shoulder to fasten men's cloaks, but were sometimes made of silver in large and elaborate designs. This bronze example from Denmark is quite small and is decorated with the heads of three Viking men with coiffed hair and drooping mustaches.

*Right* Contrasting styles in male dress: (*top*) A man of the very highest class wears an overshirt of undyed linen above baggy knee-length trousers of fine worsted yarn. His rectangular woolen cloak is fastened at the right shoulder. Another rich man wears a tailored and belted jacket trimmed with fur over a linen shirt. Strips of cloth ("puttees") bind his trousers below the knee (*center*). A slave or servant's clothing was made of coarsely woven woolen cloth. It was loose-fitting, being designed for work (*bottom*).

*Right* Pairs of oval brooches formed an integral part of female dress, and are the commonest of all brooches found in the Viking Age. Most were of rather poor quality bronze with simple designs; others – like the pair shown here – were gilded and decorated with intricate animal patterns. At the bottom of each of this pair is a perforated lug, allowing strings of beads to be hung between them. The trefoil brooch fastened an outer garment.

*Below* Both men and women wore leather shoes that were low-cut and slipper-like in shape. Men also wore ankle- and calf-high boots that laced either at the front or the side. The usual material was cattle hide, but goatskin was used for the very finest quality boots.

*Right* The dress of the high-status woman (*above*) is held in place by three brooches: the one at the neck fastens her long-sleeved, ankle-length tunic of finely pleated linen, while the matching pair pin the shoulder straps of her close fitting, calf-length woolen pinafore dress. Outdoor clothing for the rich was warm and weatherproof (*below*). This woman is wearing a long-sleeved outer garment of high-quality wool that may have been quilted with down. Trimmings of braid in contrasting colors, sometimes incorporating gold thread, were often sewn around the neck and down the front.

Depictions of men and women on various artifacts indicate that long hair was favored by both sexes; some men wore theirs tightly rolled into a bun at the nape of the neck, others had their hair shaved, while the women sometimes arranged their long flowing locks in rather complicated styles knotted on the crown of the head. Combs found in great abundance on excavated sites suggest that people lavished care and attention on their hair, perhaps with the aim of eradicating head lice. Neatly groomed beards and mustaches were commonplace for the men. Men wore trousers and a long tunic topped by a cloak, the women multi-layered ankle-length garments in both wool and linen. A single ring-headed pin or ring brooch fastened the men's cloaks at the shoulder, while the women's garments were kept in place by a pair of brooches (usually oval-shaped, though styles varied from region to region) worn one on each shoulder, with another at the neck.

**Burial customs**

For much of the Viking Age the Scandinavian peoples retained their traditional religious beliefs. They worshiped pagan gods and buried their dead according to pagan rituals, and the objects that were interred with the dead for, we assume, religious purposes, are today an invaluable source of information about the way they lived. The Vikings practiced two types of burial: cremation and inhumation. The corpse seems to have been buried or burnt in everyday clothes, and was usually provided with the personal possessions and utensils that he or she would have used in life. Sometimes the corpse was buried inside a boat or wagon. This leads to the assumption that some form of transportation was believed necessary to carry the deceased to the next world, and burial with horses (mostly found in Denmark, and at Birka in Sweden) may suggest the same thing. However, it seems clear that burial with a boat or wagon was reserved for wealthy individuals, and may merely have been the means of emphasizing the high standing and importance of the deceased person.

In rural communities in Norway and eastern central Sweden cremation was the most common form of burial until the end of the period. Cremation graves under mounds cluster around the Viking Age farms, usually on rocky outcrops. Because these places are not suitable for cultivation, the graves have not been swept away by modern agriculture and are still clearly visible today. In the absence of excavations to establish the presence of farm buildings (only recently undertaken in Sweden and still almost unknown in Norway) such graves provide the only indication of the sites of Viking Age farmsteads. They have consequently been used to pinpoint centers of population and estimate the number of inhabitants, particularly in the Mälaren region of eastern central Sweden, suggesting that the population may have increased by a half during the Viking Age.

In most cases, the body to be cremated was clothed and adorned with jewelry and fastenings for display or utility, and incinerated on a pyre. The cremated bones and melted jewellery were then gathered together and disposed of in various ways, suggesting that different religious rituals were being observed. In central Sweden, for instance, the burnt remains were usually carefully separated from the ash and charcoal of the funeral pyre and placed in a pottery vessel, which was then deposited in a pit dug into the earth; in parts of Finland they were

*Above* These burial mounds mark one of the cemeteries that surround the Viking Age town of Birka in Sweden. Burial customs varied, both regionally and socially, during the Viking Age in Scandinavia, and both cremation and inhumation were practiced. It is estimated that there are about 3,000 graves at Birka, of which some 1,100 have been excavated; many of these contain rich grave-goods that have thrown much light on the lives and activities of the settlement's occupants.

*Overleaf* Some of the richest Viking Age graves are boat-burials, but boat-shaped settings of stones may have provided a symbolic alternative. These settings form part of the cemetery at Lindholm Høje in northern Jutland. The stone outlines, which also include circles, squares and triangles, surround cremations.

## Burials in Viking Age Scandinavia

Both cremation and inhumation burial were practiced in pre-Christian Scandinavia, the former being the dominant method in Norway, most of Sweden and Finland, and the latter in southern Sweden, Denmark and Gotland. Unlike inhumations, cremations were usually covered with mounds or cairns, making them easier for archaeologists to distinguish today. The mounds might be circular, square or triangular, or even surrounded by a boatshaped setting of stones; in some areas the cremated bones were placed in pottery vessels, in others they were merely scattered on the ground. In towns and settlements, burials were concentrated in cemeteries a little removed from the centers of population; in rural areas they usually lay close to the homesteads. Great earth mounds were erected over the burials of the rich and powerful, some of whom were interred in ships and boats, as at Oseberg and Gokstad in eastern Norway and Vendel and Valsgärde in central Sweden. Such burials, however, were not confined to the highest ranks, and are particularly common in coastal Norway. Inhumed female corpses were also sometimes placed in the bodies of wagons and carts, perhaps indicating a belief that the afterlife could only be reached by making a journey.

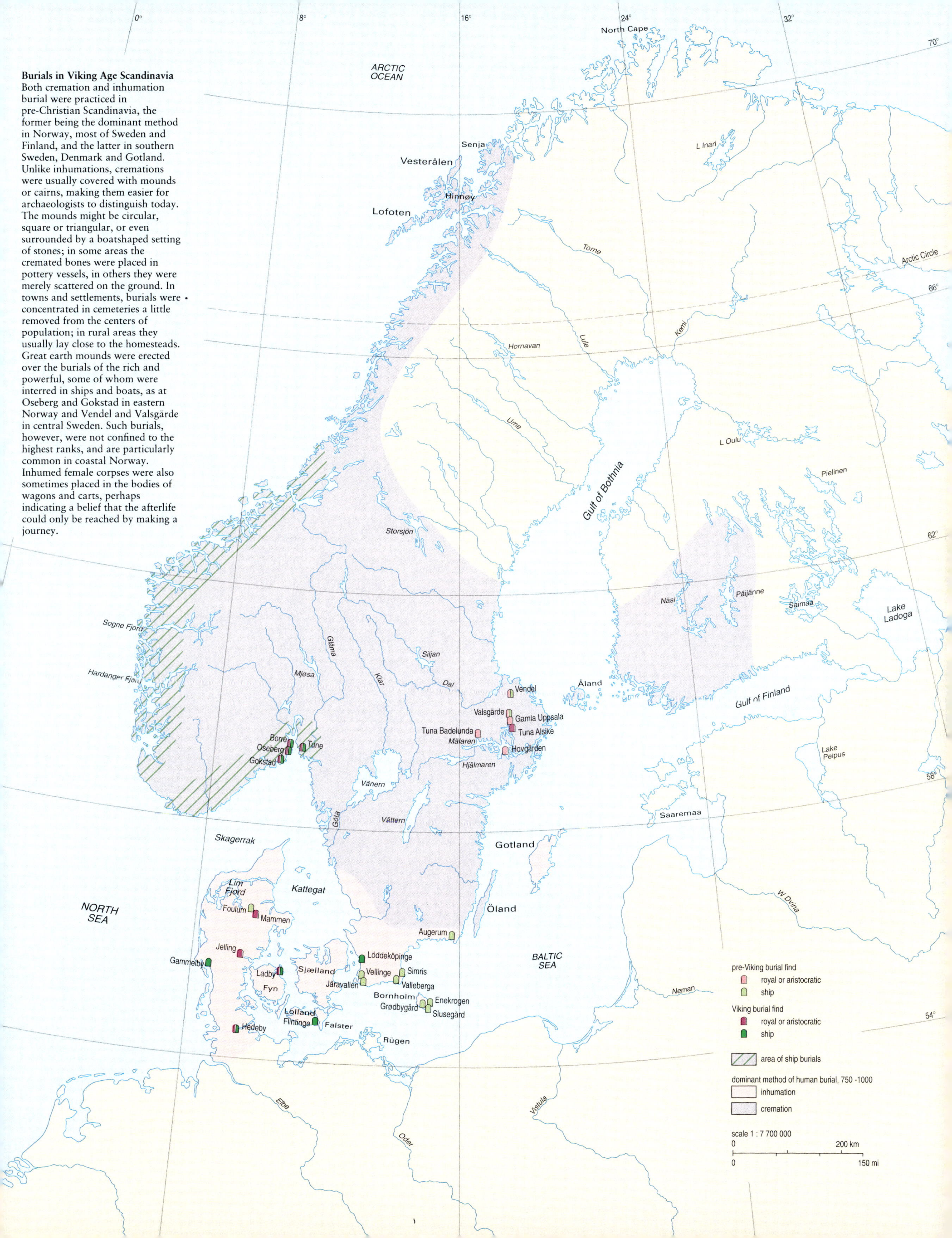

*Left* A stone-paved roadway helped travelers in the late Viking Age to cross the Risby valley on Sjælland, in Denmark. Excavations showed that the river itself was crossed by a wooden construction, beneath which were discovered a wagon wheel and a simple wooden sledge.

scattered on the ground. The cremated remains, whether buried or scattered, were then covered by a mound of earth or simply marked by stones, which were arranged in a number of different ways according to locality, again indicating divergent religious practices. At Lindholm Høje in north Jutland, for instance, and at other places, many of the graves are marked by boat-shaped arrangements of stones. In central Sweden they may be marked by circular mounds, or by triangular settings of stones, sometimes with concave sides.

The Swedish Viking influence on burials is clear on the Åland islands, where there are cremations under mounds, but in Finland itself a fusion of traditions and practices is found. In the southwest, boat-burials were common but no mounds were raised above the cremated remains, which were merely scattered on the ground. Farther inland both cremations and inhumations were covered by cairns of stones and earth. Inhumation became common in southwest Finland in the 11th century, perhaps indicative of the encroachment of Christian customs, but grave-goods continued to be buried in Finnish graves for another century.

Cremation of bodies was also commonplace in the Viking Age towns of Norway, Denmark and Sweden. The cemeteries, which sometime comprise huge numbers of graves, were placed close to the settlement. In Birka, for instance, at least 3,000 graves are known from the 200 years of the town's existence (not all of these are cremations), and there may have been up to 7,000 burials at Hedeby. Other Viking Age settlements, such as Kaupang in southeast Norway, are similarly encircled by huge grave fields. It is very probable that cemeteries also surrounded Ribe in Denmark, but only a few graves have so far been discovered.

*Right* Wooden sledges provided an important form of winter transport during the Viking Age, the largest of which were made to be pulled by draft animals. The Oseberg ship-burial in Norway contained no less than four, of which three (including this elegant example) are beautifully carved; the fourth is a plain workaday model.

The practice of inhumation raises a number of questions that are difficult to answer. With the introduction of Christianity it gradually replaced cremation everywhere, but we know it had been adopted by some of the Scandinavian peoples by the beginning of the Viking Age. In southern Jutland, where inhumation was prevalent, this may have been the result of influences from the Christianized lands to the south, but elsewhere its use is more problematic. Why, for instance, did people on the Baltic island of Gotland turn over to this essentially alien rite? We shall probably never know. Although inhumation was practiced outside these two main areas, the archaeological evidence suggests that it was a rite confined to the upper echelons of society, or to foreigners. The latter were most evident in the Viking Age towns; they brought with them their own rituals and religious beliefs. Some of the best evidence we have for inhumation graves comes from the towns of Birka and Hedeby. In the former, foreign traders came mainly from the east, from Russia or even farther afield. If the merchants were unfortunate enough to die at Birka they were buried according to the customs of their homeland. And they were mostly buried together in their own cemetery near the fortress overlooking the town.

Excavations at Birka in the 19th century uncovered numerous graves of the so-called "chamber grave" type. A pit was dug into the ground and lined with timber. The body of the deceased was then placed, fully clothed, in the chamber and was surrounded by objects of everyday use. Horses were sometimes placed in such graves, and human sacrifices are not unknown. Similarly rich chamber graves have been found at Hedeby, and the custom of interring bodies in subterranean chambers is fairly common throughout Jutland, particularly in the 10th century. These burials are the most spectacular inhumations known from Viking Age Scandinavia, but other forms of inhumation are also found. Bodies were buried in coffins, sunk into the ground in pits, or perhaps buried swathed in a birch-bark shroud. Because the bodies and their equipment were not cremated, the metal objects buried with them are often in an excellent state of preservation.

The burials described above contain the remains of ordinary men and women – some wealthier than others, whether belonging to the farming or the merchant community. The astonishing richness of objects found in the huge burial mounds of royal or aristocratic individuals have been described in an earlier section of the book. By the end of the 10th century the custom of burial with rich grave-goods had died out in Denmark and was becoming less and less common elsewhere (other than in Finland), no doubt as a result of the final triumph of Christianity over the pagan religion. From then onward the practice of inhumation in east-west orientated graves and without accompanying equipment became prevalent throughout Scandinavia, and burials can no longer be used as a source of information about daily life as well as death.

**Travel and communications**

In Viking Age Scandinavia, communication was naturally by water, along the extensive coastlines of Norway and Sweden and threading between the numerous islands along their shores. Natural harbors along the coasts provided safe overnight anchorages facilitating seaborne transport, and lake and river systems could be used to penetrate far inland into the heartlands of settlement. Stretches of impenetrable forest, bogs, and mountains posed innumerable obstacles to land travel across much of Scandinavia. Nevertheless, the Vikings did journey over land when necessary, a task made easier in winter, particularly in the north, when wet and boggy ground was frozen hard, and sledges, skis and skates could be used.

Several different types of sledge are known. The simplest and lightest was the ski-sledge. Consisting of a light body mounted on skis and pulled by hand, it must have been used to transport light and compact loads such as the furs from animals trapped in the northern areas of Sweden, Norway and Finland. Heavier sledges were used to convey bulkier goods. They were dragged by draft animals, either horses or oxen, whose hoofs were studded with iron ice-nails or crampons to give a grip on the icy surfaces. Examples of these sturdy sledges have been found in the ship burials at Oseberg and at Gokstad.

*Left* Bone skates for use over winter ice are common finds, such as these from Lund. They were made from the metatarsals of horses or cattle and were strapped to the foot with leather thongs. The skater used a stick, or sticks, like the one shown here to propel himself forward; sometimes they were furnished with an iron tip.

Skis were used in northern Scandinavia as early as the Bronze Age. At least 100 examples from all prehistoric periods are known from Finland alone, about 30 of them dating from the Viking Age. Pine was chosen to make the skis, which could be up to 2 meters long, since the natural resins in the wood lubricated the underside to make them run more smoothly over the snow-covered ground. Skates were made from the longbones of horses, cattle or elks, flattened on each surface and tied to the foot. They were not like skates as we know them today, but more like very short skis that fitted immediately under the foot. The skater propelled himself over the ice using one or two iron-tipped sticks.

At other times of the year, most people would have traveled on foot, with only the rich and important riding on horseback. Equestrian equipment – such as stirrups, spurs and bridles – was commonly included as grave-goods in high-status burials. The leather bridles have decayed, leaving only the mounts, often of ornately decorated gilded bronze, to show where they had been. The decorations from wooden harness-bows, probably used for harnessing horses to wagons, have also been found. An especially fine wagon was found with the Oseberg burial, but more everyday examples are known from Denmark where, in the 10th century, it was common practice for wealthy women to be buried in the detached bodies of wagons.

Roads were built to facilitate overland travel. The Army Road running the length of the Jutland peninsula is the best surviving example. It follows the highest ground keeping to the watershed, and comes closest to what might be called a "main road" or highway today, even though for most of its length it was an unsurfaced track. Road surfaces (nearly always of wood) were only laid down across difficult country, such as boggy land, and at their simplest consisted of brushwood and branches spread out to provide a fairly stable surface. In other cases they might be built of closely set tree trunks or even well-carpentered timbers.

Throughout Scandinavia, the innumerable rivers and streams that flow across the landscape had to be negotiated by the traveler. Until the end of the Viking Age, fords and causeways were the most usual form of crossing. Freestanding bridges do not seem to have been built until the late Viking Age. Ravning Enge bridge, some 10 kilometers south of the royal center of Jelling in central Jutland, built about 980, is an amazing structure. It is 700 meters long, 5 meters wide and could carry a weight of 5 tonnes. More than 1,000 supporting posts of oak were used in its foundations and an incalculable number of timbers made up its superstructure. It cannot have been typical of bridges built at this time; the amount of wealth and manpower involved in its construction suggests that it was built for a specific purpose, probably by King Harald Bluetooth to enhance the entry into his royal center.

Other bridges are known from 11th-century Sweden. They are mostly marked by rune-stones recording the construction of the bridge, often by a woman in memory of her son or husband or – as in the case of Iarlabanki's bridge at Täby in central Sweden – by a landowner to enhance his local prestige. These bridges are what we would call causeways today, a raised pathway of stones covered with sand or gravel affording a dry passage across a stream or marsh. It is interesting that the number of these "bridges" increases after the introduction of Christianity at the end of the Viking Age. Perhaps we have not yet discovered many earlier bridges, but it seems more than likely that with organized Christianity came the need for improved rapid communication between priests and the people they served.

## Ships and shipbuilding

Heavy reliance on waterborne travel and transport led to the Vikings becoming skillful shipwrights and excellent sailors. Their vessels ranged from the long, narrow, shallow-draft warships to the sturdier ships (strong enough to withstand the buffeting of the winds and waves) that carried settlers and their equipment westwards to the islands of the North Atlantic, and the even sturdier cargo-carrying merchant ships. A variety of fishing boats, ferries, and boats for inland journeys were also built. The stark difference in speed and

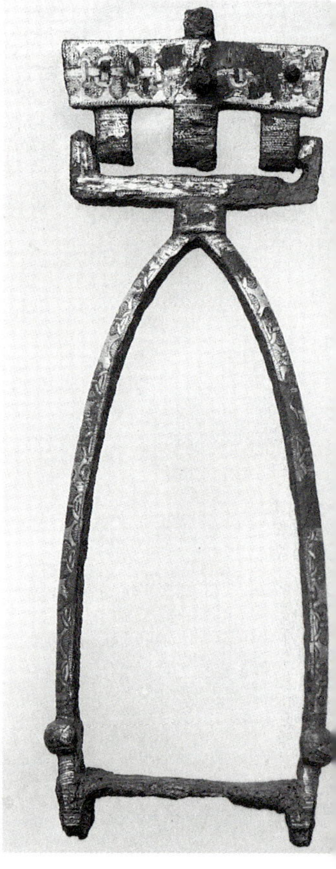

comfort between journeys by water and by land is well summed up by the German cleric Adam of Bremen writing about Sweden in the 1070s. He records that the sailing time from Skåne in south Sweden to Sigtuna on Lake Mälaren was five days, but that the overland trip took one month.

Whether large or small, the Viking ships had various features in common. They were clinker built; that is, their hulls were made of overlapping strakes (planks), joined together with iron rivets and made watertight by caulking, usually with animal hair. The hulls were built about a long and deep keel that formed the backbone of the ship; a keelson (or mast-fish) to support the base of the mast fitted above it. The stems and sterns were elegantly curved; in the most prestigious vessels the prows ended in fierce dragon heads or spirals embellished with glittering metal fittings. The rudders were like huge oars, attached to the starboard side of the stern and manipulated by the steersman using a tiller.

Both sails and oars were used to propel the ships, sometimes together. The genius of the Vikings was to combine the two methods with a truly seaworthy hull – the hull of a sail-driven vessel needs to be of wider beam and higher sided than that of a ship moved by oars alone. This problem was solved by the introduction of the keel, which gave the ships strength, stability and flexibility. In addition to this, the invention of a sailing mast that could be stepped and unstepped (put up and taken down) while the ship was in motion meant that vessels were less dependent on the vagaries of the wind. Sails were introduced from farther south in Europe just before the beginning of the Viking Age. Ships with wide square or rectangular sails are depicted on Gotlandic picture-stones dating from the 7th and 8th centuries, and there is no reason to suppose that these differed from the sails used on Viking ships; none have survived, however.

*Below* This pair of silver and copper inlaid stirrups are from a richly equipped horseman's burial at Nørre Longelse on Langeland, Denmark. Though horse harness in general is common from Viking Age burials throughout Scandinavia, stirrups and spurs are more rarely found, being high-status items; they mostly date to the latter part of the period.

Evidence of the variety of Viking ships comes to us from the chance discovery of vessels in burials, as wrecks, or submerged in harbors where they once formed part of the defenses. At Skuldelev, Roskilde fjord, on the Danish island of Sjælland, for example, five ships were sunk to form a blockade across part of the fjord in the early 11th century. Two of these ships were warships, and with another found as a wreck inside the harbor at Hedeby, they provide valuable information about this type of vessel. All three are of shallow draft, long (30 meters in the case of one of the Skuldelev wrecks) and narrow, with provision for a sail. More importantly, they clearly had seats for up to 18 pairs of oarsmen, and were obviously basically rowing boats with the addition of a sail that could be hoisted or lowered at will. The oars gave added speed, but they also made the ships more maneuverable during delicate tasks like beaching or berthing. These were the type of ship that the Vikings would have used for their startling raids upon the monasteries of western Europe.

The blockade at Skuldelev also contained the wrecks of two freight-carrying merchant ships. The larger was 16.5 meters long, built of pine, and was capable of carrying about 40 tonnes of cargo; it might well have transported furs and other commodities from the trading centers of Scandinavia to the markets in the west. Remains of other similar merchantmen have been found at Äskeskärr in western Sweden, at Kålstad near Kaupang, southwest Norway, and in the harbor at Hedeby. All the ships were wider in proportion to their length than the warships, had a hold that could accommodate goods, and relied on sail rather than oars for their propulsion. Speed was not essential. The real need was for seaworthy vessels that could cross the seas without shipwreck or foundering; oars were only necessary when the ship came into harbor and had to be brought alongside the jetty. The Äskeskärr ship, for example, only had provision for a single pair of oars.

These ships were designed to sail in the coastal waters around Scandinavia and in the open seas to the west. The warriors and merchants who set out eastwards along the rivers of Russia to Byzantium and the Caspian Sea needed vessels that were smaller and lighter than these sturdy ships, capable of being lifted out of the water and carried or dragged over portages – specially constructed routes consisting of shallow gulleys lined with timber – to avoid rapids, rocks, and other such obstacles.

The vast majority of vessels used by the Vikings were not the long-distance warships and merchant ships but a variety of small boats designed for fishing or to carry people, goods, local news and gossip from one settlement to another; some traveled along the coast but most plied the inland river and lake waterways. We have surprisingly little evidence about these vessels, but a small fishing smack or ferry boat was found in a reasonable state of preservation at Skuldelev, and the ship in the Gokstad burial carried on board three small rowing-boats including a four-oared *færing*. This was no more than 6.5 meters long. Fragmentary remains of small boats have also been found in boat-burials in Norway, Denmark and Sweden. One of these – a small rowing boat with five pairs of oars from the cemetery of Valsgärde, central Sweden – has been reconstructed and tested.

Other such reconstructions have helped experts to discover a great deal about the way Viking ships were built and how they were rigged to run before the wind and to tack. For example, some of the ships found at Skuldelev have been meticulously copied and given extensive sea trials. In the late 1980s, a replica of a ship discovered at Tingstäde Träsk on Gotland that may well have sailed along the Russian rivers was built and successfully sailed, rowed and dragged all the way to Byzantium (modern Istanbul) in Turkey, a journey that took about three months.

Unfortunately no shipbuilding yard of the Viking Age has yet been discovered, but archaeological excavations have uncovered several sites where ship repairs took place. At one such site at Paviken on the island of Gotland, traces were found of a "dry dock" in which ships could berth while undergoing repairs, together with innumerable ships' rivets and tools. A particularly interesting site has been explored on the Fribrødre river on the Danish island of Falster. Many fragmentary ships' timbers uncovered here suggest that this was a breaking yard for ships; the timbers taken from the old vessels would probably be reused to patch up other ships. The site lies in the extreme east of Denmark close to the south Baltic coast, an area that shows frequent signs of Slavic influence. We can see this at Fribrødre, for example, in the use of wooden dowels to attach the strakes, a method favored by the Slavs, rather than the iron clenchnails usually preferred by Scandinavian shipbuilders. A small vessel excavated at Hedeby that shows a similar combination of Scandinavian and Slavic building techniques was probably built in the eastern Baltic.

# Viking Ships

Ships were not just regarded by the Vikings as everyday means of transport: their significance is shown in the role they played in the religious rituals of the Viking Age. People of high social rank were frequently buried with their ships. It was the excavation of some of the great burial mounds of Scandinavia in the 19th century that first revealed to modern eyes the splendor and perfection of the Viking ship. The magnificent vessel uncovered in the 9th-century burial at Oseberg, Norway (shown right) was essentially a "royal yacht", designed for coastal and inland waters. For sheer shipwrighting skill, there is nothing to surpass the 9th-century ship found in a burial mound at Gokstad, also in Norway. This was probably the type of ship used by the early Vikings to cross the seas to their new lands in the west.

The true diversity of Viking Age ships was demonstrated in 1957 when at Skuldelev, Denmark, a group of working ships was recovered from the bottom of Roskilde fjord, where they had lain since being deliberately sunk in the 11th century to form a blockade. Differences in shape showed that while two were warships, others had specialized functions as cargo-carrying vessels, fishing boats or ferries. Enough details were preserved to suggest how the Skuldelev ships had been built, providing information about the species of timber chosen, the sequence of building stages (shown in the drawing at the top of the facing page) and the woodworking techniques used. It also proved possible to deduce how the masts had been supported, and the probable shape and size of the sails (see the drawing of Skuldelev 3, top right). Recent sea trials of fullsized reconstructions of three of the Skuldelev ships have demonstrated how well they handled under oars and under sail.

*Above* Specialized merchant ships like the one known as Skuldelev 3 were deeper and broader in the beam than the Viking warships, to make room for cargo. Decking at the ends was for the lookout (forward) and the helmsman (aft). There was little protection for the crew, but the cargo was probably covered with hides.

*Above* The 9th-century Gokstad ship can be seen in the Viking Ship Museum at Bygdøy, near Oslo, which also houses the Oseberg ship. Though the Gokstad ship is less ornate, it was superbly crafted and was found in a better state of preservation. Its seaworthiness was demonstrated shortly after its discovery in 1880 when a replica was sailed from Norway to America across the rough waters of the North Atlantic.

*Below* The magnificently decorated ship found in the 9th-century burial mound of a high-ranking woman at Oseberg was never intended as an ocean-going vessel. It has nevertheless yielded valuable evidence about Viking shipbuilding. A distinctive feature of all Viking ships was the symmetrically shaped hull, with curved stems of equal height at stern and bow. The light draft, even when loaded, allowed ships to go close into shore and far inland up shallow rivers, and the deep keel and steeply angled bottom timbers reduced sideways drift when tacking against the wind. On warships there were evenly spaced oarports for oars the full length of each sides; merchant ships had oars only at the end.

1 Sail
2 Mast
3 Attachment ring
4 Stay
5 Stern
6 Side rudder
7 Oarport
8 Priare
9 Storage for oars and spars
10 Mast support

*Above* The curved fore- and after-stems were carved from single pieces of wood and fastened to either end of the keel. The hull was built of overlapping planks (strakes) fastened to the keel and stems and to each other with iron nails. Evenly spaced floor timbers were then fastened to the hull planking, but not the keel, to give resilience, and crossbeams above each floor timber were used to support decking or rowing benches. The lower end of the mast was held fast in a mast step within the keelson – a longitudinal timber on top of the keel. In early ships the mast was supported at deck level by a massive timber known as the mast-fish, in later vessels by an upper crossbeam.

# TOWNS, TRADE AND CRAFTS

## Trade and urban growth

For more than 200 years the Vikings made use of their sailing skills and their ocean-going vessels to dominate the long-distance trade routes of northern Europe. Locally available raw materials – furs, feathers and down, timber and tar, iron ore, schist for making whetstones (for sharpening blades), soapstone for domestic cooking vessels, salt fish, sealskins and walrus ivory, and the amber found washed up along the coasts of the Baltic Sea – were all in great demand in western Europe. Furs, honey, wax, ivory and slaves (some captured in the west) were exported to Byzantium and the east. The organization of these goods for dispatch to foreign markets was an elaborate process: the raw materials had to be collected at their place of origin, transported to the coast, and then assembled into cargoes to be loaded into merchant ships. In addition, other goods were imported from farther afield for trade. Silver was one of the most important of these. Other imported goods included silk, spices and jewelry from the east, and wine, glass, pottery and weapons from western and central Europe.

The image of Vikings as traders and merchants is less romantic than their image as warriors, invaders and pirates, but it was through trade and commerce that many significant innovations and changes were introduced into Scandinavia during the Viking period. It was, for example, the development of a well-organized system of trade with internal routes centering on points of assembly and shipment that provided the stimulus for early town growth. Before then most people lived in small, predominantly agricultural settlements.

The first towns in Scandinavia were places with a relatively dense concentration of people who gained their living through trade and the manufacture of commodities mainly designed for the local market; farming was of less importance. Some of these sites may have grown up spontaneously because they stood at the intersections of communication routes, but most seem to have been deliberately founded by a king or great landowner, no doubt with the intention of acquiring revenue by imposing tolls on the commodities brought into and exported from the town. Before the beginning of the 8th century there is little sign of incipient town growth in Scandinavia, though commerce and crafts flourished at a few sites such as Helgö and Lundeborg near Gudme, probably in connection with their role as cult centers. This may reflect the lack of largescale trading before that time, but may also indicate the

*Below* A lump of amber washed up on a Jutland beach. Raw materials formed the basis for trade from Scandinavia during the Viking Age, and included such exotic luxuries as walrus ivory from the Arctic north and amber from the Baltic Sea. The latter was much used for beads, but also for amulets; they were produced in urban workshops both at home and abroad, including Ribe and Dublin.

**The Vikings as traders**
In the Viking Age, Scandinavia was at the center of an extensive trading network. The Vikings' ocean-going ships gave them command of the seaways of northwestern Europe, and smaller and lighter craft enabled them to navigate the rivers of central Europe and Russia to trade with Byzantium and with the tribes who controlled access to the great overland trade routes of central Asia. Scandinavia's raw materials were exchanged for silver and luxury goods: silks, spices and honey to flavor their food, and wine to wash it down were especially valued, as were pottery and glass vessels from the Rhineland, and Frankish swords.

*Below* Silver was one of the most coveted commodities in Viking Age Scandinavia, and was obtained from west and east by means of raiding or trading. These ornaments are from one of the most magnificent silver hoards to have been found on Gotland, which contains rings, brooches, beads and pendants, together with more than 1,000 Islamic, German, Bohemian, Byzantine and English coins.

# Hedeby

Though archaeologists first began to investigate the site at Hedeby at the beginning of the century, only about 5 percent of the area of the Viking town has so far been uncovered. Nevertheless, this is a far greater expanse than has been investigated in any other such Viking Age settlement. The layout of Hedeby's wooden-paved streets can be traced in great detail, as can the groundplans of the buildings that served as dwellings, workshops and stores for the inhabitants of this prosperous trading center. Its international character is reflected in the artifacts found there from all over the Viking world and beyond, including some from as far east as Baghdad. Excavations within the area of the harbor have greatly extended our knowledge of the nature of Viking Age shipping and the construction of jetties and harbor defenses.

*Right* The dominant feature in this aerial view of Hedeby – a pleasant rural spot today – is the curving rampart, 1,300 meters long and in places still standing to its original height of 10 meters, which is now clothed in trees. To the east (right) is the shallow inlet of Haddeby Noor and at the top are the blue waters of the Schlei fjord which connected Hedeby to the Baltic Sea. A dense patch of woodland at the north end of the rampart is the site of the hillfort that overlooked the town; the light-colored buildings at its foot house the Viking Museum.

*Left* Hedeby's busy waterfront as it would have looked in the 10th century. Merchant ships loading and unloading cargoes of various kinds are tied up alongside wooden jetties that extend out into the waters of the harbor with its defensive barrier. Evidence for the construction of the houses and jetties has been provided by the excavations that have taken place over the past decades at Hedeby.

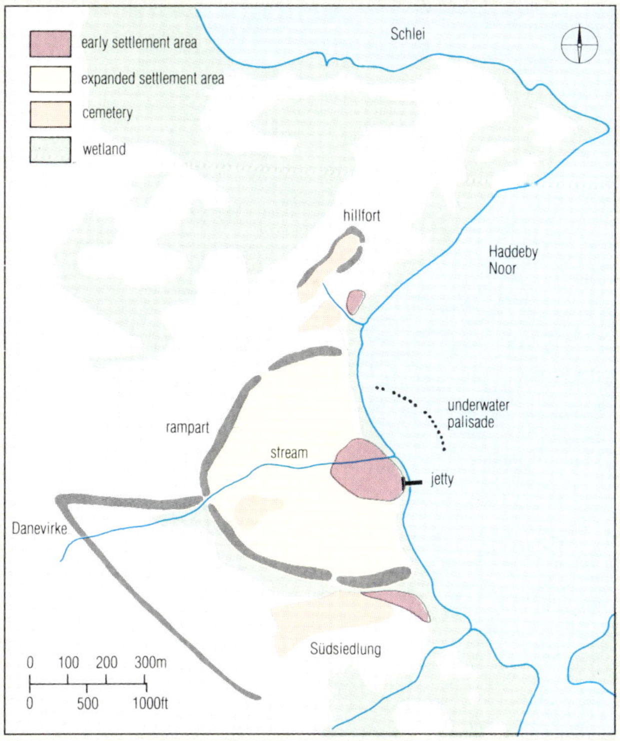


*Above* A plan of the 10th-century settlement. In the original mid 8th-century settlement, occupation was concentrated to the south (*Südsiedlung*) but by the 9th century its focus had shifted to an area around the mouth of a stream flowing out into the Noor. The only defense was the hillfort. By the 10th century the semi-circular rampart had been built up in stages until it was at least 10 meters high and enclosed an area of 24 hectares.

*Above* These silver coins, minted in Hedeby about 825, are copies of Frisian coins. The upper coin carries a picture of a ship with high curving stem and stern. The sail is furled at the top of the mast. The lower coin shows the gable of a house, the roof possibly covered with shingles and its crest crowned with animal-head finials. The slanting lines on either side are probably wall-supports of a type that are commonly found in buildings excavated at Hedeby. This coin has been pierced for later use as a pendant.

absence of rulers with power and authority to found settlements. So we cannot really say that there were towns in Scandinavia before about 700. After that date they certainly existed, and gradually increased in both number and size.

The towns founded by the Vikings in the 8th and 9th centuries were not like towns as we understand them today. They had no great public buildings built in stone, and we know little about how they were administered. They consisted of groups of wooden buildings, each containing a separate household with a dwelling-house and outbuildings within a fenced yard. Apart from the fact that the inhabitants gained their primary source of income from craft manufacture, there was little to distinguish their settlements from a village. Most of our information about these early towns comes from three sites in particular, all the subject of archaeological excavations in recent years: Hedeby and Ribe in Jutland and Birka in central Sweden. All three are mentioned by name in the 9th-century biography of Ansgar, the "Apostle of the North", who made two journeys, one in the 820s and one in the 850s, from his monastery at Corvey in north Germany to try to convert the barbarians of the north.

### Centers of trade in Jutland

The site of Hedeby (known as Haithabu in German) lies just south of the modern town of Schleswig in Germany. Today there is nothing there but open fields, with only the great semicircular rampart to show where the town once stood. Until the end of the 19th century its site was unknown to archaeologists. Mention is made of Hedeby in a written source of 808, which says that the Danish king Godfred settled a group of merchants there. This has led historians to the view that Hedeby was founded at the beginning of the 9th century. However, excavations have uncovered a small settlement, dating from the mid 8th century, to the south of what was later to become the center of the Viking Age town. It was at least partly rural in character at this date, containing some long farm buildings in which cattle were kept. By the 9th century it had been superseded by the so-called central settlement clustered around the stream that flowed through the site into Haddeby Noor, an inlet at the southern end of the Schlei fjord. In the 10th century Hedeby was surrounded by the very substantial rampart that incorporated it into the Danevirke. At its greatest extent, Hedeby covered an area of 24 hectares within the ramparts and had a population of about 1,500 individuals, bigger than other northern European trading towns of this date, but nowhere near as large as the long-established cities of the Mediterranean. An Arab merchant, Al-Tartushi, who visited Hedeby in about 950, has left a graphic description of the place and the customs of its people:

*[It] is a large town at the very far end of the world ocean. It has freshwater wells within the city. Its people worship Sirius except for a few who are Christians and have a church there...The town is poorly provided with property or treasure. The inhabitants' principal food is fish, which is plentiful. The people often throw a newborn child into the sea rather than maintain it.*

Hedeby's low-lying situation and the waterlogged nature of the soil means that organic materials such as wood, leather or textiles have survived in a remarkable state of preservation. The foundations of the houses can be clearly traced. It seems to have been a highly

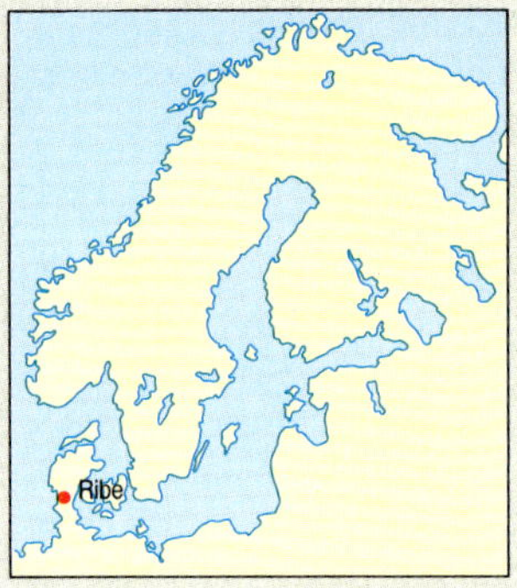


# Ribe

Ribe is one of the earliest towns of Viking Age Scandinavia. It lies about halfway down the west side of the Jutland peninsula in a sheltered position on the river Ribeå, about 5 kilometers inland from the North Sea. The small seasonal market center that grew up here in the early years of the 8th century, with temporary booths where craftsmen made and sold their goods, was thus extremely well placed to develop trading connections extending right along the North Sea coast, and it soon developed into a permanent settlement. The many silver coins (*sceattas*) found at Ribe, and probably minted there, show its importance as a center of trade in the 8th century, and its role continued for the next 200 years. From its earliest beginnings, goods arrived there from western Europe and the British Isles to be exchanged for the products of Ribe's fertile hinterland – possibly mainly cattle hides (deep deposits of cattle dung have been found among the workshop sites of the earliest settlement). Amber washed up along the Jutland shore would also have been a highly prized commodity.

From the beginning, too, manufacture was an extremely important aspect of Ribe's economy. Excavation of the debris found within the Viking Age town's industrial area has provided a wealth of information about 8th- and 9th-century production methods. Craftsmen worked in the open air crouching over simple pit hearths that were protected by windbreaks. Here they cast bronze jewelry and decorative mounts of all descriptions and made the glass beads that were produced in their thousands. Amber was worked into beads and pendants, and red-deer antler was fashioned into the combs that were always greatly in demand by Viking men and women.

*Below* Viking Age Ribe lay on the north bank of the river Ribeå (which did not then flow along its present course) on a small sandy peninsula that was slightly higher than the surrounding wetlands. Excavations in 1989 uncovered a stretch of the semicircular rampart that appears to have been built to strengthen its defenses to the north and east in the 10th century. It probably surrounded a settlement area of about 10 hectares. Later the focus of the town moved to the south bank, where the medieval town developed.

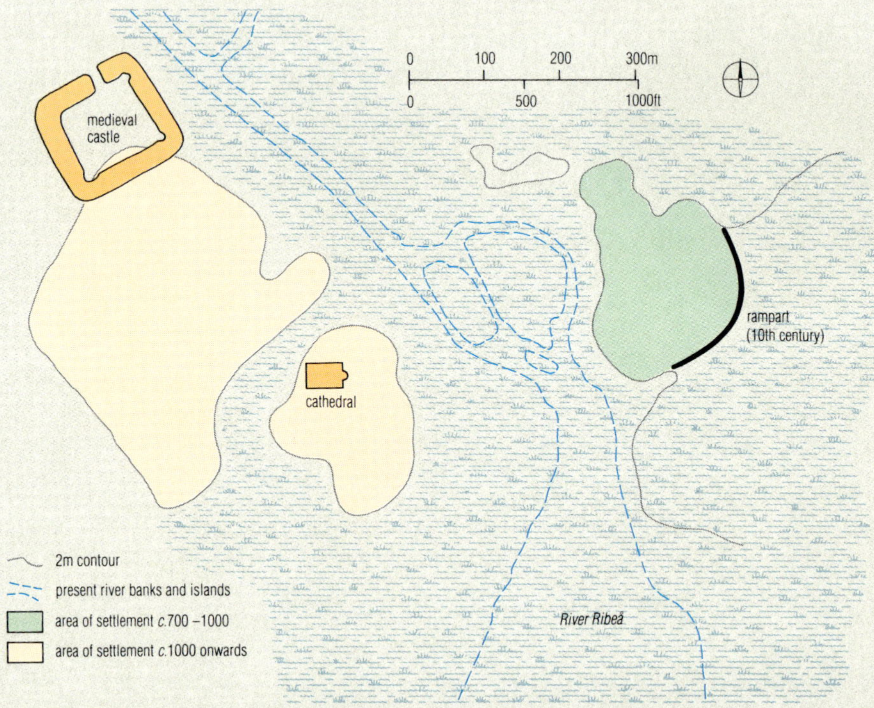

*Right* Excavation of Ribe's workshops has produced considerable evidence about manufacturing methods. Bead-making was an important craft. Raw glass (recycled fragments of broken glass or glass cubes imported from Italy) was melted and then drawn out into lengths that were softened and wound around an iron rod. The bead was molded into a round or cylindrical shape before being pushed off the rod. The debris discovered in a bead-maker's workshop in Ribe includes broken beads, discarded lengths of colored glass, some of them banded or twisted with trails of glass in other colors, and hardened drops of molten glass that fell to the ground in the manufacturing process.

*Above* The town of Ribe is still dominated by the tower of its medieval cathedral, which stands on the south bank of the river Ribeå as it flows through the lowlying countryside of west Jutland toward the North Sea. Ribe became a bishopric in 948. The site of the Viking Age town of the 8th and 9th centuries lies in the wooded area on the north bank. It was abandoned or relegated to the status of a suburb when settlement moved across the river to the area around the cathedral.

organized settlement. Rectangular houses of two or three rooms were arranged in yards surrounded by ditches and wooden fences. The short sides of the yards faced wooden-paved streets, probably essential in a place that must frequently have been flooded. The stream was canalized and lined with wooden planks. At intervals along its length short flights of steps led from the bank to the water, ending in small platforms where clothes could be washed. An abundant supply of drinking water was provided by wood-lined wells. Within the harbor area wooden jetties or piers were built out from the shore into deep water where merchant ships could tie up to unload their goods. Together with the harbor installations at other Viking Age towns, these jetties provide convincing proof that Viking ships did not always have to be beached, contrary to the view that was held in the past.

Hedeby's quantity of well-preserved artifacts enable us to build up a detailed picture of the manufacturing and trading activities of its inhabitants. It is clear that a local trading network was established in the immediate hinterland, with simple objects such as combs and jewelry being made and exchanged for essential foodstuffs with the population of rural villages such as Kosel to the east. But there is also ample evidence of Hedeby's place at the center of the expanding exchange of trade between eastern and western Europe that developed during the 9th and 10th centuries.

Goods such as silver and silk were brought to Hedeby from the east on the merchant ships that crossed the Baltic Sea. There they were exchanged for commodities from western Europe, including wine and the more mundane lava stones used to make grindstones. No waterways connect Hedeby to the North Sea. The goods must, then, have been carried overland between Hedeby and the west coast. The most probable route followed the course of the Danevirke, and it is possible that the building of the rampart that connects Hedeby to this defense work was in some way connected with the town's increasing trade and wealth. Hedeby was undoubtedly becoming an ever more attractive target for attack. Icelandic sagas record a number of fierce assaults, culminating in its total destruction by a Slavic force in 1066. Tree-ring analysis of timbers found during recent excavations in the medieval core of the nearby town of Schleswig show that building started here as early as 1071. Could this have been the replacement for Viking Age Hedeby, as historians have long suspected?

The deserted site of Hedeby is in great contrast to the modern and bustling town of Ribe on the west coast of Jutland. A small market center that sprang up on the north bank of the Ribe river in the first decade of the 8th century grew to become the leading port on the west coast of Jutland for the next 300 years. The cathedral and the core of the medieval and modern town stand on the south bank of the river. For long archaeologists believed that the town visited by Ansgar in 854 must have stood on the same site but successive excavations around the cathedral failed to reveal any Viking Age remains. Was Viking Ribe a myth? Did Ansgar never come there at all? The question was spectacularly answered by excavations that began in the 1970s when digging started at sites on the north bank of the river. It has been going on there almost continuously ever since. We now know that Ribe was indeed a flourishing settlement by the 9th century, but its center lay north of the Ribe river in an area that had declined to the status of a suburb by the end of the Viking Age. In other words, the Viking Age town was deserted and replaced by a later settlement in another location. This movement is not as obvious as the shift from Hedeby to Schleswig, but it is equally as important.

Ribe stands at a crossing of land and water routes. The Ribeå river connects the town to the North Sea and it lies on the land route that runs the length of Jutland from north to south. It was thus in an ideal position to control trade. By about 700 a small village comprising only a couple of farms stood on the riverbank. It was a magnet for other settlers who arrived within the next 10 years. They set up booths and workshops there; the land was divided up into plots, which were separated from their neighbors by ditches and fences. At first, this area was occupied only seasonally, perhaps at the time of a market or fair in the summer months. Craftsmen came to make and sell their wares (glass beads, jewelry, combs); farmers came with their cattle. The change from farming village to market center was abrupt and well-organized, and it is tempting to think that there must have been a controlling force behind it. Was there a king of Denmark at that time who felt that he would benefit from a trading center on his land? The discovery of about 300 of the small silver coins known as *sceattas* dating from this period – far more than have been found anywhere else in Scandinavia, and some of which may have been minted in Ribe itself – is further indication that the settlement was under royal control. As noted earlier, the most likely king is Agantyr.

The early 8th-century market center of Ribe was clearly a flourishing point of exchange between Scandinavia and western Europe. Finds of pottery and glass drinking vessels from the Rhineland show that wine was being imported from central and southern Germany, along with grindstones from the same area. Whetstones were brought from Norway to be re-exported westwards. Cattle were taken to market for sale to the Germans farther south. A permanent settlement began to grow up some 100 meters to the southeast of the market site, consisting of some large post-built houses, a number of smaller huts, a street and wells. This may have been the place where the governor of the market lived, and this could well have been the center around which the later permanent town developed.

By the mid 9th century, Ribe's fame and importance must have grown sufficiently to persuade Ansgar to make the journey to visit it. By that time a ditch enclosing an area of about 12 hectares seems to have marked the edge of the town. It was too narrow and shallow to be a defensive feature, and was probably a customs boundary or other legal delineation. Not until the 10th century was this ditch replaced by a true defensive structure: a much more formidable moat and an earth rampart. Before that, Ribe must have been greatly exposed to attack.

We know less about Ribe in the 10th century than we do about its earlier history. Its defenses have been revealed in part, but the layout of its streets and the buildings flanking them have yet to be discovered. However, we know from documentary sources that the first bishop of Ribe was appointed in 948. This may mark the occasion when the main area of settlement moved from the north bank of the river to the south side, around the site where the cathedral now stands. In its new position Ribe continued throughout the Middle Ages as the most important ecclesiastical and commercial center on the west coast of Jutland. It is the only town in Scandinavia to have maintained continuity of occupation from the 8th century up to the present day.

## A Viking town in Sweden

In 829 Ansgar, responding to an invitation to bring the Christian mission to "the land of the Svear", set out to sail to Birka in central Sweden. It proved a hazardous journey. At one point his ship was attacked by pirates who seized all his possessions (church furnishings and books) and forced him and his companions to abandon ship. Nevertheless, they did reach Birka, where they were greeted by King Bjorn and Herigar, the king's representative in the town (*praefectus*, as Rimbert, Ansgar's biographer, calls him). Initially, the attempt at conversion met with some success and Herigar was baptized. Some 18 months later Ansgar returned to Germany, leaving a bishop and some priests behind him. He returned to Birka in the 850s when he obtained permission to build a church and was allowed some land on which to set up a house for his clergy. We know from archaeological excavations that Birka, on the island of Björkö in Lake Mälaren, was a flourishing settlement by the time of Ansgar's first visit. It was founded sometime in the middle of the 8th century and continued in existence for more than 200 years. Then the site was abandoned and its commercial and administrative functions replaced by Sigtuna, a town founded a short distance away on the north shore of Lake Mälaren, at the end of the 10th century.

There is no town on Björkö today. It is a green and beautiful island, its grass sparkling with flowers in spring and dotted with birch trees and juniper bushes. But there are still signs of its past greatness. The ramparts of a fortress (*Borg*) stand on a rocky eminence near the lake, another rampart runs from the north coast, and more than 3,000 mounds mark the sites of Viking Age burials. More than 1,000 of these mounds were excavated in the 19th century and until recently provided most of our knowledge about Birka in Viking times.

The graves show us that Birka was at its richest in the late 9th and 10th centuries, and at its largest contained as many as 900 people, including large numbers of foreigners. These were probably merchants from the countries to the east of the Baltic Sea, as grave-goods such as dress-fittings and amulets of eastern type indicate. Silver and silks from Byzantium and the east were imported here for exchange with raw materials from northern Scandinavia, particularly furs and down. These commodities were also in demand among the wealthy aristocracy of western Europe. They were probably shipped there via Hedeby with which Birka had close connections. Birka also housed craftsmen manufacturing items such as combs and cast bronze jewelry. As at Hedeby, most of these goods would be distributed in the immediate hinterland in exchange for agricultural produce, as the island was not big enough to provide all the food the settlement needed. Some foodstuffs – such as wheat and fruit – may also have been imported from farther afield.

The reason for Birka's abandonment is far from clear. It does not seem to have been devastated by outside attack, as Hedeby was. Its geographical situation may have been an important factor in its decline. In the Viking Age Birka was accessible from the north by land routes that ran along the north-south ridges of glacial gravels (eskers), or by water. At this time Mälaren was not a lake as it is today, but an inlet of the Baltic Sea, and access for shipping was through the long narrow inlet that reaches it from the southeast, where the modern town of Södertälje now stands. This inlet was cut off from the lake by a narrow isthmus, and so ships reaching Birka had to be dragged across a specially constructed

*Above* This aerial view shows the site of the 9th-century trading center of Kaupang, in southern Norway, at the end of a fjord protected from the open sea by numerous small islands. Today the sheltered harbor, in the center foreground, is silted up. The site is surrounded by numerous burial mounds, now tree-covered, containing rich grave-goods. There is little to show us today where the settlement was, but excavations in the meadow on the right of the harbor have revealed something of its buildings and jetties, as well as evidence for its flourishing manufacturing and trading activities.

portage. The ships must have been fairly small and of shallow draft to enable them to be manhandled in this way. At the time of Birka's foundation the water level relative to the land was some 5 meters higher than it is today, but the land was steadily rising and by the end of the 10th century it had become difficult for the portage to be used by ships that were, at the same time, becoming bulkier and heavier. Another route into Lake Mälaren had to be found, through the strait where Stockholm now stands. The ships using this passage had to thread a tortuous path between myriad islands and skerries, and this fairway no longer took them directly to Björkö but north of it, to the mouth of the Fyris river where the new town of Sigtuna lay. Thus, Birka lost its essential lifeline and its economic importance.

## Market centers

Much more widespread than the towns (and sometimes mistakenly described as such) were the market centers, or *emporia* – places where manufacture and trade were carried on but where there was no permanent population or urban organization. (The early 8th-century settlement at Ribe, with its temporary booths and workshops, would have been such a center.) One of the only written accounts we have of these trading settlements comes from a 9th-century English source, which describes how Ottar, a Norwegian merchant, visited the court of Alfred the Great of Wessex, in England. He entertained his host with stories of his journeys, and Alfred was careful to have them written down. So we learn of a voyage Ottar made to Hedeby from the far north of Norway

# Birka

*Below* Though glass beads were a favorite part of female attire, glass was an exotic material in Viking Age Scandinavia. These glass playing-pieces were discovered in a grave at Birka, but were probably made in Russia. They include a figure that may represent a "king" but looks more like a bear.

Very little was known about the town of Birka on the island of Björkö in Lake Mälaren until new investigations began in the so-called Black Earth area – the area of soil darkened by its content of organic remains from two centuries of human occupation – in 1990. Important early archaeological work had been carried out here in the second half of the 19th century, but the graves in the cemeteries that flank the town on the east (*Hemlanden*) and the south soon proved a more attractive area of investigation: more than a third of Birka's estimated 3,000 burials were excavated at this time, often with spectacular results. The grave-goods from these burials provided an invaluable source of information for archaeologists, enabling them to establish a chronology for the Viking Age, to evaluate the countries with which Birka had trading links, and even to reconstruct the clothing worn by the inhabitants of the town 1,000 years ago. But it is only since the beginning of the 1990s that archaeologists have known anything about Birka's buildings.

The town was divided into plots of land divided from each other by passageways flanked by ditches. A plot might contain one or two small wooden houses, approximately 5 × 8 meters in area, and several outbuildings – workshops or stores. The buildings were timber-framed with wattle-and-daub walls. The roofs were usually of wood or thatch, but sometimes turf was used. The objects discovered in these plots tell us that some of the people living in Birka were craftsmen – jewelers and metalworkers. Some even prepared the skins of foxes and squirrels to be used for garment trimmings. Very many were merchants, as is suggested by the large quantities of Arabic coins and silver bullion that have been found.

*Below* This great hoard of silver coins, jewelry and hacked-up pieces of silver was found in the town area of Birka as long ago as 1872. Payment in Viking Age Scandinavia was made by weight of silver, and this hoard, which weighs more than 2 kilograms, must represent the accumulated wealth of a rich man, perhaps a merchant from the east. All but one of the 450 coins are Arabic in origin and were minted in various places in the Islamic world between about 718 and 977. The one non-Arabic coin was minted in Byzantium sometime between 948 and 959. Most of the rest of the hoard comprises silver arm-rings, but there are also tiny pendants and ear-rings. The hoard illustrates the close links that existed between Birka and the east up to the middle of the 10th century when supplies of Arabic coins began to dry up.

*Above* The earliest known representation of Christ in Scandinavia is this little silver-gilt filigree crucifix found in a 10th-century grave at Birka. The figure of Christ is wearing trousers and is bound to the cross with ropes.

*Right* An imaginative reconstruction of the settlement at Birka in the 10th century. The town's timber buildings are clustered within a defensive rampart, which runs up to connect with the rampart around the hillfort that dominates the town at its southern edge. The harbor is also defended with a palisade that straddles the mouth of the bay. The danger of fire in towns with predominantly timber buildings can be seen here: smoke is rising from four burning houses at the center of the settlement.

*Below* The Viking Age town of Birka in the northwest of the island of Björkö was some 13 hectares in area at its maximum extent, but in the 10th century a rampart was built to enclose only 7 hectares. At the time of the Viking occupation the island was smaller than it is today as its shoreline has been altered by fluctuating land- and sea-levels.

*Right* The "Black Earth" site of Birka is today open meadowland lying on either side of the track that runs from the shoreline (where the harbor lay) to the modern village at the edge of the trees in the background. The wooded land beyond it is Grönö, which was a separate island in the Viking Age.

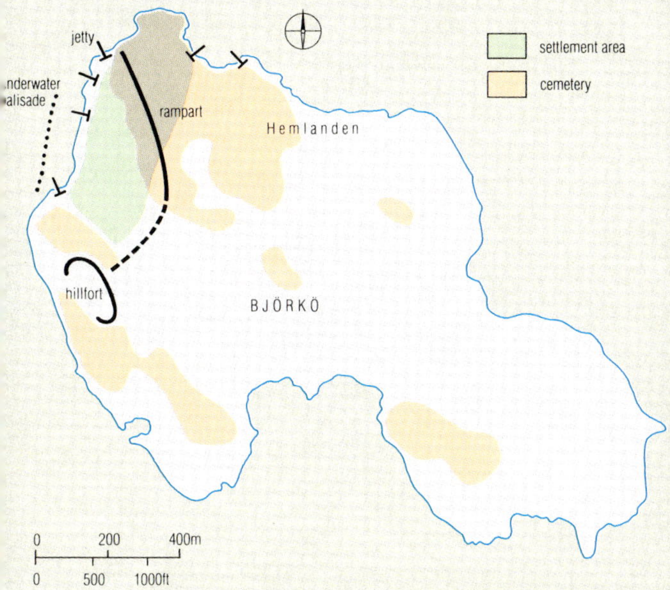

carrying precious cargoes such as walrus ivory and hides. On his way he put in at a port, called *Sciringesheal* in the Old English report, which was five days' sailing time north of Hedeby.

*Sciringesheal* has been identified with Kaupang in Vestfold on Norway's southeast coast both on the basis of Ottar's description and on the archaeological finds made there. The place-name Kaupang itself is significant. It is met with in various forms throughout the Viking world, and also in Anglo-Saxon England. In Sweden it occurs as *köping* (as in Löddeköpinge), and in England as *ceap* (Cheapside in London) or *ceping* or *cieping* (Chipping Sodbury). Basically it means market, and this seems to have been what Kaupang was.

The name Kaupang is now attached to a farm and there is no visible sign of the 9th-century settlement, though the many burial mounds in the neighborhood are of mainly 9th-century date. Today a meadow slopes gently down the shore of a fjord well protected from the open sea by islands and skerries. Smallscale excavations here have revealed a cluster of six buildings arranged roughly parallel to the shore. Finds of iron and bronze slag, crucibles and waste from glass bead-making suggest that some at least were workshops for making iron tools and simple jewelry, but the lack of domestic hearths and absence of household rubbish makes it doubtful whether any of the buildings were permanently occupied. The site of a ship-repairing yard has also been discovered; presumably it served the needs of travelers such as Ottar whose vessels had been damaged during the arduous journey along Norway's west coast. At least two wooden jetties jutted out into the water, their landward ends being built on stone foundations to secure them to the shore. A rope for tying ships alongside was also found there.

Kaupang's commercial activities may not have been on the scale of Ribe, Hedeby or Birka, but they were certainly extensive and wide-ranging. Pottery from the Rhineland, the British Isles and the Baltic countries has been found there, as have balances and weights, the essential equipment of a merchant. The imported goods were probably exchanged for local raw materials, notably schist and soapstone. The wreck of a ship with a cargo of schist whetstones has been found at Kålsund about 15 kilometers along the coast. Nevertheless, though only a tiny part of the site has been excavated, the overall impression is that this was a seasonal encampment used only in the summer for manufacture and trade. None of the characteristic features of a town, such as an organized layout of streets and houses, are seen here. Kaupang differs from true towns in other important ways: it never acquired any defenses, probably because it was no longer in existence when the need for fortifications became pressing in the 10th century, and it was not replaced by a later town. Kaupang's abandonment by about 900 may have been the result of sea-level changes or because its importance declined as Danish influence in southern Norway decreased (it had clear links with the network of trade based on Hedeby).

Kaupang is not unique. A seasonal market existed at Skuldevig, on the north coast of the island of Sjælland, Denmark, no doubt because its sheltered site provided a convenient harbor. There are signs of periodic occupation from the 8th until the 12th century, but nothing to indicate that there were ever any buildings. Open-air hearths and shallow clay-lined pits are all that remain of this transitory market; the clay-lined pits may represent the floors of the temporary shelters or tents that were erected when the market was in progress.

Because the vestigial remains left behind by such impermanent structures are so hard to identify, we have no means of knowing how many other such market centers existed in sheltered spots around the coasts of Scandinavia. However, two such sites with somewhat better preserved remains are known at Åhus and Löddeköpinge in Skåne, now in Sweden but then part of Denmark. Åhus, on the north bank of the Helge river, was founded in the first half of the 8th century as a seasonal market center specializing in craftworking, notably the manufacture of beads. The discovery of some small silver coins or *sceattas* of the type found in such abundance in Ribe attest to its importance as a trading center, but there are no indications that the settlement was ever organized on a permanent basis. Traces of buildings are few, and these are of sunken-floored huts that were easily and rapidly erected and probably never intended for fulltime occupation.

After about 50 years the site at Åhus was abandoned and refounded a few hundred meters downstream on virgin ground. This settlement covered an area of roughly 10 hectares and remained in existence from the second half of the 8th century into the early 9th century when it was abandoned in its turn, probably to be resited elsewhere. This second settlement was much more substantial than the first, with numerous buildings and a heavy dependence on bronze-working for its economy. Sherds of pottery from the south Baltic coast and the Rhineland show the extent of its trading contacts. Nevertheless, Åhus never acquired urban features.

The same is true of Löddeköpinge on the Lödde river in western Skåne where a group of sunken-floored buildings dating from the 9th century cluster within a small area inside an encircling bank. Excavations have shown conclusively that these buildings were occupied intermittently, perhaps only for a short period of time each year or at even longer intervals. There is evidence to suggest that trade was the main occupation at those times, since objects of both western European and Baltic origin have been found there. The site had been abandoned by about 900 and permanent settlement begun in a village, not a town, nearby.

Paviken on the island of Gotland seems to have been another seasonal market center. While excavations have failed to reveal any traces of large permanently occupied buildings, there is considerable evidence of trading and manufacturing activity. Arabic coins and weights indicate that it had contacts with the east, and small glass *tesserae* imported from northern Italy, which were used in bead-making, have also been found. As well as this, it had a ship-repairing yard and was a busy fishing center, if the number of fishing implements found there is anything to go by. Though there were other similar sites on Gotland, which enjoyed trading links with Sweden and the eastern Baltic, none have revealed the same wealth of evidence as Paviken. A few kilometers to the south of Paviken lies Västergarn, a site surrounded by a semicircular rampart. It may have been intended for the protection of Paviken, which was undefended, but the limited excavations that have taken place there allow us no certainty on this question.

Seasonal market centers are also known to have existed in Finland. Recent excavations at Hämeenlinna (Swedish: Tavastehus) on the shore of Lake Vanajavesi in the southwest interior of the country have uncovered an area about 6 hectares in extent containing buildings, a harbor and a rampart. The site was occupied from about 800 until the end of the 13th century and from the nature of the finds clearly served as a market center for

**Manufacture and crafts**
The growing prosperity of Viking Age Scandinavia led to increased demand for manufactured goods, both for utilitarian purposes and for items of adornment such as brooches, beads and bridle mounts. Towns and seasonal market centers were the most important manufacturing centers, with craftworking areas developing to supply the needs of the growing urban populations and of the surrounding countryside. Excavation has shown other sites to have served as centers of production for tools, weapons and objects in precious metals. Among these were the workshops housed within the 10th-century royal fortresses of Denmark. Even some farmsteads – for example, Lundbjärs and Fröjel on Gotland – had craftsmen among their inhabitants. These last two sites specialized in making the animal-head brooches favored by Gotlandic women. The most common form of female jewelry, found in large numbers over most of Scandinavia, were oval brooches; round brooches were favored mostly in Finland and central Sweden. Clay molds used in casting bronze jewelry have been found in abundance in many urban sites. Some everyday objects, notably combs made of deer or elk antler, were probably made by itinerant craftsmen who traveled from center to center producing goods on demand – this would explain why the shape and decoration of combs are virtually identical throughout the Viking world. One of the most important crafts would have been ship-building, but archaeological evidence for it is sparse. A number of ship-repairing yards, however, are known; for example at Kaupang and Fribrødre Å. Few mints were established before 1000; the number increased significantly in the 11th century with the centralization of royal power.

site shown by excavation to be 9th–11th century manufacturing center
type of product, where known
oval brooch
round brooch
animal-head brooch
other metalworking
glass
amber
bone, horn
pottery
ships
area of 9th and 10th century brooch type finds
oval
round
animal-head
location of mint
before 1000
after 1000
scale 1 : 7 700 000
0
200 km
0
150 mi
0°
8°
16°
24°
32°
70°
66°
62°
58°
54°
Arctic Circle
ARCTIC OCEAN
NORWEGIAN SEA
NORTH SEA
BALTIC SEA
North Cape
Senja
Vesterålen
Hinnøy
Lofoten
L Inari
Torne
Kemi
Lule
Hornavan
Ume
L Oulu
Gulf of Bothnia
Pielinen
Trondheim
Storsjön
Näsi
Päijänne
Saimaa
Lake Ladoga
Hämeenlinna
Sogne Fjord
Hardanger Fjord
Glåma
Hamar
Mjøsa
Klar
Siljan
Dal
Åland
Hitis
Gulf of Finland
Oslo
Skien
Tønsberg
Kaupang
Mälaren
Sigtuna
Birka
Helgö
Hjälmaren
Vänern
Lake Peipus
Göta
Vättern
Skagerrak
Lundbjärs
Gotland
Paviken
Fröjel
Aggersborg
Ålborg
Kattegat
Fyrkat
Viborg
Öland
W Dvina
Århus
Sjælland
Trelleborg
Roskilde
Lund
Åhus
Ringsted
Odense
Fyn
Ribe
Slagelse
Neman
Fribrødre Å
Lolland
Bornholm
Hedeby
Falster
Rügen
Elbe
Oder
Vistula

# Woodcarving

Wood was the natural medium for sculptors in the Viking Age to work in. Knives would always have been readily to hand, but a wider range of craftsmen's tools – chisel, gouge and file – would have been required to execute some of the masterpieces of woodcarving that are rare survivals from this period. Foremost among those that have been preserved are the many different wooden artefacts from the Oseberg burial, from the beginning of the 9th century. The rich variety of their carving opens our eyes to the skill of the artists who were working in wood at this time.

Study of the Oseberg objects shows that they are the specialist work of several accomplished carvers, and they probably represent the products of a single workshop under royal patronage in southeast Norway. One generation seems to have worked alongside the next, for some of the carvings have an old-fashioned appearance whilst others are in the forefront of the stylistic innovations that set the fashion for much that followed in Scandinavian art during the 9th century. Some show a restraint in their execution that is unusual in Viking art, whilst others have been carved in elaborate relief, with superimposed patterns visible one through the other. The surfaces were sometimes smooth or finely detailed, sometimes embellished with metal bosses – or the motifs were picked out with paint.

The designs appear to have been largely ornamental, created from stylized animals or birds. Decoration of this sort is clearly seen on the ship itself, and on the sledges. The ceremonial wagon has elements of a more complex iconography, but the unique series of five animal-head posts provides us with even more of an enigma. Without obvious function, they are generally assumed to be cult objects. The placing of four of them in the burial-chamber itself might well mean that they were somehow possessed with protective powers.

*Right* The prow of the Oseberg ship coils gracefully to a snake's head, turning the vessel into a true "sea-serpent". Both faces of the prow and stern are carved above the waterline with friezes of contorted animals, each slightly different from the next, with which it interlaces. There can have been few ships so lavishly carved as this; it was probably a royal yacht designed for use in sheltered waters.

*Right* One of a pair of animal-head posts, carved in high relief, which was found with two others in the Oseberg burial-chamber. The canine teeth are covered with metal plates, as are the eyes, whilst the decoration that fills all the available surface is further embellished with numerous tinned nails. The animal ornament is not confined to the underlying scheme of oval panelling, but writhes about in a way that makes it hard to understand the designs, though they are in fact always kept under control. This characteristically vigorous style replaced the style that is seen on the ship itself.

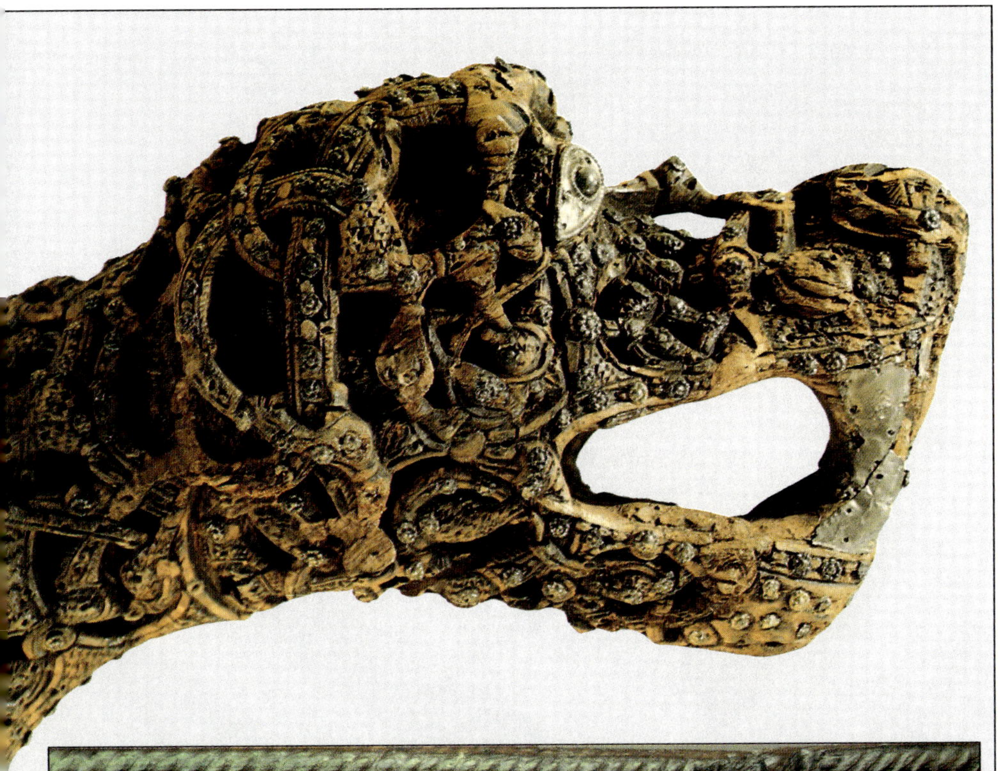

*Above* This figural scene is carved on one long side of the Oseberg wagon-body (another is shown on the front). Pictorial representations are rare in Viking art, and the significance of these is unknown. The scene shows a woman of authority with flowing hair and an elaborate necklace. She is restraining an armed man from attacking a man on horseback, who is accompanied by his hound. The rest of the wagon-body is carved with ribbon-shaped animals, interlacing to form decorative friezes.

*Left* One of four semi-naturalistic carved men's heads that form the terminals of the cradle that held the Oseberg wagon-body. Three-dimensional carving and human representation were both rare in Viking art. Though fearsome in aspect, the man's mask-like face, with its staring eyes, is shown with a sweeping mustache and well-trimmed beard, whilst a close-fitting cap covers his hair. A distinctive artistic personality can be seen at work in the creation of these four heads, each of which is different. Their significance, however, is lost to us today.

the surrounding neighborhood: there is no evidence that the site ever developed wider trading contacts. However, two market centers on the coast – Turku (Swedish: Åbo) and Uusikaupunki (Swedish: Nystad) – were drawn into a larger network of trade through their proximity to Sweden. Similarly, the Åland islands in the middle of the Gulf of Bothnia midway between Finland and Sweden traded extensively with mainland Sweden, Estonia and Gotland, but though there was a market center in the Viking period, no true town grew up there until early modern times.

## Viking crafts

As well as being farmers, sailors, traders and marauders, the Vikings were skilled craftsmen producing – in addition to items for everyday use – fine jewelry, elegant and practical weapons, intricate wood-carvings and incised stones. The high standard of their workmanship can be seen in their handling of many different materials, from precious metals to antler and bone. Most of the archaeological evidence shows that crafts were mainly carried on in the towns and market centers, and a wide variety of skills was practiced. Leather was tanned and made into shoes, scabbards, belts and other articles. Wool and linen were woven into cloth on upright looms and tailored into garments. Wood was carved into a multitude of household objects, particularly bowls and other containers, and also made into boxes and chests, many of which were provided with locks and strengthened and decorated with metal mounts. In contrast to later periods, pottery was little used and evidence for urban pottery-making is only fully attested in Hedeby; some may have been made in the countryside in a very primitive fashion. In many households the vessels used in food preparation were of soapstone; it was quarried in Norway, probably roughed out at the quarries themselves, and finished at the places to which the stone blocks were exported.

## Iron-working

Iron was of paramount importance to the Vikings, being used to make tools and weapons, for shipbuilding, and for many other purposes. The iron ore found in bogs and lakes was often of rather poor quality, but was nevertheless a valuable source of raw material. The ore was smelted in simple bloomery furnaces close to its source in the countryside. The resultant raw iron was then fashioned into bars and transported to centers either in towns or in the countryside where smiths converted it into tools and other artifacts. The discovery of a wooden tool chest in a bog at Mästermyr on Gotland shows that a wide selection of tools was available to blacksmiths. The nails and rivets they produced would have been in great demand in the shipbuilding and ship-repairing yards where some of the most skilled of all the Viking craftsmen worked.

The most highly regarded craftsmen of all were the weaponsmiths on whose strong, sharp and flexible swords and elegant but deadly spears the success of the Vikings in battle depended. Working with intractable materials under great difficulties, they had the highest status of all Viking craftsmen and must have been well rewarded for their labors and skill. They often worked for an individual master, providing him and his retainers with new weapons and refurbishing and sharpening the old ones. Unfortunately, no workshop used by a weaponsmith has yet been discovered; our

knowledge of the skill and techniques involved comes from the finished products themselves.

The weaponsmiths knew precisely the qualities of the materials in which they worked, selecting one type of iron for the core of the weapons, another for the cutting-edges, and often welding strips of differing hardnesses together to improve the flexibility of the blades, particularly swords. This pattern-welding technique was most widely practiced in the earlier part of the period.

### Gold, silver and bronzework

Gold and silver were used to make jewelry and other adornments for the high-ranking members of society. Gold was more prized than silver, being rarer, and was acquired by melting down jewelry (and perhaps coins) that originated in continental Europe. In the centuries before the Viking Age, gold coins of the late Roman period had arrived in large quantities in Scandinavia, particularly Gotland and southern Jutland, and some of these may have been used by Viking Age goldsmiths to make neck-rings and arm-rings, and also brooches, which were elaborately decorated with filigree and granulation.

Silver was used to inlay patterns into other metals, particularly iron, as on the Mammen ax, and was also used for brooches, pendants and chains as well as the neck- and arm-rings of various standard weights that plainly served as a form of currency in a period when coinage was little used. They are mostly found in silver hoards: many are plain and simple, but others consist of plaited and elaborately twisted silver wires. The innumerable scraps of chopped-up rings (known as hacksilver) that have been widely found are also an indication that commercial transactions were paid for in silver by weight. Merchants' scales, used for weighing cut pieces of silver, are frequently found in Viking Age graves in Scandinavia.

Until the middle of the 10th century, most of the silver entering Scandinavia came from the silver mines of Transoxiana in central Asia, then part of a great territory ruled by Muslim Arabs that stretched from Baghdad to the borders of India. The silver was brought to Scandinavia usually in the form of coins. These are known as Kufic coins from the script (named after the town of Kufah in present-day Iraq) used for their inscriptions and would be melted down. Some silver arrived in Scandinavia in the form of ready-made jewelry, such as the Permian rings imported from the Volga region of Russia. By the end of the period these supplies had been replaced by silver from mines in central Europe.

Below the upper ranks of society, men and women had to make do with jewelry of baser metals, usually bronze, sometimes gilded in an attempt to make it seem finer. Fragments of clay molds used for casting bronze have been found on a number of sites, particularly in Ribe, Hedeby and Birka, suggesting that the bronzesmiths were predominantly urban dwellers. They must have been important members of the manufacturing community, producing not only bronze jewelry but other objects of everyday use such as pins and needles, keys and lock cases, and were called upon by the wealthier members of society to supply decorative mounts for their harnesses and plaques to attach to wooden chests and the like. On

*Above* A small selection of the tools, including those used both for iron-working and for carpentry, contained in an oak chest that was found at Mästermyr on Gotland. The chest also contained raw materials, as well as part-manufactured and finished products – more than 200 objects in all. Its owner was clearly a smith who could work in iron and bronze, as well as being a joiner and wheelwright. He may have been a traveling craftsman who lost his tools while crossing a great bog.

*Right* Silversmiths melted coins and scrap silver to fashion rings and brooches, as well as other types of ornament. Many of the neck- and arm-rings are made of twisted, or even plaited, rods, as can be seen amongst this selection from the Sejrø hoard, Denmark. Note also the filigree-decorated disk brooches, as well as some hacksilver fragments used for payment by weight. The Sejrø hoard also contained 146 assorted coins, most of which are Arabic (from central Asia) and date its concealment to the second half of the 10th century.

the whole, however, their wares were not of very high quality and were probably made to meet the needs of local consumers.

The best evidence we have for their methods of production comes from Ribe, where remains from bronzesmiths' workshops from about 800 have been found in abundance. Here, and probably elsewhere, the bronzesmiths worked in the open air, protected from the worst of the weather merely by a fragile windbreak. Little was needed in the way of furnishings: a small forge (usually a simple pit) fueled by charcoal, on which the bronze ingots or scrap would be melted in crucibles, and an adjacent hearth in which a mold could be kept warm while the molten bronze was being poured into it. The bronzesmith's portable equipment consisted of crucibles, molds, models for the finished products, tongs for holding the red-hot crucibles, and small files and chisels for retouching the finished product once it had cooled and had been freed from the mold.

The crucibles were made of sand-tempered clay to withstand the intense heat needed to melt the bronze.

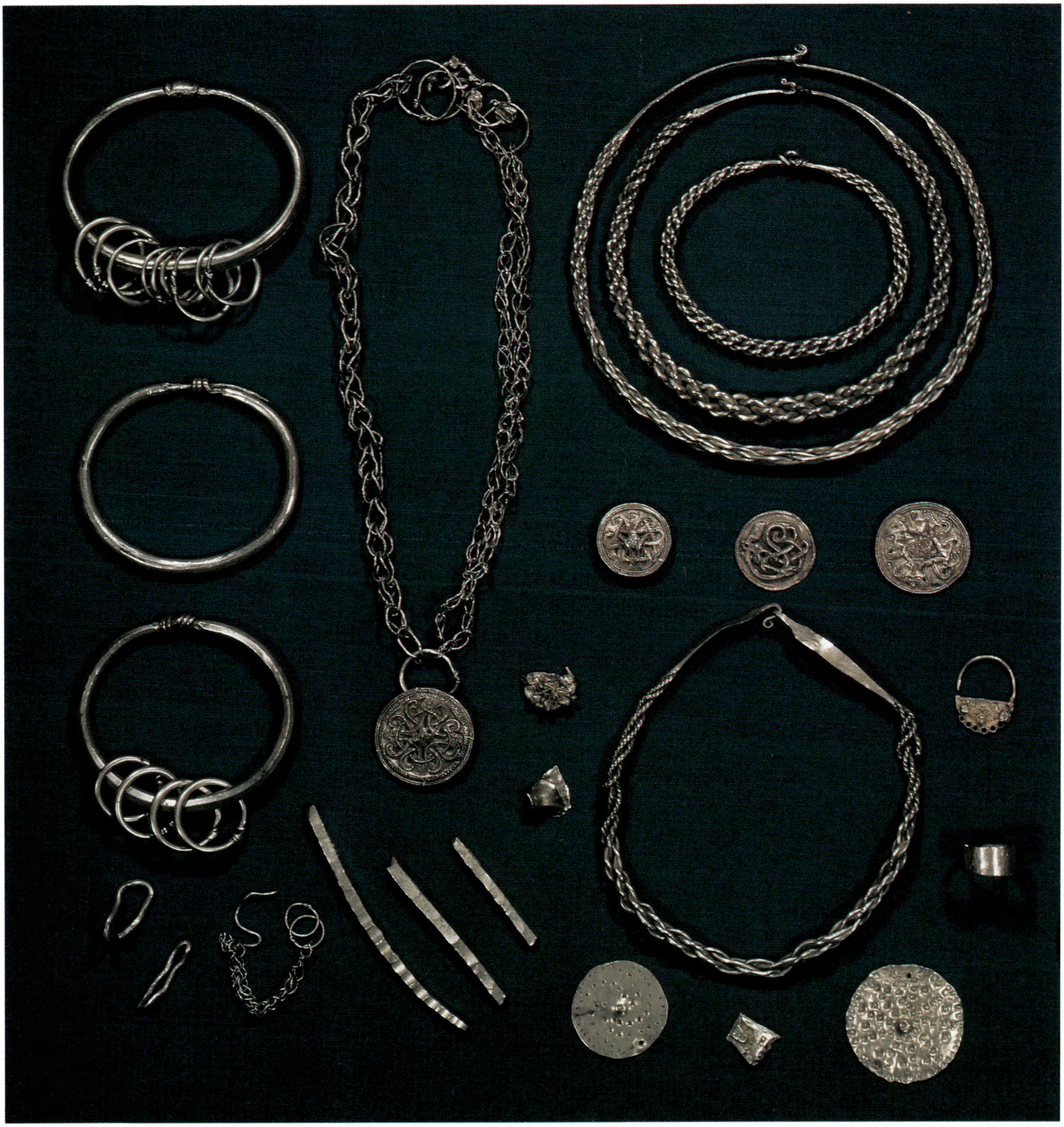

# Ornamental Metalworking

Much ornamental metalwork, women's brooches in particular, was mass-produced during the Viking Age. This normally involved the manufacture of a series of clay molds from a common master, each of which was then used once, rather than the repeated use of a single mold. This is because the normal clay mold had to be broken open in order to release the cast ornament before it was finished by hand (see below).

A mold for use in this way could be made from either a newly-created model or, more often, an already finished object. However, during the latter part of the Viking Age, there is evidence that mass-production of ornamental metalwork was also carried out by means of multiple casting in molds carved out of antler, or even wood. These could be used for casting lead alloys (pewter), which had a sufficiently low melting point not to destroy the mold itself. The cheap brooches produced in this manner seem to have found a ready market in the developing towns.

Another form of mass-production was utilized by jewelers working for wealthier patrons able to afford gold or silver. A die was used to impress foils with basic designs in relief, which were then decorated with exquisite filigree work. Such ornaments – amongst the most skillfully made products of the Viking Age metalworker – can readily take their place alongside the finest pieces from the Middle Ages.

*Below* Oval brooches were the commonest type of Viking Age jewelry, used in pairs to fasten the shoulder straps of female dress. Most were mass-produced, cast in bronze in two-part clay molds, which were discarded in pieces after use, such as these from a jeweler's workshop in Ribe, Denmark.

*Right* This gold disc brooch (much enlarged) is one of two found at Hornelund in Denmark (c.1000). It is made from two plates, the upper impressed with a die before being embellished with filigree work; the plant ornament is influenced by styles from western Europe.

*Below bottom right* A jeweler's die (patrice) of the type used for the manufacture of gold filigree ornaments, such as the pendant from Hedeby shown on its right.

*Left* The manufacture of a pair of oval brooches required two clay molds to be made, each in two parts. First, a master mold impressed with an old brooch (or one newly shaped in wax) is used to cast a pair of wax models (1), which are covered in clay (2). The wax is melted and poured out, and then wax pegs inserted for the pin fittings (3). Next (4) a piece of wax-impregnated cloth is pressed into the mold to determine the thickness of the final brooch; the other side is then built up with clay over the cloth (5), the mold heated to run off the wax and the cloth removed; finally, the two parts are reassembled (6) and sealed ready for use. The molten metal is poured into the heated mold (7), which is broken open once it has cooled down (8), and the brooch is then removed for finishing (9).

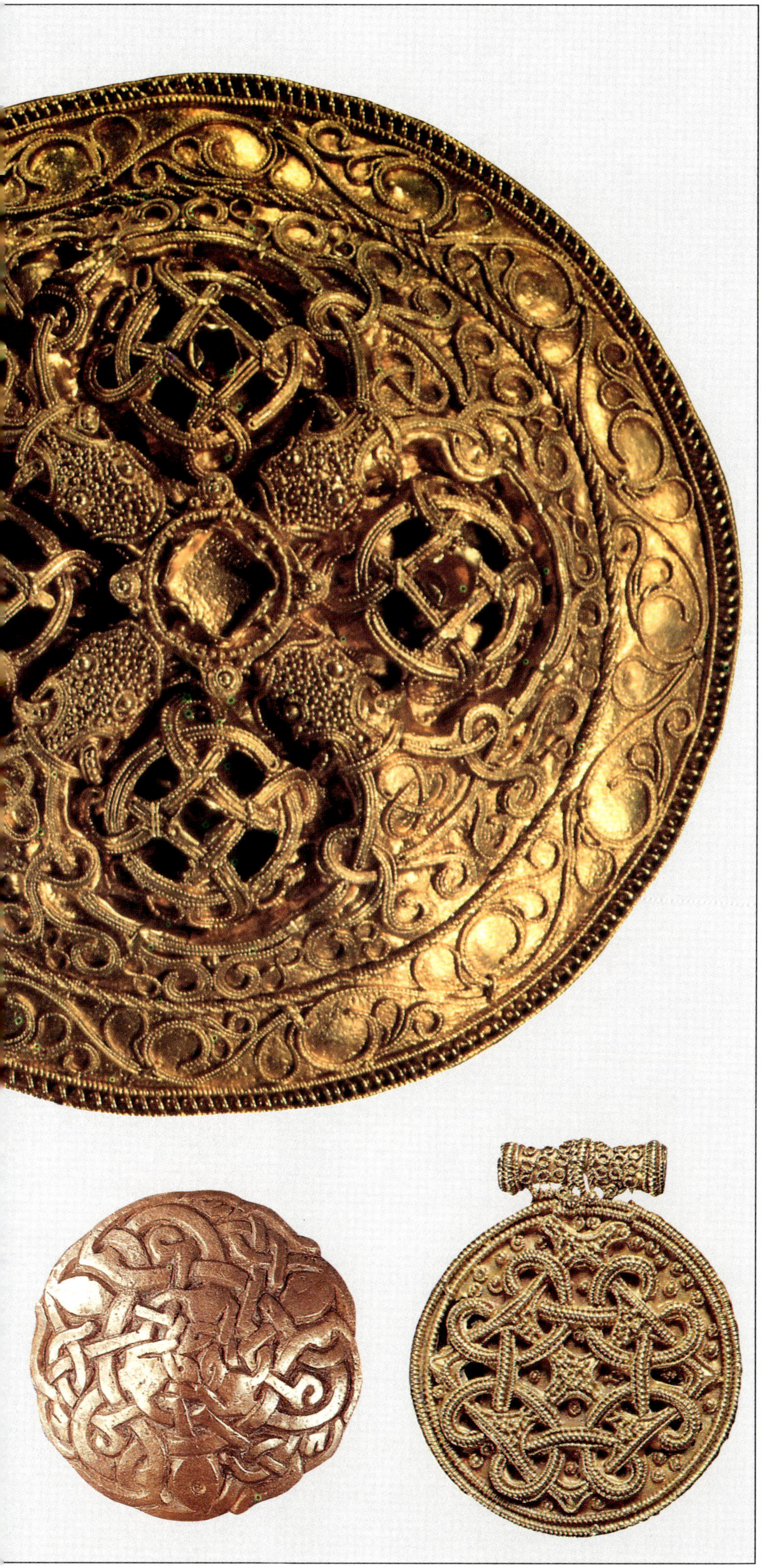

They were usually roughly cylindrical in shape, with a small lug near the lip that could be gripped by the tongs. When the bronze was in a liquid state the crucible was lifted out of the glowing embers of the forge with the tongs. A steady and careful hand was needed to pour the molten metal into the neck of the mold (the ingate) to make sure it filled all the intricate lines of the pattern that had been impressed into the clay, and to avoid any air bubbles being formed. The mold was then left to cool down gradually beside the hearth. When the metal within it had cooled and solidified, the mold was removed from the hearth and broken open to reveal its contents. The newly cast brooch or plaque was then finished off by filing away any excess metal, and further decoration could be added at this stage. If the object were to be gilded, it too would be done at this time.

The broken pieces of the mold were usually just thrown down on the ground around the hearth. Thousands of discarded pieces have been found in excavations, providing evidence of how the molds were made. A model (often an actual brooch, or else a specially made lead prototype) was pressed into a slab of prepared clay, or thin layers of clay were applied to its surface, to produce a master. Liquid wax was then poured into the master and removed when cold and set. A number of identical wax positives could be made from one master. The upper part of the mold was made by pressing clay around the wax positive, and heating it. As the wax melted, the design it carried was left in the hardened clay. A piece of woolen cloth covered in wax was placed in the hollow cavity of the mold, and more clay pressed on top to form the back. The whole was heated once more and after the wax had melted out the two halves were separated and the textile removed. The two parts of the mold were then reassembled and covered with a thin mixture of clay and water to fix them together firmly. The mold would be placed in the hearth to heat it up before the molten bronze was poured into the cavity left by the textile plug. This prevented it from cracking with the heat of the molten metal.

Using this method, many identical items could be made from a single master cast. One of the most common bronze ornaments was the oval brooch, many hundreds of which have been found in upper-class women's graves from the 9th and 10th centuries. These brooches were not worn merely for ornament, but were an integral part of a high-status woman's apparel, one being worn on each shoulder to fasten her dress. At least two of each design were therefore usually made, but so many have been found bearing identical patterns as to suggest that they were virtually mass-produced. Nevertheless, though an individual bronzesmith may have been especially skilled in making one particular type of object, the finds from the workshops at Ribe show that he would have been capable of turning his hand to practically anything that demanded casting in bronze.

**Bead-making**

Glass beads were also made in their thousands. Most evidence for the craft comes from the 8th and 9th-century towns or market centers – Ribe, Åhus, Paviken and Kaupang – and the methods used were always identical. Sherds of glass from drinking vessels originally imported from the Rhineland provided the raw material (cullet) from which the beads were made, and small cubes of brightly colored glass, sometimes covered with gold leaf, were added to achieve different shades and hues. These glass cubes, or *tesserae*, were probably made in northern Italy for use in church mosaics. They provide graphic evidence of the distances over which commodities were transported at this period. Rough lumps of blue glass were also imported for use in this craft.

Like the bronzesmiths, the bead-makers probably worked in the open. Their equipment was also simple: a hearth, iron rods for forming the beads, and a number of small metal dishes. The cullet was melted on the hearth, and a small lump of molten glass was

*Left* A selection of Viking Age necklaces and pendants found on Gotland, including gold, silver and colored glass beads. At the top and bottom are pendants of imported rock crystal in delicate silver mounts of Slavic character. The set of 32 "fish-shaped" pendants forming an elaborate collar, at center, represents a jewelry fashion unique to Gotland; they are made of gilt bronze with applied silver plates inlaid with niello.

*Above* Comb-making was a skilled craft. Evidence of specialist workshops has been found in excavated Viking towns. The methods of manufacture were standardized and the single-sided shapes are very similar across the Viking world. Antler was the most usual material, favored for its natural strength; the back- and toothplates were held together with iron rivets.

then transferred to an iron rod. This was twirled around while the glass solidified slightly before being rolled on a flat surface to form a cylindrical or spherical bead, which was then slipped off the rod to harden. Additional threads of colored glass could be applied at this stage to make polychrome beads and a more complex technique was used to produce mosaic beads, which involved fusing and then slicing multi-colored rods of glass. Bead-making workshops can be recognized by the debris surrounding the hearths – blobs and thin threads of different colored glass that fell to the ground in the manufacturing process. Some of the iron rods have also been discovered. At Paviken, Gotland, one rod still had a bead attached to it; the glass may have cooled down and hardened before it could be slipped off the rod.

Beads were also made in other materials, notably amber – the orange and tawny colored lumps of fossilized pine resin that were picked up on beaches around the Baltic Sea and (in much smaller quantities) along the North Sea coast of Jutland. Although much of it was sent overseas to the markets of the west, many carved amber beads have been found in Viking Age graves. Gaming pieces, pendants and amulets were also carved out of amber.

### Comb-making

Combs are found in great numbers in all excavated Viking Age towns, and are also common in graves. They must have been owned by all ranks of society: some are extremely beautifully decorated (some of the finer ones even had bronze inlays), and others quite plain. From the numbers found, the Vikings seem to have carried a comb with them at all times, and to have both used and dropped them frequently.

The comb-makers were highly skilled and specialized craftsmen who must always have had a buoyant market for their wares. Comb-making was predominantly practiced in towns, and both the raw material from which the combs were made (red deer antler in southern Scandinavia, elk antler farther north), together with whole and fragmentary combs and semi-manufactured articles have been found.

The combs were made of a number of different pieces that utilized almost the whole of the antler. A pair of back-plates was shaped from long straight pieces, given a slightly curving ridge and decorated with geometric patterns. They were then attached one on either side of a series of thinner rectangular slabs, and these were finally filed into teeth. Whatever the material used, Viking Age combs are remarkably similar in shape and method of production, and virtually identical examples have been found throughout almost all the Viking world from Dublin in the west to Novgorod in the east. This has led to the suggestion that the comb-makers were itinerant craftsmen, traveling from place to place to make and sell their wares wherever there was a demand.

### Art-styles

The Vikings loved ornament. All their artifacts, including their ships and buildings, were densely packed with the restless movement of decoration, often taking the form of highly stylized animals. The very characteristic art styles that they favored grew out of what had gone before, but during the Viking Age foreign influences were incorporated to produce highly original designs of typically Scandinavian form. It was not until the coming of Christianity that European influences came to dominate, and the last Viking styles were superseded by western European Romanesque art and architecture.

Most of our information on Viking art comes from the objects that were buried in graves. We thus have rather a one-sided picture, because the things that have survived are mainly of metal or stone. Only a few examples of wood-carving and decorated textiles have fortuitously been preserved to show us that jewelers were not the only artists and craftsmen to produce spectacular items. For the purposes of study and comparison, the art of the Vikings has been classified by experts into separate styles, named for the place where an object carrying the specific motif or group of motifs that identifies that particular style was first discovered. The beautiful and barbaric art of the Vikings can be enjoyed and appreciated for itself. It is also a very useful tool for archaeologists who use the gradually evolving styles as chronological indicators to date archaeological structures and features.

The Broa style, named after a burial at Broa on Gotland, decorates objects that were made and used in the second half of the 8th and a little into the 9th century. As with all the styles, it is made up of highly stylized animal motifs, either ribbon shaped and entwined in tendrils or with more rounded bodies. A new type has little paws that grip – a motif that is called the "gripping beast". "Gripping beasts" are also present in the Oseberg style, current from about 800 to 875. The objects in the Oseberg ship burial, dated to 834, that gives the style its name include most of the few wood-carvings preserved to us from the Viking Age and convey some idea of the great wealth of wood-carving that has been lost.

Some gilt-bronze harness mounts found in a burial mound at Borre, Norway, give their name to the Borre style, which was used to decorate articles of personal adornment for a hundred years after 850. It is a more formalized and geometric style than those that went before, one of its characteristic motifs consisting of a chain of interlocking circles and squares called the ring-chain. The style is found not only in Scandinavia; both the true Borre style and variants of it decorate objects that have been discovered in Viking settlements overseas, from Iceland to Russia.

The same is true of the four remaining Viking art-styles, though often objects found outside Scandinavia display a debased and provincial form of the style. The Jellinge style of the first half of the 10th century, named from a silver goblet found in the burial in the north mound at Jelling in Denmark (tree-ring dated 958/9), is characterized by S-curved ribbon-shaped animals that interwine and overlap each other. An ax unearthed from the Mammen burial, also in Denmark and dated by tree rings to 970/1, typifies the Mammen style of the second half of the 10th century. Like the Ringerike style, largely confined to stone and named after the district of southeastern Norway that was the source of reddish sandstone used for carved stone memorials, it is noted for seminaturalistic animals almost obscured by interlacing plant tendrils.

The final Viking Age style, the Urnes style, originated about 1050 and continued throughout the Viking world into the 12th century. It is named from the 11th-century stave-church at Urnes on Sogne fjord, Norway, whose magnificent wooden carvings are yet another reminder of the great skill of the Viking craftsmen. Its main motif consists of an elegant quadruped in conflict with a snake-like creature.

# Viking Art

Scandinavian art of the Viking Age was primarily decorative, its patterns based on various stylized animals, though there were periods when ribbon interlace or plant motifs became popular. Viking art was open to influence from western Europe, but foreign ideas were borrowed selectively and adapted to Scandinavian taste. The essential continuity in its development can be readily traced, though there seem to have been short periods of artistic innovation, usually followed by longer periods of conservatism. One such period of change took place during the 8th century (the "Broa style"), laying the foundation for Viking art proper that begins with the "Oseberg style"; another was in the 10th century, with the creation of the so-called "Mammen style", seemingly under the patronage of King Harald Bluetooth and the Danish court at Jelling.

It is customary today to divide the sequence of Viking art into six successive styles: Oseberg-Borre-Jellinge-Mammen-Ringerike-Urnes. But as a new style came into fashion, it did not immediately replace the old. At the same time, much of the mass-produced jewelry was hardly in the mainstream of artistic development. A major innovation during the late Viking Age was the introduction of stone sculpture. Earlier there had been only the picture-stones of Gotland. Otherwise few pictorial scenes have survived from Viking Age Scandinavia, the Oseberg tapestry being a notable exception.

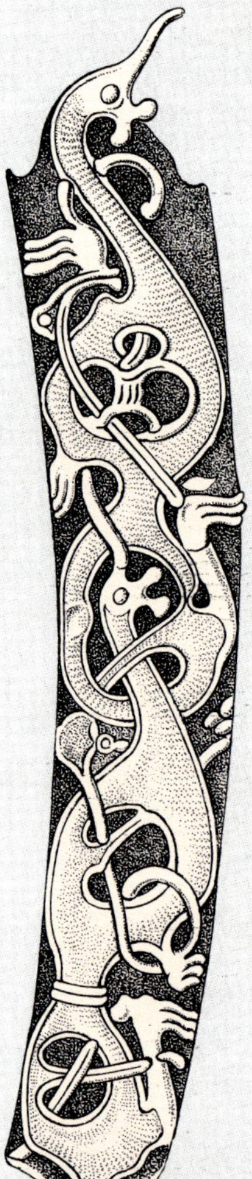

*Far left* Gilt-bronze harness-mounts from Broa, Gotland, of late 8th-century date, display a mixture of native animal-art and of other animals and birds introduced from western Europe, notably a distinctive "gripping beast". The Broa motifs are used for the Oseberg carvings, as on the ship *(left)*. These form the basis for the 9th-century Oseberg style.

*Above* A pendant from a Swedish hoard (buried c.940), in the form of a Borre-style "gripping beast", with mask-like head, pretzel-shaped body and gripping paws. The "gripping beast", probably of Anglo-Saxon origin, entered Scandinavian art during the 8th century, and long remained popular, though in the Borre style geometric ribbon-interlace motifs were much favored.

*Below right* The memorial erected by King Harald at Jelling in the 960s was a unique stone monument in Denmark at the time. It was soon imitated, as was the new motif that fills one of its faces: a lion entwined by a snake. This new dominance of a single motif is characteristic of the style named for the ornament on the Mammen ax, which flourished during the second half of the 10th century, developing a lush version seen on the ivory panels of the Bamberg casket, Germany (*right*).

*Below* The final phase of Viking art has been named the Urnes style for the magnificent wood carvings on the Urnes stave-church in Norway. Stylized animals are once again the most important motifs and form the basis for elegant designs that have the appearance of multi-loop patterns. A fine example in metalwork is provided by this small silver brooch from Lindholm Høje in Denmark, though such openwork brooches have been found throughout Scandinavia. The style, which originated during the mid 11th century, continued in use into the 12th, when the fashion for European Romanesque decoration spread into Scandinavia.

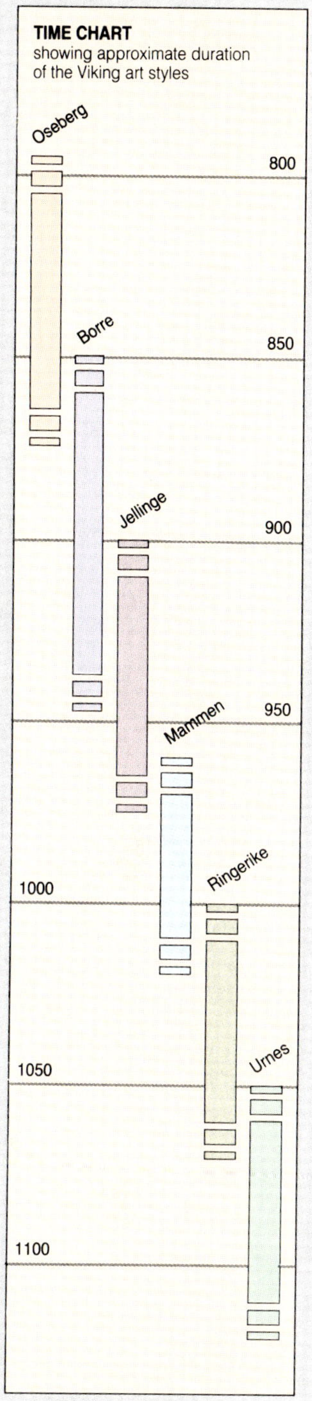

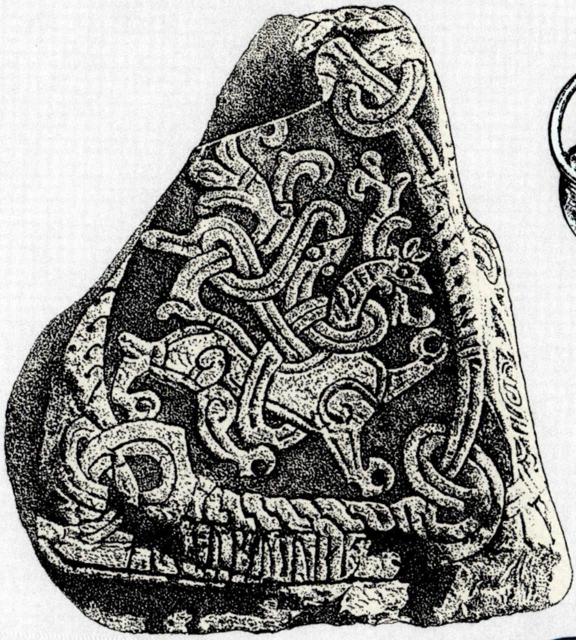

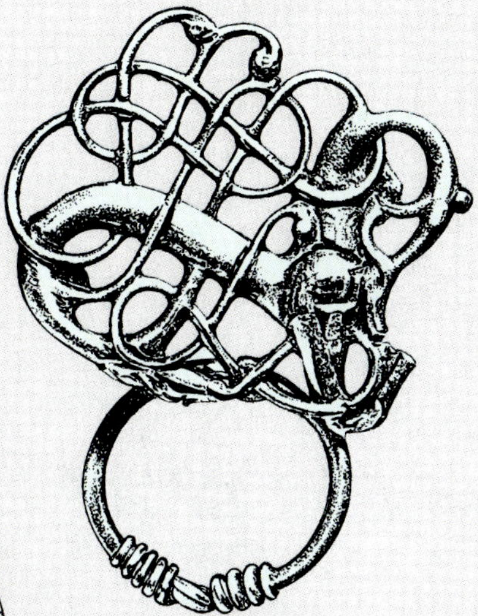

*Left* The Jellinge style is named for the S-shaped animals on the silver cup from the royal burial-chamber in the north mound at Jelling, Denmark. These ribbon-like animals are intertwined to form an open interlace pattern, as seen also along the length of a harness bow (*above left*) from Mammen in Denmark. This terminates in open-jawed animal-heads, each having a "gripping beast" in its mouth; the horse's reins passed through the central hole. The Jellinge style flourished during the first half of the 10th century, overlapping both the earlier Borre and the succeeding Mammen styles.

*Left* The Heggen weather-vane from Norway is probably from the prow of a Viking ship; this face displays two lion-like beasts, descended from that on the Jelling stone (*above center*), but with tightly clustered tendrils forming their manes and tails in the manner of the Ringerike style. This flourished during the first half of the 11th century and a typical example is provided by the Vang stone (*right*), from southeast Norway, on which the beast is of lesser importance than the plant motif. Foliate patterns of western Europe origin were dominant during this one phase of late Viking Age art.

# LEARNING AND RELIGION

*Left* A fearsome mask adorns this runestone from Århus in Denmark: the inscription relates that "Gunulv and Øgot and Aslak and Rolf set up this stone in memory of Ful, their partner. He met his death ... when kings fought."

## The oral tradition

It is hard for people brought up in a culture of books to understand how literature and learning can exist without them. Yet, though the Vikings had no books until they came under the influence of Christianity, this does not mean they had no literature, or even learning of a sort. Ari Thorgilsson (1067–1148) wrote his *Book of the Icelanders* (a history of Iceland) in the early 12th century and had to describe events that had taken place some 250 years earlier. He had no written records to guide him, so got his material, as he tells us, "from the accounts of Teit, my foster-father, the most knowledgeable man I ever knew, son of Bishop Isleif, and of my uncle Thorkel Gellisson, whose memory went far back, and of Thurid Snorradottur who was not only well-informed but also completely trustworthy." In other words, he relied on the testimony of witnesses passed on by word of mouth from generation to generation: the oral tradition.

The Icelander Snorri Sturluson also relied on folk-memory to write his history of the Norwegian kings early in the 13th century. In his introduction to the work he informs us, "At the court of King Harald [about 900] there were poets, and people still know their poems, and the poems of court poets of all the kings who have since ruled Norway. And we put most trust in what is said in those poems recited before the rulers themselves or their sons. We assume to be true what is said there about their exploits and battles. Because it is the poet's custom to praise most the man they are reciting to. But nobody would dare to tell the man tales of adventures that everyone – the man himself as for that – knew to be nonsense or falsehood. That would show contempt, not praise."

This is one sort of learning the cultured Viking had: a knowledge of the history of the great men of his people, as contained in the poems recited in the royal hall. The songs of the skalds, the professional court poets, were in very complex form, with elaborate rhyme, rhythm and alliterative schemes. Sentences intermingled, and a specialized wording was used, removed from the idiom of daily speech. The poets often made reference to the adventures or characteristics of the pagan gods of Scandinavia, which their listeners were expected to recognize. To understand the poems was hard; to produce them very hard. A court poet needed lots of training and considerable memorized knowledge. So did his audience.

Another range of learning was in the law. The Vikings were a people who had great respect for the law – though that is not how they are usually thought of today. Law was made and administered by the local assembly (thing), and preserved in the memories of its elder statesmen. It controlled society and kept in check the ambitions of great men if political power and authority were there to enforce it. If the Icelandic sagas are anything to go by, legal procedure was complicated and precise, and methods of judgment in both civil and criminal cases – there was in effect no difference between them – depended on rigorous adherence to a proper code of practice. A case could be lost if it were pleaded in the wrong form, if assessors were wrongly chosen, if it were presented to the wrong court. Therefore success in the law depended on learning gained by listening rather than reading, by sitting at the feet of older lawmen, by committing to memory the details of past judgments and by observing the practices of the courts.

## Runes

For all that they had no books, the pagan Vikings were not illiterate. They used a script composed of letters called runes. It is fashionable today to attribute to the users of the runic alphabet all sorts of magical powers. This is nonsense. Runes were merely a simple alphabetical script that could be adapted to various purposes: memorial, legal, practical. Magic was only

# Iarlabanki's Causeway

Iarlabanki's causeway is a long, raised road that runs across clayey flatland between Täby and Vallentuna, some 15 kilometers north of Stockholm. It gets its name from a local landowner who had it built in the 11th century. We know this because Iarlabanki also erected a group of rune-stones celebrating his local importance and achievements. Four of the stones that survive mention his "bridge". Apparently they stood in two pairs at either end of the causeway; two remain at its north end. They have closely related texts: "Iarlabanki had these stones raised in his own lifetime, and he made this causeway for his soul's sake. Alone he owned the whole of Täby. God help his soul." On the other stones we learn that he owned the whole district, made a meeting-place, and cleared a path. He was clearly eager to record his personal fame and his act of Christian charity in helping travelers by improving the road system of his neighborhood.

*Below right* The view looks down the causeway from the northern end, which is flanked by the two rune-stones still in their original position; they are 6.5 meters apart. The standing stones seen farther along the causeway are uninscribed; other, smaller stones once marked its length. The causeway was built of stones covered with sand and gravel, nearly a third of a meter in depth.

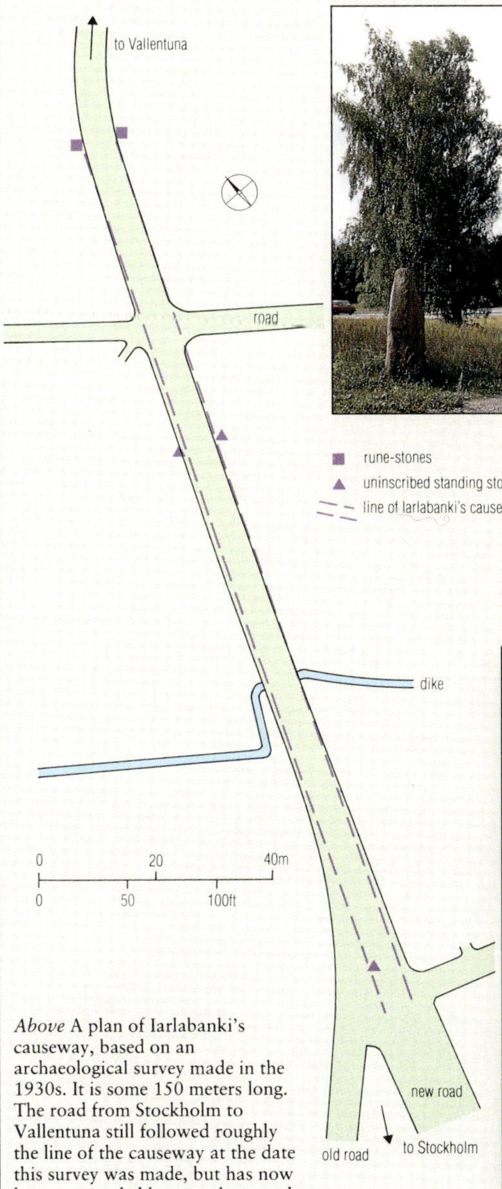


*Above* A plan of Iarlabanki's causeway, based on an archaeological survey made in the 1930s. It is some 150 meters long. The road from Stockholm to Vallentuna still followed roughly the line of the causeway at the date this survey was made, but has now been superseded by a modern road.

*Below* Iarlabanki's stone is a Christian memorial, and appropriately has a central cross. The inscription, in "long-branch" runes, is cut on the bodies of two snakes. The text is in two sections, beginning at the snake's head and curling round to the tail.

one use the Vikings put it to, and not a specially important one at that. Nor was runic specifically a Norse script. Early runes are found in various parts of Europe – in England, the Low Countries, Germany and central Europe, as well as Scandinavia and the larger Viking world. But it is in the north that runes survived longest and have left most examples. They appeared there long before Viking times and remained in use well after the introduction of Christianity and the roman script, indeed into early modern times.

In Scandinavia, too, they developed characteristic, much simplified letter forms. Runic script consists of straight lines rather than curves, and is usually believed to have been developed for cutting on wood, since straight lines are easier to cut into a material with a strong grain. Soon runes were being used on other materials: on bone, metal, and stone. At one time the runic alphabet had 24 letters, but by the beginning of the Viking Age the number had been reduced to 16. These were not enough letters to represent all the sounds of the Norse languages, so spelling was very idiosyncratic. This makes Viking runic texts hard to interpret.

The most striking examples of Viking runic writing are to be seen on the rune-stones. These may take the form of free-standing upright stones or boulders, rock-faces with texts cut on them, or groups of stones in some ceremonial formation, one or more of which bears an inscription. Most of the texts appear to have a memorial purpose, though modern scholars suggest that some of them may have legal implications. Typically, a rune-stone inscription records publicly the death of an important person (sometimes a death far from home) and so makes it clear that the heirs take over the estates. Often there is detailed reference to the lands the dead man owned, and his relatives are named and the relationship defined. Such an inscription is found on a stone at Hällestad, Skåne, Sweden: "Asgaut raised this stone in memory of Ærra his brother; and he was Toki's retainer. Now shall stand this stone on the mound."

But a runic text can be more elaborate than this, and give details of a man's achievements, the circumstances of his death, his relationship to important people, the extent of his land-holding, and so on. For instance, the rune-stone from Dalum, Västergötland, Sweden states: "Toki and his brothers raised this stone in memory of their brothers. One of them met his death in the west, and the other in the east." Or the mysterious Rada stone, also from Västergötland: "Thorkel set this stone in memory of Gunna his son, who met his death when the kings did battle together." We can only wonder which kings these were.

Sometimes runic epitaphs, like those of later times, break into verse. One from Gripsholm, Södermanland, Sweden, is part of a group recording a disastrous Viking expedition to a place called Serkland (a region of dark-skinned peoples – presumably Arab territory) that ended with the death of a number of adventurous young men, and runs like this:

*Tola had this stone put up in memory of his son Harald, Ingvar's brother:*

> *Like men they traveled far for gold*
> *And in the east they fed the eagle,*
> *In the south they died, in Serkland.*

Some rune-stones are avowedly pagan, ending with a sentence such as "May Thor hallow these runes." But rune-stones continued in Christian times, and there may

# Runes

The Scandinavian runic alphabet has its own peculiar letter order and takes its name, *futhark*, from its first six characters. In the Viking Age there were two main versions, but they were not kept distinct, and forms of the one *futhark* sometimes invaded the other. The two types are known as long-branch runes (sometimes called Danish runes) and short-twig runes (also known as Swedo-Norwegian or common runes). Because they were designed for incising into wood or stone, rather than being written with a pen, runes are usually made up of straight lines – a single vertical stave and one or more sloping staves or bows. No distinction is made between capitals and lower-case letters. The short-twig runes are simpler than the long-branch, and they may have developed for writing less formal inscriptions – letters, ownership marks, graffiti and so on.

The early *futharks* were inefficient, for there are not enough individual characters to represent all the sounds of a language, and they were not well distributed. There were no letters for the two common vowels *o* and *e*, for example, though there were two variants of *a*. Among the consonants, there were no specific characters for *d*, *g* and *p* – *t*, *k* and *b* were used instead. Runic spelling was therefore imprecise, with only approximate representations of sounds. Spelling was also inconsistent, different rune-masters representing a word in different ways. As a consequence, runic texts are often difficult to interpret. Toward the end of the Viking Age this deficiency was noticed and new runes were created to fill the gaps.

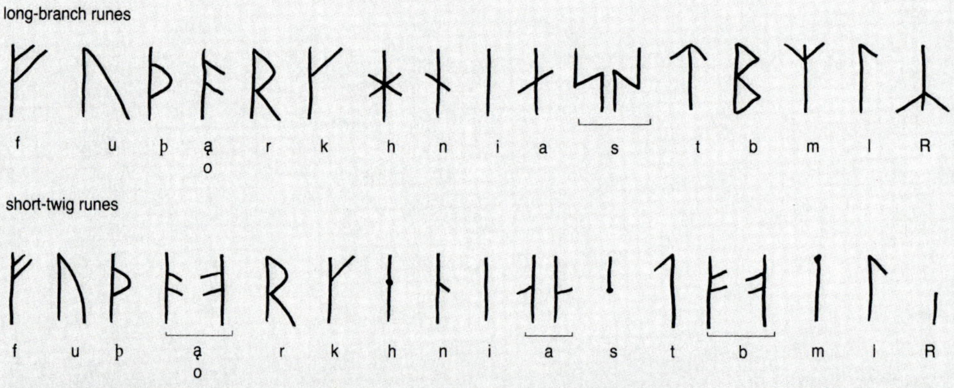


*Top right* Stylized drawings of long-branch and short-twig *futharks*. The forms that distinguish one type from the other are *h, n, a, s, t, b* and *m*. Long-branch runes *(top)* were employed usually in Denmark and occasionally elsewhere, often on monuments. Short-twig runes *(below)* were commonly used in Norway and Sweden and their colonies. A mixture of the two scripts seems to have been typical of runic monuments on the Isle of Man. These two types, known together as the shorter *futhark*, developed from the older *futhark* of 24 letters in the century before the Viking Age. The two rune-rows were used throughout Viking times, but were gradually superseded by Roman script as Christianity penetrated the Scandinavian world.

*Right* This formal group of stones at Björketorp, Blekinge, Sweden (formerly part of Denmark) still stands on its original site. Two of the stones bear no inscription. The third, which is 4 meters high, has a runic text whose language shows it to be very old indeed, perhaps as early as the 7th century. Its runic letters are archaic in form. The inscription is imperfectly understood, but it speaks of "runes of might" and invokes a curse on anyone who destroys the memorial. The purpose of this stone setting is unknown.

*Below* A comb-case made from deer's antler, from Lincoln, England, tentatively dated to the 10th or 11th century. It has an inscription in long-branch runes: *kamb: koþan: kiari: þorfastr* ("Thorfastr made a good comb").

*Above* This graceful rune-stone, nearly 3 meters high, comes from Dynna, Hadeland, in Norway. On its face are Christian symbols. Above, the three magi ride their horses beneath the Christmas star; below, shown sideways on, is the nativity scene, with a kneeling horse beneath. The runic inscription, commemorating a girl called Astrid, is incised along the edge of the stone, and is read from the base upwards.

be an appeal to the Christian God, as on the Valleberga, Skåne, stone: "Sven and Thorgot made these monuments in memory of Manni and Sveni; may God help their souls, and they lie in London."

A lord might put up a stone in memory of a retainer killed in his service, as a king did at Hedeby, south Jutland: "King Svein set this stone in memory of Skarthi, his man, who had traveled in the west but now met his death at Hedeby." This records the occasion in the 11th century when the Danish king Svein besieged and captured Hedeby from an occupying force. Sometimes if a man did not trust his successors or lord to put up a stone he raised one himself, like the one at Väsby in Uppland, Sweden, which records that "Ali had this stone put up in his own honor. He took Cnut's *Danegeld* in England. May God help his soul." Taking part in a Viking raid on England was hardly a Christian act, but Ali thought it an episode in his life worth recording. For the historian, it is important evidence that the Viking army commanded by the Danish king Cnut had Swedish mercenaries in its ranks.

And of course it was not only men who were commemorated on rune-stones, though they certainly predominate. The most splendid of the Norwegian rune-stones comes from Dynna, Hadeland. It is a tall slender pillar decorated with carvings of the three magi (wise men), the Christ-child and the Christmas star. The text records an act of Christian charity, building a bridge to help the weary traveler: "Gunnvor, Thryrik's daughter, built a bridge in memory of her daughter Astrid. She was the handiest [most skillful] girl in Hadeland."

There are inscriptions on other objects than stone, though these are often enough prosaic statements of ownership, like the one on a box of Celtic workmanship found in Norway (exactly where is unknown) with the text "Rannveig owns this box." More interesting is a verse text on a silver neck-ring from a Viking hoard found at Senja, Troms, Norway. It reads:

*We paid a visit to the lads of Frisia*
*And we it was who split the spoils of battle.*

The Rök stone in Östergötland is among Sweden's most impressive rune-stones. It has the longest known inscription, which has been tight packed into every available space. Carved in short-twig runes, it is a priceless literary document – written by Varin in memory of Væmod, his dead son – from the early Viking Age. It contains an eight-line verse as well as complex allusions to lost lays and legends.

Runic inscriptions are common in some parts of Scandinavia, rare in others; why this should be we do not know. It may be an indication of relative densities of population, but it is also likely to reflect social or political conditions – some classes of society may have been more conditioned to putting up runic memorials than others; in some regions there may have been more spare money to spend on such luxuries. It is estimated that some 2,500 runic inscriptions dating from before 1300 survive in Sweden alone, many fewer in Denmark, perhaps 350, and fewer still in Norway outside the late Viking Age towns that are now being excavated. However, the Vikings also left inscriptions in some of the areas they colonized: in west Russia, on the north German coast, in Orkney, Shetland and the Hebrides, in Ireland and the Isle of Man, and in certain regions of England and the mainland of Scotland. Yet there are surprising gaps, for there seem to be no Viking runic inscriptions from Iceland or Normandy, though both were settled by Vikings. The Isle of Man, in the Irish Sea, is a special case, for though it is tiny it has 30 or so surviving rune-stones and the names that appear on the inscriptions suggest an intermingling of Norse and Celtic-speaking peoples. Here again the rune-stones have preserved historical information that is not available to us from other sources.

The runic script was essentially a practical one, for a Viking could find a piece of wood anywhere, and he would always have a knife at his belt. The letter forms are easy to learn and easy to cut. But the script could hardly be used to write down longer texts, though occasionally a poem of up to eight lines might be cut on a stick or even a standing stone. A memorial to a Danish leader at Karlevi on the Swedish island of Öland preserves a stanza in the elaborate verse form called *dróttkvætt* ("court meter"), much used by the skalds.

**The Icelandic sagas**

Though one meaning of the Icelandic word *saga* is "history", not all the works we now call sagas are historical in content. However, what historical accounts we have of Viking Age Scandinavia come largely from the two principal types of prose narrative, the *Kings' Sagas* (*Konunga sögur*) and the *Sagas of Icelanders* (*Islendingasögur*). Because these were written mainly in the 13th century, that is nearly two centuries after the end of the Viking Age, their reliability as historical evidence needs careful scrutiny.

The *Kings' Sagas* begin with some purely legendary tales of early Scandinavian rulers and continue with a life of the first king of all Norway, Harald Finehair, whose government began, by traditional dating, in 870. Then follows the full succession of Norwegian kings to the end of the Viking Age and beyond. Harald had many sons,

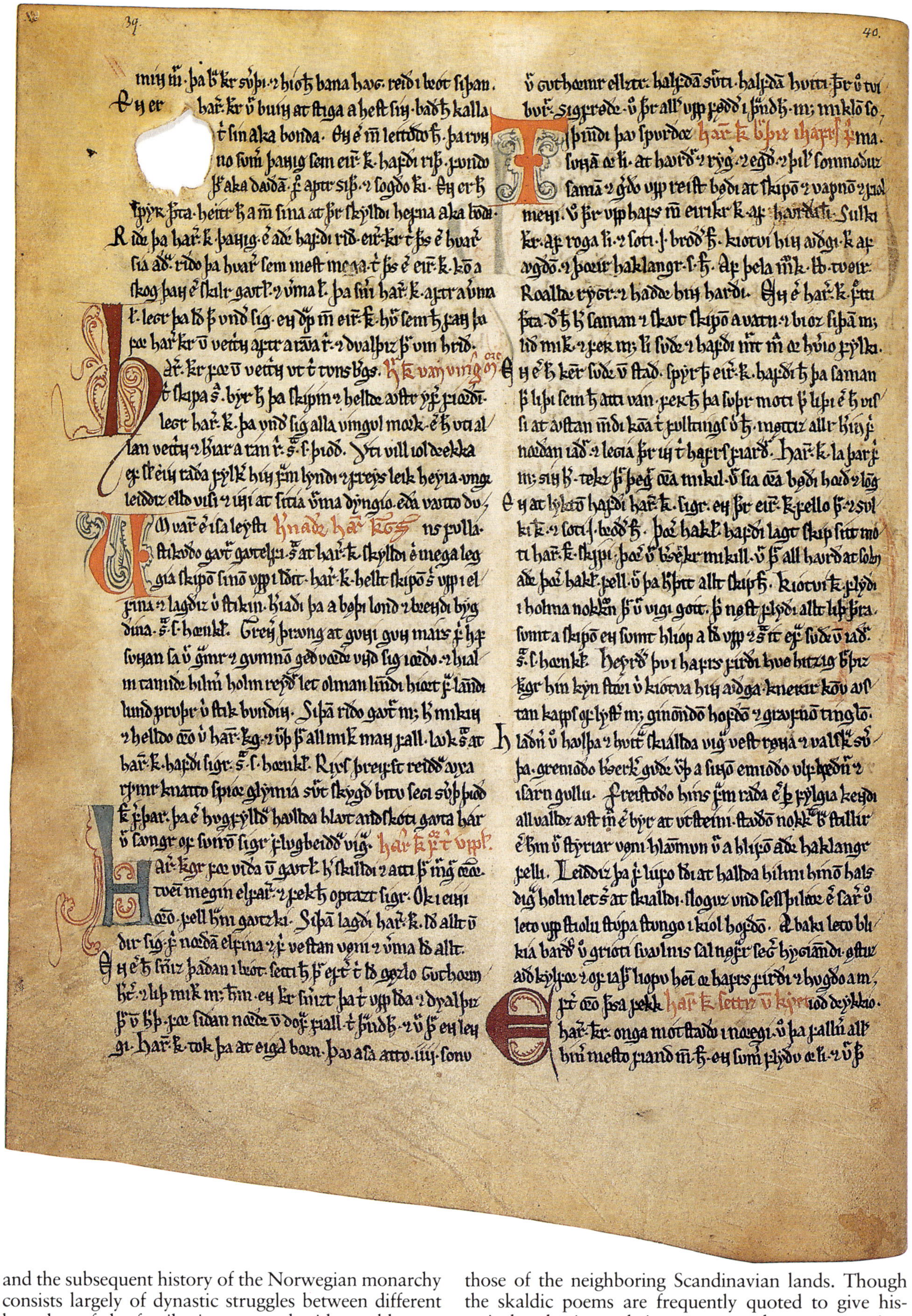

*Left* A page from Harald Finehair's saga in an early 14th-century Icelandic manuscript of Snorri Sturluson's *Heimskringla – The Circle of the World* – written by him about 1230. This prose chronicle of the kings of Norway from legendary times to 1177 is the masterwork of the *Kings' Sagas*, furnished with liberal quotation from skaldic poetry. In his prologue Snorri explains the importance of these poems as an historical source, most particularly "if the metrical rules are observed in them and if they are sensibly interpreted".

and the subsequent history of the Norwegian monarchy consists largely of dynastic struggles between different branches of the family, interspersed with troublesome periods when powerful non-royal families, like that of the great Earl Hakon of Lade (now a suburb of Trondheim), controlled much of the country. There was often trouble with the powerful free farmers and land-owners who dominated the provincial assemblies of early medieval Norway. The sagas also tell something of the relationship between the rulers of Norway and those of the neighboring Scandinavian lands. Though the skaldic poems are frequently quoted to give historical authority to their statements, the saga narratives are episodic and full of personal anecdotes, giving prominence to the adventures of Icelanders at the Norwegian court.

The *Sagas of Icelanders*, on the other hand, tell stories about the early colonizers of Iceland (in the period 870–930) and their successors over a couple of generations. They are concerned with the nature of the early

*Right* This rune-stone was raised, about 1000, in memory of a chieftain named Sibbe, at Karlevi on the island of Öland. The last part of its inscription preserves the only stanza of skaldic verse that is known to have been written during the Viking Age, in the elaborate *dróttkvætt* meter.

settlement and the problems of survival in an intimidating environment, the attempt to impose the rule of law, and the conflict between this and traditional methods of settling disputes between powerful clans, such as the blood-feud and payment of compensation. They are often called Family Sagas because their plots center on family relationships and marriage alliances. They vary in length from a short tale to what almost amounts to an extensive novel, as in the case of *Njal's Saga*, for example. Some, like the *Saga of Egil Skallagrimsson*, tell of the exploits of Icelanders abroad, whether as merchants and adventurers or serving as poets at the courts of Scandinavian rulers. Others, like the *Saga of Gisli Sursson*, describe the hunted life of the outlaw in Iceland, and his struggle to survive. Others again confine themselves to the early history of a particular region, such as *Eyrbyggjasaga*, which is set in the peninsula of Snæfellsnes in western Iceland.

The *Sagas of Icelanders* are written in a plain, straightforward narrative style. This, together with their details of daily life and working conditions in medieval Iceland, give them an air of authenticity that has led some readers to regard them as historically accurate accounts of life in the Viking Age. Modern opinion, however, tends to regard them more like historical novels, often based on fact or local tradition but elaborated with post-Viking invention.

### Skaldic poetry

Though skaldic verses were, as we have seen, occasionally cut in runes on stones or sticks, most of our knowledge of them comes to us in quite another way. With the coming of Christianity, the Scandinavians acquired the use of the roman script and soon began to write down texts in the Norse language: the earliest surviving transcripts we have are from the 12th century, after the end of the Viking Age. One of the main topics that interested the Scandinavians – in particular the Norwegians and Icelanders – was the history of their own countries. As we have seen, this provided the subject matter of some of their most important medieval prose literature, the *Kings' Sagas* and the *Sagas of Icelanders*. To provide themselves with material, the writers of these sagas turned to the poetry of the skalds that dealt with historical topics, as the Icelander Snorri Sturluson tells us he did.

As we have seen, skaldic poetry was written for public performance and passed on by recitation and remembering. Its characteristic forms – the rhymes and alliterative patterns – must surely have been developed to aid memory by helping to keep the shape of each verse in the reciter's mind. The 12th- and 13th-century saga-writers quoted this poetry to illustrate their prose, add vigor to its action or justify their statements, and so it has been preserved to us. Because the verse was difficult to understand and complex in form, later copyists wrote down stanzas without fully understanding them and often got bits of them wrong. Other prose writers would invent bits of verse to add weight to their stories or give them the appearance of authenticity, and these passages must be distinguished from the genuine Viking quotations. For all these reasons the study of skaldic texts is full of problems.

Some of the poems that survive are what the Icelanders called "loose verses," single stanzas that comment upon contemporary circumstances or incidents. Others take the form of groups of stanzas that make up longer poems, often recited in honor of kings or war leaders. They have different degrees of formal elaboration, sometimes with a refrain, sometimes not. Clearly there was an etiquette involved in the way a poem was presented and it must have been important to know which leader was entitled to a *drápa* – that had a refrain – and which one could be fobbed off with a *flokkr*, that did not.

Unfortunately there are no contemporary reports of how a skald performed his poem before his chosen leader and we have to rely on later stories. These may contain a good deal of invention. Obviously a praise poem to a great king had to be performed in public – there was no profit in praising a man in private. This meant that the poem must compete with all the hubbub of the royal hall, so it was common to begin with a request for silence. Then would follow a series of stanzas defining the king's qualities, usually warlike and successful. It would be wise for the poet to praise the king's generosity as well, for after all the poet was a professional and expected to be rewarded. A major poem might have 20 or more verses and a three-part structure with parallel opening and closing sections framing a central group of stanzas and refrains.

Not all poems contained praise, however. The skald was less dependent on his patron than other courtiers, for he was not a permanently attached member of the royal retinue, and so could sometimes be persuaded to pass on unpalatable advice to him. Sigvat Thordarson was the poet at the court of the 11th-century Norwegian king Magnus whose father, Olaf Haraldsson, had tried to bring Christianity to Norway and had been killed in battle against rebel landowners at Stiklestad near Trondheim in 1030. When Magnus came to the throne he began to take revenge on those who had opposed his father, and made himself exceedingly unpopular. A group at court chose Sigvat for the task of pointing out to Magnus the folly of his actions. In a poem called "The Plain-speaking Verses" Sigvat warned Magnus of the dangers he ran if he did not amend his ways, and defined the qualities a good king should have.

Skaldic poetry differs from much other early Norse literature in that the names of the poets are known; verses are attributed to individual skalds. What survives comes mainly from western Scandinavia, and the poets are Norwegian or, at a slightly later date, are often Icelanders. Some poems survive from the Danish court. There were presumably Swedish skalds – though we do not know their works – and minor courts, such as that of the Orkney earls, also had their poets.

**The Eddas**

The difficult, often bizarre, language of skaldic poetry and the complexity of its meters led the poet and historian Snorri Sturluson to assemble, perhaps in the 1220s, a handbook for such young poets as wished to compose similar verse. This is the work called the *Prose* (or *Younger*) *Edda*, one of the most important works surviving from medieval Iceland. It is divided into three sections. The last one is called "the list of meters" and contains over 100 examples of different verse patterns with Snorri's commentary and descriptions of them. The first and second parts are concerned with the content and language of skaldic poetry. They provide an explanation of the mythological and heroic references contained in the poetry, and of the words that are used to define different poetic subjects.

For much of his information here Snorri relied on another type of early poetry, that of the *Poetic* (or *Elder*) *Edda*. Eddic poetry is anonymous, and is usually much simpler in form than skaldic. The greater part of it is preserved in a single manuscript called the Codex Regius, formerly in the Royal Library, Copenhagen, but now kept in Reykjavik, Iceland. Occasional poems of the same type are also found in a few other manuscripts. The Codex Regius was written in the 13th century but the material it contains comes from a wide period of time and apparently from various countries. Some of it is almost certainly from the Viking Age. The poems are on diverse topics. Some of them are mythological, relating tales of the pagan gods of Scandinavia, of the beginning and end of the world, and recounting traditional wisdom. Others are heroic, telling of the famous exploits of the great kings and warriors of the early Germanic peoples of continental Europe.

It is from the Eddic poems – and Snorri's retelling of them – that we get much of our information of the pagan myths and beliefs of early Scandinavia, including the names of the gods, their relationship to one another and their struggles with hostile powers. We have to be careful how we use the information, though, for our source is a literary not a scientific one. Some of the poems may have been written after the coming of Christianity – nor should we assume that pagan mythology was the same in all parts of Scandinavia.

*Above* Drangey Island in Skagafjordur, northern Iceland, is the location of an important episode in *Grettir's Saga*. The hero, Grettir the Strong, is outlawed for a killing and, as a last resort, takes refuge on the remote island of Drangey – a natural fortress, with cliffs on all sides – where he is able to feed on seabirds and their eggs, as well as the sheep put there for the summer grazing. Ultimately his enemies, unable to get at him any other way, contrive his death by witchcraft.

*Right* A 14th-century Icelander's impression of the death of St Olaf in 1030, at the battle of Stiklestad in Norway, from the *Flateyjarbók*. This miniature is framed in the opening initial of the saga devoted to his life, written in the early 13th century. The marginal illuminations at the bottom of the page illustrate some of the legendary exploits of the earlier Norwegian king, Olaf Tryggvason, who is depicted killing a wild boar and a sea-ogress.

# The Pagan Gods

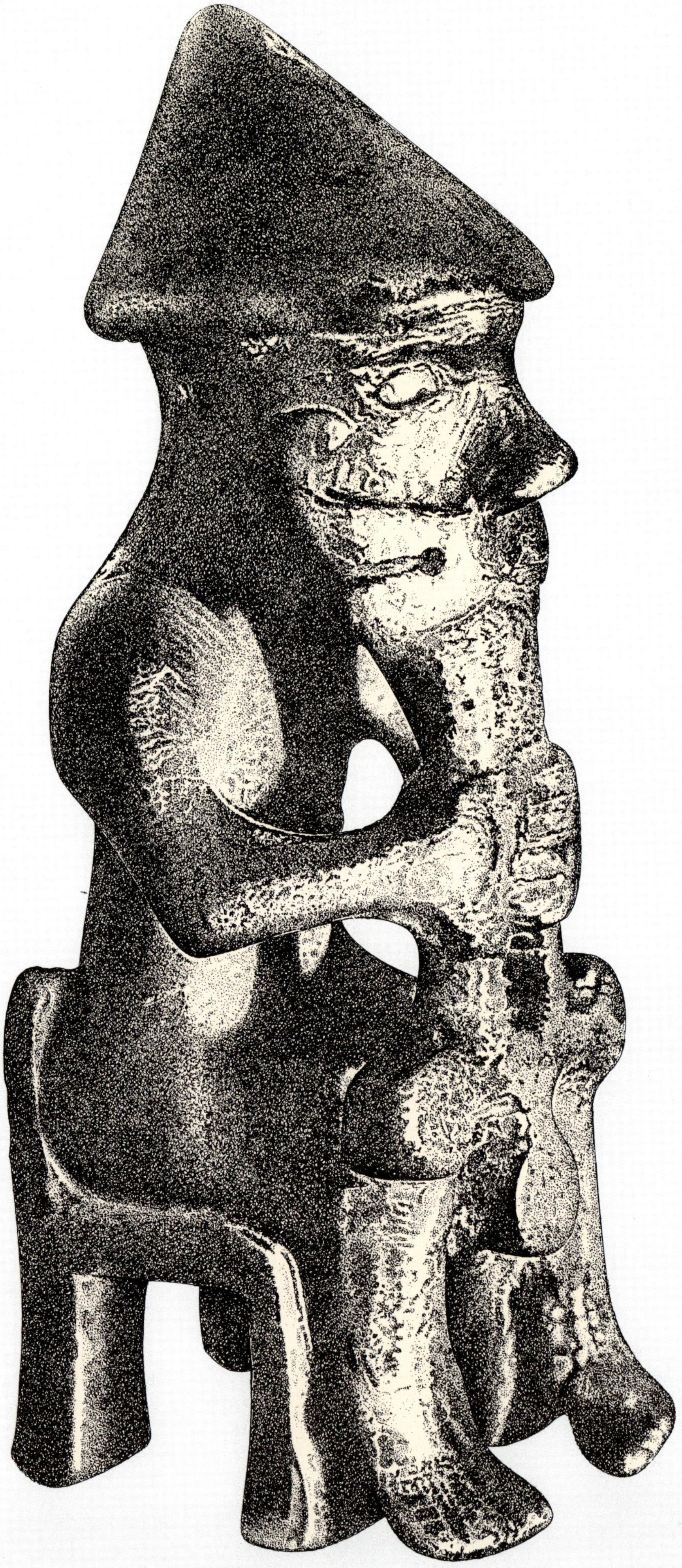

The pagan gods and goddesses of Scandinavia form two groups. Most belong to the race of Norse gods called *Æsir*, but there is an important – and indeed influential – smaller group known as the *Vanir*. The two groups have very different qualities and ways of behaving, and the distinction between them seems to go back to pre-Viking times. In later Norse myth the gods are shown as two warring tribes who, after a long period of conflict, come to an agreement, each giving the other hostages. This explains the presence of the *Vanir* – the gods of wealth, fertility and physical delight – among the *Æsir*.

Niord and his son and daughter, Freyr and Freyia, are *Vanir*. Niord is a god of sea-travel and mercantile enterprise, of money and property, while his offspring are deities of fruitfulness and sexual love: Freyr and Freyia have an incestuous relationship that is not accepted among the *Æsir*. The *Vanir*, and particularly Freyia are connected with the practice of *seiðr*, a form of magic that enabled its practitioners to control others and to gain special knowledge, but also brought with it effeminacy, a condition that was unacceptable to most Norsemen.

The larger group of gods, the *Æsir*, includes some of the most famous of Norse deities, notably the two great gods Odin and Thor. These stand in contrast to one another. Odin is a complex figure with many attributes, some of them sinister. He is powerful but treacherous, and skilled in magic. In disguise he often intervenes in the affairs of men. He is something of a god of war for he supports great warriors, but often ends by betraying them to their deaths. In later stories he is shown as the god of the professional soldier. His famous weapon is a mighty spear Gungnir, and he rides an eight-legged horse called Sleipnir. He dwells in the hall Valholl, into which he gathers famous fighting-men who are killed in battle in preparation for Ragnarök, the final day.

Thor is a simpler and less intelligent deity, more the god of the common man. He is physically powerful; armed with his great hammer Miollnir, he fights giants and demons and defends Asgard, the stronghold of the gods. In some of his adventures he is accompanied by the god Loki, who is an ambiguous figure, sometimes appearing as a witty and mischievous companion, but also as a wicked and treacherous figure whose actions will eventually end the rule of the gods at Ragnarök. It was Loki who arranged the killing of the god Baldr, the beautiful and beloved.

Among the less well-known gods is Tyr, god of warriors. Only one great myth survives about him – he is one-handed because the wolf Fenrir bit off the other hand when trying to escape from a snare set by the gods. Another little-known god is Heimdall. He guards the paths into Asgard, and will sound his warning horn at the opening of the great day of Ragnarök. We also know the names of numbers of goddesses including Frigg, consort of Odin, Nanna, who is Baldr's wife, and Sif, married to Thor. However, only Freyia figures largely in the surviving myths.

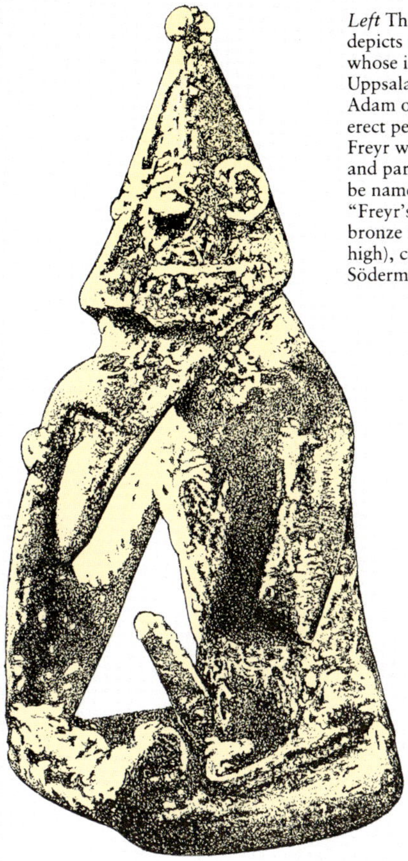

*Left* This phallic figure probably depicts the fertility god Freyr, whose idol in the temple of Uppsala was represented (says Adam of Bremen) with a great erect penis. As a god of fruitfulness Freyr was a patron of the farmer, and particularly fertile fields would be named after him: *Freysakr*, "Freyr's cornfield". This small bronze figurine (6.9 centimeters high), comes from Rällinge, Södermanland, Sweden.

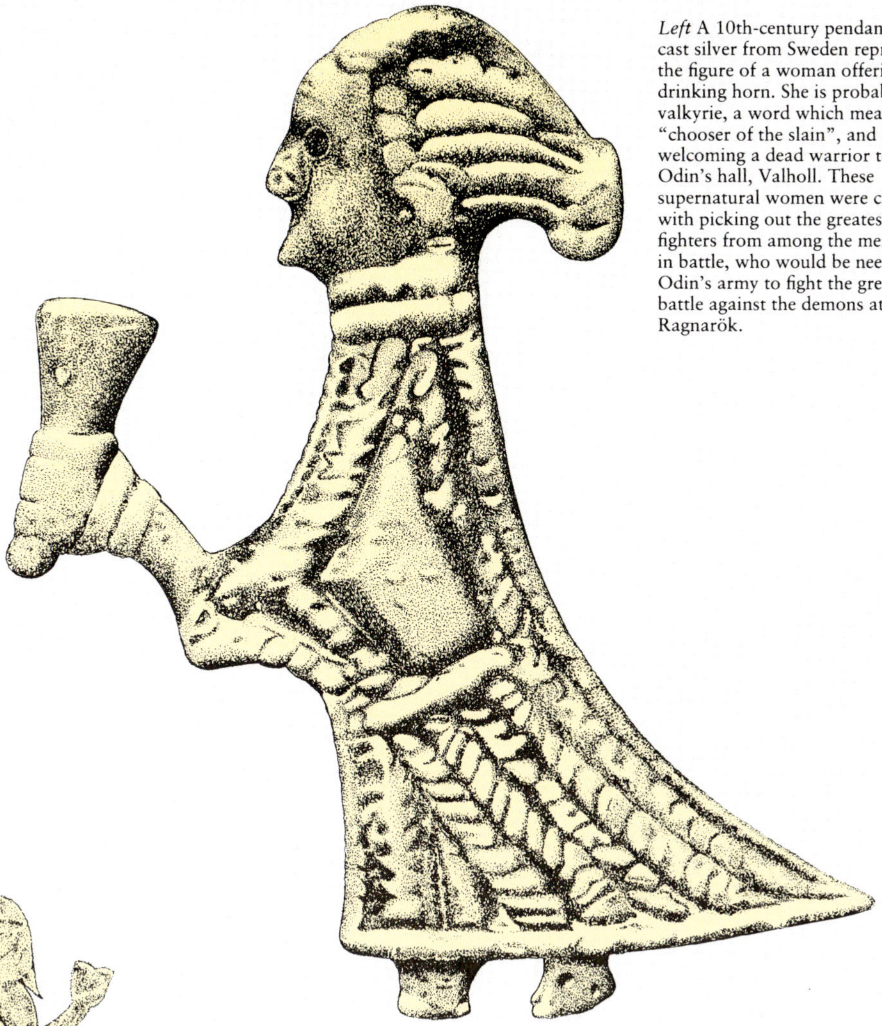

*Left* A 10th-century pendant of cast silver from Sweden represents the figure of a woman offering a drinking horn. She is probably a valkyrie, a word which means "chooser of the slain", and is welcoming a dead warrior to Odin's hall, Valholl. These supernatural women were charged with picking out the greatest fighters from among the men killed in battle, who would be needed for Odin's army to fight the great battle against the demons at Ragnarök.

*Left* This small bronze figurine (6.7 centimeters high) from northern Iceland probably represents the god Thor holding his hammer Miollnir – one of the greatest treasures of the gods since it helps Thor defend them against the giants and monsters who intend to destroy them. It was made by one of the dwarfs, a race noted for their craftsmanship. Thor wields it both as a missile and as a striking weapon, and it presumably represents the thunderbolt.

*Above* This detail from an 8th-century picture-stone from Tjängvide on the island of Gotland shows a man riding an eight-legged horse; it probably represents Odin's horse, Sleipnir. Described as "the best of steeds" in an early poem, Sleipnir was the result of a union between the god Loki (disguised as a mare) and a giant stallion.

*Right* This figure of a fighting-man has a helmet surmounted by a boar's figure. The god Freyr had a boar called Gullinbursti ("Golden-bristled") crafted by the same dwarf who made Thor's hammer. It could gallop faster than any horse and illuminated the darkest night with the glitter of its bristles. The boar on this helmet may indicate a fighter under Freyr's protection. One Old Norse word for a noble fighting-man, *iöfurr*, literally means "wild boar".

*Left* Legendary treasures in the Norse myths are often attributed to the work of dwarves; here one such dwarf is depicted at his forge, in a detail from a 12th-century baptismal font on the island of Gotland.

**Myth and legend**

Among the most powerful Norse myths are those that explain the beginning and end of this world. Not surprisingly, neither is very precise. In the beginning there was nothing, a void only, but this lay between two regions, one freezing and misty called Niflheim, one hot and sparkling called Muspell. A river flowed into the great void, and froze over, layer upon layer. Where the hot and cold areas touched, the ice melted and formed a frost giant, Ymir, from whom are descended all the frost giants of the world. Then it formed a cow, Audhumla, that licked the salty frozen ice. As it licked, a figure of human shape was formed out of the block, and this was Buri, from whom most of the great gods are descended. The gods Odin, Vili and Ve killed Ymir, and from his body made the structure of this world, of the sea, the sky and clouds: within this world dwell a variety of creatures, the gods themselves, men, dwarfs, elves, giants of various sorts.

There also live a number of sinister monsters who will put paid to the gods on the final day, which is called Ragnarök. The most famous are the wolf Fenrir and the World Serpent, Midgardsorm, also called Iormungand. For the greater part of time these monsters are kept secure, Fenrir bound and chained to a rock, Iormungand at the bottom of the sea. When Ragnarök comes they will emerge from their captivity and join with the forces of darkness, the evil god Loki and an obscure group of fire-demons and giants. These will attack the gods, who will fall after a valiant defense, and the world will be consumed by fire. The gods have foreseen this, and indeed Odin has collected an army of great warriors in his great hall of Valholl from among the heroes killed in battle, but he knows before he starts that his resistance is in vain, and that he and all his kin are doomed. This is a suitable mythology for a warrior race, one in which killing and treachery are commonplace, and in which a great man displays his greatness by struggling against a fate that he knows is inevitable.

The Norse myth of the creation of mankind is a primitive one. Three gods, Odin, Hoenir and Lodur, were walking by the seashore and came upon two logs, presumably driftwood. They picked them up and gave them human shape, one male, one female. Then each god added human characteristics: breath and life; understanding and movement; speech, hearing and sight. From these two beings, says Snorri, descend all people. But humans are social animals and there survives a curious poem, *Rigsthula (The Lay of Rig)*, which describes how social distinctions came about in this world. The great god Heimdall was walking through the world, and took on himself the name of Rig. He went to three houses, belonging to a poor, middling and rich couple in turn. In each he ate with the couple and stayed three nights, sharing their bed. In each case the wife gave birth to a child nine months later. From the poor wife descended the slave class, from the second the free working class, from the wealthy the class of nobles and eventually royalty. According to this myth, then, Heimdall was the progenitor of humankind in its social capacity.

A number of myths relate to the gods themselves. One of the most powerful tells of the beloved god Baldr, of whom the sinister Loki was so jealous that he contrived his death. Baldr was invulnerable to weapons made from any material except mistletoe, which was so insignificant it had not been included in the oath not to harm the god. Loki learned of this, and contrived that the blind god Hod should shoot a mistletoe shaft at Baldr, which killed him. The gods tried in vain to bring Baldr back from the abode of Hel, goddess of the dead, but he remains there until, in one version, he shall return again after Ragnarök. This is the "dying god" myth, familiar to students of comparative religion.

Another common myth-type is the "sacred marriage", wherein the god of fertility mates with the earth to make it fruitful. This is represented in Norse legend by a tale of the god Freyr and his love for a giant-girl Gerd. Freyr saw her first when he was sitting in Odin's great throne, Hlidskialf, from where the whole world could be viewed. He fell so deeply in love with her that he could neither sleep nor drink, and sent his servant Skirnir to make proposals to her. Skirnir's reward would be to receive Freyr's famous sword, which could fight of its own accord. The messenger made the dangerous journey to the giant-haunted north, offering sumptuous gifts to the giantess. When she rejected them he resorted to threats, and at last got Gerd's promise to be Freyr's bride. So the story had a happy ending – but it left Freyr without his sword, and thus he will not be able to use it to defend the gods at Ragnarök.

For the poets who recorded these myths, the most important concerned the poetic mead, the drink that gives the inspiration to create great poetry. It was originally compounded by a pair of dwarfs, Fialar and Galar, who killed a giant called Kvasir and mixed his blood with honey, thus making mead. The drink later came into the possession of a giant Suttung who kept it in three cauldrons. Odin coveted the mead and stole it from Suttung by seducing his daughter Gunnlod, who let him have a drink from each cauldron. However,

*Below* This scene, on the rune-stone at Altuna church in Uppland, Sweden, illustrates the legend of Thor in which he goes fishing for the World Serpent. Thor's hammer is at the ready, but his left leg has been driven through the bottom planks of the boat, so violent is the struggle when the Serpent first seizes his hook, baited with an ox-head.

*Above* Amongst the enigmatic scenes on one of the Gotlandic picture-stones from Ardre is one that may illustrate an incident from the tale of Volund (Wayland) the Smith, recounted in the *Edda*. Volund has been captured by a king who forces him to work in the royal smithy; he takes his revenge by killing the king's sons and seducing his daughter before escaping in the shape of a bird. On the right of the smithy (indicated by the hammer and tongs), are two headless corpses, whilst to the left is a bird-like form and the figure of a woman.

Odin drained the contents dry, then flew away in the form of an eagle. Suttung pursued him, also in eagle's guise, but Odin managed to get to Asgard (the realm of the gods) and spewed the mead out into the pails and jars that the gods had got ready. From there Odin is able to dispense it to any of his favorites.

### Sacrifice, worship and belief

Today we have no way of knowing how far these literary myths represent what the Vikings actually believed or acted upon in their daily lives. The Vikings themselves did not record details of their pagan religion, and the Christians who came into contact with them were reluctant to describe paganism or give it any credit; if they did mention it, it was usually in pejorative terms. The 10th-century English chronicler Æthelweard speaks of Vuothen, the ancestor of the Anglo-Saxon kings, and says that "the unbelieving Northerners (which is to say the Danes, Norwegians and [Swedes]) are overwhelmed by such great temptation that they worship him as a god even today." (Æthelweard is here equating Vuothen with Odin.) The 11th-century English homilist Ælfric wrote a sermon "On false gods" in which he pointed out that Jupiter "is among some nations called Thor, one whom the Danish peoples love most of all."

The only pagan temple of which we have detailed information is that at Gamla Uppsala, in central Sweden, which was described by the German churchman Adam of Bremen in the 11th century. He says that the temple building was gilded throughout. The temple contained idols of three gods; the most powerful, Thor, sat in the middle with Odin and Freyr on each side. Adam goes on to define the different attributes and qualities of these gods, as the Swedes believed them to be. Thor presides in the air, governs thunder and lightning, winds and rainstorms, fine weather and crops; his figure holds a scepter. Odin (whose name, says Adam correctly, means "fury"), controls warfare and courage, and his idol is an armed figure. Freyr is the god of peace and physical delight, and his figure has an immense penis. Each god has his own priests, and the people sacrifice to the gods for appropriate benefits, to Thor in

# The Legend of Sigurd

1

2

3

*Above* The decorative doorway from Hylestad church in Norway contains scenes from the Sigurd story. Left to right, they show: (1) Sigurd, helmeted as a hero should be, testing Regin's swords by chopping at an anvil with them. The first sword has just broken, and Regin in the background is setting about making the second. (2) With an assistant to blow the bellows, Regin is working the metal of the blade of the third sword. This was made from the metal fragments of Sigmund's great sword Gram, which had only shattered when Odin posed his spear before it in battle and broke it. (3) Sigurd, protected by his shield from the dragon Fafnir's venom, takes Regin's advice and stabs upward at the serpent's belly. (4) Regin has fallen asleep, nursing the sword, while Sigurd is roasting Fafnir's heart, threaded onto a spit, over a fire. He has just burned his hand, and is licking it to soothe it. As he swallows the dragon's blood he finds himself able to understand what the birds round about are saying. (5) Sigurd takes the birds' advice and slaughters Regin. The written versions say that Sigurd decapitated him, but here he takes an independent line and simply slashes him in two. (6) Grani, Sigurd's splendid horse, carries Fafnir's treasure on his back. Two of the birds who have advised Sigurd are sitting among the foliage.

The stories and characters that are the essential matter of Norse legend derive from the Germanic tradition of central Europe, but it is in the literature of medieval Scandinavia that they are most fully preserved. It was to the Norse myths that the German composer Richard Wagner (1813–83) turned for the inspiration for many of his musical dramas and operas, particularly the adventures of the two great Germanic heroes, Siegmund and Siegfried, father and son. The story of Sigurd (Siegfried) is told in several of the poems of the *Poetic Edda*, and Snorri Sturluson also summarizes it in his *Prose Edda*. It is most easily accessible to the modern reader in the 13th-century prose tale, the *Saga of King Volsung and his descendants* (*Volsunga saga*).

Sigurd was the posthumous son of the great hero Sigmund. He was put out to foster with a smith called Regin, who came from a family skilled in magic. Regin made Sigurd discontented with his lot in life and encouraged him to improve it by seeking the treasure that was guarded by a dragon called Fafnir. In fact, Fafnir was Regin's brother and they had quarreled over the ownership of the treasure. Regin set about making a sword for Sigurd to kill the dragon with, but the first two he made shattered when Sigurd tried them out, so Regin made him a third, out of the fragments of his father Sigmund's ancient sword. This proved to be perfect – both sharp and tough.

Regin accompanied Sigurd to the heath where Fafnir was lurking. They found the tracks that Fafnir made when he went to his watering-hole. They were enormous, and Sigurd became apprehensive. Regin advised him to kill the scaly monster by digging a pit and hiding in it so that when the dragon came to drink he could stab it in its soft underbelly. This Sigurd did. When the dragon was dead, Regin came forward to claim some of the treasure since he had supplied the sword. Regin and Sigurd quarreled, but Sigurd finally agreed to Regin's request that he should cut out the dragon's heart, roast it and give it to Regin to eat.

Sigurd roasted the heart on a spit. When the juices began to splutter out, he tested the heart with his finger to see if was done. His finger was scalded and he put it in his mouth to cool it, so drinking some of the heart blood. This instantly gave him the ability to understand the language of the birds twittering to each other in the bushes nearby. They revealed that Regin intended to betray Sigurd and take the treasure for himself and suggested that Sigurd should cut off Regin's head. He followed this counsel, and afterward ate some of Fafnir's heart, before jumping on his horse Grani – a magnificent animal that had been sired by Odin's steed Sleipnir and chosen with Odin's advice. He traced the dragon's tracks back to its lair where he found the heap of gold and other treasures – more than two or three ordinary horses could carry between them, yet he was able to load all the treasure on to Grani's back without difficulty. He did not know that the treasure had had a curse placed on it that would bring disaster to anyone who possessed it.

Riding away, Sigurd came to a king's hall where he met a woman, Brynhild, with whom he fell in love, and they exchanged rings and vows of mutual fidelity. After lingering there for some time, Sigurd went in search of further adventures and came with his treasure to the court of a King Giuki who had three sons, Gunnar, Hogni and Guttorm, and a beautiful daughter, Gudrun. He made a great impression and Grimhild, their mother, schemed to unite Sigurd to their family. She gave him a magic potion that made him forget Brynhild so that he fell for Gudrun and married her; to bind the alliance, Sigurd, Gunnar and Hogni swore an oath of blood-brotherhood.

In turn Gunnar set out to win Brynhild, and Sigurd agreed to help him. She lived in a hall surrounded by a barrier of fire and had vowed to marry only the man who could ride through the flames to claim her. Gunnar could not do this, but Sigurd, with his great steed Grani, could. So Sigurd and Gunnar exchanged shapes and Sigurd, disguised as his friend, won Brynhild. They slept together, but Sigurd put a naked sword between them to preserve their chastity. He took from Brynhild the ring he had earlier given her when they became betrothed, and this he later handed over to his wife Gudrun. Gunnar and Brynhild were married and came to live at Giuki's court. Not till then

*Right* Like so many of the Swedish rune-stones, this example from Drävle, Uppland, has its inscription cut on a serpent. The carver has interpreted this as the dragon Fafnir and, at the top of the stone, has carved Sigurd stabbing it in the belly.

4

5

6

did Sigurd's memory return, and he recollected his earlier contract of love with Brynhild.

Gudrun and Brynhild quarreled over who had the finest husband. Brynhild boasted that hers was the greatest as he had ridden through a ring of fire for her, and Gudrun then revealed the deception that had been practiced on Brynhild – that it was Sigurd in Gunnar's shape who had won her – and proved it by showing Brynhild her own ring that Sigurd had passed on to Gudrun. Brynhild was savagely angry and plotted revenge. She told Gunnar that she knew that it was Sigurd who had won her, and aroused his jealousy by revealing that she and Sigurd had slept together within the flame barrier, but did not mention the sword that had lain between them. So she encouraged Gunnar to plot Sigurd's death. He drew his brother Hogni into his schemes, arguing that with Sigurd dead they would succeed to his treasure and to the power that he wielded. But as Sigurd's blood-brothers they could not in propriety kill him themselves. Their third brother, Guttorm, was not bound to Sigurd in any way, and he agreed to do the killing in return for high honors. Guttorm twice went to Sigurd's chamber while he was still in bed, but each time Sigurd looked at him with his piercing eyes, and he was afraid to do the deed. The third time Guttorm approached him, Sigurd was asleep, and Guttorm drew his sword and stabbed him. Sigurd jerked awake and picking up his sword, threw it at Guttorm. It sliced him in two. Gudrun, in bed beside Sigurd, awoke drenched in blood to find him dying in her arms. As she cried out, Brynhild heard her and laughed aloud.

Brynhild now taunted the brothers by pointing out that without Sigurd they would be greatly weakened in battle, and she revealed to Gunnar that Sigurd had put the sword between them as they lay together, and so had kept faith with him. She collected her wealth together, gave it all to her attendants, and stabbed herself. As she lay dying she asked to be burned on the funeral pyre beside Sigurd, with a drawn sword between them. This was done, and the cursed treasure remained with Gunnar and Hogni, waiting to achieve its next nefarious deed.

time of famine and plague, to Odin for victory, to Freyr for fruitful marriages.

According to Adam, the temple served as a center of national worship. Every nine years there was a major festival, which everyone from all the Swedish provinces, including baptized Christians, had to attend. Sacrifices were made of male victims, including dogs, horses and men, to placate the gods, and their bodies, all mixed up together, were suspended from the trees in the sacred grove near the temple. Adam quotes the evidence of "a certain one of the Christians" who had seen 72 bodies of various creatures strung up in the grove. From this it seems that Adam had his account from eyewitnesses, and that this pagan cult continued in Sweden later than in other Scandinavian lands. However, Adam may also have been influenced by biblical accounts of temples.

The evidence of place-names provides some additional information about pagan sites. For instance, Odense in Fyn, Denmark, is "Odin's *vi*" (meaning sanctuary). Torshov, a name that occurs several times in Norway, means "Thor's temple". For the most part, however, we are reliant on later Scandinavian sources for the details of pagan worship and belief, and these must be treated with great caution. In the early part of his history of the Norwegian kings, *Heimskringla*, Snorri Sturluson describes the customs that Odin established for the northern peoples: "He decreed that all the dead should be burned, and put on the funeral pyre with all their possessions. He also said that everyone should come into Valholl with all the property that he had on the pyre, and he should also enjoy the use of what he himself had buried in the earth, and the ashes should be carried out to sea or buried in the earth, and mounds should be raised in memory of men of rank...And there should be a sacrifice at the beginning of winter for a successful year, and at midwinter for regeneration, and a third in summer which was a sacrifice for victory."

Elsewhere Snorri tells the story of a sacrificial feast that got the Christian king of Norway, Hakon the Good (934–60), into trouble. It was the king's traditional role to preside at this feast, which was held each year in the fall, and eat the ordained meal of horseflesh. However, Hakon could not reconcile this with his Christian faith – good Christians did not eat horse-meat. He wished to sup apart with his friends, but was forced to come into the great hall and sit in the high-seat, the place of honor. Instead of pledging to Odin he made the sign of the cross over the drinking-horn, and only escaped censure when a supporter gave the excuse that he was making the sign of Thor's hammer. Altogether it was a disastrous day for Hakon, and one that cost him dear in political support. The following winter when a major sacrificial feast was held at Trøndelag, the local farmers forced Hakon to take part willy-nilly, to eat the pagan meal of horse-liver and to drink without signing the cross over the cup.

Modern scholars have tended to play down the importance of the major celebrations so richly – and perhaps imaginatively – described in the sagas, and to emphasize instead the more local aspects of worship. Like the Germanic peoples in general, the Scandinavians had no distinct priestly caste: the priest was also a secular leader, the head of a household or of local society. Here the *Sagas of Icelanders* are of particular importance, though again their late date and Christian background may make their information unreliable. Nevertheless, they strongly imply that the Norse pagan religion was closely linked to the yearly cycle and to the secular social hierarchy. The local leader was called a *goði*, a word originally meaning "priest" but which, in Iceland at least, denoted secular distinction as well. The word also turns up as a title of rank (perhaps a religious one) in a Danish runic inscription.

The 13th-century *Eyrbyggjasaga* describes one such local *goði*, and despite its late date, it probably contains a good deal of genuine evidence that had been passed on through the oral tradition. The saga tells of a Norwegian landowner Thorolf, nicknamed Mostrarskegg, who was a great devotee of the god Thor – hence his name. He lived in the late 9th century, when King Harald Finehair was bringing southern Norway under royal control at the expense of the old free-farmer families. Unhappy at political developments, Thorolf consulted his "beloved friend" Thor who advised him to emigrate. Thorolf therefore collected his dependents, and took down his "temple" – which probably means the great hall of the family homestead. The main beams were loaded onto his ship and the family group set off for Iceland.

As the ship approached the island, the posts that had supported the seat of honor in the hall were thrown overboard. These represented Thorolf's

*Top* This reconstruction of the pagan temple at Old Uppsala is from Olaus Magnus' *History of the Northern Peoples*, published in 1555. It is based on the description by Adam of Bremen, from the 1070s, who commented on the golden chain that surrounded the roof, as well as an adjacent evergreen tree and a holy spring in which human victims were sacrificed by drowning.

*Above* The god Thor was symbolized by his hammer: this soapstone mold from Trendgården in Jutland, Denmark, meant that the local smith could give his 10th-century customers a choice between a Thor's hammer or a Christian cross.

authority as head of the household and also probably as a priest of Thor; the figure of Thor (or possibly his name or symbol) was carved on one of them. The saga tells us that "Thorolf made the agreement that they would settle in Iceland wherever Thor directed them to land." Accordingly, when the posts were washed up on a headland on the west coast, a place that Thorolf named Thorsnes (and which is still its name), Thorolf staked his claim to land here, and here he built a temple. The saga's description of the temple sounds suspiciously like that of a Christian church, and so is not now generally accepted, but it contains some distinctive details: "In the middle of the floor stood a pillar like an altar, and on it lay a penannular ring, twenty ounces in weight, and all oaths should be sworn on it. This ring the priest should wear on his arm at all legal meetings." (We know from other sources that the swearing of an oath on a holy ring had particular importance in Norse society.) "On the pillar should also stand a sacrificial bowl, and in it sacrificial 'twigs'... they were used for sprinkling from the bowl the blood that is called *hlaut*, that is the blood shed by the beasts that were dedicated to the gods." The saga-writer mentions one further aspect of the holiness of this area, a sacred mountain nearby "that he [Thorolf] called Helgafell [Holy Mount], and he believed that when he died he would go into that mountain and all his family on the headland there." That Thorolf established his legal meeting-place on the point of the headland where Thor, represented by the seat-posts, came to land, is confirmation of the close link between religion and social organization.

## The conversion to Christianity

By the beginning of the 9th century, Scandinavia was one of the last remaining strongholds of paganism in northwestern Europe. The Vikings would have come into contact with Christianity in various forms and guises in the course of their journeys overseas as pirates, colonizers and traders; for example, the Vikings who made the long journey along the rivers of Russia to the Black Sea would have encountered the churches of eastern Christianity when they visited Byzantium to do business there, or else to serve in the Greek emperor's personal guard. The sagas tell us that Vikings trading in Christian lands were sometimes ready to accept token Christianity to ease their relations with their clients.

Norse settlers abroad were likely to be influenced by the local religion, and this seems to have led to an intermingling of beliefs. One of the first colonizers of Iceland was Helgi Eyvindarson, called Helgi the Skinny because he was brought up in the Hebrides and as a lad was very short of food. He was, we are told, "very mixed up in his faith; he believed in Christ, but prayed to Thor on sea-journeys and in tough situations." In the Isle of Man 10th-century runic inscriptions in the Scandinavian tongue appear on Christian cross-slabs, some of which have additional sculptured scenes taken from pagan Norse myth, strongly suggesting a confusion of religious beliefs. At Killaloe in Ireland a fragment of a stone cross commemorating a Norseman Thorgrim has inscriptions cut both in runes and in ogham, the old Celtic alphabet. Most remarkable of all, though Viking invaders killed the Anglo-Saxon Christian king of East Anglia, Edmund, in 870, by the end of the century Danish settlers in the region were issuing a St Edmund memorial coinage.

It is clear from a number of incidents that some western leaders used Christianity as a means of diplomacy to bring the Vikings over to their side. This is what Alfred the Great of England did in 892/3 when,

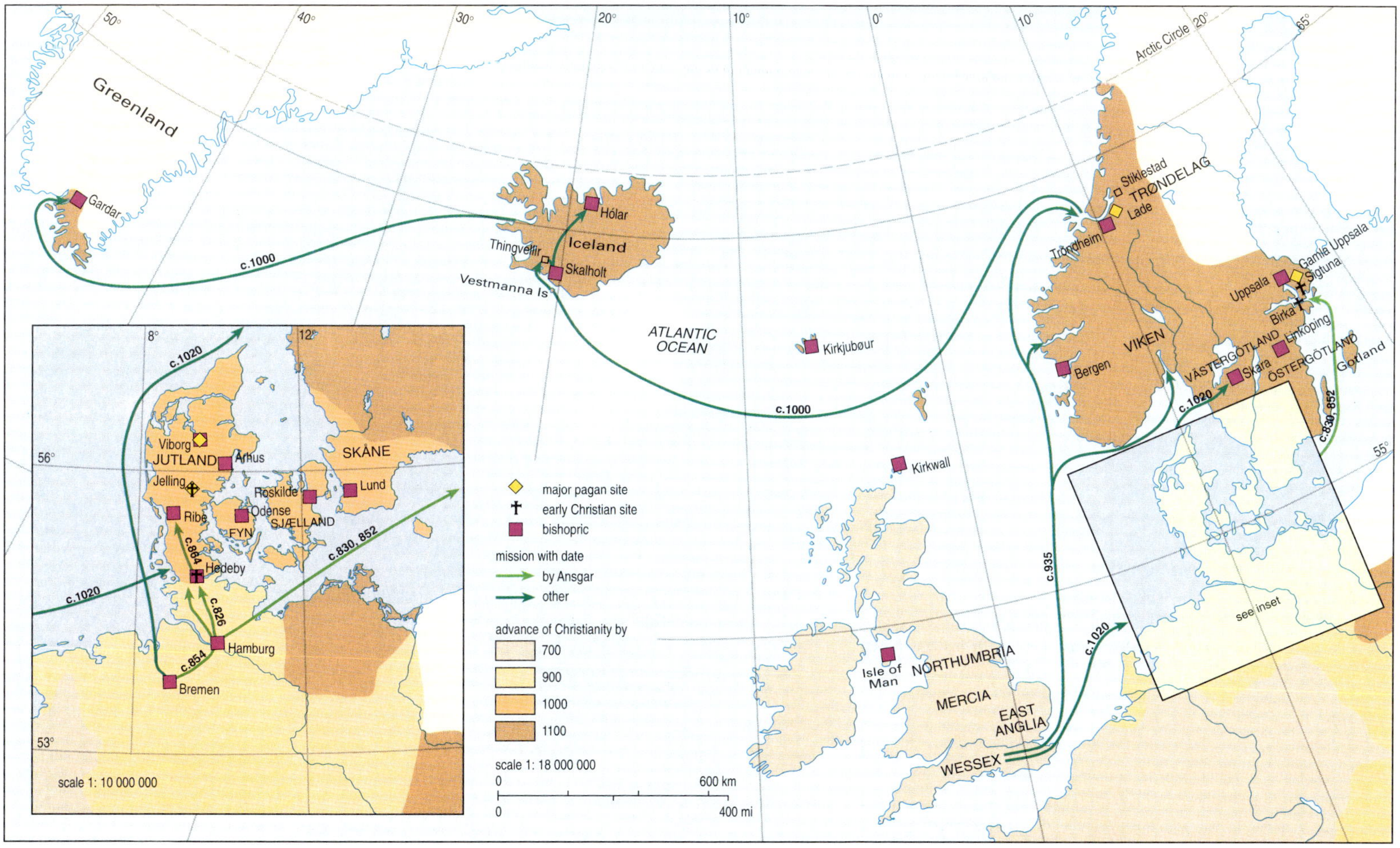


**The spread of Christianity**
The earliest attempts to convert the pagan Scandinavians to Christianity were made in the 8th century by Frankish missionaries to Jutland. We have documentary evidence of the missionary journeys of Ansgar who visited Jutland and central Sweden in the mid 9th century, founding churches at Hedeby and Birka, but his efforts do not appear to have been long-lived and it was not until a century later that the Danes became formally Christian in the reign of Harald Bluetooth, who had his royal center at Jelling. It was in western Europe that many Norwegians first came into contact with Christianity, but though exiled members of the Norwegian royal dynasty were converted there, often for political reasons, early attempts to introduce the new faith into Norway met with mixed success: Lade in Trøndelag was a particular center of resistance. English missionaries were active in Norway during the 10th century, but it was only after the death of Olaf Haraldsson (St Olaf) at the battle of Stiklestad (1030) that Christianity became the official religion. From Norway Christianity spread to Iceland and Greenland at the beginning of the 11th century. Sweden was the last country to become Christian, and its conversion was not completed until well into the 11th century.

*Left* King Olaf Haraldsson (1015–30), who was violent in the repression of paganism in his kingdom of Norway, met what came to be regarded as a martyr's death at the battle of Stiklestad. Pilgrims were soon flocking to his burial place at Nidaros (Trondheim). This 14th-century painted wooden panel, now housed in the cathedral at Trondheim, depicts the royal saint, symbolized by an ax, surrounded by scenes of his death and subsequent enshrinement.

according to the *Anglo-Saxon Chronicle*, there were two Viking armies operating in southern England, a smaller one camped at King's Milton and a large one with a base at Appledore, both in Kent. In order to prevent them joining forces, Alfred and his deputy, Æthelred, stood as godfathers to the two sons of Hastein, the leader of the smaller band of invaders, binding him further by giving him money and extracting oaths and hostages. But it did not work. Hastein still ravaged Alfred's kingdom, and, says the chronicler indignantly, even the province that was administered by Æthelred. Over a century later the English king Æthelred the Unready was more successful. In 994 he made a pact with Anlaf (Olaf Tryggvason, later king of Norway) who in alliance with the Danish king Svein Forkbeard had launched an assault on the kingdom. Æthelred gave Anlaf tribute, but also stood sponsor to him at his confirmation: "and", the *Chronicle* adds, "Anlaf promised that he would never come back to England again with hostile intent – and what's more, he kept his promise."

More far-reaching were the diplomatic strategies of Athelstan, king of England from 924 to 939. According to the Icelandic *Saga of Harald Finehair*, he took into his court the boy Hakon, Harald's son, a tradition that is consistent with the character of Athelstan as given in English sources. Thus Hakon is nicknamed "Athelstan's foster-son" in Norse accounts. Athelstan brought the lad up as a Christian, and on the death of his father supported him in his claim to the Norwegian throne, in opposition to his elder half-brother Eric Bloodax. Hakon ousted Eric in about 935, and tried to bring Norway over to Christianity, but he came up against the opposition of the Norwegian free-farmers who were suspicious of any innovations, fearing they were an attempt to infringe their rights. So Hakon was ultimately unsuccessful, and his funeral ode, composed after his death from wounds received in battle in 960, is pagan in tone. Nevertheless the presence of the occasional English name – Sigefridus of Glastonbury, for instance – among those who became bishops in Norway in the 10th century suggests that a serious missionary effort by the English church took place at about this time.

From now on Christianity had an important role in Norwegian religion and politics, though Hakon's immediate successors were not particularly inclined toward it. Indeed, the great earl Hakon of Lade who ruled the country toward the end of the 10th century was notorious for his pagan sympathies. He was replaced in 995 by Olaf Tryggvason, a most charismatic leader who in the five years that he ruled Norway was, says tradition, eager to reintroduce Christianity. He had been converted during a long exile abroad in early life (though there are several conflicting accounts of where this had occurred) and had – as we have seen – been confirmed in England. To what extent Olaf was a committed Christian, however, or to what extent he used the new religion as a means of political coercion to bring the free-farmers

*Right* The conversion of Sweden to Christianity can in part be charted by the distribution of runic memorials incorporating crosses in their designs and Christian sentiments in their inscriptions. This memorial (and combined title-deed) is carved on a rock face at Nora in Uppland. The text is contained within the ribbon-like body of a one-legged beast that balances on a central cross whilst in combat with a snake. Its elegant composition forms a classic Urnes-style design of late 11th-century date.

# Jelling

Dominating the market town of Jelling in eastern Jutland are two great mounds that are among the most impressive monuments from Viking Age Scandinavia. Between them stands a medieval stone church. The mound to the north is the largest burial-mound in Denmark, but its burial-chamber – dated to about 958 by tree-ring dating – is empty. The purpose of the south mound is more uncertain: it never held a grave and was probably a memorial. Midway between them are two rune-stones. The inscription on the smaller one reads: "King Gorm made these monuments in memory of his wife Thyra, Denmark's adornment." The larger one says: "King Harald ordered these monuments to be made after his father Gorm and his mother Thyra. It was this Harald who won for himself all Denmark and Norway and made the Danes Christians." This stone clearly refers to Harald Bluetooth who became Christian about 960. The likeliest explanation is that after his conversion he moved the body of his father Gorm, a pagan, from the north mound to a grave in the church that he had built.

*Above* This silver cup is one of the few objects found in the burial-chamber of the north mound. Elaborately decorated with animals, it is of high quality and suggests the splendor of the grave-goods that must have been buried with Gorm.

*Below* The two great mounds at Jelling are on either side of the present churchyard surrounding the medieval church. On a line that joins the top of the mounds, and exactly halfway between them, stand the two rune-stones, one erected by Gorm, the other by Harald. Below the south mound are the remains of an earlier stone setting.

*Top right* The two Jelling rune-stones are an important source of information about Denmark's 10th-century royal dynasty. To the left is the small memorial erected by Gorm to his queen. To the right is the boulder that Harald put up to celebrate his parents – and himself. It is elaborately carved on all three of its faces.

*Right* In this view of Jelling, the nearer of the two mounds contains Gorm's burial chamber. The rune-stones can be seen just on the other side of the church.

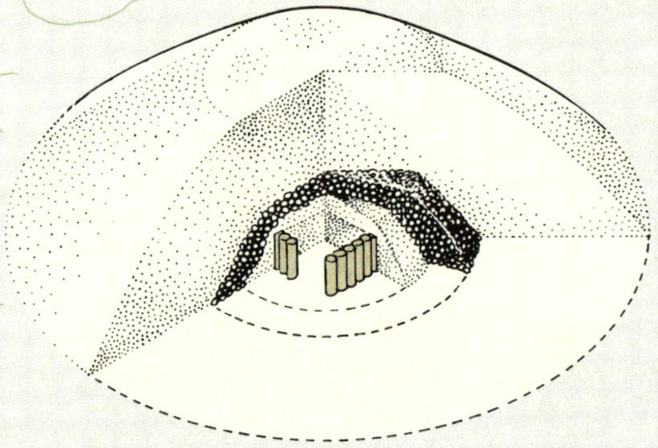

*Below* A cut-away of the north mound. The burial-chamber was dug into an existing mound, perhaps of Bronze Age date. This was covered with a layer of stone packing and then with earth.

of Norway under royal control is a matter of interpretation. Certainly his methods showed a muscular approach to Christianity, with the burning of temples and physical attacks being carried out on eminent pagan leaders. After his death in battle in the year 1000, there was another anti-Christian reaction – at least according to some Norse writers.

The triumph of the new religion came in the reign of Olaf Haraldsson (1015–30), the king who was later to become St Olaf of Norway. The many sagas that were written after his death in battle at Stiklestad, north of Trondheim, tell of his vigorous and often merciless attacks on heathens in Norway. As one says: "King Olaf held a meeting with the heathen sub-kings... When he found that they were unwilling to accept Christianity, he had nine kings taken prisoner one morning; some he had blinded, some maimed in other ways, some he outlawed. King Olaf laid such stress on all men in his kingdom being Christians that he offered them the choice: be killed, leave the country or take baptism." More important is the fact that he managed to bring Christianity into the legal codes of Norway after a major council meeting held in Hordaland about 1024, and that he encouraged the activity of English missionary bishops in Norway and its neighboring lands – Sigafrid, Grimkil, Rudolf and Bernard are all known to us by name. Olaf's death in battle came to be interpreted as a martyr's death, and pilgrims thronged to his place of burial at Nidaros (Trondheim).

Of the introduction of Christianity into Iceland we have a more authoritative account, given us by the historian Ari Thorgilsson in his *Book of the Icelanders*. As we have seen, Ari obtained his material from oral accounts that can be traced back to the time of the conversion. He tells how Olaf Tryggvason tried to bring Christianity to Iceland, sending a turbulent priest called Thangbrand on a mission of conversion. The Icelanders, perhaps indignant that a Norwegian king was trying to impose his authority on their country, were in the main not sympathetic, though some leaders of the community accepted the new teaching. Thangbrand's departure from the country under a cloud, after brawling with hostile Icelanders, angered Olaf so much that he threatened reprisals against anyone from Iceland who came to his court.

Two leading Icelanders responded to this pressure by agreeing to put the case for Christanity to the annual assembly at Thingvellir. In the debate that followed, Christians and pagans concluded they could not agree but must accept different religions and different laws. At this point the "lawspeaker", the chairman of the assembly, intervened. Though a pagan, he argued that there could not be two legal systems in the same land, as that would lead to anarchy, and proposed a compromise that everyone should become formally Christian, but that the pagans should be allowed to retain some of their old customs and to sacrifice to their gods in private. This was accepted, but shortly afterward the concessions to paganism were abolished. The first bishop of Iceland, Isleif, was the son of one of the first converts. His son succeeded him, settling the episcopal see at Skálholt in the south of Iceland. Later a second bishop, Jon, was consecrated, with his see at Hólar in the north.

Christianity reached Greenland in a similar way, introduced by Leif, son of the colony's founder Eric the Red, in the early 11th century. Returning to Greenland from Norway, where he had become a Christian convert, Leif brought a priest with him to teach the new faith. Despite a conflict of opinion with his father, who clung to the old pagan ways, Leif's party gained the ascendancy. An episcopal see was established at Gardar in the south of the country, a place described by a 15th-century pope as being "at the end of the world".

### German missionaries

The conversion of the eastern Scandinavian nations, the Danes and the Swedes, took a different course. Here the important forces were the Frankish empire to the south, and the episcopal see of Hamburg-Bremen at the neck of the Jutland peninsula in particular. Tentative efforts were made to spread Christianity northward in the 8th century, but it was not until the 9th, through the work of Ansgar, "the Apostle of the North," that any success was achieved.

Of Ansgar, a monk of Corvey abbey in Westphalia, Germany, we have a contemporary Latin biography written by his colleague and successor, Rimbert. After the exiled Danish king Harald Klak was baptized at Ingelheim in the Rhineland in 826, Ansgar was given the opportunity to travel with him to preach Christianity. The only success of this first ministry was the founding of a small school, perhaps at Hedeby in the south of Jutland. A second opportunity came in 829 when Ansgar was summoned to lead a more adventurous mission to Sweden. It was on this occasion that he visited the influential trading town of Birka on Lake Mälaren, where he set up a mission station, converted the local prefect, Herigar, and built a chapel.

Ansgar returned to the imperial court late in 831 and was made the first archbishop of Hamburg (moving to Bremen after Hamburg was destroyed by Vikings in 845). The pope entrusted Ansgar with the task of bringing the Danes and Swedes to Christianity, and a bishop, Gaudbert, was dispatched to Sweden but later expelled "by the zeal of the pagans". In the 850s Ansgar returned to the north, founding a church at Hedeby to minister to the small Christian community already there, and in 852 went again to Sweden. The king and the local legal communities of Birka and Uppsala authorized him to preach and build a church at Birka. A final journey to Denmark in 854 strengthened the church at Hedeby, and led to the founding of a second at Ribe. Yet the effects of Ansgar's mission were to prove shortlasting, and by the end of the 9th century Sweden and Denmark had lapsed again into paganism.

Political considerations led the Danes back to Christianity – pressure from the German emperor on Denmark's southern border in the first half of the 10th century. We know less than we would like to about this period of Danish history, and often have to rely on late sources. From these we learn that Archbishop Unni of Hamburg-Bremen led a mission to the king of Denmark in the 930s, but he turned out to be an obstinate pagan called Gorm. Not until the reign of his son and successor, Harald Bluetooth, did the Danes become formally Christian, about 960. According to one version, Harald's conversion took place after the missionary Poppo had proved through an ordeal by fire the greater power of his religion. It is this conversion that Harald boasted of in his inscription on the greater of the two Jelling rune-stones. Bishoprics were established in Hedeby, Ribe (where Odinkar ministered for 40 years in the early 11th century) and Århus. Thereafter, despite a lapse in the early years of the reign of Svein Forkbeard (987–1014), Harald's son and successor, Denmark was at least nominally Christian, with further bishoprics being established in Roskilde and Lund. Indeed, in one of his Christian moments Svein sent an English bishop, Gotebald, to the church in Skåne. Under Svein's son, Cnut (reigned 1018–35), who was also king of England, the church received further reinforcement from English missionaries – Bishops Bernard in Skåne, Gerbrand in Sjælland and Reginbert in Fyn – and thereafter there were both English and North German influences on Danish Christianity.

*Above* The first face of the great rune-stone set up at Jelling by King Harald Bluetooth of Denmark carries the major part of the runic inscription that celebrates his parents – and himself. The text carries on around the bottom of the other two faces, one depicting the crucifixion of Christ (shown on the previous page) and the other a scene of a lion-like beast intertwined with a snake (page 99).

In Sweden the process of conversion was later and more drawn out. This was partly due to the divided nature of its population. The people of Östergötland and Västergötland in the south were closer to the Christianizing influence of mainland Europe, while the Svear, living in central Sweden around Lake Mälaren, remained entrenchedly pagan. Individual 10th-century kings admitted Christian missions to the land, and King Olof Skötkonung (reigned 990–1021/2) accepted baptism and extended the spread of Christianity, founding the first Swedish bishopric at Skara in Östergötland.

Successive rulers furthered the Christian cause, and the religion reached gradually into the various provinces of the land, with bishoprics being founded at Uppsala and, at the end of the Viking period, at Linköping. This spread is charted in the inscriptions on runic memorial stones. Texts incorporating Christian sentiments appear from the early 11th century in southern Sweden but a good deal later in the more central parts of the land, where forms of paganism seem to have held out for a long time. Indeed, in the later 11th century there were times when Christian bishops were scared to occupy their sees. The great pagan temple at Gamla Uppsala appears to have lasted relatively long into the "Christian" period of Swedish history, and it seems likely that it formed a center of opposition to the new faith.

# PART THREE

# THE VIKINGS OVERSEAS

# WESTERN EUROPE

## The first raids in England, 793–865

*793: In this year dire portents appeared over Northumbria and sorely frightened the people. They consisted of immense whirlwinds and flashes of lightning, and fiery dragons were seen flying in the air. A great famine immediately followed those signs, and a little after that in the same year, on 8 June, the ravages of heathen men miserably destroyed God's church on Lindisfarne, with plunder and slaughter.*

With these words, taken from the *Anglo-Saxon Chronicle*, the Vikings first appear in the annals of English history. Over the next three centuries they were to dominate events in the country to such an extent that the Anglo-Saxon kingdoms were brought to the brink of destruction. So strong an imprint was left on the English landscape by the Scandinavian presence that traces of it survive even today.

Though the raid on the monastery of Lindisfarne is the first one recorded in the documents that we possess, it is likely that contacts between England and Scandinavia had existed for much longer. Even in the pre-Viking period of the 7th and 8th centuries, certain resemblances between art-styles in England and Scandinavia surely indicate a degree of contact across the North Sea. At this time England was divided into a number of kingdoms and subkingdoms, and it is possible that some of them may actually have been founded by people of distant Scandinavian origin. The most dramatic evidence we have of this comes from East Anglia, where certain objects, particularly the helmet and shield, from the great 7th-century ship burial at Sutton Hoo are almost identical with those from contemporary Swedish sites such as the Uppland cemeteries of Valsgärde and Vendel. Though the Sutton Hoo warrior and his kinfolk were probably not Scandinavian, there seems no doubt there was a conscious association, through the use of objects and symbols, with a Scandinavian cultural tradition. The reasons behind this may lie in an identification with the pagan beliefs of the Scandinavian homelands. At the time of the Sutton Hoo burial, Christianity was gaining a strong foothold in England, and the Swedish objects such as the helmet – perhaps used as symbols of aristocratic or even royal power – can be seen as deliberate anti-Christian statements of solidarity with the older, pagan ways. It should not be forgotten that paganism persisted in Sweden well into the 11th century.

This attempt to keep the early religions alive in England failed, and by the end of the 8th century, when the first Viking raids occurred, the country had been wholly Christian for well over a hundred years. If the former identification with Scandinavia had not been forgotten, it was certainly not maintained. Indeed, contemporary English written sources, such as the *Anglo-Saxon Chronicle*, make no distinctions between Scandinavians from Denmark, Norway or Sweden. They are all usually referred to as *Dene* – "Danes" – or more simply described as heathens.

Several enigmatic documentary references from around the time of the Lindisfarne raid may concern Viking activity. We know for example that King Offa of Mercia in the center and south of the country, then one of the most powerful of the kingdoms, ordered the defense of the south coast against a threat from unspecified pagan warriors in 792, and an entry in the *Anglo-Saxon Chronicle* for the year 789 tells us that sometime in the reign of King Beorhtric of Wessex (786–802) three ships carrying Scandinavians arrived at Portland in the southwest. These northmen were possibly traders; their recorded killing of a royal officer may

*Left* The sculptor who carved the weapon-brandishing warriors on this 9th-century grave-stone from the monastery at Lindisfarne may have been deliberately evoking the devastating Viking raid of 793. The iconography of its other face is most likely a reference to the Day of Judgment – and the first Viking raids on England were seen by the church as a Judgment.

*Right* The 6th-century Sutton Hoo helmet was very probably made in Sweden and so serves as a reminder of the Scandinavian links with England that existed before the end of the 8th century when the violence of the Vikings first erupted across western Europe.

*Left* Offa's Dyke is the most impressive structure of its kind in Europe – a great bank and ditch constructed during the reign of King Offa of Mercia (757–96) as a frontier against the Welsh. However, the first phase of the equivalent earthwork defense that cuts across the base of the Jutland peninsula, known as the Danevirke, was probably built over a generation earlier.

*Below* Viking loot: this gilt-bronze mount, with its 8th-century Anglo-Saxon ornament in the form of a cross filled with interlace and stylized animals, was prised from the cover of a holy book for use as a pendant. It was found in a woman's grave at Bjørke in western Norway.

well have been the result of a misunderstanding rather than premeditated violence. Like the Lindisfarne raiders, the Portland Vikings seem to have been Norwegians, and there is a marked Norwegian element in many of the early attacks on the British Isles. However, even at this early date it is likely that the Viking ship crews contained warriors of more than one nationality, adding further to the English confusion about the identity of their persecutors from the north.

As the news of the devastating Viking attacks spread, the English reaction was clearly one of horror and shock. Shortly after the destruction of the church associated with St Cuthbert at Lindisfarne, the eminent cleric Alcuin, who was an official at the court of the emperor Charlemagne at Aachen, wrote to the king of Northumbria: "Never before has such terror appeared in Britain as we have now suffered from a pagan race, nor was it thought that such an inroad from the sea could be made. Behold, the church of St Cuthbert spattered with the blood of the priests of God, despoiled of all its ornaments; a place more venerable than all in Britain is given as prey to pagan peoples." In 794, the year after the Lindisfarne raid, a second Northumbrian monastery at either Monkwearmouth or Jarrow (the annals are unclear) was burned by Viking raiders. It was this disregard for the sanctity of the church more than all other aspects of the Vikings' ferocity that inspired such dread in their Christian victims. As pagans, the Vikings were regarded by many of the English annalists as a judgment from God for the sins of the people, and the predictions of the Prophet Jeremiah echoed through the bitter wars that followed: "Out of the north an evil shall break forth upon all the inhabitants of the land."

After the initial violence of the 793 raid, England was left in virtual peace for 30 years and more while the Viking fleets concentrated their attacks on Ireland. This was to be but a brief respite, since the 830s saw the Scandinavians take a renewed and more lasting interest in England. After a successful summer spent raiding along the Frisian coast (the modern Netherlands) the previous year, a large Danish force landed in 835 on the isle of Sheppey in the Thames estuary from where they ravaged the surrounding area. From then on until 850 the south coast was devastated by a series of attacks, including raids on London and Rochester, Kent. Pitched battles were fought with Vikings in Dorset and at Southampton, and raids were also carried out on the east coast in the kingdom of Lindsey and farther north in Northumbria.

In 850 the Viking impact on England took a graver turn. Before this date, the raiding fleets had been a purely seasonal phenomenon, plundering during the summer as the opportunity arose and then returning to Scandinavia for the winter; the raiders had also remained highly mobile, their success stemming in part from the fast-response and shallow draft capabilities of their longships, which enabled them to mount sudden attacks deep inland along the river systems and then withdraw with the loot before an organized retaliation could be launched. However, in 850 a Viking force over-wintered in England for the first time, on the island of Thanet at the mouth of the Thames. From this year until well into the 11th century, England was to be never entirely free from a Scandinavian presence. In the 15 years up to 865 regular attacks continued, and in that year reference is made for the first time to the payment of *Danegeld* – a term used to describe a sum demanded from the English by the Scandinavians as protection money, upon the payment of which the people would be left in peace. The Vikings had discovered that extortion was potentially even more lucrative than fighting, and had fewer hazards. As with many such agreements in many cultures, the terms of the peace were as often broken as kept, and the *Danegeld* of 865 was typical in this respect. Following a payment made by the people of Kent, the *Anglo-Saxon Chronicle* tells us that "under cover of that peace and promise of money the army stole away inland by night and ravaged all eastern Kent."

The following year, in 866, the largest Viking army yet seen in the country arrived in England. The *Anglo-Saxon Chronicle* refers to the host simply as the *micel here*, an enigmatic phrase that is usually translated as "Great Army". After several years' fighting in the Carolingian empire, a large force of Danes had come to England in pursuit of a new objective – permanent settlement. The advent of the "Great Army" marked a turning point in the Vikings' relations with England, and the beginning of what is often termed Phase Two of the Scandinavian raids, the change from sporadic attacks to campaigning armies.

**Viking armies in England and continental Europe**

Almost all our contemporary accounts of the initial Viking raids were written as the "official" histories of particular kingdoms or states and, for the most part, by

*Below* The account of the years 862–74 in the *Anglo-Saxon Chronicle*. This series of annals (or yearly entries of events) seems to have been compiled initially in the late 9th century, though it contains earlier material. It is the primary historical text for our knowledge of Viking activity in Anglo-Saxon England.

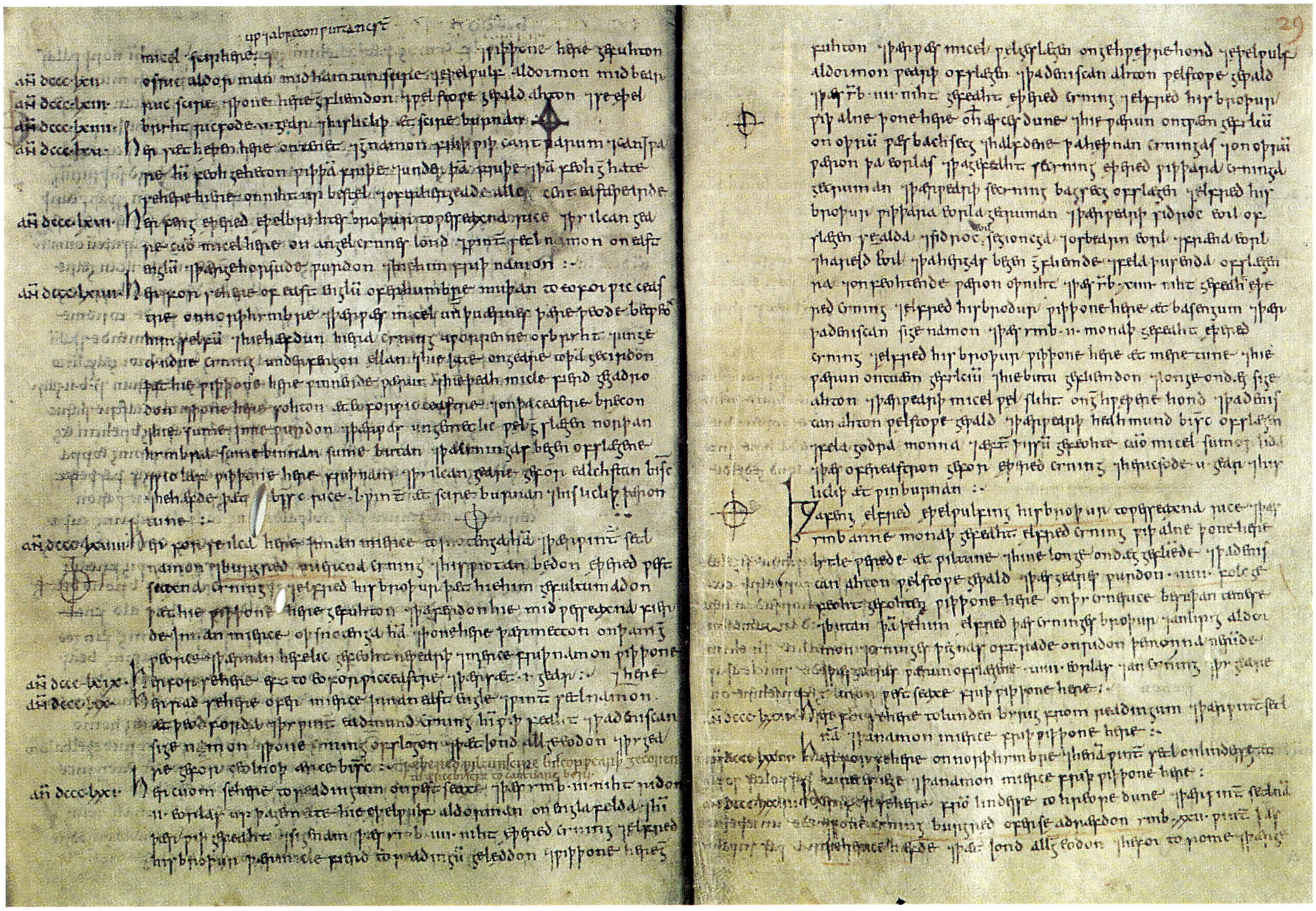

Viking raid 793-865
campaign led by Bjorn Ironside and Hastein, 859-862
monastery or settlement raided by Vikings
793-833
834-850
851-865
Arab fortification
political boundary, 814
Anglo-Saxon kingdoms
Celtic kingdoms
Carolingian empire
Galicia and Asturias
Byzantine empire
Abbasid caliphate
NORWAY
SWEDEN
DENMARK
NORTH SEA
Shetland
KINGDOM OF THE PICTS
Iona
STRATH-CLYDE
Rathlin I
Dunseverick
Bangor
Lindisfarne
Tynemouth
Inishmurray
Clonmacnoise
Clonfert
Lorrha
Louth
Duleek
IRELAND
Skellig Michael
Cork
Beggary I
NORTHUMBRIA
WALES
MERCIA
EAST ANGLIA
London
WESSEX
Portland Bill
CORNWALL
Quentovic
St Omer
Ghent
Dorestad
Utrecht
FRISIA
SAXONY
Elbe
Cologne
Rhine
EASTERN SLAVIC TRIBES
WESTERN SLAVIC TRIBES
MORAVIA
Amiens
St Wandrille
Rouen
Bayeux
Paris
Evreux
Meaux
Chartres
Seine
BRITTANY
Le Mans
Orléans
Fleury
Angers
Loire
Blois
Tours
Nantes
Noirmoutier
Bourges
CAROLINGIAN EMPIRE
BAVARIA
Danube
CARINTHIA
ATLANTIC OCEAN
Saintes
Clermont-Ferrand
Périgueux
Bordeaux
Valence
Rhône
Po
LOMBARDY
Luna
Pisa
Toulouse
Narbonne
St Eulalia
GALICIA AND ASTURIAS
Ebro
Corsica
DUCHY OF BENEVENTO
Sardinia
Tagus
EMIRATE OF CORDOBA
Lisbon
Balearic Is
MEDITERRANEAN SEA
BYZANTINE EMPIRE
Sicily
Cadiz
ABBASID CALIPHATE
scale 1 : 8 000 000
0
300 km
0
200 mi
10°
0°
10°
57°
50°
43°
36°

**Viking raids in western Europe, 8th and 9th centuries**
In the last decade of the 8th century, raiders from Scandinavia struck at targets in Britain, Ireland and the Carolingian empire with startling and unparalleled ferocity: Lindisfarne, on the northeast coast of England, was attacked in 793, the tiny island of Iona in the Hebrides in 795, and the Frisian coast in 799. The Vikings soon identified the rich monasteries and religious houses as prime sources of loot, and these places bore the brunt of their aggression. In the first decades of the 9th century it was Ireland and Frisia that suffered most heavily, but after 835 the fleets moved south to plunder along the south coast of England and around the Seine and Loire estuaries in France. From the middle of the century Viking forces over-wintered both in England and in France, and the raids were planned with a high degree of organization, the armies moving across Europe and between England and France along a regular route of destruction. A few raiders ventured as far as Spain. In 859 Bjorn Ironside and Hastein took a fleet through the Strait of Gibraltar and into the Mediterranean, where it spent two years looting in North Africa, southern France and Italy before returning to its base on the Loire in 862. However, the organized and effective resistance of the Arabs in Spain deterred other Viking expeditions from entering the Mediterranean through the Strait of Gibraltar, and after 862 most of the raids were confined to France and central Europe.

the people who were themselves the targets of Scandinavian aggression. The picture they present may differ subtly from the reality. When referring to the Viking forces the English sources usually number them by the ship-load, and figures of 200 to 300 ships are not uncommon. These figures are highly problematic, as they may represent a more-or-less accurate attempt to record the true numbers, or be a wild exaggeration intended to minimize the failure of the Anglo-Saxon armies (it is less humiliating to be defeated by overwhelmingly superior forces). There is also no reason to suppose that the various annalistic entries are consistent with each other.

We cannot be certain how many armed warriors each ship held, both in terms of simple capacity and also bearing in mind the probability that space was taken up by cargo, supplies, horses and non-combatants; clearly, too, ships differ in size. A more subtle bias is similarly present in the terminology of the English sources. When the *Chronicle* mentions a *here* (normally translated as army or host) this may be intended as an exact statement of size. However, we simply do not know what sort of numbers the writer had in mind. That an "army" may have been very different from our modern conception of the word is shown by a reference in the 7th-century law codes of King Ine of Wessex, which describes any armed force numbering more than 35 men as a *here*. Added to this, the documents' indifference to distinctions between Scandinavian nationalities has already been mentioned. Thus we are presented with information that depicts an undifferentiated mass of "Vikings", all intent solely on murder and destruction, and of uncertain numbers.

Archaeologists and historians are still unsure about many aspects of the nature of Viking military forces. What is certain is that the uniform mass of raiders and conquerors described in the written sources conceals a highly variable range of men (and perhaps women) of different nationalities, organization, leadership and motives. The initial raids were most probably carried out by a few ships' crews on the look-out for opportunistic rewards. Their captains may have been minor chieftains with their friends and retainers, perhaps banding together with others of similar type to form small flotillas of four or five ships. Alternatively, the raiders may have been confederations of warrior farmers and small landowners, joining together to outfit a ship and sharing the proceeds to supplement their agricultural income. Indeed, we know from runic inscriptions that similar raids often took place within Scandinavia itself, with attacks on neighboring districts. The composition of these early raiding fleets probably changed from year to year, with some Vikings returning again and again to familiar targets but others preferring subsequently to stay at home to take possession of their inherited property or simply to settle down. Warriors lost in combat would have been replaced by new recruits. There seems no reason to postulate any particularly organized or co-ordinated structure for the fleets of the early-mid 9th century, in marked contrast to those that fought in England after 865.

In terms of numbers of ships, there is a clear change in the documentary references at this time. Before this date, the accounts talk of small groups of up to 23 vessels (perhaps an exact count), while after 865 larger rounded numbers of between 80 and 350 are given. While these latter may be decimal multiplications of the earlier numbers, or vague approximations of a "big" fleet, there is a marked correlation between the fleet sizes given in both English and Frankish sources, indicating that the Viking fleets numbered at least many tens of vessels. A ship's fighting crew is conventionally estimated at between 30 and 60 warriors, giving totals for the larger armies of the later 9th century of probably no more than 1,000; this figure has recently been supported by calculations of the population capacities of Viking field fortifications, such as winter camps, which also number around 1,000. Such a small force might seem insufficient to threaten an entire country, but battles were usually fought between armies of armored and experienced Scandinavian mercenaries on the one hand and hastily-organized Anglo-Saxon peasant militias on the other. Furthermore, the Scandinavians had the advantage of surprise and mobility, while many terrified English people clearly perceived their pagan foe as agents of the Antichrist; it is worth remembering that the Aztec civilization of Mexico was destroyed by a far smaller Spanish force in similar circumstances.

It is evident that a far greater level of organization and centralized control was present in the Great Army and other Viking forces campaigning in England after 865 than before it. Though we do not know precisely how these hosts functioned, the *Anglo-Saxon Chronicle* contains several enigmatic references that hint at the networks of logistics and supplies that must have been a necessary part of the Great Army's movements: in 866 the East Anglians make peace with the Danes and provide them with horses, while in 896 a second army is mysteriously supplied with a full complement of ships. In European sources such as the *Annals of St Bertin*, we even find *Danegeld* payments specifically detailed to include food, wine and provisions. On several occasions the army was actively assisted by various disaffected factions among the English, and references in the *Anglo-Saxon Chronicle* to "great civil strife" may conceal a level of political turmoil far greater than the pro-Wessex annals would wish to make explicit. Even more surprisingly, the sources also contain evidence of some degree of diplomatic contact between the Great Army and the Wessex dynasty itself, for the occasion on which King Alfred the Great (reigned 871–99) and the ealdorman Æthelred (a high-ranking nobleman) stood as godfathers to the two sons of the army commander Hastein clearly involved negotiation. The larger Viking forces thus seem to have maintained themselves through an effective combination of itinerant violence and extortion, and judicious diplomacy and collaboration.

As for the actual members of the armies, the combination of political strife, increasing state control and centralized power, and changes in social organization within the Scandinavian homelands in the late 9th century must have produced large numbers of young men without land or hope of immediate inherited wealth, and plenty of exiled would-be kings to lead them. That the large armies were perceived as an active threat to the Scandinavian kingdoms is undoubted, as major wars ensued on several occasions when exiles returned home after many years campaigning abroad, having won enough silver to recruit a large personal army. The famous Viking leaders Olaf Tryggvason and Eric Bloodax both made attempts on the Norwegian crown in this way. It is no coincidence that it is at this time that we see for the first time the names of individual Scandinavian commanders recorded in connection with the army – their names distorted by Old English spellings, but still recognizable as the same career soldiers whose names also occur in European and even Arab sources – men such as Hastein (Hæsten in the English sources, Hásteinn in Old Norse), Healfdene

# Repton Winter Camp

After 850, the Vikings are known to have built winter camps while campaigning in England or Frankia, but no such site had ever been found until archaeologists excavating a fine Anglo-Saxon church at Repton in Derbyshire, England, unexpectedly uncovered a massive ditch and earthen rampart. This originally ran in a D-shape against the river bank to form a fortified enclosure centered on the church. Viking burials were found around the church, and coins dated the features to around 873–74 – exactly the years, so the *Anglo-Saxon Chronicle* tells us, that Repton was the site of a Viking winter base. West of the rampart, a former Saxon mortuary chapel had been emptied and leveled to be reused for a mass burial of at least 249 people. Their bones had been stacked around the walls, and at the center was the burial of a male Viking of very high status. The chapel had then been covered by a low mound. Nearly all the bodies in the mass burial were male and of non-local physical type – presumably members of the Viking army that wintered at Repton. They did not die of battle injuries, so it seems likely that the army was devastated by disease that year. The Repton winter camp is so far unique, and forms a rare monument to the Viking wars with Wessex.

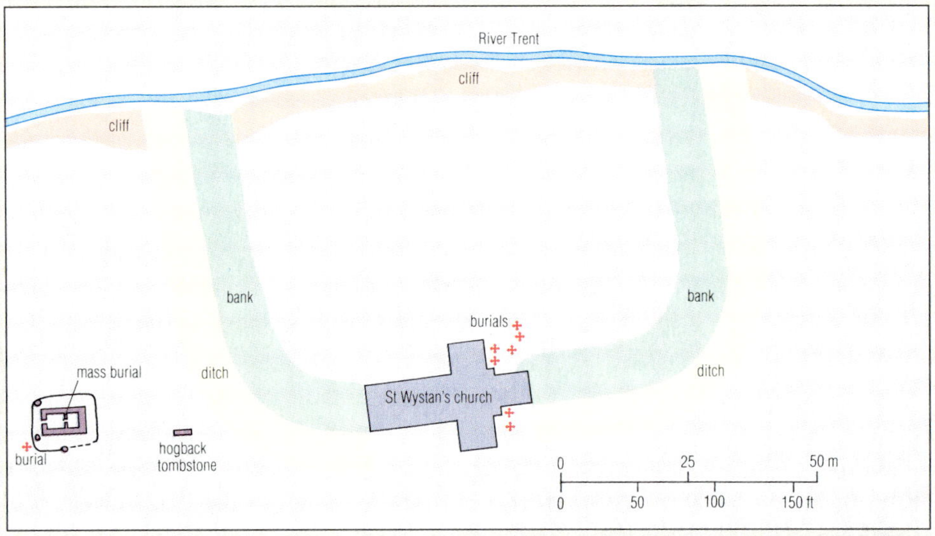

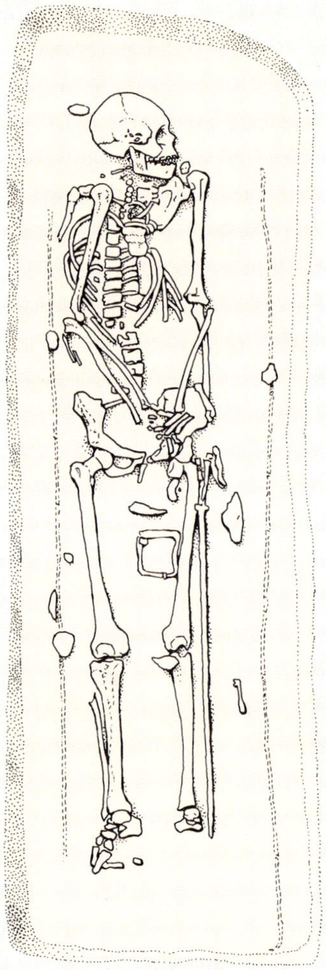

*Left* A school now occupies the site of the Repton camp, raised on a bluff above the river Trent. Excavations were conducted there every summer between 1974 and 1988. As is clearly seen from the plan (*above left*), the D-shaped enclosure built by the Vikings used the natural landscape to its advantage, being protected by the cliff on the river bank and incorporating St Wystan's church as a fortified gateway. The mound containing the mass burial would have been a prominent landmark outside the walls of the winter camp.

*Above* Among the Viking burials near the church was that of a man, age 35–40, killed by a massive blow to the hip, who was buried with his weapons and equipment. His grave was covered with a cairn of stones. Among the finds were a sword (*above left*) and scabbard, two knives, and an elaborate belt set. As a pagan, he wore a Thor's hammer necklace and had been buried with a small bag containing the tusk of a wild boar and the legbone of a jackdaw, perhaps as magic charms.

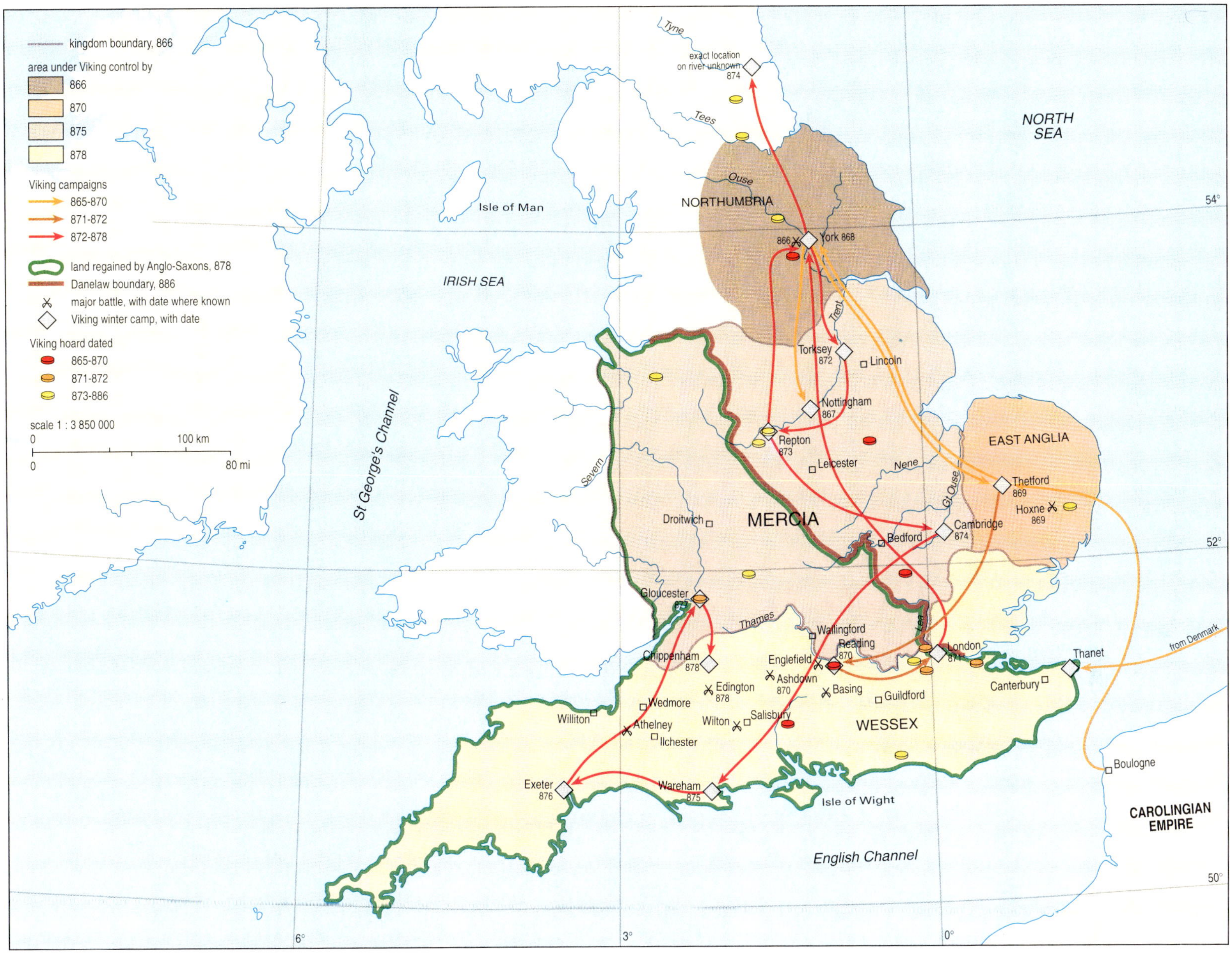


**The Viking campaigns in England, 865–885**
In 865 the over-wintering of a large Scandinavian army in England – the "Great Army" – marked the beginning of a new phase in the Viking campaigns: for the next 30 years there was almost continual fighting as the Scandinavians consolidated their hold over large parts of the country. The first area to fall into their hands in 866 was Northumbria. The old Roman city of York was made the base from which the Vikings launched a series of campaigns against the other Anglo-Saxon kingdoms: first East Anglia and then Mercia were overrun, and in 878 it was the turn of the southern kingdom of Wessex. However, Alfred the Great was able to rally his forces to defeat the Vikings at the battle of Edington and later that year secured their withdrawal through a treaty made at Wedmore. In 885 the Viking commander Guthrum renewed the attack against Wessex, but the threat was again contained and the treaty of 878 renewed, leaving the Vikings in control of the north and east of England, an area that came to be known as the Danelaw.

(Hálfdan) and Guthrum. By mapping the movements of forces according to their named leaders, it has proved possible to see at least traces of individual command units within the armies. As members of the army dropped out to return to Scandinavia they doubtless brought news of the rich pickings to be had in Europe, thus ensuring a steady flow of warriors to replace them. The armies evidently did not operate in complete isolation from civilian life, since the *Anglo-Saxon Chronicle* contains several references to the Danes' wives and children being left in protective fortifications in Viking-held areas while the army was on campaign. This is supported by the fact that females account for as many as 20 percent of the skeletons excavated at the site of the winter camp at Repton occupied by the Great Army from 873–74; the tentative suggestion that these women are of a different physical type from the males intriguingly hints that they may have been native English camp followers who had taken partners among the Viking army, adding a further dimension to the nature of Anglo-Scandinavian collaboration.

During the late 9th century several different Viking armies were operating in western Europe, each with an array of leaders, nationalities and objectives – fighting for money, land and political power, or for a combination of these. These forces may even have had completely different command structures, since an army fighting on the Loire told Frankish messengers that they had no commander but made their decisions on a communal basis, while a Danish army on a raid into Sweden is recorded as casting lots to decide on strategy. The Viking armies sometimes fought each other or combined in temporary pacts, and there was certainly a continual interchange of warriors between them. Thus in contrast to the two-dimensional picture of pagan killers conveyed by the written sources, we should see in the Viking armies a complex, shifting network of power structures and alliances, interacting on several levels with the peoples of England and continental Europe.

## Armies and settlement in England, 866–892

The landing of the Great Army in East Anglia in 866 marked the beginning of the long and bitter wars between the Vikings and the kingdom of Wessex. The turmoil and uncertainty of these years can be seen in the archaeological record, as large numbers of coin hoards have been found. These may have been buried in an effort to make them safe from Viking attack. Coin hoards are notoriously difficult to date accurately and interpret – there are many reasons for hiding valuables, and the hoards give few clues as to the identity of their owners – but the fact that so many hoards were unrecovered has grim implications for the fate of those who buried them. Although the entries for these years in the *Anglo-Saxon Chronicle* are among the most detailed for the whole period, we are still unable to follow the campaigns with precision. Given its nature as the court history of the West Saxons (i.e. Wessex), it is not surprising that the *Chronicle* concentrates on events in southern England, but the geographic gaps that appear in the annals may be due to an altogether different reason. During the late 9th century the West Saxon kingdom was seeking to expand its power over the neighboring English kingdoms of Mercia and East Anglia. The territories of the East and South Saxons and the kingdom of Kent had already been absorbed by Wessex in the 820s, with Cornwall added 10 years later. By the reign of Æthelred I, who succeeded to the throne in 866 at the time of the Great Army's arrival, the West Saxons were already casting their eyes north and east. Thus the wars against the Vikings took place not solely in a context of national defense – there is no doubt that on many occasions the Wessex armies were fighting for nothing less than the independent survival of the Anglo-Saxon people – but also in the context of an expansionist struggle against the other English kingdoms. While this may perhaps diminish the heroic stature usually afforded to Alfred and his descendants, it goes a long way to explain the readiness of the East Anglians and Northumbrians to form alliances with the Scandinavians, and their preference for Danish rule above control from the south.

Having made peace with the East Angles in 866, the Viking host moved north the following year and laid siege to the old Roman town of York. After heavy fighting, both within the walls and outside, the Northumbrians suffered a devastating defeat. With all the English leaders killed in the fighting, the Vikings installed a puppet king. For several decades after this the Viking army was to have a secure base in Northumbria (stretching from the Humber estuary to the Scottish lowlands) from which to launch its attacks on the rest of Britain. Having made an abortive attack on Mercia in 868, the Vikings consolidated their hold on Northumbria the following year and in 870 launched a massive campaign against the East Angles. The Anglian king, Edmund, was killed and the whole of East Anglia fell quickly to the Danes.

The Viking army did not settle in one place, but moved around the country in the summer months fighting as they went, and building fortified camps in which to spend the winter. They now controlled the north and east of England, with only Mercia in the center and Wessex in the south still holding out. In 871, after five years of war, the Viking army launched what it must have hoped would be the final push against the West Saxons. The Danes divided their forces into several divisions and were met by the Wessex armies under King Æthelred, his brother Alfred and ealdorman Æthelwulf. The Danes and Saxons fought five battles in the early summer, some only days apart. Both sides suffered heavy losses. Nine Viking *jarlar* (earls) were killed together with one of their "kings" – in reality probably an exiled army leader – while the English lost five earls and many other prominent leaders including Æthelwulf and even a bishop who was fighting with the army. On 15 April King Æthelred died, and Alfred succeeded to the West Saxon throne. Within a few months of his succession Alfred's armies had met the Vikings nine times, and at the end of the year the exhausted opponents made a temporary peace, the Scandinavians withdrawing to London the following year.

The years 872–74 saw the Vikings change targets. Their efforts were now directed against Mercia, which fell to them after three years of fighting. In 875 the Great Army divided again, one part moving northwards from the Humber into southern Scotland to attack the Celtic kingdoms of Pictland and Strathclyde, while the other host maintained its grip on central England. This latter army was defeated by the West Saxons in 876, only narrowly escaping to Exeter, but the northern Vikings began a process that was to have far-reaching effects: "and that year Healfdene [the Viking commander] shared out the land of the Northumbrians, and they proceeded to plow and to support themselves" is the *Anglo-Saxon Chronicle*'s gloomy observation. For the first time a Viking army had established permanent settlements on English soil. In 877 the southern Viking army followed the example of their comrades and divided out the Mercian lands.

An embattled Wessex now stood alone. In 878 the southern Viking army commanded by Guthrum overran that territory too. Alfred and the remnants of his forces scattered into the fens and marshes of Somerset, in the southwest, from where they continued a desperate guerrilla war against the Danes. All through the early part of the year Anglo-Saxon refugees streamed into Alfred's camp at Athelney, until all that remained of the armies of Wessex and Mercia were united under his command. Just after Easter the English counterattacked and met the Danes at Edington. The Vikings were decisively defeated, and Alfred made peace with them at Wedmore, Somerset, in a ceremony that involved the baptism of Guthrum and the other Scandinavian commanders. Between 879 and 885 Wessex was left in

*Top* The Latin legend on this Viking silver coin invokes St Edmund, the East Anglian king (the large A in the center stands for *Anglorum* – "of the Angles"). Though Edmund was murdered by the Danes in 870, his cult as a martyr swiftly became established amongst them, and coins of this type – copying a design from his own reign – were apparently being struck in the Danelaw, principally in East Anglia, by the 890s, continuing into the early 10th century.

*Above* King Alfred the Great (871–99) was not only a capable military leader who saved Wessex from the Vikings, but also a distinguished scholar. This penny was struck for Alfred in London after its re-occupation, probably in the 880s, though some have argued that London had been retaken as early as 878, after the peace of Wedmore.

*Left* Following his struggle for survival in the 870s, and his treaty with the Danes, Alfred initiated a program for the revival of religion and learning in Wessex. The Old English inscription around this elaborate jewel is to be translated "Alfred had me made". The purpose for which the jewel was made is unknown, but one possibility is that it formed the handle of a manuscript pointer (*æstel*), such as Alfred caused to be sent to every bishop in his kingdom with a copy of his translation of the *Pastoral Care* of Pope Gregory I: in his preface, the king lamented the decay of learning in England. Another suggestion is that it formed the head of a scepter or wand of office. The figure on the jewel has been interpreted both as a represention of Sight and of Christ in the personification of Holy Wisdom. It was found near Athelney, Alfred's one-time refuge in the marshes of Somerset.

**The Viking campaigns in England, 892–895**
The period of relative peace after 885 saw the construction of a chain of *burhs*, or fortified strongpoints, across southern England. Each one was within about 32 kilometers (12 miles), or a day's march of its neighbor. They proved highly effective in defense when the Vikings under Hastein renewed their raids against Wessex in 892. For the next three years, the English and Scandinavian armies engaged in a series of skirmishes as they chased each other back and forth across the country. In 894 the Viking armies built a fortified camp on the river Lea north of London, and it was here that Alfred decisively defeated them, leading to their withdrawal to Bridgnorth, and subsequently back into the Danelaw.

peace. Guthrum's forces withdrew to East Anglia where they settled and began to farm, and in 880 the greater part of the army crossed the Channel to easier pickings in the Carolingian empire.

The Vikings did not return until 885 when Guthrum broke the peace of Wedmore and sailed to England with half the army, leaving the rest in Frankia. They encamped at Rochester in Kent, and harried the surrounding region. Alfred was quick to respond, having had six years of comparative peace in which to consolidate his rule and prepare his forces. The English fought the Vikings on land and in several sea battles (the latter with limited success, as the Danes were more experienced in fighting at sea). By 886 the threat was contained. The original treaty that had been made in 878 was renewed, and we are fortunate that its terms have survived in a later manuscript. The Anglo-Scandinavian frontier was defined as running "up the Thames, and then up the Lea, and along the Lea to its source, then in a straight line to Bedford, then up the Ouse to Watling Street". The land north and east of this border was ceded to Viking control, and became known as the Danelaw.

From the establishment of the Danelaw until his death in 899, Alfred ruled Wessex in a divided land with the armies of the Scandinavian Danelaw an ever-present threat to the north. During the last 10 years of his life, Alfred gradually rebuilt the centers of religion, learning and culture that had been destroyed or neglected during the long Danish wars, and ensured their continued survival by means of a chain of fortified strongpoints built across southern England. These *burhs* seem to have been a combination of refuge points for the population in time of war, fortified markets and administrative centers. They had permanent garrisons and carefully planned street layouts, usually on a grid system; it is in these settlements that we see the origins of many of the earliest English towns.

## The second wave of Danish attacks, 892–900

The program of military and civil engineering instituted by King Alfred after the treaty of Wedmore was to be fully tested at the end of his reign. In 892, the section of the Danish army that had remained behind in 885 left Frankia and returned to England. Now under the command of the veteran warrior Hastein, the Vikings arrived in Kent in two armies, building fortifications and storming a *burh* that was under construction. The following year saw a complex series of events, as the Vikings raided deep into Wessex, fighting skirmishes everywhere with Alfred's troops

but rarely meeting in pitched battle. On occasion, the East Anglians and Northumbrians seem to have fought side by side with Hastein's Danes, apparently preferring to live under Danelaw rule than under the domination of Wessex.

Both the Scandinavians and the English had many forces in the field, but these often failed to intercept each other as they crossed and recrossed southern England. Despite many blunders on the English side, the chain of *burhs* held firm and the Vikings made no real headway. Eventually the Wessex forces managed to coordinate their efforts and the Danes were successfully besieged on the banks of the river Severn near the Welsh border. After fierce fighting, the Scandinavians fled north to Chester with the English armies in pursuit. Using tactics familiar from more recent wars, the Danes crossed into the safety of the Danelaw and moved across Northumbria and down into East Anglia. As the Anglo-Saxon armies turned again and followed the frontier southeastwards, Hastein's forces gathered in Essex. Simultaneously, a division of the Viking army that had been attacking the southwest by sea "turned homewards", as the *Chronicle* puts it, sailing east to ravage Sussex. The two Viking forces joined up on the Lea, and built a fortress there, from which they harassed the region.

Throughout most of the following year, 895, the Scandinavians remained in their base above London engaging in only minor skirmishings. However, in the late fall Alfred laid a complicated siege involving several fortifications and a blockade of the river, denying the Danes access to their ships. The Viking army fled north, while the English captured or destroyed the entire Danish fleet. This seems to have been a decisive victory, since the Viking army dissolved itself the next year, its members joining their comrades

*Above* Some of the Wessex *burhs* reused Iron Age or Roman forts, others lay within the restrengthened walls of Roman towns. A number – such as Wallingford in Oxfordshire – were new towns, built on open sites within a rectangular rampart. This aerial view of Wallingford reveals the rectangular outline of the *burh*'s Anglo-Saxon ramparts, running down to the river Thames in order to control a crossing-point against the Danes; the line of the High Street, parallel to the river, is also clearly visible. The *burhs* were the most effective weapon employed by the English in their war against the Danes, probably requiring as many as 27,000 men to defend them. They also served as administrative and commercial centers.

*Above* Amongst the first coins struck in the eastern Danelaw were clumsy – and lightweight – imitations of the coins of King Alfred: this example is based on one of his silver pennies minted in Oxford.

in the Danelaw and settling in East Anglia and Northumbria; a few who could not afford to buy land and settle joined the Scandinavian armies that were fighting on the continent.

In the latter years of the 9th century, the power of Wessex was consolidated yet further and its strength reinforced by a still more ambitious program of *burh* construction. Though the Danelaw remained firmly in Scandinavian hands and seems to have functioned as a more-or-less cohesive unit, the English did not have to contend with a major army raiding beyond the frontier. Alfred died in 899, leaving a legacy of a strong and unified English state gathering its forces for the long process of recovery of the north and east.

## The Danelaw

The same problems that make it difficult to establish the precise nature and organization of the Viking armies in England carry over into any attempt to explore the Scandinavian settlement of the Danelaw. Healfdene's Vikings who shared out the land and started to plow it in 876 are of course the same people who occupied the Danelaw during the later 9th century. If we are unsure of their character as members of the army, then we are equally unsure as to who actually settled in the conquered territories. The main questions center around the scale and density of the Scandinavian settlement, and the structure of Danelaw society. We do not know how the Danelaw

*Right* The devastation of the Northumbrian island monastery of Lindisfarne during the Viking raid of 793 was far from complete, as is demonstrated by the survival of the relics of St Cuthbert (now in Durham Cathedral), as well as of the Lindisfarne Gospels (in the British Library). This magnificent gospel-book, written and illuminated there about 700, exemplifies the cultural achievements of the "Golden Age of Northumbria", which were brought to an abrupt end by the Danish conquest in the latter part of the 9th century.

**The Scandinavian presence in England**
The archaeological evidence for the Scandinavian settlement of England – remarkably sparse by comparison with the written sources – nevertheless throws some light on the occupation of the Danelaw. In particular, the integrity of its frontier is clearly shown in the heavier concentration of different types of Scandinavian place-names in the north and east, with some isolated patches in the west. The same pattern is repeated in the find-spots of hogbacks. The excavated remains of Viking Age towns and rural settlements, together with burials containing Scandinavian artifacts, present many problems since the identification of ethnic groupings in archaeological material can be far from certain. The notable lack of large quantities of recognizably Scandinavian objects, however, almost certainly indicates the rapid adoption of native English customs, lifestyles and burial practices by the incoming settlers. The question of the density of Scandinavian settlement and the numbers of individuals involved is still the subject of much debate.

was organized administratively and socially, and the precise character of the relations between the native English population of the area and the newcomers are also far from clear.

The dramatic impact that the creation of the Danelaw made on the English land and people, recorded in the historical sources, is confirmed by the total lack of documentary information concerning the area during the later 9th and early 10th century. Though the *Anglo-Saxon Chronicle* makes occasional reference to Viking movements within the Danelaw, there are no surviving sources from within the region itself. Since the days of the Venerable Bede in the 8th century, Northumbria had been a center of monastic scholarship and this complete dislocation of a literary tradition, and of the ecclesiastical and administrative apparatus within which it functioned, are telling testimony to the totality of the Scandinavian takeover: to all intents and purposes, the Danelaw is a historical black hole after 886.

The distribution of place-names that contain Scandinavian elements, as recorded in the *Domesday Book* commissioned by William the Conqueror in 1085, supports this view. The names can be of many types, each with a distinct meaning. Among the principal groups are those with the ending *-bý* (such as Selby and Derby); this suffix is found in places throughout Denmark and southern Sweden where it usually refers to a village, and in Norway where it refers to an individual farm, or even an area of cultivation. We also find names containing Scandinavian personal names (for example, Grimsby, "the village belonging to Grim"), or descriptive topographical names (Snaefell, "snow mountain"). A later type of place-names with the ending *-thorp* (Swainsthorpe) may indicate a phase of secondary settlements, perhaps expanding outwards onto marginal land as prime agricultural areas became heavily populated. Though the dating of these names is problematic, as some may come from the Middle Ages proper rather than the Viking period, their distribution is striking. When combined on a single map, their distribution coincides exactly with the known frontiers of the Danelaw, to such an extent that the border could be drawn with reasonable accuracy even if the terms of the Wedmore treaty had not survived.

Further levels of information in the place-name evidence are more difficult to interpret. Firstly, we do not know if the named settlements were new foundations, or simply a new name for an existing place. Nor can we be sure that all such names were actually coined by the Vikings, since it is likely that the English language contained Scandinavian elements before the 9th century, and this influence certainly continued into the medieval period, long after actual ethnic distinctions had become blurred. Furthermore, place-names as they are recorded in official documents are usually decided not by those living in a settlement, who have no need to name it, but by outsiders who need to refer to it for purposes such as taxation. The Scandinavian place-names contain regional groupings of different types, which seem to indicate expansion at later stages of settlement and the transfer of land into private ownership. However, much work still needs to be done before this information can be confidently ordered into a pattern and, as yet, this aspect of Danelaw studies remains inconclusive.

The documentary sources, though meager, do shed some light on the Scandinavian territories. The *Anglo-Saxon Chronicle* mentions a loose confederation of towns known as the Five Boroughs, which comprised Derby, Stamford, Leicester, Nottingham and Lincoln, all in central England. (A single reference to Seven Boroughs may be the Five plus two others, or a completely different group about which we know nothing.) These centers were all fortified and seem to have acted in a similar way to the Wessex *burhs*; indeed, it is likely that the latter were used as the model for the Danelaw towns. Excavations in some of the Boroughs, notably Lincoln, have revealed tantalizing glimpses of urban communities, with town plots laid out along planned streets and tenements. The houses and workshops indicate thriving mercantile settlements, with both local and long-distance trade networks stretching to the Scandinavian homelands and even beyond to Byzantium and the Middle East. The fact that this trade centered on the areas under Scandinavian control, as opposed to a countrywide network, is demonstrated by the distribution of certain artifact groups, such as pottery of the type that is known as Stamford ware. This is found almost exclusively in the area of the Five Boroughs and must surely reflect the range of their political influence. Assuming that the pottery was made for local consumption, then its restriction to this area is further confirmation of the Danelaw's boundary.

Standing alone as a counterpart to the Five Boroughs of the southern Danelaw was the kingdom of York, an area with flexible (and perhaps originally ill-defined) boundaries. Historically, we know much more about this northern kingdom than about the Five Boroughs, partly due to its closer ties with the Scandinavian homelands and with the Viking colonies in Ireland and the North Atlantic. Through the political upheavals of the 9th and 10th centuries the rulers of York changed from Danes to Norwegians, and trading and political links shifted westwards toward the Irish Sea and the Viking strongholds in Dublin and the Isle of Man. During this period the Kingdom of York also passed several times into temporary Anglo-Saxon control.

As a constant factor throughout this period of disruption lies the city of York itself, dominating the flat plains of the Vale of York, and commanding the main north-south land route through England. The town was refortified by the Danes shortly after their takeover, and flourished as one of the main defended market centers of northern Europe, to which merchants traveled from all over the Viking world. In recent years, excavation of the Coppergate site and others has revealed the cramped tenement dwellings and workshops that housed the ordinary working population, allowing us to see behind the kings and warriors recorded in the documents to the daily lives of a Viking Age community.

Of life outside the towns, we know much less. Only a handful of rural settlements have been excavated within the southern Danelaw and the Kingdom of York, and none of these can be definitely assigned to Scandinavian occupation. In the north, the best preserved is a farmstead complex excavated at Ribblehead in Yorkshire. Here, a longhouse similar to those found in Norway lay adjacent to a small bakery and smithy, at the center of a system of field enclosures. Similar sites have been investigated nearby at Bryant's Gill and Simy Folds, also in Yorkshire, and all three settlements seem to have practiced a mixed economy of agriculture supplemented by limited craftworking. A further isolated cluster of longhouses has been found on Lindisfarne at Green Shiel, post-dating the destruction and abandonment of the monastery after the 793 raid. No artifacts have been found to shed light on the ethnic origin of its inhabitants, the domestic finds being of everyday types common throughout early medieval Europe. The only other non-urban site to have been investigated north of the Humber is the community at Wharram Percy, where a number of small farming units seem to have gradually united into a nucleated village structure in the later Viking Age.

Within the southern Danelaw, several sites have been excavated, but again without revealing the nationality of their occupants. Some of them consist of a fortified enclosure surrounding a central long hall with several ancillary buildings (for example, at Goltho near Lincoln and Sulgrave in the south Midlands); but it is not clear whether they belonged to Anglo-Saxon landowners seeking to defend their property against Viking attack or were the sites of new settlements built by Scandinavian incomers. Whatever the identity of their owners, these small fortified residences may almost certainly be regarded as the forerunners of the manorial complexes of the medieval period and their establishment may reflect widespread changes in the patterns of land division and ownership occurring at this time. A scatter of small hamlets of the Wharram Percy type and some larger complexes have also been found in the Danelaw, for example at Little Paxton, St Neots in Cambridgeshire and Raunds in Northamptonshire.

At a very small number of sites we may actually be able to see the settlers themselves, in the finds of burials containing objects of recognizably Scandinavian type. The fact that these graves contain artifacts at all marks them out as pagan, and therefore distinguishes them from English burials of that date, for Christian burials do not include grave-goods. The limited numbers of such pagan burials in all probability testifies to the speed with which the Viking immigrants either adopted Christianity or at least followed the local conventions regarding burial; most of their number are almost certainly interred in the churchyards of Anglo-Scandinavian England, and are therefore archaeologically invisible to us. Amongst the burials that do survive are 17 graves containing typical male equipment such as weaponry and 3 inhumations with female jewelry, together with a scatter of other burials with Scandinavian artifacts. Almost all these graves are confined to the Danelaw, with the majority within the Kingdom of York. All the burials are single

# York

*Right* The excavations at the Coppergate site in the late 1970s and early 1980s provided detailed information about Viking York. Four tenement plots were excavated, stretching from the street frontage back toward the waterfronts on the Foss river. Over three periods of Anglo-Scandinavian occupation from the late 9th to 11th centuries, successive rectangular timber buildings lined Coppergate in rows, sometimes two-deep, their short sides facing toward the street. The clay floors and hearths were covered with the debris and finished products left by the craftsworkers who lived in them – leatherworkers, antler comb-makers, woodturners and metal smiths (*below right*). In one of the buildings the remains of a coin mint were found. The plot and street boundaries have survived almost unchanged since the Viking Age and, as the Jorvik Viking Center, the whole site has been preserved in its original location in the basements of the modern shops that are the successors to the Viking Age ones. Here visitors ride through a reconstruction of the 10th-century streets (*below*).

The old Roman city of York in the north of England is located at the confluence of the Ouse and Foss rivers, and lies on the main north–south landroute through England. The town, first occupied by the Great Army in 866, served as a Scandinavian stronghold in the north for almost a century, except for brief periods when it was recaptured by the English. York – which they called *Jórvik* – was sometimes ruled directly by the Vikings and sometimes by their puppet English rulers. Scandinavians seem to have settled in large numbers, reorganizing the street plan (the roads mostly have Scandinavian names, even today), repairing and extending the Roman city wall, and constructing waterfront quays. Excavations of Viking Age York have uncovered dozens of houses and workshops, with all the material culture of a thriving market town and trading center: with other Danelaw towns like Lincoln, York was the link with the merchants of the Scandinavian homelands, acting as the principal point of import for goods such as German pottery and the wine it contained, Norwegian whetstones and Byzantine silks. Archaeologists have found objects from as far away as the Arabian Gulf. Nearer at hand, trade also seems to have been conducted with the English during lulls in the war. Mints were set up, producing coins bearing both Christian and pagan symbols – a duality reflected also in the stone sculpture of the region. Several pieces of stone grave markers found near the medieval cathedral bear elaborate carvings in Scandinavian styles, and Viking burials have been excavated at St Mary Bishophill, a late Viking Age church and the oldest surviving church in the city.

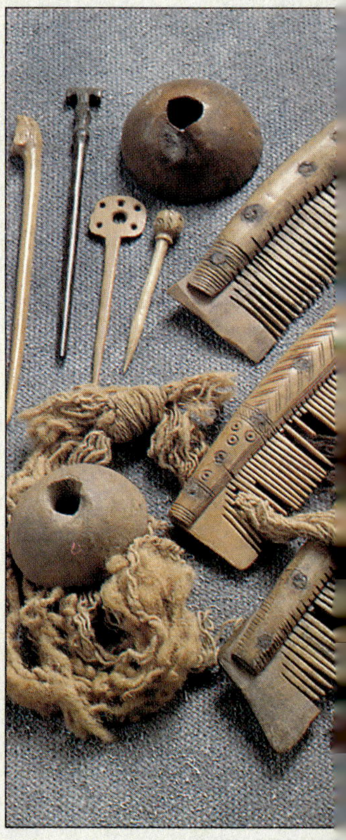

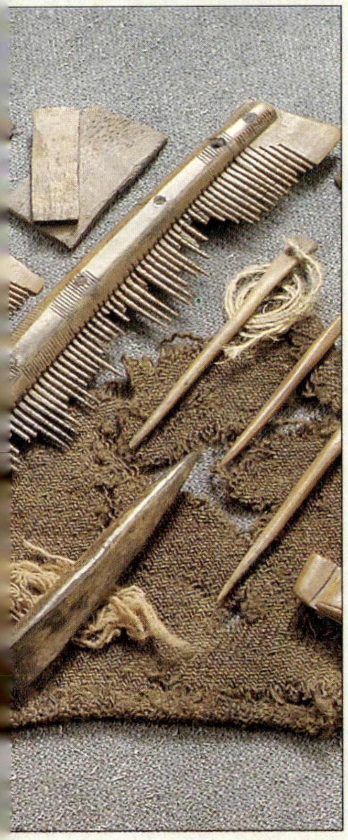

inhumations (though sometimes found in small groups of up to eight). However, the mass army grave at Repton and a unique group of 60 burial mounds at Ingleby in Derbyshire, the only site where Viking cremations have definitely been found in England, are notable exceptions.

**Cultural exchange**

Consideration of the level of interaction between the Scandinavian settlers and the native population presents a number of intriguing possibilities, and leads to the conclusion that what took place was not just a question of integration and assimilation, but led to the creation of a distinctive Anglo-Scandinavian culture. It is in the sphere of religion and belief that we see this demonstrated most graphically. Apart from the burials described above, there are very few instances of recognizably pagan practice in Viking Age England. However, considerable quantities of weapons and other artifacts such as horse equipment have been dredged from rivers, notably from the Thames at London Bridge and Oxford. While these objects may have been simply dropped or lost during battles, it seems more likely that the deposits are deliberate offerings to the gods, such as occur in large numbers in the peat bogs of Denmark and southern Sweden. A notable site of this kind has been excavated at Skerne in Humberside in northern England, where the skeletons of at least 20 horses, cattle, sheep and dogs were found around the pile supports of a bridge, along with metalwork and weapons.

Contrasting with this fragmented picture, considerable evidence of the Scandinavian conversion to Christianity has survived, principally in the form of stone sculpture. Anglo-Saxon England already had a flourishing tradition of carved stone crosses and burial markers by the time of the first large-scale Scandinavian settlements, but from the early 10th century onwards we see new elements appearing in the sculpture. New elements appear in the crosses, and Scandinavian art-styles are found increasingly among the decoration. Particularly striking are the new iconographic images that the Scandinavians seem to have introduced, including the depictions of armed warriors shown surrounded by weapons that are found on the Middleton crosses in North Yorkshire, for example. They were perhaps intended as symbols of military prowess and power, reinforcing the Scandinavians' control over the area. In a still more graphic example, a cross fragment from Weston, also in North Yorkshire, shows an armed warrior grasping a female figure by the neck – incidentally the only contemporary depiction of violence against a woman found anywhere in the Viking world.

The Scandinavians seem to have taken stone carving out of its monastic preserve and placed it in a secular environment, using it for purposes of political ideology and propaganda as well as for conventional commemorative purposes. Interestingly, several ostensibly Christian monuments incorporate scenes from pagan Norse mythology. For example, episodes from Ragnarök – the end of the world in which all the gods and people are destroyed – are shown on the shaft of the great cross at Gosforth, Cumbria. It has been argued that these scenes are intended to represent the triumph of Christ over the devil and his agents, here identified with the gods of the old religion, but this is by no means certain, and the monuments may even have served a dual role in which an active purpose was ascribed to the pagan imagery. A further type of stone monument, known as "hogbacks" from their distinctive ridge-back form, is found only in Britain and may be regarded as an example of Viking colonial sculpture. Probably used as grave covers, many of the hogbacks are in the form of houses with the roof and walls clearly depicted; some are also flanked by huge bears, grasping the "gables" of the house. Though a very few have crucifixions carved on them, most of the hogbacks include no Christian iconography at all and their religious orientation (if any) is uncertain.

Taken together with the other archaeological and place-name evidence, the stone sculpture suggests that

*Above* This striking image of a helmeted Viking warrior surrounded by his weapons (shield, sword, ax and spear), carved on one of the stone crosses at Middleton in North Yorkshire, demonstrates the novel manner in which some of the newly-converted members of the Danelaw aristocracy were commemorated on their 10th-century Christian memorials. Presumably the intention was to reinforce their authority over the local population.

# Anglo-Scandinavian Styles

Stone sculpture in the north of England bears witness to the cultural interchange that took place between the Anglo-Saxon population and the Scandinavian settlers. The former had a well-established tradition of erecting carved stone crosses and Christian burial markers, and these attracted the attention of the Viking overlords as they were themselves converted to Christianity. York in particular was a lively center of Anglo-Saxon carving and the craft continued to flourish under Viking rule, absorbing elements of Scandinavian fashion. The sculptors were influenced by the late 9th- and early 10th-century Borre and Jellinge styles of Viking art favored by their new patrons, who wanted the sculptures to depict themselves as a warrior aristocracy as well as to show familiar episodes from Norse mythology. The types of stone monument did not change greatly, except for the introduction from the Celtic West of the ring-headed cross and the invention of the curious "hogback" – a form of house-shaped tombstone. This blending of Scandinavian taste with Anglo-Saxon tradition gave rise to a distinctive 10th-century art in northern England, also reflected in metalwork, that is properly described as "Anglo-Scandinavian". A similar situation developed in southern England during the reign of the Danish king Cnut in the 11th century, when the Scandinavian Ringerike style was introduced. It is less clear, however, why the later Urnes style should have found some favor in post-Conquest England.

*Right* This cross, still standing in Gosforth churchyard in Cumbria, reflects the conversion to Christianity of the 10th-century Scandinavian settlers in northwest England. The ring-headed form of the cross-head is of Celtic derivation, but the decorative motifs include a ring-chain pattern inspired by the Scandinavian Borre style. The complex iconography combines the Crucifixion with episodes from Ragnarök – the end of the world of the pagan Scandinavian gods.

*Below* The sculptor rejected this piece of work, carved on a slab of limestone, before he had completed it. The fragment was excavated at Coppergate in York and belongs to the mid 10th century. It displays two interlocked beasts, with contoured bodies, characteristic of the Scandinavian Jellinge style of animal ornament.

*Above* This gilt-bronze brooch (much enlarged) was found at Pitney in Somerset in the southwest of England. Its classic combat-motif, executed in openwork, exemplifies the Anglo-Scandinavian version of the Urnes style that was fashionable in Scandinavia from the mid-11th to the beginning of the 12th century. The central design consists of a coiled ribbon-like animal, whose plain body has a beaded border, which is being bitten across the neck by a snake; the bodies of both animals end in plant-like tendrils. The scalloped border suggests Romanesque influence, giving it a late 11th-century date.

*Top right* A group of 26 sculptures at Sockburn in Co. Durham, northeast England, dates from the 10th century when the burial ground of an Anglo-Saxon monastery was taken over by the Vikings. This warrior, armed with a spear and wearing a helmet, demonstrates clearly the tastes of the new Scandinavian aristocracy who wanted to see themselves commemorated in stone. The decorative schemes of the Sockburn carvings are repeated on the sculpture found elsewhere in the area, and together represent the products of a workshop operating in the Tees and Leven valleys.

*Right* The Ringerike style introduced into southern England during the reign of Cnut had sufficient similarities to the contemporary English "Winchester style" for it not to be surprising that some Anglo-Saxon artists drew upon it for inspiration. A psalter thought to have been written at Winchcombe Abbey in Gloucestershire has decorated initials in both Winchester and Ringerike styles – and some that are mixed. The animal-head on this letter "d" is closely paralleled on the stone from St Paul's churchyard (page 210); its tightly intertwined tendrils are also characteristic of the true Ringerike style.

*Left* A fine example of a hogback tombstone from Ingleby Arncliffe in North Yorkshire, which has large muzzled end-beasts clutching the gable-ends of a house-shaped monument, with a curved roofridge. Its form seems to have been inspired by Christian shrinetombs and other house-shaped reliquaries; the curious niche in the side may imitate a shrine opening for the faithful to touch the relics. Hogbacks originated in the 10th century in the areas of Scandinavian settlement in northern England, especially Yorkshire and Cumbria, from where their use spread to Scotland.

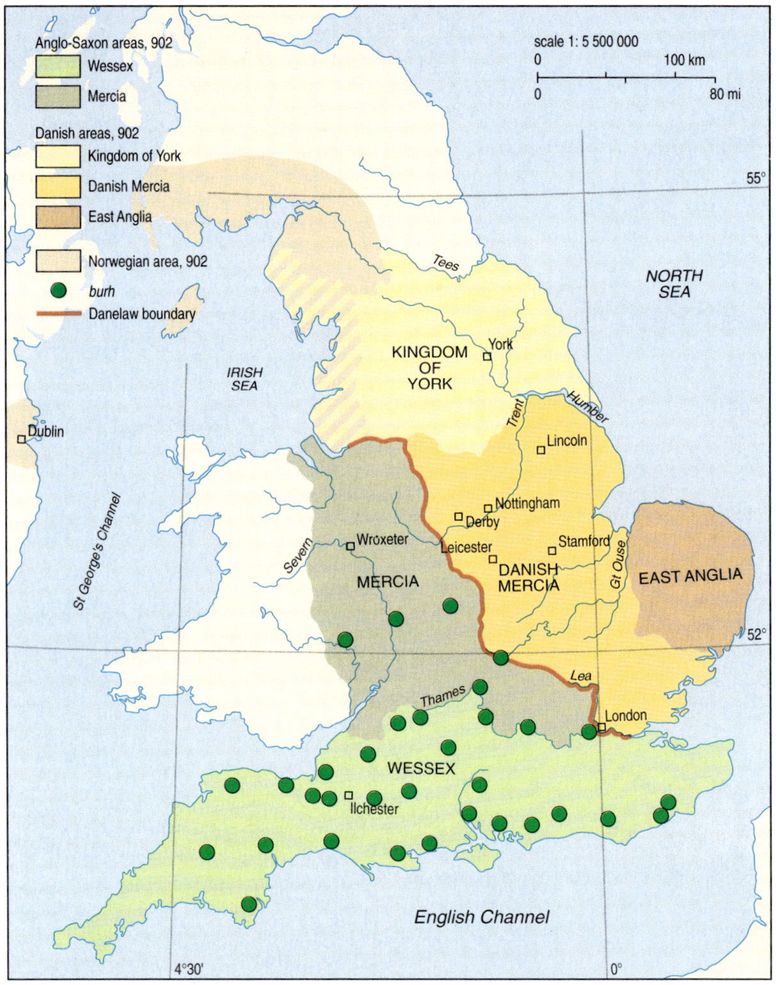

Anglo-Saxon areas, 902
Wessex
Mercia
Danish areas, 902
Kingdom of York
Danish Mercia
East Anglia
Norwegian area, 902
burh
Danelaw boundary
scale 1: 5 500 000
0
100 km
0
80 mi
55°
52°
4°30'
0°
NORTH SEA
IRISH SEA
St George's Channel
English Channel
Tees
Humber
Trent
Severn
Thames
Lea
Gt Ouse
Dublin
KINGDOM OF YORK
York
Lincoln
Nottingham
Derby
Leicester
Stamford
Wroxeter
MERCIA
DANISH MERCIA
EAST ANGLIA
London
WESSEX
Ilchester


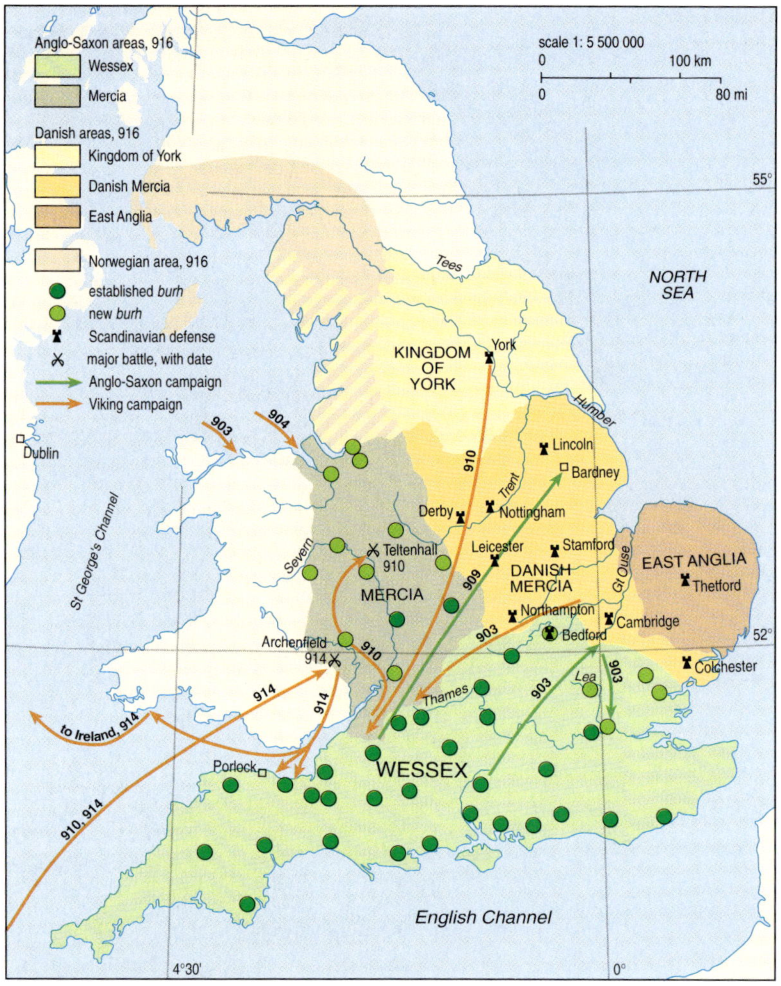

Anglo-Saxon areas, 916
Wessex
Mercia
Danish areas, 916
Kingdom of York
Danish Mercia
East Anglia
Norwegian area, 916
established burh
new burh
Scandinavian defense
major battle, with date
Anglo-Saxon campaign
Viking campaign
scale 1: 5 500 000
0
100 km
0
80 mi
55°
52°
4°30'
0°
NORTH SEA
St George's Channel
English Channel
Tees
Humber
Trent
Severn
Thames
Lea
Gt Ouse
Dublin
903
904
910
909
914
to Ireland, 914
910, 914
KINGDOM OF YORK
York
Lincoln
Bardney
Derby
Nottingham
Leicester
Stamford
Teltenhall 910
MERCIA
DANISH MERCIA
EAST ANGLIA
Thetford
Northampton
Cambridge
Bedford
Colchester
Archenfield 914
Porlock
WESSEX


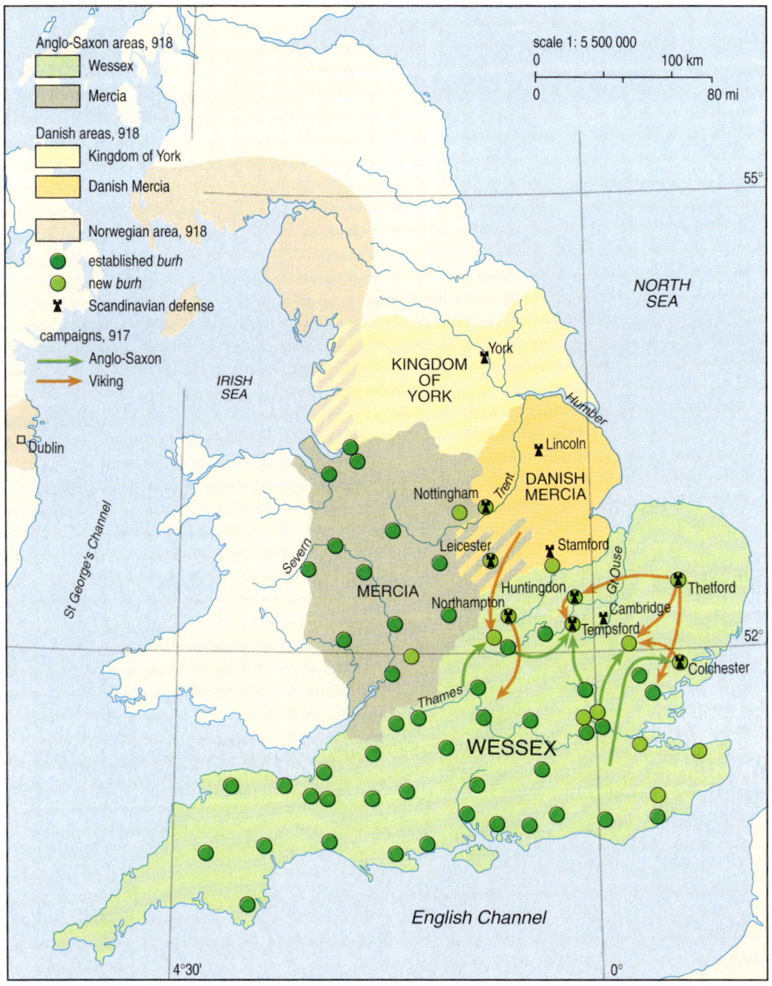

Anglo-Saxon areas, 918
Wessex
Mercia
Danish areas, 918
Kingdom of York
Danish Mercia
Norwegian area, 918
established burh
new burh
Scandinavian defense
campaigns, 917
Anglo-Saxon
Viking
scale 1: 5 500 000
0
100 km
0
80 mi
55°
52°
4°30'
0°
NORTH SEA
IRISH SEA
St George's Channel
English Channel
Humber
Trent
Severn
Thames
Gt Ouse
Dublin
KINGDOM OF YORK
York
Lincoln
DANISH MERCIA
Nottingham
Leicester
Stamford
MERCIA
Northampton
Huntingdon
Thetford
Cambridge
Tempsford
Colchester
WESSEX


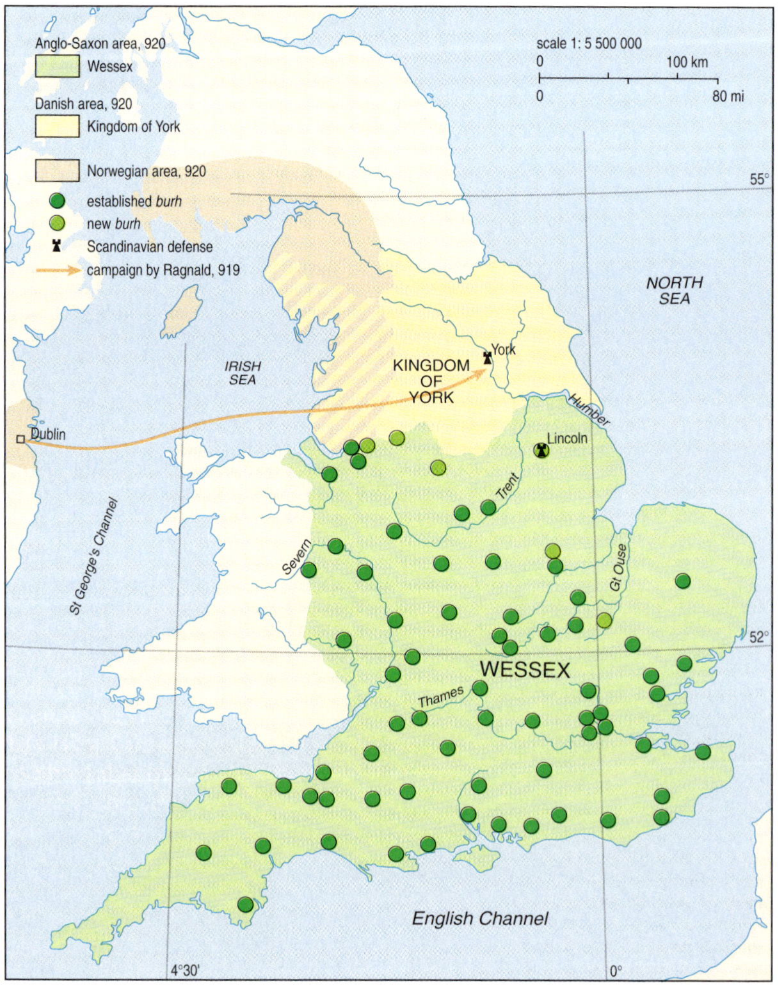

Anglo-Saxon area, 920
Wessex
Danish area, 920
Kingdom of York
Norwegian area, 920
established burh
new burh
Scandinavian defense
campaign by Ragnald, 919
scale 1: 5 500 000
0
100 km
0
80 mi
55°
52°
4°30'
0°
NORTH SEA
IRISH SEA
St George's Channel
English Channel
Humber
Trent
Severn
Thames
Gt Ouse
Dublin
KINGDOM OF YORK
York
Lincoln
WESSEX

**The recovery of the Danelaw**
Between 902 and 921 the Anglo-Saxon kingdom of Wessex launched a determined series of military campaigns with the dual objective of retaking the Danelaw territories and expanding its influence at the expense of its English neighbors, particularly Mercia. The successors of Alfred the Great and the rulers of Mercia continuously raided the Scandinavian-held areas, isolating and neutralizing the different Viking armies one by one. The Scandinavian response was rendered ineffective by the network of fortified *burhs*. As the northern territories fell, the Wessex dynasty consolidated its hold over the newly won lands by building more *burhs* and settling large numbers of people in them. This program was also extended into Mercia. By 921, only the Viking Kingdom of York survived intact, saved by an alliance with Ragnald, the Norwegian king of Dublin. In the Midlands, Mercia had effectively vanished and had been absorbed by Wessex, which now ruled the whole of England south of the Humber estuary.

the Scandinavian settlers firmly and swiftly established themselves in their newly won lands and ruled the Danelaw and Kingdom of York with a well-defined sense of identity and purpose. While the size of their settlements is still not known to us with any degree of accuracy, the English and Scandinavian populations must clearly have interacted to a quite considerable extent, and in the northern and eastern parts of England we find compelling evidence of a rapid cultural fusion and transformation.

## The Anglo-Saxon recovery of the Danelaw, 902–954

At the beginning of the 10th century, both the Anglo-Saxon and Scandinavian peoples were exhausted by decades of war. However, as the Danes consolidated their hold on the Danelaw, Wessex – now ruled by Alfred's son Edward – began a slow campaign of attrition against the Danes, with continual small incursions over the frontier. Major campaigns were mounted in 903, 906 and 909 when the Vikings allied with English leaders who were hostile to the Wessex throne, but Edward's armies held firm.

The English strengthened their frontier defenses with an increased program of *burh* construction, securing an unbreakable line of retreat, and as the frontier was pushed slowly north they consolidated

*Right* The Cuerdale hoard, buried about 905 beside the river Ribble in Lancashire, is the largest Viking treasure known from Britain or Scandinavia, consisting of some 7,500 coins and a mass of hack silver to a total weight of about 40 kilograms of bullion. Amongst the hack silver there is much of Hiberno-Norse origin, suggesting that a good part of its contents had been transferred from Ireland to northwest England after the Vikings were expelled from Dublin in 902. However, many of the coins had been freshly minted in the Viking Kingdom of York. Perhaps some of the wealth of both kingdoms was being gathered together prior to an attempt to reestablish the Vikings in Dublin.

*Left* This early 9th-century fresco in the Oratory of St Benedict at Malles in Italy shows a bearded Frankish nobleman holding his sword. The early Viking raiders in mainland Europe turned the factional quarrels that divided the Frankish warlords to their own advantage.

the territory they had won back by building *burhs* as they went. Both parties were troubled by external threats during this period; the Mercians were forced to repel attacks from the Celts in Wales, while the Danish armies came under increasing threat from the Norwegian Vikings who had settled in Ireland. Some of their number moved into western Northumbria and the northeast Midlands after the Irish succeeded in expelling the Norse from Dublin in 902. They quickly began to compete with the Danes for power in the north, and this internecine fighting certainly weakened the effectiveness of the Vikings' defenses against the advancing English armies.

Mercia was allied to the West Saxon dynasty through the marriage of Edward's sister Æthelflæd to the Mercian leader Æthelred, but the process of reconquest went hand in hand with the expansion of Wessex. On Æthelred's death in 911, Edward gained control of the Mercian lands around the Thames valley and used them as a base to reconquer the whole of Essex by 916. The most dramatic events however were to come the following year. In 917 Edward and Æthelflæd, who had assumed control of Mercia on her husband's death, were ready to launch their decisive campaign, and in the summer they marched north to meet a Danish army that had been harrying across the frontier of the Danelaw earlier in the year. By late fall the Danish forces had collapsed in a chain reaction leaving the English in command of the Midlands and Cambridgeshire, with only East Anglia holding out under Danish control, but this, too, fell in 918.

Two events in 918 and 919 set the pattern that was to shape events in the rest of the century. The death of Æthelflæd led to the final consolidation of Wessex and Mercia after the Mercian successor was quickly deposed, and shortly afterwards Danish power in England suffered a grievous blow when Ragnald of Dublin stormed York and took the city. The last of the Danelaw territories fell in 920. Wessex rule, now synonymous with English rule, reached to the Humber, and the Kingdom of York formed part of a Hiberno-Norse power block extending across the Irish Sea to Dublin with a Norwegian and Celtic cultural orientation that reached west and north to the Viking colonies of the North Atlantic.

The final stage of the English counterattack unfolded during the reign of Edward's son Athelstan, who came to power in 924. After strengthening the borders to the west, Athelstan launched a concerted attack on the Kingdom of York in 927. Through a series of judicious alliances with the Celtic rulers in Scotland and Wales, Athelstan ruled a united kingdom that extended far to the north of the modern English border. However, in 937 this was threatened by a massive alliance of the Dublin Vikings and the Celts who gathered from all over northern Europe to launch a coordinated last-ditch campaign to restore the Scandinavian conquests and defeat the English once and for all. The two armies met at an unidentified place, called *Brunanburh* in the accounts, in a clash so fierce that later Celtic writers who recorded the whole campaign in poetry and stories were to remember it simply as the "Great War". After some desperate hours the English forces won the battle, with the result that opposition to English rule was neutralized for the remainder of the century. Nevertheless, the English hold on the north remained insecure, and on Athelstan's death in 939, it was temporarily lost to the Dublin kings who took direct control of the kingdom of York again and imposed a series of puppet rulers. It was internal quarreling, however, that brought about the disintegration of the Norse kingdom, and in 954 the last Viking king of York, Eric Bloodax, met his death at the battle of Stainmore.

Nearly a century after the Great Army had settled in England in 866, the Scandinavian conquest of England was finally halted. The political structure of the country had been changed forever. The fragmented Anglo-Saxon kingdoms that had faced the Vikings in the 9th century had disappeared, and the process of recovery had brought about the unification of England into the single kingdom we recognize today.

## The Vikings in Frankia

*The number of ships grows: the endless stream of Vikings never ceases to increase. Everywhere the Christians are the victims of massacres, burnings, plunderings: the Vikings conquer all in their path, and no one resists them: they seize Bordeaux, Périgueux, Limoges, Angoulême and Toulouse. Angers, Tours and Orléans are annihilated and an innumerable fleet sails up the Seine and the evil grows in the whole region. Rouen is laid waste, plundered and burned: Paris, Beauvais and Meaux taken, Melun's strong fortress leveled to the ground, Chartres occupied, Evreux and Bayeux plundered, and every town besieged."* **Ermentarius of Noirmoutier, c.860.**

Frankia, or the Frankish or Carolingian empire, all describe the European territory ruled by the Carolingian dynasty of kings and emperors descended from Charlemagne (?742–814). It reached its fullest extent

*Right* This page from the *Annales Xantenses* records some of the events that took place in western Europe in 842: amongst them are Viking attacks on Frisia and Frankia, and also the death of one of their leaders. At the bottom of the page, the sentence begins with reference to one of their kings, by name of Rorik (*rex eorum nomine RORIK*).

during the reign of Charlemagne's son, Louis the Pious (778–840), when it stretched from the Pyrenees across the whole of France to the present-day Low Countries, into northern Germany, and down into the Italian peninsula.

The first recorded Viking raid in Frankia occurred in 799, followed by isolated attacks on unprotected targets through the first four decades of the 9th century. The raids followed a similar pattern to those on England, and indeed the history of Viking involvement in Frankia is closely linked to events in the Anglo-Saxon kingdoms. Periods of heavy Viking activity in England often meant a brief respite for the Franks – and vice versa – since the same Scandinavian armies often campaigned on both sides of the English Channel, coordinating their efforts to exploit the riches of the Christian west to the full. As in England, too, steps were taken to try to stop the Vikings. Charlemagne, for example, issued orders that the major river bridges should be fortified as barriers against the raiders' fleets.

The earliest Scandinavian raids were concentrated on Frisia, in the area of modern Belgium and the Netherlands. At this time Frisia's coastal settlements at Quentovic and Dorestad were among the major market centers of northwestern Europe, from where vessels sailed across the English Channel to Britain and eastward into the Baltic Sea. Frisian merchants had been trading here with both Scandinavians and Slavs since long before the Viking Age, and evidence of their presence has been found at Hedeby and other Viking settlements.

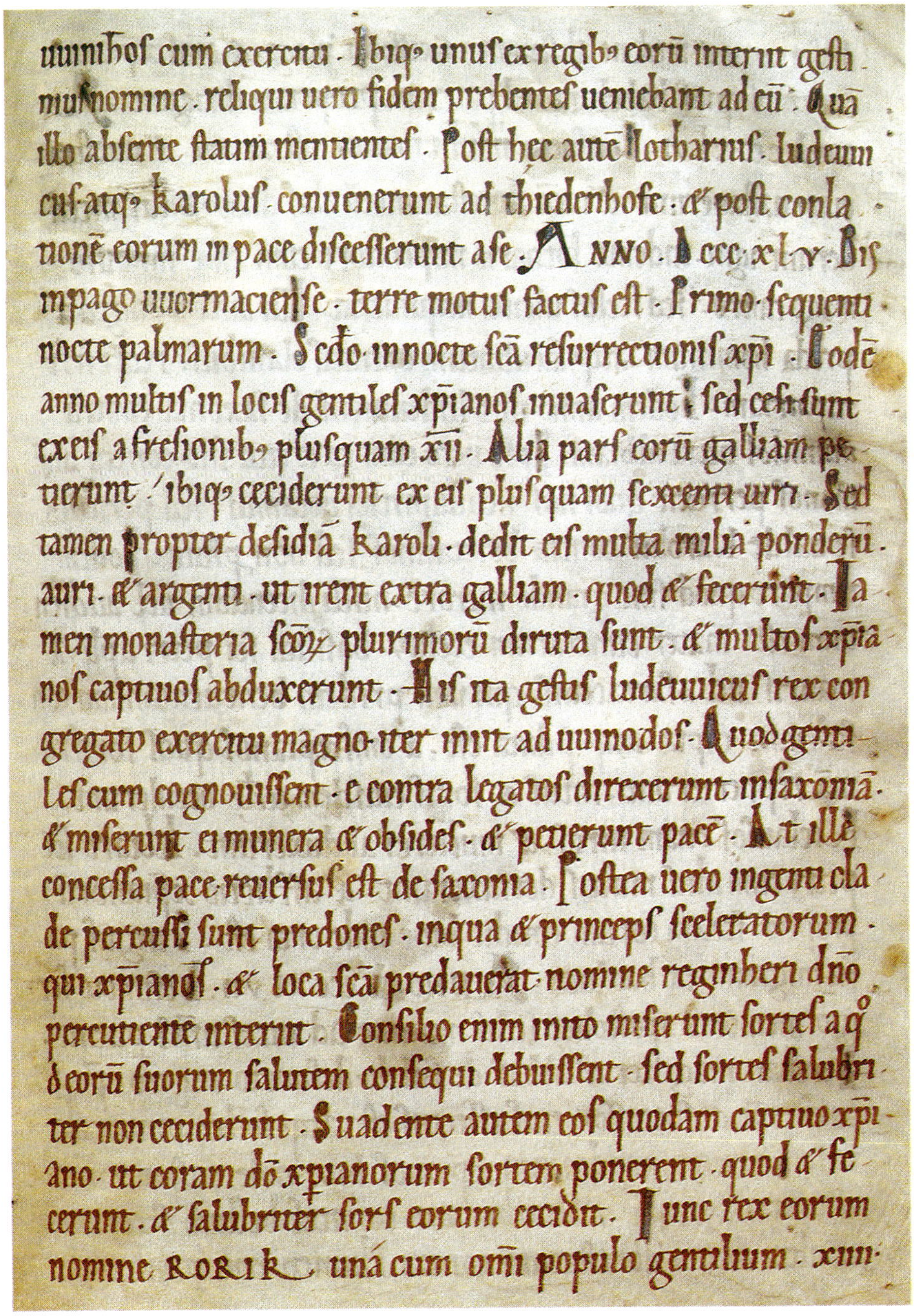
uuinibos cum exercitu. Ibiq; unus ex regib; eorũ interiit gesti
nus nomine. reliqui uero fidem prebentes ueniebant ad eũ. Qua
illo absente statim mentientes. Post hec autẽ Lotharius. ludeuui
cus atq; karolus conuenerunt ad thiedenhofe: & post conla
tionẽ eorum in pace discesserunt a se. ANNO. Dccc xl v. Bis
in pago uuormaciensi. terre motus factus est. Primo sequenti
nocte palmarum. Scdo in nocte scã resurrectionis xpi. Eodẽ
anno multis in locis gentiles xpianos inuaserunt; sed cesi sunt
ex eis a fresionib; plusquam xii. Alia pars eorũ galliam pe
tierunt. ibiq; ceciderunt ex eis plusquam sexcenti uiri. Sed
tamen propter desidiã karoli. dedit eis multa milia ponderũ
auri & argenti. ut irent extra galliam. quod & fecerũt. Ta
men monasteria scõr. plurimorũ diruta sunt. & multos xpia
nos captiuos abduxerunt. His ita gestis ludeuuicus rex con
gregato exercitu magno iter init ad uuinodos. Quod genti
les cum cognouissent. e contra legatos direxerunt in saxoniã.
& miserunt ei munera & obsides. & petierunt pacẽ. At ille
concessa pace reuersus est de saxonia. Postea uero ingenti cla
de percussi sunt predones. in qua & princeps sceleratorum.
qui xpianos. & loca scã predauerat nomine reginheri dño
percutiente interiit. Consilio enim inito miserunt sortes a quo
deorũ suorum salutem consequi debuissent. sed sortes salubri
ter non ceciderunt. Suadente autem eos quodam captiuo xpi
ano. ut coram dõ xpianorum sortem ponerent. quod & fe
cerunt. & salubriter sors eorum cecidit. Tunc rex eorum
nomine RORIK. unã cum omi populo gentilium. xiiii.

The wealth of the Frisian ports made them prime targets for Viking raids, and both Dorestad and Quentovic were destroyed several times. The former seems to have borne the brunt of the onslaught – as soon as the town was rebuilt after a raid, it would be attacked again, and the annals say that it was burned to the ground four times in three years. Some Vikings were settled temporarily in Frisia as early as 826, when a grant of land to a Scandinavian commander called Harald is recorded. The island of Walcheren at the mouth of the river Scheldt served as a fortified Viking base, and the whole of Frisia was overrun on several occasions. From about 838 onwards, however, the focus of Scandinavian raiding moved farther west to the Atlantic coast.

On the death of Louis the Pious in 840 the Frankish empire was divided among his sons Lothar, Louis the German and Charles the Bald, and never again reached the peak of cohesion and power that had been achieved in the early years of the 9th century. Soon civil war had broken out and the empire was partitioned still further as an ever increasing number of factions appeared as contenders for the vestiges of Frankish imperial power. These included the various descendants of Louis the Pious, as well as a number of independent warlords, intent on carving out their own territory. All of these elements had their own armies and retinues, and fighting was frequent between fathers, sons and brothers. When the Vikings first appeared in earnest on the European mainland, their commanders were able to exploit this volatile situation, just as they turned the fragmented state of the Anglo-Saxon kingdoms to their advantage in England.

After 841 two major Viking fleets operated in Frankia, one based on the Seine, the other on the Loire; several other independent Viking leaders acted in isolation or joined the larger fleets for major raids. After the mid 9th century the highly mobile raiding fleets no longer went every summer to Frankia; instead the two main campaigning armies overwintered there, just as happened in England, with a further force encamped on the Somme river. In 850, for example, a Danish fleet under the command of Rorik – the brother of the Harald who had settled in Frisia in the 830s – was ceded Dorestad in return for protecting the northern coasts. This early parallel to the establishment of Normandy was shortlived, but while it lasted the Danes of Dorestad proved just as treacherous as the Norman Vikings were to do: Rorik's son Godfred raided from the Rhine to the Loire in the course of the next decade.

However, though the empire as a whole was severely harassed by the Scandinavians, with widespread destruction of its monasteries and towns, the Carolingians never faced a concerted Scandinavian attempt at total conquest as happened in England. Given the scale of the empire and the fragmented nature of its power structures such an undertaking would have been unlikely to succeed, but a further

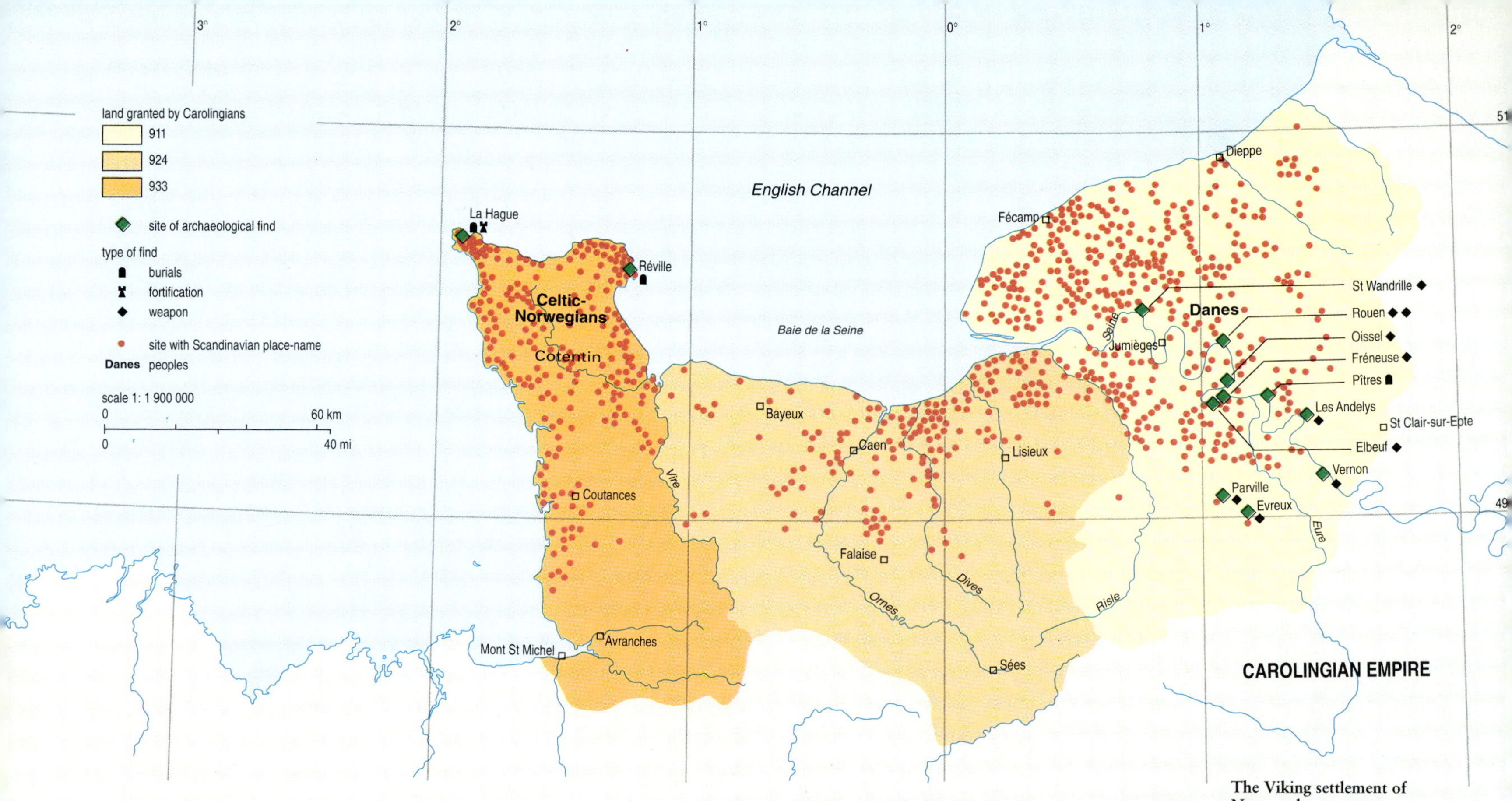


**The Viking settlement of Normandy**
The scatter of Scandinavian place-names that survives in Normandy today is an indication of how thoroughly the region was occupied after 911. Settlement appears to have moved outward from two centers, with a concentration of mainly Danish names in the east around the Seine estuary and a mix of Celtic-Norwegian names in the north of the Cotentin peninsula.

reason may be found in the effect that this fragmentation had on the Scandinavians themselves. Certainly, the lack of a coordinated Frankish defense facilitated the Vikings' operations, but the numerous Carolingian factions were able to play the Scandinavian armies off against each other to such an extent that they often found themselves fighting against each other in the civil wars. In these circumstances, instead of aiming at outright conquest, the larger Viking armies organized their efforts to effect a greater degree of planning in their raids, moving across Europe almost to a system along a regular route of destruction and looting. Through a combination of simple raids on wealthy monasteries, trading centers and villages, and the extortion of protection money in the *Danegeld* payments familiar from England, the Viking armies were able to sustain themselves comfortably on a life of peripatetic violence. In a very real sense, the Viking operations in Frankia acted as a training ground and sometimes a base for their attacks on England, since all the forces involved in the wars with Wessex had fought at some time in mainland Europe.

The Scandinavian impact on Frankia has left little trace in the archaeological record, with almost all the material confined to Normandy and Brittany in the northwest. Indeed, the clearest evidence we have of Viking activities in mainland Europe comes from Scandinavia itself, where many Carolingian objects have been found in hoards and in burials – almost certainly seized as loot or forming part of the great *Danegeld* payments. According to the Carolingian documentary sources, more than 19,500 kilograms of silver and 300 kilograms of gold were received by the Vikings as part of these bribes. Though many Frankish coins have been found in Scandinavia, the quantity is nowhere near large enough to account for the massive *Danegelds* recorded, implying that much of the coinage was melted down and recast as silver objects. It has, however, been suggested that the Viking armies may simply have spent their money while campaigning in the west.

Viking activities in Frankia largely ceased after the end of the 9th century. When the Great Army shifted its focus of activity to England in the 890s, the orientation of Scandinavian interest in western Europe shifted with it. Only in the settlements established in the early 10th century in northern Neustria (later to become the duchy of Normandy), and in the short-lived Viking colony in Brittany did the Scandinavian presence continue in mainland Europe.

*Above* There is only slight archaeological evidence on the continental mainland of western Europe that bears witness to the Viking presence there. However, this characteristic pair of standard oval brooches dating to the beginning of the 10th century was found in a Scandinavian woman's grave at Pîtres on the river Andelle in Normandy.

*Left* Amongst the quantity of Carolingian silverwork carried off from Frankia to Scandinavia was this ornate 8th-century vessel. It was found in a field at Fejø, Jutland, together with five smaller drinking cups.

### Rollo and the settlement of Normandy

The early history of Normandy is far from clear, and must be pieced together from fragmentary later sources and tangential contemporary material such as legal documents and property charters. At the beginning of the 10th century the Frankish ruler Charles the Simple (879–929), no doubt in desperation at the scale of the depredations being carried on by the Viking army based on the Seine, which had been raiding far upriver into the interior, offered them the grant of an area of land in the north of his kingdom if they would agree to settle there and defend it against other Viking attacks: in this way he hoped to neutralize them as a threat in the future. The leader, a Norwegian named Rollo in the Frankish sources (identified in later Scandinavian sagas as *Göngu-Hrólfr* – "Hrolf the Walker"), accordingly accepted the land between the Epte and Risle rivers in the east of what is Normandy today. According to a later Norman source the agreement was signed at St Clair-sur-Epte after a battle fought at Chartres in 911, but though Rollo initially kept his word and repelled a few shiploads of marauders, he soon led his followers on further raids themselves, striking deep into the Frankish heartlands. By 924, when he handed power to his son William Longsword, Rollo had gained control of an area reaching as far west as the river Vire. William completed this process of conquest in 933 when he seized the Cotentin peninsula, and Normandy acquired the geographic boundaries it has today.

Though a Norwegian himself, Rollo's army seems to have been principally composed of Danes. They appear to have dispersed rapidly through their newly won lands, and to have settled in several enclaves broadly based around Rouen, Bayeux and Cherbourg, to judge by the concentration of Scandinavian place-names in these areas. On the basis of these names, it would seem that there was a significant proportion of Celtic speakers among the Viking immigrants, perhaps pointing to a Hiberno-Norse or Hebridean element among the army. In the early days of the Norman settlement, the immigrants seem to have quarreled frequently among themselves, and the province was severely wracked by feuding, culminating in the murder of William Longsword in 942. But under his successors it managed to maintain a high degree of unity and cohesion, avoiding many of the problems that had weakened other Viking colonies such as the Kingdom of York.

As in England, interaction between the native Franks and Scandinavians led to the rapid formation of a distinctive local culture and a true Norman identity, accelerated by an early conversion to Christianity in the mid 10th century. However, two burial sites of Scandinavian character have left a material record of the pagan beliefs of the first Normans. At Pîtres, near Rouen, a woman was buried with typical Scandinavian oval shoulder brooches and pottery, while a number of stone burial settings in the form of longships were discovered on the beach at Réville near Cherbourg in the 1960s. It is difficult to date these monuments since they contain cremations and there are no accompanying grave-goods, but the form of the settings is exactly paralleled in burials found throughout Viking Age Denmark and Sweden.

The Viking settlement of Normandy has left few other recognizable archaeological traces, but a notable exception is the remains of a large earthen-banked fortress on the very tip of the Cherbourg peninsula at La Hague. This may have been a maritime base for a group of early 10th-century Vikings. The violence of the initial Scandinavian contact in the region is attested by finds of contemporary swords, axes and spearheads dredged from the Seine and its tributaries, either deposited there as thank-offerings or lost in battle.

The rapid integration of the Scandinavians and the native Franks, coupled with the pressing problems that faced the Carolingian rulers elsewhere in the empire, hampered their efforts to reconquer Normandy. The settlement flourished and became the duchy of Normandy – the title *dux* ("duke") is first recorded as being used by the Norman ruler Richard II in 1006 – and the strength of the new duchy increased until it reached its zenith of power with the conquest of England in 1066.

### The Viking occupation of Brittany, 914–936

The tiny province of Brittany held a unique position in early medieval Europe, as its fiercely independent Celtic population had acted as a small thorn in the side of the Frankish kingdom since the Merovingian period (5th to 8th century). The Breton rulers continued to do the same in the 9th century. The first Viking raids on Frankia coincided with the successful invasion and conquest of Brittany by Charlemagne's armies. After a series of consolidatory campaigns, Louis the Pious appointed a Breton called Nominoe as imperial representative in the province. He remained loyal to Louis as long as he lived, but after Louis' death in 840, the Breton leader rebelled. Throughout the remainder of the 9th century the Bretons proved a major irritant to the Frankish rulers, acting as one more element in the complex network of vicious Carolingian power politics.

Brittany suffered the effects of the Viking raids in a similar fashion to the rest of the empire, with fleets fighting at various times against the Bretons or in alliance with them in attacks on the Franks. The Carolingian rulers in their turn attempted to play off the Scandinavians and Bretons against each other. Brittany was particularly unfortunate in that the main base of the Loire Vikings was situated at the mouth of the river on the island of Noirmoutier – the site of the once-prominent monastery that was destroyed by the Scandinavians early in the 9th century – close to the Breton capital at Nantes.

Though not immune to their own civil wars, Nominoe and his successors proved strong war leaders and kept the Viking armies in check, despite the province being temporarily over-run on several occasions. However, with the death in 907 of the most successful of the Breton rulers, Alain the Great, the resulting power vacuum saw an immediate escalation of Viking attacks. After the settlement of Normandy from 911, the possible targets for Viking looting expeditions in the traditional manner had narrowed to one – Brittany – and the remnants of the great mercenary armies of the later 9th century seem to have converged on the region. They were aided by Rollo's Seine army and left well alone by the Franks who were only too happy to see their old enemies fighting each other. After seven years of increasingly severe assaults, Brittany finally fell to a vast Norwegian army in 914. The Breton nobility and much of the clergy fled to the court of Athelstan in England, while the countryside was laid waste and many of the population enslaved.

From 914 until the end of the Viking colony in 936 we have no documentary sources whatsoever originating in Brittany. The character of the Viking takeover seems to have been very different from that in other Viking colonies such as the Danelaw and Normandy: there is no evidence of trading activities – normally so characteristic of the fiercely competitive Scandinavian warrior-merchants – and no sign either of agricultural settlement or of newly established rural centers. Instead the occupation appears to have been a purely military one, an extended spree of violence and looting by the last truly Viking army operating in Europe. Such an anachronism could not last for long, deprived as it was of allies, external trade and supplies. In 936 the exiled Bretons launched a seaborne invasion with English aid and the grandson of Alain the Great, Alain Barbetorte, drove the Vikings from Nantes. However, three more years of bitter fighting were needed before the Scandinavian army was finally routed, and the Breton dukes restored to power.

The short occupation, so unusual in the Viking world, has left equally exceptional archaeological monuments. In the first half of the 10th century a magnificent ship grave was constructed on a headland facing the sea on the small island of Groix off the southern Breton coast. A longship with a smaller ship's boat inside was dragged along a processional way of standing stones to a specially cleared area of turfs, and then filled with a rich assemblage of objects including weapons, riding gear, gold and silver jewelry, ivory gaming pieces, smith's tools and farming equipment. The bodies of an adult male and an adolescent – possibly a human sacrifice – were placed in the ship, which was surrounded by 24 shields, and the vessel was then set on fire, the ashes covered by a mound. The Groix ship burial is the only one of its kind in Europe, built at a time when the other Viking armies had already become Christian, and thus represents a glorious throwback to a pagan past that had been gone for more than a generation.

The second major archaeological discovery to have been made in Brittany in recent years is the excavation of a circular fortress at Péran near St Brieuc. This seems to have been either defended or attacked by a Scandinavian force in the early 10th century. The high, earthen ramparts of the fort have been burned, vitrifying them in some places. Among the remains discovered there were a Viking sword and other weapons, bucket-like vessels similar to those found in the Groix ship, and a coin minted in Anglo-Scandinavian York between 905 and 925. It is highly likely that the Camp de Péran was the site of a fierce battle between Scandinavians and Bretons during the liberation of Brittany in 936, and as such provides us with a unique frozen moment in the history of the Vikings in Frankia.

With the destruction of the Nantes army in 939 the Viking adventure in Frankia was over. Though isolated raids continued sporadically into the 11th century, fleets and armies on the scale of those employed in the 9th-century wars with the Franks were never seen again. The empire and its Breton neighbors had barely survived, like the Anglo-Saxon kingdoms across the sea. Unlike them, however, they would not have to face a second wave of Scandinavian aggression in the early 11th century. Instead, a lasting Scandinavian presence remained in mainland Europe in the shape of the duchy of Normandy, which would slowly form its own counterpart to Frankish rule and come to dominate the whole of western Europe in the later years of the century.

**The Vikings in Spain and the Mediterranean**

A number of the Viking raiding fleets that made their way down the Atlantic coast did not stop off in France but continued south to attack the territories of the Arab Umayyad emirates (the Moors) in what are now Spain and Portugal. The first known raid occurred in 844, when several towns were sacked and Seville was temporarily occupied. However, the Arab defenders put up such fierce resistance that the Vikings were quickly repulsed, their forces almost destroyed. This lack of success seems to have discouraged other Scandinavians from followng their example, and it was 15 years before another assault was made.

The second Scandinavian intervention in Spain formed the prelude to the most ambitious Viking voyage yet undertaken; indeed, only the journey of Ingvar the Far-Traveled to the Black and Caspian Seas in the 11th century stands comparison with it. In 859, a fleet of 62 ships set out from the Viking bases on the Loire under the joint command of Bjorn Ironside and Hastein – both famous Vikings who had fought with the Great Army in England and France – their objective nothing less than to sack the city of Rome. The fleet ravaged all along the Spanish coast, penetrating farther than the 844 raid and sacking many Moorish cities. Passing the straits of Gibraltar, the Vikings then raided along the North African coast, southern Spain and the Balearic Islands before wintering on an island in the Camargue in the Rhône delta, which gave them a base from which to plunder southern France.

By this time, the Scandinavians were laden with almost more loot than their ships could hold. Their decision to press on to Rome had an element of conscious glory-seeking about it; fame was a preoccupation of the Viking warrior, and Bjorn and Hastein's campaign must clearly be viewed in this light. Reaching Italy, they sacked Pisa and finally Rome itself – or so they thought: they had missed their target by more than 300 kilometers, destroying Luna on the Ligurian coast instead. Their movements after that are uncertain, but by 861 their fleet was again attempting to pass Gibraltar. In the narrow straits they fought a pitched battle with Arab ships equipped with Greek fire, a type of primitive napalm thrown from catapults that could set a ship ablaze in seconds: the Vikings escaped only narrowly. The next year, having raided along the French coasts on the way, Bjorn and Hastein reached their base on the Loire again. They had lost two-thirds of their ships, but had come home fabulously wealthy.

The third and final Viking raid on Spain took place in 866. A few towns in the far north of the country were attacked, but the Arabs quickly ejected the raiders. The effectiveness of the Arab armies and fleets, together with the heavily fortified Moorish towns, the towers of which were defended by missile-throwing war machines that were unfamiliar to the Vikings, meant that the Vikings met with little success in Spain, with the exception of the 859 expedition.

The difficulties of the Gibraltar passage – Bjorn and Hastein were lucky to have got through – prevented the western route to Byzantium from being opened up for trade. Some trade may have developed between the Spanish Moors and the Scandinavians – we know that a Moorish delegation was sent north after the 844 raid – but there is no archaeological evidence to support the presence of such activity. Contacts between the Moors and the *majus* ("fire worshipers", as the Arabs called the Scandinavians) were minimal after the 9th century.

**The Vikings in Brittany**
The Celtic population of Brittany fought strongly to maintain their independence from the domination of their Frankish neighbors in the Carolingian empire. During the 9th century, the region's monasteries and churches fell prey to frequent Viking attack. The raiders followed a well-traveled route westward along the coast from Normandy and round into the mouth of the Loire, where the island monastery of Noirmoutier was taken over as a Viking base from 836. The attacks intensified in the early 10th century, and in 914 the whole region was overrun and occupied by a pagan Norwegian army. Brittany was the last of the Scandinavians' colonizing efforts in Europe, flourishing briefly at a time when most other Vikings had long since settled and become Christian.

# THE CELTIC WORLD

## The Viking impact in Scotland

In common with many other areas of western Europe at the end of the 8th century, Scotland suffered from seasonal raiding by Vikings along its coasts. As in England and Frankia, church property was particularly at risk. Attacks are noted against a number of monastic centers, and the abbey on the tiny island of Iona, founded in 563 by the Irish St Columba, was raided three times in a little over ten years, in 795 (two years after the first recorded Viking attack on Lindisfarne), 802 and 806: the danger was such that some of the community retreated to Kells in Ireland (established in 807) for safety.

Scotland at this time was inhabited by three distinct subgroups of the Celtic peoples, who were distributed throughout northern and western Britain, the Isle of Man and Ireland and had close cultural and linguistic links with the Celtic population of Brittany in northwestern France. The Scots formed the kingdom of Dalriada in the west of Scotland, the British inhabited the kingdom of Strathclyde to the southeast, whilst the Angles of Northumbria (a non-Celtic group) occupied the rest of lowland Scotland. The Picts were scattered throughout eastern and northern Scotland, being most concentrated between the Firth of Forth and the river Dee and in the far north.

The Scots had originally occupied the present area of County Antrim in Northern Ireland, known as Dalriada, and crossed the short sea gap to Argyll in western Scotland some time in the late 5th century. Though some of their strongholds have been identified, they are difficult to distinguish from Pictish forts farther east, and little is known about the Scots archaeologically. The Picts were given their name by the Romans in the 3rd century AD (*pictus* is the Latin term for "painted") when it was applied to all the peoples living north of the Antonine Wall, a substantial turf embankment built by the Romans that ran east–west from the Forth to the Clyde; the name possibly refers to their habit of body-painting or tattooing. To the Romans, the Picts were a problem, and numerous raids across the wall are recorded. Unfortunately the meeting in the 8th century between the Picts and the Vikings is less well documented, but the archaeological record suggests that it might not all have been as violent as is often assumed.

The Picts were farmers, settled in lowland areas. Their seamanship, which so troubled the Romans, was put to the best advantage in the exploitation of fishing catches. Politically, they were a confederation of tribal groups with highly distinctive traditions. Their houses were often built in a cellular form, resembling a clover-leaf or a figure-of-eight. They buried their dead in kerbed cairns of rectangular or circular shape, and have left a visible record of their presence in the form of carved stones, termed symbol stones, embellished with enigmatic animal and human figures. Christianized in the 6th and 7th centuries by missionaries from Ireland, by the 8th century they were raising decorated crosses of Celtic design.

*Right* The rocky coastline of one of the tiny islands of the Inner Hebrides, off the west coast of Scotland. Though the Northern Isles – Orkney and Shetland – attracted the first Viking settlers from Norway during the early 9th century, others soon established themselves in the Hebrides – known to the Norse as "the Southern Islands" – which lay on the Viking sailing route from Norway to Ireland.

*Left* The ruined Broch of Gurness (or Aikerness) on the mainland of Orkney represents the remains of a type of Iron Age fortification that is characteristic of northern Scotland and the islands. The site has revealed evidence not only of subsequent Pictish settlement but also of a Norse presence – including a female Viking grave. In the background, across Eynhallow Sound, is the island of Rousay where a complete Viking cemetery has been excavated at Westness.

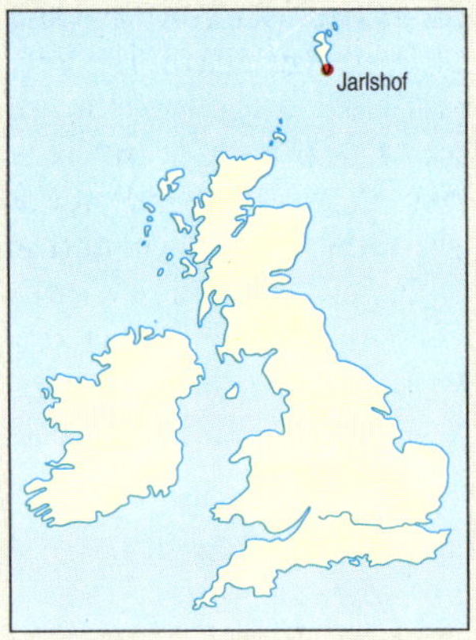


# Jarlshof

The farming settlement of Jarlshof, on the West Voe of Sumburgh at the southern tip of Shetland, is one of the most impressive Viking sites in northern Scotland. Its name, however, owes nothing to its Norse associations: it was invented by the 19th- century novelist Sir Walter Scott in his novel *The Pirate*. Excavations at Jarlshof have revealed layer upon layer of occupation going back some 6,000 years: it was an attractive place to settle, as the Vikings who arrived in the 9th century found. They used the stones of earlier Pictish buildings to build their own farm complex. Jarlshof possessed several other advantages, including an abundant supply of peat for fuel and a quarry that provided soapstone, an important commodity. The sheltered bay offered safe anchorage, and ships could be manhandled over a narrow strip of land nearby to avoid the dangerous waters to the south. The first Viking settlers at Jarlshof probably came from southwest Norway, and the indented coastline must have seemed very similar to the fjords of home.

*Right* A man's head and a small bird scratched on a slate found at Jarlshof. This vivid sketch is possibly the portrait of a real person, thought perhaps to be Pictish.

*Below* The earliest Viking farmstead at Jarlshof, dating from early in the 9th century, consisted of a simple two-room dwelling built of stone and turf – sufficient for the needs of a single family – with a number of outbuildings, including a bath house or sauna, a smithy and storehouse. The byre for the animals was at this time separate from the main building, but in a later rebuilding it was incorporated into the dwelling house – a true longhouse.

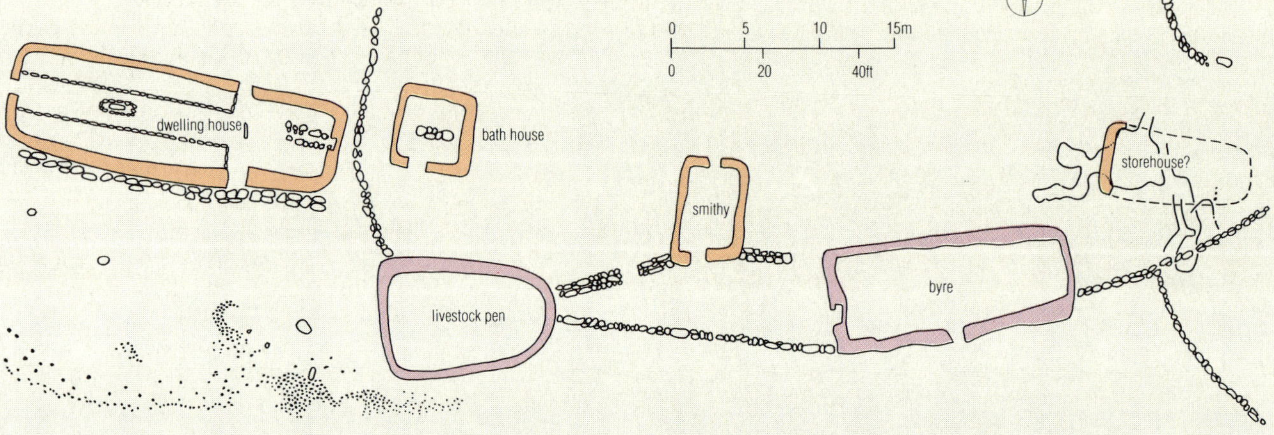


*Right* This aerial view clearly shows the many phases of occupation at Jarlshof, going back thousands of years. Superimposed on the round forms that date from the Bronze and Iron Ages are the long rectangular outlines of the buildings of the Norse settlement. Dominating the site are the medieval ruins to which Sir Walter Scott gave the romantic name of "Jarlshof" or "Earl's mansion".

Many of the everyday objects used by the Picts were unique to them and were sometimes incised with small symbols and ogham inscriptions. A number of manufacturing centers have been identified. At one on the Brough of Birsay in the northwest of Orkney, penannular brooches (that is, in the shape of an almost complete ring) appear to have been made that are similar to those found in the Pictish silver treasure hoard from St Ninian's Isle, Shetland.

Only a small handful of sites have so far produced evidence of the actual meeting between the Picts and Vikings. They present a varied picture. Discoveries at Birsay (including the nearby site of Buckquoy on the Orkney mainland) indicate that Pictish sites here were occupied by the Vikings, who seem to have adopted, and adapted, local styles and may have intermarried with the local population; there seems therefore to have been some sort of coexistence. At Skaill in the east of Orkney, however, a more violent meeting is suggested, and this may also have been the case at the Udal in North Uist in the Outer Hebrides. At other sites (for example, Freswick Links on the east coast of Caithness on the Scottish mainland) there is no evidence of occupation during the crucial centuries around the arrival of the Vikings, though there are signs of Pictish settlements and fields beforehand and of late Norse occupation afterward.

Study of the place-name evidence does however clearly indicate that the Viking takeover of the native areas of occupation was extensive. Place-names including elements such as *-bólstaðr* meaning a farm (as in Kirbister, Orkney; Scrabster, Caithness; or Embo, Sutherland), *-kví*, an enclosure for animals (as in Quoyloo, Orkney) and *-dalr*, a valley (Scorradale in Orkney) are clearly of Scandinavian origin. The distribution of such names is most concentrated in the north. Virtually all the place-names in Shetland, Orkney and northeast Caithness are Scandinavian in origin, and only a few examples of the earlier Pictish names have survived. The most notable of these include the element *papa* ("father"), denoting the presence of monks or priests (as in Papigeo, Caithness). The derivation of the Pentland Firth, the name that was given to the strait separating Orkney from the Scottish mainland by the Vikings, is *Péttlandsfjørðr*, or the Firth of the Picts. Scandinavian place-names are

more generally scattered throughout Sutherland and the Hebrides. It is within all these areas that the bulk of the archaeological evidence for the Vikings in Scotland has been found.

**From raiders to farmers**

That Viking raiders were active in Orkney before any largescale settlement took place there is indicated by a sentence in the *Saga of King (Saint) Olaf*: "It is related that in the days of Harald Finehair [c. 870–c. 940], the king of Norway, the islands of Orkney, which before had been only a resort for Vikings were settled." The date of the actual settlement is, however, open to debate, though an Irish source relates that Rognvald, a Norwegian chieftain who had been driven from home by trouble, became established in Orkney by about 860. While these written references could easily relate to events that took place after the initial settlement, it is certainly difficult to argue, on the basis of the available archaeological evidence, for a date for largescale settlement that is any earlier than the mid 9th century.

The period of true Viking activity (conventionally beginning with the first raids in the 8th century and coming to an end in the late 10th century) in Orkney is a very short episode indeed in the long history of Scandinavian influence there, which lasted until the 15th century. It is not surprising that the evidence is somewhat fugitive for the primary period of actual settlement, which ended, if the *Saga of the Orkney Islanders* (*Orkneyinga saga*) is to be believed, as early as 874 with the establishment of the earldom of Orkney, including Shetland and Caithness. According to its version of events:

*One summer Harald Finehair sailed west to punish the Vikings, as he had grown tired of their depredations, for they harried in Norway during the summer, but spent the winter in Shetland or the Orkneys. He subdued Shetland and the Orkneys...he fought there many battles and annexed the land farther west than any Norwegian king has done since. In one battle fell Ivar, the son of Earl Rognvald. But when King Harald sailed home from the west, as compensation for his son he gave to Earl Rognvald Shetland and the Orkneys. Earl Rognvald, however, gave both lands to his brother Sigurd...*

The saga was of course written at a much later date, but it is clear that the imposition of earls (usually connected to the Norwegian royal house) marked the beginning of an era of direct political control from Norway, though limited raiding by individual war leaders no doubt continued for some time.

Inconclusive as our information is about the early Viking settlement of Orkney, the picture is nevertheless clearer here than it is elsewhere in Scotland. Little is known about the start of settlement in Shetland. However the primary phase of Viking occupation at Jarlshof at the southern tip of Shetland, the most visually impressive of all the Viking sites in Scotland, has been dated by some to about 800, though such an early date in the 9th century is controversial. The farm complex at Jarlshof is part of a multiperiod grouping of stone buildings with functions varying from dwelling house to barns and byres. Another site formerly identified with the early phase of Viking activity in Shetland, Underhoull on Unst, is of greater structural simplicity, and its building plan suggests that it is more probably of Late Norse date. It seems to have been a smaller farm unit than Jarlshof, though economically similar, and it was probably occupied for a shorter time-span.

The dwelling house from the second phase of building at Jarlshof, still in the Viking period, included an integral byre for animals, an element of construction that was brought to Scotland from the more extreme climes of Scandinavia. In later rebuildings, separate buildings again housed the animals, but it is interesting to note that the integral byre – as in a true longhouse – remained in use in the north of Scotland into the last century. From the limited evidence available, the early Viking settlers appear to have practiced a mixed style of farming, raising cattle and sheep with some cultivation of bere (barley) where conditions allowed. Fishing, grew in importance as the settlements developed but was probably limited in extent in these early days. This way of life would not have differed markedly from that followed in Norway at the time. Indeed, the topography of Shetland is quite similar to the Scandinavian homelands: Orkney, however, was a gentler environment, and considerably more attractive to incoming settlers.

In the mainland areas of Scotland, known Viking Age settlement is limited to a handful of sites. The *Saga of the Orkney Islanders* implies that settlement of Caithness took place from Orkney, probably in the 10th century, which may seem surprisingly late. After all, the distance between Orkney and the mainland is small – some 11 kilometers at the nearest point – and the one can be clearly seen from the other. Furthermore, the island of Stroma, whose name means "island in the stream", would have acted as a stepping stone for the move to Caithness. Yet despite extensive excavation, it has not proved possible to identify evidence of early Viking settlement in Caithness; it seems that the *Saga of the Orkney Islanders* may have been accurate after all.

The only other excavated site on the Scottish mainland that has yielded evidence of settlement in the Viking period, though not necessarily of a primary nature, is at Whithorn in the southwest lowlands. Here the buildings are of wood and are clustered tightly together. They differ in plan from others found so far in Scotland, and bear closer similarities to Viking buildings excavated in Dublin, Ireland. The site has yielded debris from the manufacture of antler combs, while a number of cat skulls found there indicate that cat skins were processed to make fur trimmings for garments.

In the Hebrides, excavation at the Udal on North Uist indicates early Viking settlement including a small defensive site (presumably against the native Picts), superimposed on the distinctive Pictish cellular structures that have already been discussed. At Drimore, South Uist, a single fragmentary stone structure has been excavated that is likely to relate to Viking Age activity; it is probable, however, that there are more buildings at the site awaiting investigation. Geographical distance placed the Hebrides outside the political orbit of the earldom of Orkney, and (as with Whithorn) contacts were mainly with the Viking trading centers around the Irish Sea – in Ireland, the Isle of Man, northwest England and Wales – ensuring that there was a greater, or at least more obvious, bias toward trading activities than elsewhere in Scandinavian Scotland.

That settlement in Scotland in the Viking period and beyond was predominantly rural in character cannot be in doubt. To date, no concentrations of population that can be termed urban, such as existed at York in England or at Dublin in Ireland, have been identified. The discovery of buried hoards of silver and gold, together with coins – mostly from England but also of Arabic origin – are indications that a barter economy was in existence here as elsewhere in the Viking world: many hoards contain items of jewelry, in some cases badly damaged or cut, as well as "ring-money" – pieces of plain silver in the form of simple arm-rings that served as units of currency. The largest Viking silver hoards in Scotland have both been recovered from Orkney, from Skaill and Burray. Payment by weight of silver or gold would have been made through merchants who carried portable scales for the purpose. Such items are not common in the British Isles outside the major trading centers, such as York, but a number have been found in pagan graves in the Hebrides, supporting the view that trade was an important activity in the west of Scotland.

**The Scandinavian presence in the Celtic world**
The distribution of Scandinavian place-names in northern and western Scotland and around the Irish Sea shows clearly the areas of greatest Viking influence. The Scottish islands and the Isle of Man have a rich archaeological record, including settlement sites, carved stones, graves and hoards. In contrast to the rural settlement of Scotland, the Vikings in Ireland founded a number of urban trading centers along the coast, the most important of which was at Dublin. They traded extensively with the native Irish, as is demonstrated by the number of Viking Age coin hoards found throughout the country.

*Below* These massive brooches and rings form part of the largest Viking silver hoard known from Scandinavian Scotland: a remarkable 10th-century treasure consisting of over 8 kilograms of prestige ornaments, together with cut-up fragments and a few coins. It was discovered by chance in 1858 in the mouth of a rabbit burrow at Skaill, in Orkney.

Viking settlement
Viking find
carved stone
hoard, ring or brooch
isolated burial
cemetery
Picts tribe or people
land over 200m
concentration of Scandinavian place-names in Scotland and the Isle of Man
Viking influence in Ireland
Howth Scandinavian place-name
area of settlement
scale 1 : 3 850 000
100 km
80 mi
9°
6°
3°
0°
61°
59°
57°
55°
53°
Underhoull
Clibberswick
Sandwick
Papa Stour
Shetland
Jarlshof
Fair Isle
Westness
Tuquoy
Pool
Skaill
Birsay
Gurness
Orkney
Orphir
Brough of Deerness
Kirkwall
Pentland Firth
Robertshaven
Freswick
CAITHNESS
Lewis
Outer Hebrides
North Minch
SUTHERLAND
St Kilda
ROSS
Moray Firth
The Udal
North Uist
Little Minch
Picts
Drimore
South Uist
Isle of Skye
Spey
Barra
Rum
Eigg
Dee
GRAMPIAN MOUNTAINS
DALRIADA
Tay
Tiree
Mull
ATLANTIC OCEAN
Kiloran Bay
Scots
NORTH SEA
Colonsay
Jura
Firth of Forth
Ballinaby
Islay
Britons
Lindisfarne
Firth of Clyde
Isle of Arran
Angles
Rathlin I
STRATHCLYDE
Tyne
Larne (Ulfrecksfjord)
ULSTER
Lough Neagh
Aspatria
Solway Firth
Whithorn
Tees
L Erne
Irish
Gosforth
Strangford
see inset
Isle of Man
CONNAUGHT
Carlingford
IRISH SEA
Lough Derg
Lambay Island
LEINSTER
Leixlip
Howth
Shannon
Dublin
Irish
Wicklow
Arklow
Limerick
Smerwick
MUNSTER
Suir
Wexford
Waterford
see map on p.134
Cork
Saltee Islands
The Skelligs
Dursey I
Isle of Man
4°40'
4°20'
54°20'
54°10'
Kirk Andreas
Vowlan
Lezayre
Ballaugh
Maughold
Kirk Michael
Block Eary
Manx
Injebreck
St Patrick's Isle
Tynwald site of Thing
Castal Ballgawne
Doarlish Cashen
Braaid
Braddan
Malew
Cronk ny Merriu
Cass ny Hawin
Close ny Chollagh
scale 1 : 570 000

Pagan graves provide one of our most accessible sources of information for the Viking period in Scotland. They are generally dated to the late 9th and 10th century and are distinguishable by the presence of grave-goods of Scandinavian origin; in some cases, locally produced items were also included in the assemblage of goods. Such burials have a wide distribution in Scotland, and include the graves of men, women and occasionally children. The evidence suggests that the people buried in these graves were members of early settlement groups rather than warriors killed in raiding skirmishes. For example, the fact that the oval brooches in a woman's grave at Kneep in Lewis, Outer Hebrides, had been repaired, or that brooches of a rather earlier date are included, suggests that these items were heirlooms.

Several rich graves have been excavated in Scotland. Some, such as those at Castletown in Caithness and at Kiloran Bay on Colonsay in the Hebrides, are considered to be isolated burials, but some at least are parts of larger cemetery groups. Two fine boat graves with male burials accompanied by weapons have been excavated at Westness, Orkney, and a grave at Scar on Sanday, also in Orkney, contained a single boat with three occupants and very rich grave-goods, including a rare whalebone plaque. Most of the objects recovered from such burials are normally thought to come from southwest Norway, the traditional homeland area of the early settlers in Scotland. However, a much more northerly origin is suggested for the plaque and a brooch from Scar – perhaps even beyond the Arctic Circle in northern Norway.

As in all parts of the Viking world, the total number of known settlements and graves of Scandinavian origin is grossly inadequate for the number of individuals who must have been settled in Scotland at this time. However, cultural assimilation with the native population makes it increasingly difficult, after the initial period of settlement, to identify Scandinavian burials with any degree of certainty from the grave-goods alone, and clearly there is much that remains to be discovered in this area.

**The Isle of Man: a rich archaeological record**

Located in the middle of the Irish Sea, off the northwest coast of England, the Isle of Man is well placed to attract cultural influences from a wide area. A small island, only about 48 kilometers from north to south by 16 kilometers east to west, its upland interior is crowned by Snaefell, meaning "snow mountain" – the name given it by the Vikings. A large coastal plain lies to the north, and a relatively fertile coastal fringe surrounds the island as a whole. Good agricultural land and an abundance of natural harbors undoubtedly served to attract Viking adventurers, added to which were a number of major monastic centers such as Maughold, though these are unlikely to have been as wealthy as those in Ireland or England. The documentary record, however, is silent on early Scandinavian activity in Man – a Viking attack on *Inis Patraic* (Patrick's Island) mentioned in the *Irish Annals* of 798 is now taken to refer to the island of that name in Dublin Bay rather than St Patrick's Isle, Peel, off the west coast of the Isle of Man. Nevertheless, the material evidence of Viking occupation in the island is very extensive; it is particularly rich in archaeological sites, including settlements, burials, carved stones and silver hoards.

There can be no doubt that the pre-Viking Celtic

*Left* The only Viking cemetery to have been fully excavated in Scotland is at Westness on Rousay, in Orkney. It included the richest female grave known from Scotland, as well as two male boat burials: in the one shown here the prow and stern were packed with stones to create a central chamber for the body. Amongst other pagan graves at Westness was one of a woman (*bottom left*). Her skull shows signs of having been trepanned; she was buried with a comb below her right arm and spindle whorls by her side, as well as with a sickle and a bronze brooch.

*Right* The Viking settlers on the Isle of Man were converted to Christianity during the 10th century and adopted the use of memorial stones. This fragmentary cross-slab from Andreas is carved with a pagan scene on one face, counterbalanced by a Christian scene on the other. Here is represented the triumph of Christ over the Devil: a bearded figure holding a cross and book tramples a knotted snake underfoot.

population of the island was Christian. This is clear from the number of surviving carved stones with Christian symbols including a particularly fine crucifixion slab from the Calf of Man. Additionally, a network of Christian sites – small chapels or keeills – has been identified on the island, several of them with associated cemeteries of stone lintel graves. At Balladoole, a Viking boat burial is located immediately on top of an earlier cemetery. However, evidence of pre-Viking domestic settlement is confined to a few sites only. Some Viking buildings were constructed within the confines of already existing promontory enclosures, such as at Cronk ny Merriu. At other Viking sites – for example, at the Braaid or Close ny Chollagh – the distinctive circular structures of pre-Viking settlements have been identified.

Though it has been argued that some elements of earlier settlements continued in use into the Viking period, the overwhelming preponderance of Norse place-names suggests that once again, as in northern Scotland, the local population was almost totally submerged by the Viking incursion. However, it is possible that many of these names are of a later date than the Viking Age, and follow a naming tradition that had been established by the Scandinavians. Some place-name elements from the earliest phases of Viking activity, such as *-setr* and *-bólstaðr*, which are widely found in Scotland, are rare in Man, and it has been pointed out that *-setr*, meaning a shieling, an upland summer pasture, could be more commonly represented in Man by the Gaelic element *-ærgi* (as in Block Eary). The distribution of Scandinavian topographical names is widespread through the island; for example, the flat northern plain is still known as the Ayres, from the Norse meaning "a gravelly flat expanse". Place-names ending in *-bý* (as at Jurby or Sulby) are also commonly found.

The known Viking Age settlements on Man are varied in form. Cronk ny Merriu, as already mentioned, reuses an Iron Age promontory site; it is visible as a

*Right* The oval of stones marks the outline of an important Viking boat burial at Balladoole in the Isle of Man; it is on the site of an early Christian graveyard that lies within an Iron Age enclosure. The vessel was about 11 meters long and contained the skeletons of both a man and a woman. However, the grave-goods - including stirrups and spurs – showed this to have been a male burial , and the accompanying female body may provide evidence of the rite of suttee, or female sacrifice – possibly a slave.

*Left* The small promontory fort at Cronk ny Merriu, Isle of Man, overlooking the entrance to Port Grenaugh, was first constructed in the Iron Age. However, this aerial view shows the excavated remains of the later Norse house that was built behind the massive rampart – a subrectangular building with three doorways, side benches and a central hearth.

small, almost rectangular building containing benches and a central fireplace: Close ny Chollagh, Cass ny Hawin and Vowlan are similar sites. Farther inland, sites of greater complexity have been identified. At Doarlish Cashen, some 210 meters above sea level, the grass-covered foundations of three buildings grouped around a yard, have been found. The settlement was initially identified during a survey for potential shieling or transhumance sites, and the fact that an area of marginal agricultural land should have several structures visible was of great interest; excavation suggested that at least two of the buildings were likely to be Norse in date. One small dwelling of almost rectangular form was found to be a small Norse-type farmstead of a kind that is characteristic of the Isle of Man. Though badly damaged, the threshold stones remained in place to show that there were doors in the two long walls, with a possible third in one of the short walls. There was a large area for the fire, the debris of which was scattered over most of the floor. Traces of a bench to each side of the hearth completed the interior arrangements of this small upland house, which had its yard to one side. Nearby, a small corn-drying kiln was excavated, and the other buildings, which were only surveyed, were suggestive of a larger farming complex. A funnel-like entrance to the yard could have assisted the management of cattle, but the presence of the corn-drying kiln suggests that livestock farming was not the only activity. No doubt kilns existed at other settlements on the island, but no other has yet been discovered.

It has been argued that the small size of the dwelling at Doarlish Cashen, which measured only 7 by 3 meters, indicates that it was a poor settlement, and indeed the lack of objects recovered during excavation does little to alter this view. Much larger buildings are found lower down in the valleys where there was probably more pasture and a less extreme climate to contend with: for example, one at the Braaid measures 21 by 9 meters, and the house at Cass ny Hawin is also quite sizable – about 10 by 4.5 meters. The site at the Braaid is somewhat controversial, for it has dwellings in the form of a substantial stone roundhouse (probably of native Manx construction) with two adjacent rectangular ones. Use has been made of huge slabs, far larger than those seen at other sites on Man, and this, coupled with the overall massive scale of the complex, suggests that it may have been something more substantial than simply a farmstead.

The pagan burial evidence from Man is of great interest. Boat graves such as those at Balladoole and Knock y Doonee are reminiscent of those at Westness and Scar in Orkney. The vessels are about 5 to 6 meters in length and usually contain male burials,

*Right* An abandoned Norse farmstead at the Braaid, Isle of Man, comprises a large bow-sided dwelling and a rectangular building of massive construction. This may have been a second house, but was more probably a large stable or byre. The adjacent roundhouse, in the native Manx style, was presumably in use when the Vikings took over. Unfortunately, excavation revealed nothing, apart from some constructional details, to help in the interpretation of this site.

probably of Vikings who arrived in the first phase of the island's settlement. The positioning of the grave mounds, usually in a prominent location in sight of the sea and overlooking good farming land, may indicate the location of the original farming settlements. Spears and swords are commonly found in these burials; less usual was the inclusion of a female companion, but evidence of the rite of suttee, known to have been practiced elsewhere in the Viking world, is found in two Manx burials, at Balladoole and, most poignantly, at Ballateare, where the young woman had a badly slashed skull. She may have been a slave, but the archaeological record only reveals that she was buried without goods in the upper part of a mound erected over her master's grave.

Excavations on St Patrick's Isle, Peel, revealed the remains of a cemetery that includes six pagan Viking graves. Some of them are cut through early Christian stone slab graves, suggesting the continuing use of a pre-Viking cemetery. Among the Viking burials is the so-called "Pagan Lady of Peel", discovered in a stone slab grave surrounded by a wide variety of grave-goods, including a cooking spit, comb and beads. The significance of this find lies in the fact that it is the only Norse female burial yet found on the island and represents a rich addition to the corpus of graves from this period in the British Isles as a whole. Little is known about the position of women, but the nature of the grave-goods indicates that the "Pagan Lady of Peel" was someone of considerable importance, perhaps even a local landowner in her own right. The number of rich male graves on Man suggests very strongly that there was a social hierarchy of influential landowners, each with an attendant household. There has been considerable debate about the way land was divided in the island in the Viking period. The present parish system is thought to follow the Norse land divisions, and these may in part have been based on an earlier system.

The landowners were probably the people who commissioned some of the carved standing crosses and other stones that are one of the more significant elements of the Norse legacy in the Isle of Man. Today some of these stones are found inside the local parish churches, having been brought there from the surrounding area at some time in the past. Many are pre-Viking in date and are worked with typically Celtic, elaborate ring-headed cross motifs. However, a larger number of Viking Age carved stones survive, chiefly from the 10th century.

The remarkable skill of the craftsmen, combined with the quality of the local slate and the rich elements of imagery that are portrayed, make these stones a unique record for the period. The inclusion of motifs from Norse mythology, such as the dragonslaying from the Sigurd legend, on an elaborately carved Christian cross highlights the degree of cultural exchange that took place with the native population. Christianity had probably become the dominant religion of the Scandinavian settlers by the middle of the 10th century, but some of those who adopted the outward forms of Christianity would have found it hard to give up the familiar stories of the gods they had brought with them from the homeland (just as grave-goods may have continued to be included in the burials of nominal Christians). It may even be that elements of paganism were consciously adapted to convey parts of the Christian message – the dragon being associated with Satan, for example. Whatever the case, pagan themes continued to hold a central

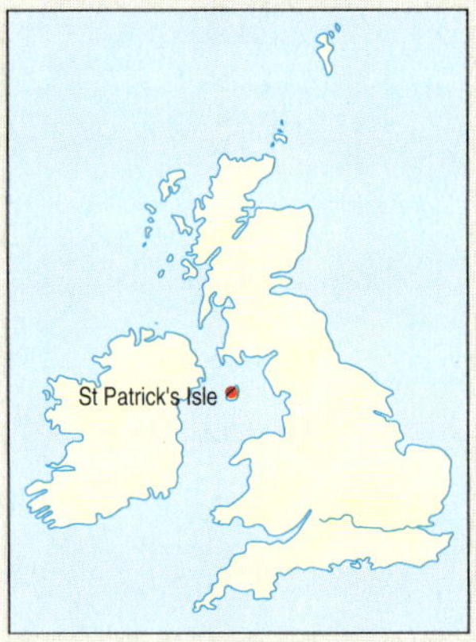


# St Patrick's Isle

St Patrick's Isle, or Holmepatrick, at Peel is a tidal islet that controls the entrance to the only sheltered harbor on the west coast of the Isle of Man – the site of Peel Castle. Occupied since prehistoric times, in the late Norse period it became the site of the cathedral of the Norse diocese of Sodor and Man, under the archbishopric of Nidaros (later Trondheim) in Norway. The diocese, like the Kingdom of Man and the Isles (established in the 11th century), embraced all the Hebrides – the *Suðreyjar* or Sudreys. Recent excavations on this major archaeological site have resulted in numerous discoveries of all periods, including an early Christian cemetery that contained several well-furnished Viking Age burials.

*Below* Amongst the Viking Age burials excavated in the Christian cemetery was the only Norse female grave to have been found in the Isle of Man. The fully-dressed body had been laid out in a slab-lined grave into which were put a wide selection of grave-goods denoting the high-status of the so-called "Pagan Lady of Peel".

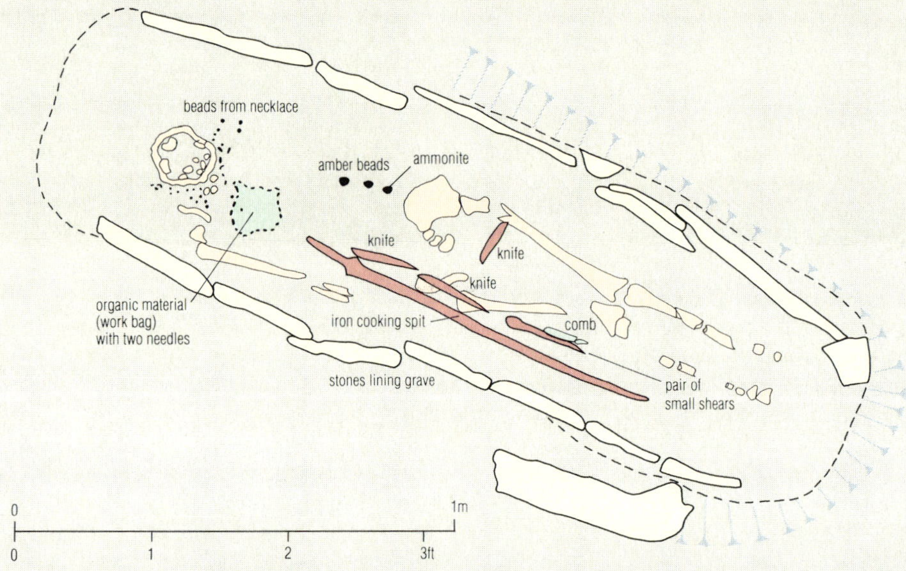

*Right* For a short period during the 11th century, silver pennies appear to have been struck for the rulers of Man, in imitation of the contemporary Hiberno-Norse coinage of Dublin. The mint must have been linked to the seat of political power – then most probably located on St Patrick's Isle at Peel.

*Below* A spectacular necklace containing over 60 glass and amber beads was around the neck of the "Pagan Lady" when she was placed in her grave. Beside her was laid an iron cooking spit, a goose wing and a bunch of herbs, as well as her workbag, which held a pair of needles. She was equipped with her comb and household shears, perhaps hanging together from a belt. There were also two knives, one of which has a silver inlaid handle.

*Right* Within the walls of Peel Castle are situated the roofless Gothic remains of St German's cathedral, built in the 12th century. The early Christian cemetery was discovered on its north side; it continued in use throughout the Viking Age into the medieval period. The Irish-style round tower and its adjacent church were built in the 10th or 11th century.

place in the Norse culture of the Isle of Man, producing some striking juxtapositions. On a slab at Andreas, for example, a depiction of Odin, shown with spear and raven and his foot in the jaws of the wolf Fenrir, is counterbalanced by a Christian figure, possibly a cleric, holding a book and a cross.

In several cases, runic inscriptions are an element of the crosses: on one of the earlier examples a man named Gaut boasts that he "made this [presumably the cross] and all in Man". It is likely that some inscriptions were added later to the carvings. Wherever they appear, they provide a direct link between the modern reader and both the carver and the literate Scandinavian settler who was his patron.

Some 20 hoards of Viking Age silver have been recovered from the Isle of Man. Most combine coinage with ornaments. The period when they were buried stretches from the early 10th (more certainly from 960) to the late 11th century. Periods of warfare and threats of attack from other Vikings in the Irish Sea area – at times in the 10th century the island came under the direct influence of the Dublin-based Norse – or even just from greedy neighbors, must have led people to take the precautionary measure of hiding their valuables. The hoards recovered today are of course the ones that were never retrieved, suggesting that all too often there was a violent and tragic outcome to events.

**Wales: a staging post for trade**

Some of the Viking raiders who were active in the Irish Sea area from the 790s onward turned aside to attack Wales, particularly Anglesey and along the north coast, and around the southwest coast into the Bristol Channel. At this time, the native Celtic peoples of Wales were divided into several kingdoms, including Powys, Gwynedd and Dyfed. They were predominantly farmers: no towns or similar concentrations of population have been identified, and only a small number of pre-urban centers have been distinguished. Monasteries, however, housed large numbers of people; as in Ireland, they possessed extensive agricultural estates, as well as being centers of scholarship and craftsmanship. Their wealth would have acted as honey-pots to the Vikings, and there is evidence that some of the large monasteries such as Carmarthen,

Llancarfan, St David's, Caldey and Llantwit had been burned and plundered.

Asser, the Welsh-born monk and biographer of King Alfred the Great, tells us that in 878 a Viking force over-wintered in Dyfed in the southwest, probably for the first time. This was the beginning of a major series of raids against Wales over the next few decades. In 914 a great naval force led by two Scandinavian earls sailed north from Brittany to ravage the west coast; there were unsuccessful attempts to head inland. During the following 40 years there was a respite, for the Welsh had a strong leader in Hywel Dda (Howell the Good) of Gwynedd, and the Vikings kept away until after his death in 950. By 980, however, the Viking menace had increased in violence: the cathedral at St David's was sacked four times between 982 and 989, and the raids continued beyond the end of the century despite attempts to keep the Scandinavians at bay by paying *Danegeld*. Even in the late 11th century St David's was subjected to a spate of attacks from Dublin-based Viking fleets.

The significance of Wales to the Scandinavians lay in its geographical position – an integral part of the western searoute, close to Ireland and the Isle of Man and providing a staging post on trading routes to centers of Scandinavian domination in England. It may be no coincidence that the largest silver hoard, probably associated with merchant activity, found in Wales came from near Llandudno, within easy reach of Viking settlements in northwest England. The distribution of other coin and silver hoards is generally coastal. Amongst the earliest is one from Bangor, deposited about 925, which includes Arabic coins. Isolated single coins are more scattered in their distribution and their presence is perhaps an indication of commercial activity. The *Irish Annals* suggest that Viking merchants from Dublin may have traded in Welsh slaves, horses and probably honey and wheat in the 10th and 11th centuries, very likely in exchange for Irish furs, hides and coarse woolen cloth.

There must have been some actual settlement by the Vikings in Wales, even if only confined to the coastal areas, but other than place-name evidence, there are no records of this. The Scandinavian influence is particularly felt on place-names in southwest Wales: Colby for example combines a personal name with the settlement element *-bý*, and Scollock, Milton and Fishguard also include Scandinavian elements. Given the concentration of place-names in these areas, it seems likely that coastal trading centers were established, perhaps at Milford Haven and Swansea, with some inland rural settlement in Pembrokeshire. The names of islands and navigation points along the north coast of the Bristol Channel are also clearly Norse in origin: Lundy (meaning "puffin island"), Flat Holm, Steepholm and Skokholm (in which the element *holm* stands for a small island) and Skomer and Caldy Islands all fall into this category. North Wales has fewer Norse names, though Bardsey Island, Great Ormes Head, Priestholm, and even Anglesey (Ongul's Isle) are Scandinavian in origin. Anglesey, lying off the north coast, would have been a particularly vulnerable target for attack, prey to the Vikings based in the Isle of Man as well as those in Ireland, and so the recovery of a hoard of Viking silver arm-rings and a possible Viking grave is no surprise.

Wales contains a number of finely-worked stone crosses whose decorative motifs reflect the way Celtic and Scandinavian influences merged around the Irish Sea. Particularly fine examples are found at Penmon (Anglesey) and Nevern and Carew (Pembrokeshire). Even in the pre-Viking period, crucifixion slabs carved in Wales were strongly influenced by Irish patterns. In the Viking Age examples, panels of elaborate interlace patterns, reminiscent of styles seen in the Isle of Man and elsewhere with all the available areas around filled with carved motifs, are combined with the ring-headed cross so commonly found in the Celtic areas around the Irish Sea.

### The Vikings in Ireland

According to the *Irish Annals*, the first Viking raid along the Irish coast took place in 795 at a place called *Rechru*. This is now most usually identified as Rathlin Island lying just off the northeastern tip of Ireland. Intermittent attacks followed until the 820s, when the scale of attacks was increased. Movement inland is recorded from about 830, the first overwintering is reported on Lough Neagh in 839, and the first permanent settlements (known as *longphorts*) were established in 841 at Dublin and possibly at Annagassan, Dundalk Bay.

There was plenty to attract the Vikings to Ireland. The greatest concentrations of settlements were the large monastic complexes, sometimes termed "cities", which were located amidst a landscape of scattered farms. Other major centers of wealth were located in the crannogs – man-made islands in marshy or wet areas. One of these, at Lagore, is mentioned in the *Annals* as being a royal center that suffered catastrophic damage at the hands of the Vikings in 934. Though the primary economic activity of the Celtic population was farming, finds of imported goods such as pottery from western France discovered on sites ranging from royal centers such as Lagore or Knowth to the more humble ring-forts, or enclosed homesteads, that were the predominant type of rural settlement, show that Ireland was part of an extensive trading network. On a number of sites, the discovery of such things as debris from antler working, tools for smithing, crucibles and molds for working precious metals and glass-making equipment provide evidence of a variety of manufacturing activities.

The most important centers of craft production, however, were the monastic "cities". These were extensive settlements within large enclosures, with multiple churches to serve the religious and lay populations of the monastic community. From the mid 10th century, stone towers became a distinguishing feature of these sites. They served as belfries, but some people have suggested that they were also built as defenses in response to the Viking raids. Housed within the monasteries were the craftsmen – stonecarvers, ornamental metalworkers, glassworkers and scribes producing illuminated manuscripts – whose artifacts are the most lasting legacy of the rich culture of the early medieval Irish church. These beautiful items, intended both for monastic consumption but also to meet the demands of local patrons, brought the inevitable attentions of the Vikings. The monastic centers contrasted sharply with the small, austere hermitages that were also typical of the Celtic church in Ireland and were found mostly on the rocky west coast (as at Church Island or Skellig Michael, Co Kerry) but even these were not immune from Viking attack. It is clear that many precious church objects were removed from Ireland to Scandinavia during the raiding period, but the scale of this removal is difficult to gauge and, indeed, our view is colored by the fact that the written accounts of the raids are provided by churchmen.

*Above* This house-shaped shrine – with an unknown Norwegian provenance – is of 8th-century Irish type, though the style of decoration suggests that it was most probably made in the Scottish-Pictish area. It appears never to have been buried, whilst its contents demonstrate that it was serving its original function as a reliquary, or container for sacred relics, in the Middle Ages. A runic inscription on the base, stating that "Rannveig owns this casket", shows it to have been in Norse hands by about 1000.

Until comparatively recently our understanding of the Vikings in Ireland was mostly based on the discovery of isolated finds, together with scattered literary references. From these we know that the Vikings established the first true towns in Ireland, at Waterford, Wexford, Limerick, Cork and Dublin. These places served as trading posts on the long sea route that linked the Scandinavian homelands and their western colonies with westernn Europe and the Mediterranean. Here goods such as slaves and wolf hounds were gathered for export in exchange for silver. The rulers of the Viking towns therefore looked to the sea rather than the land for their livelihood, which was got by raiding and trading around the Irish Sea. Close relations were maintained with the Scandinavians of Man and the Hebrides.

The Viking occupation of Ireland was therefore different in kind from that of the other Scandinavian colonies. There appears to have been little rural settlement. It is not impossible that Norse settlers in the countryside lived in buildings of adapted local type. This means that they would be identifiable in the archaeological record only by the recovery of Viking artifacts. However, such finds can also be taken as evidence of cultural contact between the town-dwelling Vikings and the local inhabitants, so it is difficult to attribute rural settlements to either Vikings or Irish with any certainty. The distribution of Viking pagan graves may be an indication of how far Scandinavian influence spread outside the towns in the early days of the settlement. Apart from major cemeteries at Kilmainham-Islandbridge near Dublin, however, graves are present only as isolated finds. A mound burial at Donnybrook, also by Dublin, and a possible boat burial at Ballywillin, Co Antrim, represent single examples of traditions that are seen much more widely elsewhere in the Irish Sea region, and indeed in the larger Viking world.

Outside the towns, Viking influence seems to have been restricted to the immediate hinterlands, where there must have been considerable interaction with the rural population who supplied the townspeople with fresh produce. In Dublin, for example, cattle would be

driven into town from the countryside, and crops would be exchanged for manufactured items. The townspeople also relied on the surrounding area to provide timber for building and raw materials for craft manufacture, so the interchange must have been wide-ranging. Some 120 Viking Age coin, silver and gold hoards are known in Ireland. These are indicative of great wealth. Of the known hoards, 80 consist only of coins; many of these have been found on native Irish sites, and consequently support the view that economic relations existed between the Vikings and the Irish. The Irish lacked a coinage before the 12th

*Right* Viking burials at Kilmainham and Islandbridge, upriver from the site of 10th-century Dublin, resulted from the establishment of a *longphort* on the Liffey in the mid-9th century, most probably on the site of an Irish monastery. This contemporary painting illustrates some of the grave-goods dug up there in the 19th century, including several swords with ornamented hilts, spear- and ax-heads, shield bosses and women's bronze brooches, together with some gaming pieces.

# Dublin

The excavations that have been carried out in the Wood Quay area of Dublin, on a site between the river Liffey and Christchurch cathedral, since 1960 have uncovered evidence of the Viking Age town that is of exceptional quality because of the waterlogged nature of the ground. It has been possible to identify some of the wooden dwelling houses of the Viking inhabitants, which stood within fenced plots, together with ancillary buildings – latrines, byres, animal pens, workshops and storehouses. The swampy nature of the ground was clearly always a problem: broken furniture and doors were laid down as duckboards in the streets between the plots, which must have been trampled by the cattle brought in from the surrounding countryside. Being made of wood, the houses had to be rebuilt every 10 to 20 years, and because the property boundaries were unchanging the new houses were built on the same site as the old: turf was laid down on the earlier foundations to provide a firm footing. As a result, there are several successive layers of habitation within the Viking Age period of settlement (c.920–1100) – as many as 13 in Fishamble Street alone. Furthermore, when the Anglo-Normans reclaimed land at the river's edge in the 13th century, they used the domestic debris of the Viking settlement as infilling. The careful examination of all this material has provided a rare insight into the everyday life of the Viking Age town, providing evidence of different activities such as wood- and bone-carving and leatherworking. The wealthiest members of the Viking community, identifiable by their larger houses and rich artifacts, appear to have lived in the area of the cathedral, on higher ground that would not have been susceptible to flooding.

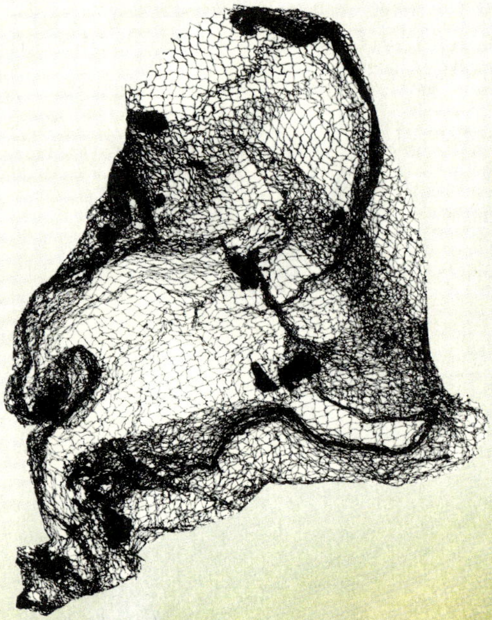

*Below* A silk hairnet, found in Fishamble Street, is evidence of Viking Dublin's far-reaching contacts – the yarn, and probably the method of manufacture, suggest an origin in Byzantium or farther east.

*Left* A coin of Sihtric Silkbeard, the ruler of Viking Dublin who established the first mint in Ireland about 997.

*Below* A reconstruction of a street in 10th-century Dublin, based on the excavations in Fishamble Street. It shows a series of adjacent tapering plots, each with a wooden dwelling and, in some cases, outbuildings. The plots, separated by wattle fencing, follow the natural lie of the land.

*Left* Waterlogged conditions have ensured the survival of many wooden items such as turned vessels and staves for barrels. This crook, found in Fishamble Street, is more elaborate. It is very finely worked in a distinctive Dublin version of the Ringerike style of decoration current in 11th-century Scandinavia.

*Above* Archaeologists at work at the eastern end of Dublin's modern High Street – one of several Viking Age sites that have been excavated in Dublin: Wood Quay and Fishamble Street lie nearby. The well-preserved remains of an 11th-century timbered footpath, similar to ones that have been found in Scandinavia and elsewhere in the Viking world, have been uncovered, and the picture shows very clearly the heavy, badly drained clay soils that have preserved so much of Viking Age Dublin. This part of the settlement appears to have been where the craftworking area of the town was located, and many artefacts were discovered here.

*Left* A fragment of bone found in High Street, elaborately carved in the Ringerike style as a craftsman's practice piece.

century and the Dublin-based Vikings only started minting their own coins in about 997. Consequently, until the end of the 10th century the coin hoards consist of imported coins from English, Frankish and Arabic sources.

There are other indications of cultural interchange with the local Irish population. The distinctive ringed pin of the Irish was adopted and manufactured on a large scale by the Vikings. Examples have been found as far north as Iceland and as far west as Newfoundland. Brooches of penannular form, beautifully executed in Ireland, were also copied, often in much cruder variants, by the Scandinavians. The Vikings found much else to covet in Ireland, especially the fine metalwork that was brought back to Norway from the early raids. In the later Viking period, Scandinavian styles of decoration such as the Ringerike and Urnes were modified in Irish workshops. A sword cross-piece from Smalls reef, southwest Wales, for example has decoration in the distinctive Irish Urnes style, and the Ringerike style can be seen on wooden artifacts from Dublin. Though carved stone decoration shows signs of modified Hiberno-Norse elements, this style is not as common in Ireland as on the other side of the Irish Sea. It may be, though, that wood was more favored as a medium for carving than stone, and so examples have not survived. Isolated runic inscriptions on stone, such as one known at Beginish in the west of Ireland, must suffice to fill this gap in the material evidence.

**The Vikings of Dublin**

Much more is known about Dublin than about any of the other towns of Viking Age Ireland, if only for the reason that it is here that the bulk of archaeological investigation has been carried out. The Vikings were attracted to the site by its location at an important ford on the river Liffey, which formed the boundary between the kingdoms of Brega and Leinster. In 841 they established a *longphort* at a site that has not been located, but which could well have been that of the Irish monastery at Kilmainham. No occupation levels earlier than the 10th century have been discovered in the extensive excavations undertaken in Dublin since the 1960s. We know that the Norse were temporarily expelled from their first settlement in Dublin in 902, and that many of them settled in northwest England and the Isle of Man. They returned in about 917, and it is clear that Dublin was then refounded on the site that it still occupies today.

During the 10th century Dublin grew rich on trade with other centers around the Irish Sea, such as Chester and Bristol. Excavations have revealed a number of well-preserved wooden buildings from the Viking Age. Many of these housed the workshops where blacksmiths, leather-workers, comb-makers and wood-carvers plied their trade. The wealthy rulers of Dublin took advantage of the uncertain situation in England at this time to extend their power across the Irish Sea, claiming authority over the Isle of Man and seizing control of the Kingdom of York from the Danes. This they held until 952. In 980, however, they were defeated by the Irish of Munster at the battle of Tara, and a large tribute was exacted from the town. Subsequent unrest amongst the Norse in Ireland led the Waterford Vikings to assume control over Dublin for a brief time in 994 and the latter was never again able to regain the pre-eminent position it had previously enjoyed among the Irish Norse.

# THE NORTH ATLANTIC

As we have seen, a number of the Vikings who left Norway to raid along the coasts of Scotland and Ireland remained there as farmers. Soon some of them – or some of the second generation of settlers – were looking west again, this time to destinations in the North Atlantic: the Faeroe Islands, Iceland and, finally, Greenland and North America. Others made the journey directly west from Norway. Many would argue that chance played the most significant role in the Vikings' westward migration, but from this distance in time it is hard to know how far necessity and purpose, rather than just curiosity and the prevailing winds, drove them on in the search of new lands.

There can be no doubt that the voyages were risky. It was necessary to overcome the natural hazards of the North Atlantic, such as icebergs, and not surprisingly we hear of ships and their crews being lost en route. We know little about the Vikings' methods of navigation. In coastal waters they would have used known landmarks to steer by, and out of sight of land they probably judged their position in relation to the home port or point of destination by using some sort of standard measure, such as a calibrated stick or handspan, to estimate the apparent height above the horizon of the sun by day or the Pole Star at night ("latitude sailing"). A body of knowledge about routes, sailing times between known points, tides, winds and currents would have gradually been built up to be passed on orally from generation to generation, but this would not have been available to the first adventurers who crossed the unknown waters of the North Atlantic. The saga writers were in no doubt about their courage, whereas later successful landings went unrecorded as commonplace events.

The significant factor about the westward movement across the North Atlantic, as opposed to the Viking voyages farther south, is that the prime motivation appears to have been settlement – land-taking and exploitation – rather than raiding and looting. These new lands were unpopulated. This affects the way we view these events today. Unlike the Viking incursion into western Europe, where contemporary chroniclers from amongst the local populations were on hand to describe their acts of piracy, there was no one to provide a first-hand account of what happened in the North Atlantic. Our documentary information is supplied chiefly by the sagas, which – as has already been noted in earlier chapters – were written down long after the event, and most likely after the story had been embellished in transmission.

For all the sagas' celebration of Viking prowess, Norse sailors were not the first people to have reached the islands of the North Atlantic. The Irish monk Dicuil, writing in France in 825, tells us in the *Book of the Measurement of the Earth (Liber de Orbis Mensura Terrae)* that from about the year 700 it was the custom for certain intrepid monks to cross the uncharted waters in their frail vessels (probably simple leather boats known as currachs), settling on whatever uninhabited island they reached first and building

*Below* The midnight sun in Iceland is testimony to its northern latitude, just touching the Arctic Circle. The first inhabitants of this remote volcanic island in the North Atlantic were Irish hermits in the 8th century, but the arrival of Norse settlers in the 9th century caused them to flee. By the mid-10th century Iceland was fully populated and organized as an independent republic. The first farmers had to bring their own livestock, as Iceland's isolation is such that they encountered only one native mammal – the polar fox – though seabirds (and their eggs) were numerous, providing them with an important source of food.

themselves simple cells in which to live as hermits, devoting their lives to God. The Vikings who encountered these monks in the Faeroe Islands, and in Iceland as well, called them the *papar* – the fathers. As befitted their lifestyle, the hermits apparently fled the incomers; Ari Thorgilsson tells us they left behind them books, bells and croziers. The evidence of their occupation, however, is scanty. Beyond the writings of Dicuil and Ari, there are only a few place-name survivals and fugitive archaeological remains.

### The islands of sheep

It is Dicuil who provides us with our first historical glimpse of the Faeroe Islands, a cluster of steep-sided islands lying in the North Atlantic midway between Shetland and Iceland:

*There are many other islands in the ocean to the north of Britain which can be reached from the northernmost British Isles in two days' and nights' sailing, with full sails and an undropped fair wind... A certain holy man informed me that... he came to land on one of them. On these islands hermits who have sailed out from Scotia* [Ireland] *have lived for roughly a hundred years. But... now because of Norse pirates they are empty of anchorites, but full of innumerable sheep and a great many seafowl.*

From this we learn that there were sheep on the islands even before the arrival of the Norse in about 860–870; it is consequently not surprising that the settlers named the islands *Færeyjar*, or Sheep Islands.

It is left to the *Saga of the Faeroe Islanders* (*Færeyinga saga*) to provide us with the identity of the initial Norse settler:

*There was a man called Grim Kamban; he was the first man to settle in the Faeroes. But in the days of King Harald Finehair a great number of people fled* [from Norway] *because of his tyranny. Some settled in the Faeroes and made their home there, while others went to other uninhabited countries.*

Despite the saga writer's assertion that he was a Norwegian, the Celtic name form Kamban suggests that Grim may have been a Scandinavian settler from the Hebrides or Ireland.

A number of simply incised cross-slabs, as found for example on Skúvoy, together with a scattering of place-names containing the element *papa*, have traditionally been taken as supporting Dicuil's account of the presence of Irish monks in the islands. However, no associated archaeological finds have been made at the sites of the *papa* names, and the simple form of the incised crosses does not in itself prove their early date. More recently it has been argued that pollen samples from the island of Mykines show that cereals were being cultivated on the island in the 7th century. However, the dating of the pollen samples has been disputed. If all three elements of information could be established without doubt, the evidence to support Dicuil's account would be persuasive indeed. But in the light of our present understanding of the archaeological record, it is not possible to argue the case

*Above* The Faeroe Islands, approximately midway between Shetland and Iceland, must have presented a bleak prospect to the first Norse settlers in the 9th century. Sheer volcanic cliffs rise steeply from the sea, and the islands are naturally treeless due to the strong westerly winds and frequent storms.

**Viking Age settlement in the Faeroe Islands**
In the Viking Age, as today, settlement was restricted in the main to the islands' narrow coastal fringes. However, the distribution of the place-name element *ærgi* – meaning a shieling or upland grazing – strongly suggests that some of the farming population moved to temporary shelters in the summer when the flocks of sheep were taken to upland pastures. A comparatively large number of Viking Age settlements – both individual farmsteads and groups of dwellings – have been investigated, including in recent years some upland farms, but – except for Toftanes – they are generally poor in finds from this period. Only two groups of pagan Viking Age graves are known.

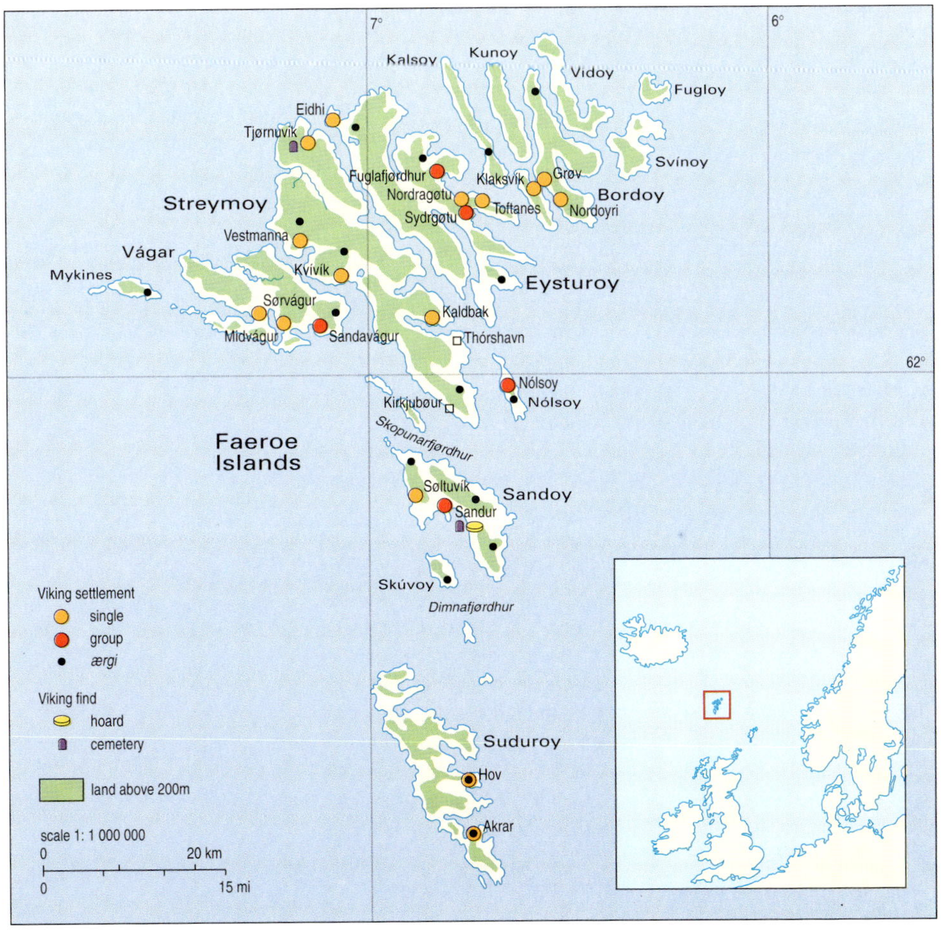


for any settlement traces on the Faeroes earlier than those of the Viking era.

The *Saga of the Faeroe Islanders* tells us the names of the individual colonizers as well as the places where they settled on the various islands: for example, we know that a certain Thrand had his homestead at Götu on Eysturoy. Though the reliability of the source as a whole is now questioned, and it cannot be used as an accurate guide to the early settlement phase, or *landnám*, of the Faeroe Islands, the locations named in it have been plotted to reveal striking similarities to modern settlement patterns. However, given that the steep gradients of the islands, which rise abruptly from the sea, restrict the area of land available for building, this is perhaps unsurprising. While this correspondence of settlement areas assists the archaeologist in the identification of sites, it can also create problems, for few people are keen to have excavations carried out within their houses or gardens.

Some 16 Norse sites have been excavated in the Faeroes, but few have produced artifacts dating from the initial Viking settlement; the bulk of the datable objects recovered belong to the 11th century. The earliest evidence of settlement, from the last years of the 10th century, have been found at Kvívík and Fuglafjørdhur. However, part of the site at Kvívík, built close to the shore, has been eroded away by wave action, and it has been suggested that some earlier settlement sites may have been destroyed in this way.

The farmstead at Kvívík is the best preserved of the Viking Age remains to be seen in the Faeroes today. It consists of a substantial subrectangular dwelling house with thick stone and turf walls standing to a height of about 1 meter and contains a large central hearth and ember pit. Though one end of this structure has been lost to the sea, a side entrance remains in one of the surviving walls, leading out directly to an adjacent stream. Immediately alongside this building is a byre, also now incomplete because of sea erosion, which must have held about a dozen cattle in stone stalls. Traces of the turf sods and birch bark that formed the roof have been discovered – a method of roofing that the settlers brought with them from Scandinavia and which remained in common use in the Faeroes until recent times. Carbon-14 dating of these traces confirms an early date in the settlement phase for the building. Houses in the Faeroe Islands were also built with wooden and stone walls, constructed in the same way as in the Scandinavian homelands, though this required the importation of timber to these treeless islands.

Both Kvívík and Fuglafjørdhur, which is a similar though less well-preserved site, lie within the boundaries of modern settlements. At Toftanes, south of Leirvik on Eysturoy, where a larger area was available for investigation, four buildings, some showing signs of having been rebuilt, have been excavated. These major excavations have added greatly to our understanding of the economy of the Faeroe Islands in the primary settlement phase. The complex consists of a dwelling with central hearth, a storehouse and two more structures, probably including a kitchen. An exceptionally large number of finds – some 500 in all – were recovered, including soapstone bowls (possibly brought over from Scandinavia), glass beads, schist whetstones and, most interestingly of all, because of the rare nature of the evidence, a number of well-preserved wooden items, among them a gaming board. Carbon-14 dating of these items confirms that

*Below* Excavation at Kvívík on Streymoy has revealed the classic example of a Faeroese Viking Age farmstead, comprising a dwelling, some 20 meters long, and – parallel to it – a byre for the cattle in winter, both built with thick walls of earth and stone. The house has a side door, giving access to the adjacent stream, and a central paved hearth; its interior would have been lined with wood, whilst the roof of turf and birch bark was supported on two rows of posts. A toy horse was amongst the finds made here (*left*), a stallion carved out of fir wood; the toy boat of willow, shown above it, is from another Viking Age settlement at Argisbrekka on Eysturoy.

the site was occupied in the 9th and 10th centuries. The animals kept on the farm were predominantly sheep, as is still the case in the islands today, but some cow and pig remains have also been found.

Toftanes was evidently a farming complex of considerable size and importance. In the spring and summer months the animals would be taken from farms like this to upland grazings or shielings. This farming system, in use in Norway, was readily adopted in other mountainous regions by Viking farmers; we have already seen its presence in Scotland and the Isle of Man. In the latter case, the Celtic place-name element *ærgi*, may provide evidence of a Viking Age shieling, and this is often the case in the Faeroe Islands, too – possibly an indication that the original settlers came from western Britain, as Grim Kamban may have done. Recent archaeological investigation has concentrated on these upland farms. At Argisbrekka, for example, a number of houses made with turf walls, very different in construction from other Viking Age buildings on the islands, have been discovered, and it is suggested that this was a temporary summer settlement, with the main farm in the vicinity of Eidhi, the nearest village.

The recent discovery of a group of pagan graves at Sandur on the southern island of Sandoy has provided fresh evidence of early Viking presence. Excavations close to the church here have revealed extensive settlement remains, including an important series of early timber churches, the earliest of which is associated with an 11th-century hoard of coins. This site occupies an area of low-lying, free-draining land, very different from the sheer volcanic basalt and tufa slopes of the more northerly isles, and it has clearly had a history of settlement as long as any in the Faeroes. For all its notable concentration of Viking Age remains, however, the site is not mentioned in the *Saga of the Faeroe Islanders*.

*Below* Iceland has the largest glaciers and the greatest volcanic activity in Europe. Its interior consists largely of a barren plateau, covered with ice, lava and ash, so that settlement is mostly confined to the coastal areas, particularly in the southwest and south where the Gulf Stream moderates the climate.

Until discovery of the pagan graves at Sandur, virtually the only other known Viking burials in the Faeroe Islands were at Tjørnuvík, at the northernmost point of Streymoy. Here a group of graves marked by stone settings was uncovered in an area of land-slippage at the head of an inlet. They were so poorly furnished with grave-goods that it has been suggested that the people buried there were the victims of a shipwreck. A simple bronze ringed pin of the 10th-century Irish design that became a ubiquitous fashion amongst the Vikings confirms the cultural identity of these individuals. The distribution of these ringed pins from Newfoundland to Scandinavia is evidence of a network of cultural contacts linking the Viking colonies of the North Atlantic.

### Iceland – the land of ice

Iceland lies in the mid Atlantic about 800 miles from the coast of southwest Norway. It would have taken some time between a week and a month for ships setting sail from the Scandinavian homelands to reach it. Even with stops in Shetland and the Faeroe Islands, the journey would have been fraught with danger. Iceland's largely inhospitable landscapes have been formed by volcanoes and ice; lava fields and glaciers cover nearly three-quarters of its surface, and farming land is limited to the coastal fringe and valleys of the south and southwest. Nevertheless, from about 860, Viking settlers began to arrive here in very large numbers, in a settlement movement that appears to have come about under very different circumstances

from those that brought Shetland and Orkney, or the Faeroe Islands, into the Viking sphere of influence. Iceland's medieval historians believed that it was King Harald Finehair's ruthless subjugation of Norway's free farmers that led many of them to seek political freedom in the new land to the west; others have argued that the colonization was prompted by land shortages at home. There is no doubt, however, that some of the original settlers came from Britain and Ireland. Once again it is Dicuil who provides the earliest written account of the island. The accuracy of his description of such natural phenomena as the midnight sun is convincing evidence of the reliability of his eyewitness sources:

*It is now thirty years since priests* [clerici] *who have lived in that island from the first day of February to the first day of August told me that not only at the summer solstice, but in the days on either side of it, the setting sun hides itself at the evening hour as if behind a little hill, so that no darkness occurs during that very period of time, but whatever task a man wishes to perform, even to picking the lice out of his shirt, he can manage it precisely as in broad daylight. They deal in fallacies who have written that the sea around the island is frozen... but after one day's sailing from there to the north they found the frozen sea.*

This and other documentary references to the northern wanderings of Celtic saints such as St Brendan suggests that there was settlement on "Thule" (now identified as Iceland) some 60 to 70 years before the advent of the Vikings. However, there is no strong archaeological case to support a pre-Viking presence in Iceland. A few *papa* place-names in the southeast of Iceland have been the cause of much discussion, but recent excavations on the island of Papey have failed to locate any traces of settlement that can definitely be dated earlier than the 9th century. Evidence once supposed to support pre-Viking activity on the Vestmanna Islands is now generally disputed. In the past, the presence of small

*Below* Geysers and hot springs (like the one shown here) are a striking element of Iceland's varied landscape – in marked contrast to its glacier ice. Reykjavik – "Steamy Bay" – the site of one of the earliest Viking settlements, was so named on account of the vapor rising from the many hot springs in the southwest of the island.

*Right* In 12th-century Iceland, a remarkable book – known as *Landnámabók* – was compiled to provide an account of the 9th- and 10th-century Norse settlers and their families, where they came from and where they settled on the island. It contains invaluable information about the country's origins and earliest history, but survives almost only in changed and expanded later copies; this version was written out in the late 17th century.

*Below right* This bronze disk brooch with long chains and pendants – one of several such found in Iceland – is of a 10th-century type that is most common in northern Scandinavia.

bells in a few pagan graves was said to indicate a pre-Viking Irish presence in Iceland, but this too is now in question as no parallels have been found to exist in Ireland. The bells may have been amulets. In any event, as in the Faeroe Islands, the arrival of the Norse caused the *papar* to move away.

The Norse arrival in Iceland is described in the *Book of the Icelanders (Islendingabók)*, written by Ari Thorgilsson, the so-called "Father of Icelandic history", in the early 12th century, but it makes no mention of the Scandinavians who are credited with the discovery of Iceland – the Swede Gardar Svavarson and the Norwegians, Naddodd and Floki. Their names come to us through two early Latin sources, the *History of Norway (Historia Norvegiae)*, written about 1170, and the *History of the Antiquities of the Kingdom of Norway (Historia de antiquitate regum Norvagiensium)*, about 1180. Floki is supposed to have given Iceland its name – chosen because of the harshness of the first winter he spent there and the drift ice he saw to the north. It seems from this and other stories that several voyages may have been made to Iceland before the main period of settlement. The *Book of the Settlements (Landnámabók)*, originally compiled by Ari with others in the first half of the 12th century, is the main source of information we have

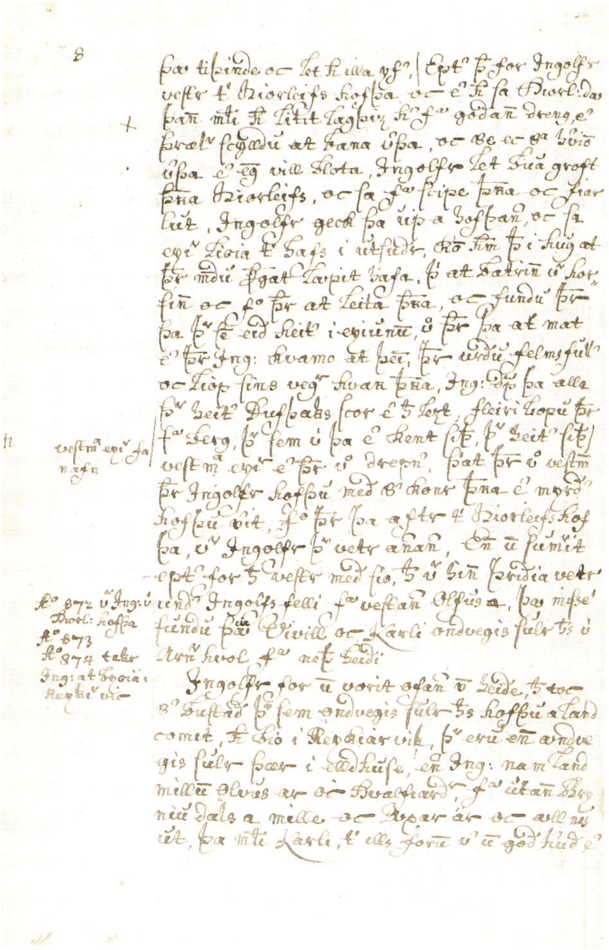

concerning the *landnám* or settlement phase, providing the names and biographies of 430 settlers with details of their land-claims. It is thus a unique source, or combination of sources, and among other things has proved of great use to archaeologists in indicating to them where the early settlements might be located.

According to the *Book of the Settlements*, the first permanent settler on Iceland was a man called Ingolf. When he sighted land he is reported to have flung the carved wooden pillars of the high-seat that he had brought with him from his home in Norway into the ocean to see where they would wash ashore. It took him two or three years to locate their landing place, but he eventually found them at a place in the southwest of Iceland that we know as Reykjavik. The island's capital today, it gained its name, which means "steamy bay", from the natural hot springs in the vicinity. Though excavations in the heart of the old town have uncovered Viking Age remains, nothing has been found that links them directly with Ingolf's original farm.

According to Ari Thorgilsson's information, the settlement of Iceland was completed in 60 years between 870 and 930. Many of the first settlers were pagan, and a number of burials with fine grave-good assemblages have been discovered. However, there are nothing like enough to represent the original population, for it has been estimated that some 20,000 people came to Iceland during the settlement period, with the population rising subsequently to about 60,000. Every inch of fertile land was exploited by the Norse farmers, and those arriving after the main period of settlement were left with only a choice of poor land. One such latecomer was Eric the Red, a murderer and political outcast from Norway.

# Stöng

*Below* This hemispherical bowl recovered in the excavations at Stöng is made of local volcanic tuff, a more readily available material than the soapstone that was characteristically used to make bowls of this type in the Scandinavian homelands.

In 1939 excavations at Stöng, in the Thjórsá valley of southern Iceland, uncovered the remains of a small farm complex dating from the Late Viking Age. It was buried beneath layers of volcanic debris thrown out by Mount Hekla. This had kept the turf walls, which had been built on top of stone foundations, in an excellent state of preservation. Investigations carried out at a later date discovered structural remains from two earlier phases of occupation beneath these buildings, and it is possible that Stöng, one of several Norse sites in the area, dates back to the initial phase of the Icelandic settlement, described in the *Landnámabók*. In 1974, to coincide with the celebration of the 1,100th centenary of the Icelandic settlement, a reconstruction of the hall at Stöng was built in a more accessible location a little way from the site.

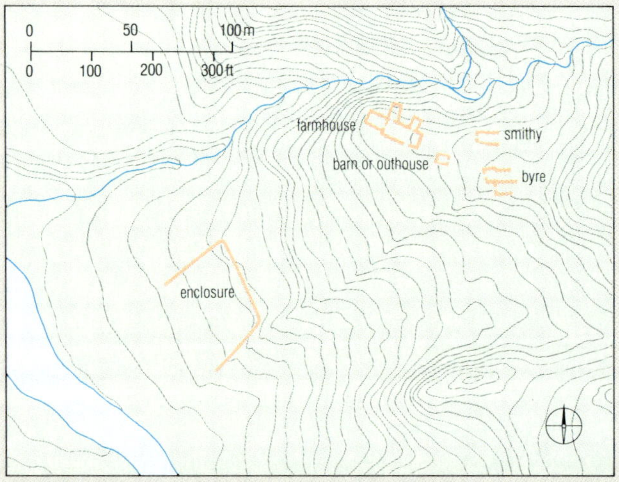


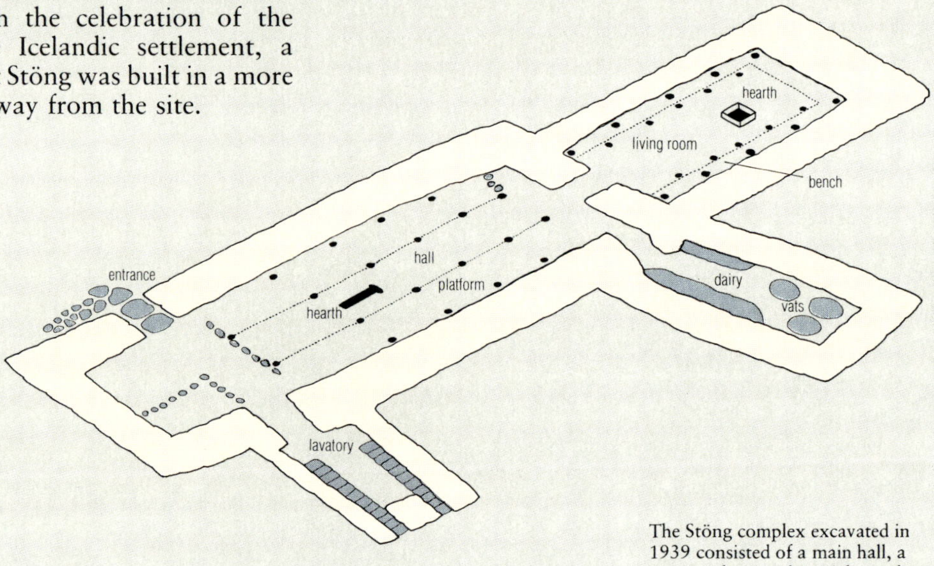

The Stöng complex excavated in 1939 consisted of a main hall, a separate byre with upright cattle stalls, a possible barn and a smithy for working the local bog iron; an enclosure for animals lay close to the fast-flowing stream (*above left*). It is hard to imagine how the site would have appeared in the Norse period, as lava and pumice now mask the original contours of the land. Because the turf and stone walls were so well preserved by the protective layer of volcanic debris, it has been possible to reconstruct the hall at Stöng with a high degree of accuracy (*left*). Squares of turf were stacked neatly on low stone foundations to build the outer walls: the roof covering was also of turf. The walls and roof were lined with an insulating layer of timber. The interior of the hall (*above*) was divided into two main rooms, each provided with a central hearth and sleeping benches: this heat-conserving arrangement is found in later medieval houses in Iceland. Two offshoots on one side of the hall are conventionally described as a dairy and a lavatory, but recent investigation suggests that wool processing took place in one of them, and that urine was used to prepare the fleeces.

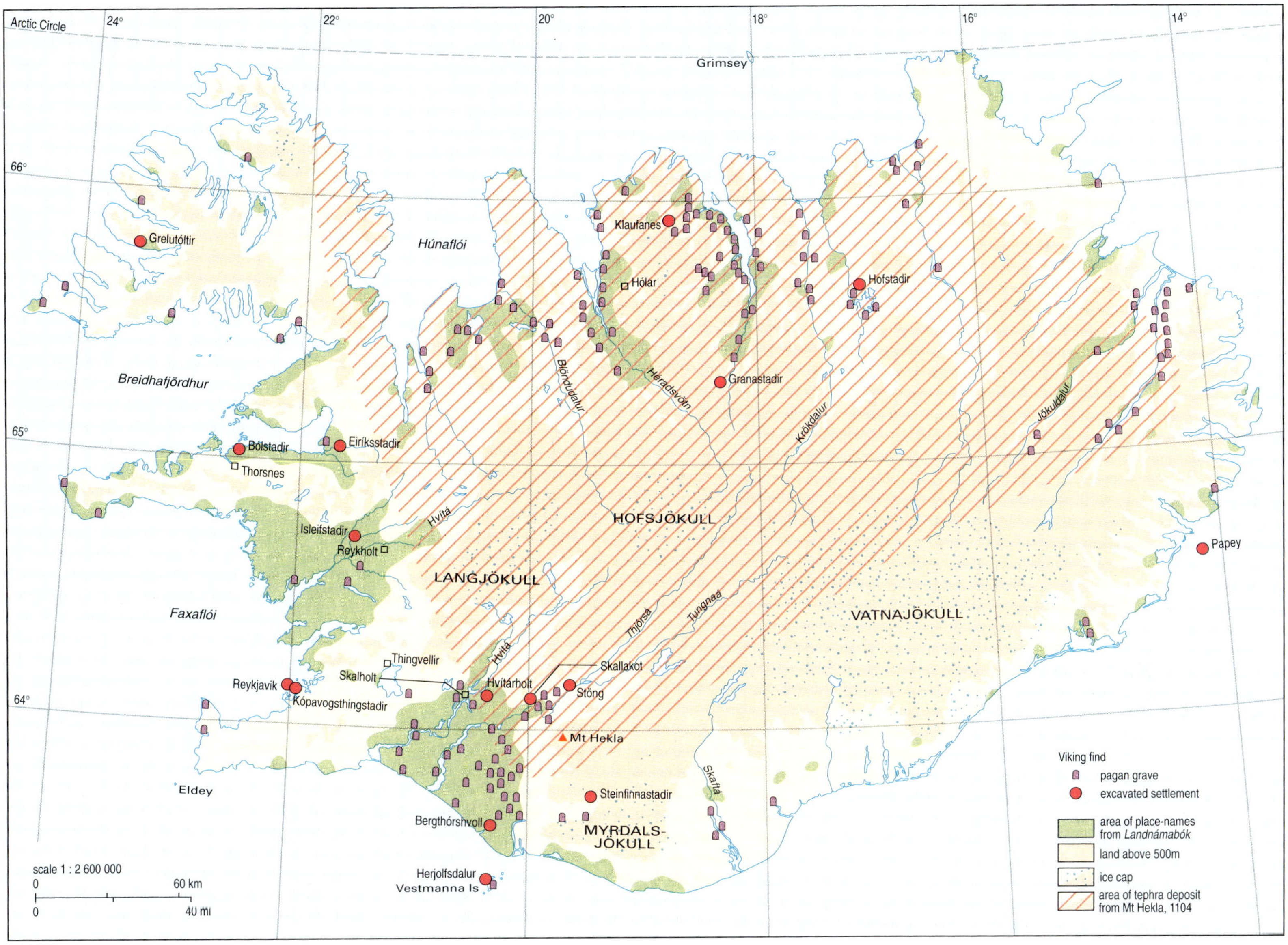


**Viking Age settlement in Iceland**
Analysis of the landholdings of the first generation of settlers from Scandinavia listed in the *Landnámabók* shows that they were most concentrated in the southwest and western coastal fringes of the island and along the long river valleys of the north. This is strikingly corroborated by the archaeological evidence as demonstrated in the distribution of Viking Age burials and excavated settlements. Occupation in the early years of the Viking settlement was particularly dense in the lower Thjórsá valley, then free of the layers of tephra that overwhelmed it when Mount Hekla erupted in the Middle Ages.

Because so much of Iceland's interior was covered in inhospitable ice or lava, Norse settlement was concentrated in the coastal fringe and broad valleys, particularly in the southwest of the island. The once densely populated Thjórsá valley is today a wasteland covered with layers of volcanic debris known as tephra, thrown out by Mount Hekla, one of Iceland's largest volcanoes. This is known to have entered upon a phase of activity at the end of the Viking period, and several farmsteads belonging to the Viking Age and slightly later lie beneath a blanket of ash. In many cases it is possible to give a date to their destruction since individual tephra layers have been identified with documented eruptions, though the datings are not as accurate as was once thought. For a long time one of the most significant of these eruptions was thought to have taken place in 1104. It was this that was supposed to have brought about the abandonment of the farmstead at Stöng, at the northern end of the Thjórsá valley, first excavated in 1939. However, recent reinvestigation has revealed that there were several successive periods of occupation of this site. Two structural groups underlie the one that was uncovered in the original excavation, and occupation continued into the 12th or 13th centuries. A distinctive layer of tephra from a late eruption has been built into one of the uppermost turf-walled structures, and current opinion suggests the cataclysm originally dated to 1104 may in fact have occurred nearly a century later.

One of the most significant aspects of the Viking settlement of Iceland was the establishment of a general judicial assembly: the Althing. This was an open-air meeting of all the island's free men, held every summer for two weeks at a site that became known as Thingvellir. The Althing was presided over by the lawspeaker, who was elected by the local chieftains or *goðar*, and it provided the forum for making laws and dealing with complaints. Traditionally, the first meeting of the Althing was supposed to have taken place in 930, and this date was held to mark the birth of Iceland as an independent nation, free from royal control of any kind: writing in the late 11th century, Adam of Bremen noted that "the Icelanders have no other king than the laws".

The Althing was the vehicle for all major decisions concerning the colony as a whole. Christianity, for example, was officially introduced after lengthy discussion at the Althing in 1000, though provision was made for pagan practices to be carried on in private by those who so desired. Below the level of the Althing were the regional Things, which met regularly to decide local matters and hear grievances. It was at one of these, the Thorsnes Thing, that Eric the Red, whose fiery temper matched the color of his hair, was outlawed from Iceland in about 980 for murder.

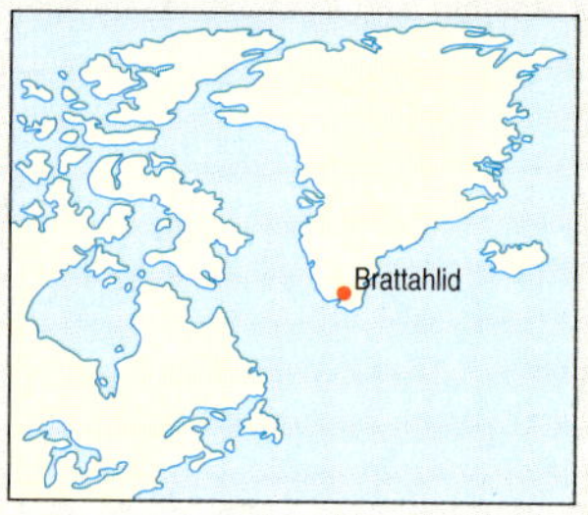


# Brattahlid

It was at Brattahlid, on a steep slope overlooking Eiriksfjord, that Eric the Red built his farmstead at the end of the 10th century. This was to become the center of Greenland's Eastern Settlement. Known now by the Inuit name Qagssiarssuk, meaning "Little Strange Creek", the remains of three large farm complexes and a meeting place, or Thing, are still visible there today. Though one of the farm complexes has become popularly known as "Eric the Red's farm", most of the stone structures belong to the 13th and 14th centuries, at the end of the Eastern Settlement's period of occupation. Nevertheless, archaeologists have revealed the traces of earlier structures below the visible ruins. More positively identified has been the site of the turf church built by Eric's wife Thjodhild after her conversion to Christianity by their son, Leif the Lucky.

*Below* Groundplan of the turf and stone building traditionally described as Eric the Red's farm. The walls are late in date, but are built on earlier foundations. Its small rooms and thick walls are a response to the harsh climate. Extra heat would have been provided by the animal byre at the end of the hall, the oldest part of the building.

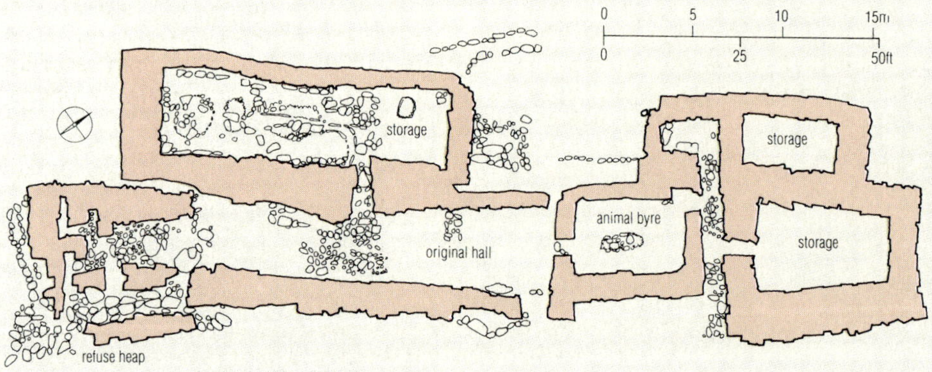


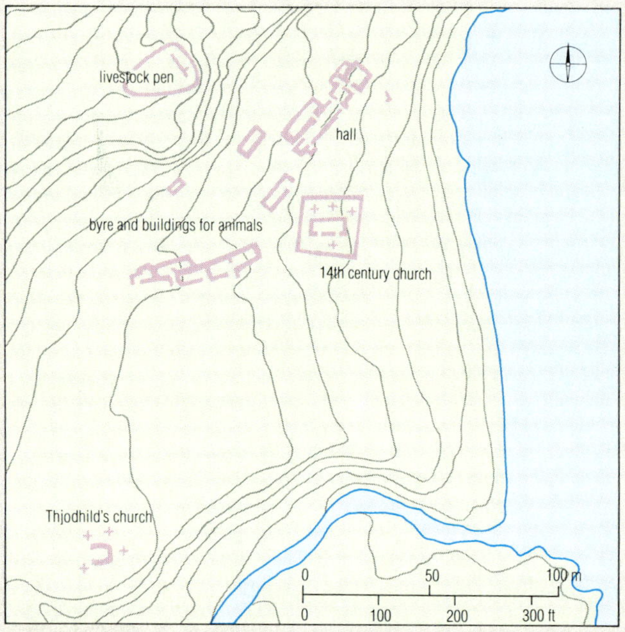


*Above* The large farm complex to which the hall shown left belonged sprawled across a pleasant slope overlooking Eiriksfjord at Brattahlid. The buildings visible today were built over several centuries. The church, standing next to the hall, is the most impressive, and in its present form dates from the 14th century. The other buildings shown here are byres, stables and livestock pens. To the south, nearer to the stream, is the site of the turf church that was built by Thjodhild on land away from the main settlement.

*Left* Iron was a precious commodity in Norse Greenland and thus tools would have had to have been looked after most carefully: this wooden box for sheep shears was found in a byre at Sandnes in the Western Settlement.

*Right* Greenland's inner fjords provided sheltered land for the Norse settlers and scope for agriculture. A period of comparatively mild climate throughout the North Atlantic region during the Viking Age made life there easier then than now, and thus all the more attractive for colonization.

## Greenland

After his banishment from Iceland, and unable to return to Norway, Eric sailed west once more to look for an unnamed land that had been sighted, but not visited, some 60 years earlier by a man called Gunnbjorn Ulf-Krakuson who had been blown far off course by wild storms on his way from Norway to Iceland. Eric was successful in his quest. Three years later he returned to Iceland with talk of a land that he called Greenland. He had come in search of settlers to found a new colony there, and the saga tells us he gave it this name to make it sound more attractive. This has been called the biggest confidence trick in history, yet the summertime visitor to Greenland today is struck by the amount of green land to be seen, especially along the coastal fjords and inland valleys of southern Greenland. Perhaps Eric has been somewhat maligned; when compared with the holding of poor land he had been given in Iceland, Greenland may well have been appropriately named.

We are told that Eric collected enough volunteers to make up an expedition of 25 ships, and in about 985 these set sail from Iceland to Greenland. Only 14 of the ships completed the journey, rounding Cape Farewell to reach the sheltered fjords of Julianehåb bay, as it is called today, where there was safe harborage, good fishing and land for pasturage. Here the Eastern Settlement was established. Eric selected the most favorable sites for himself, and his farm at Brattahlid at the head of Eiriksfjord became the settlement's political center. Some members of Eric's original band of settlers sailed on for some 650

*Above* A loomweight incised with Thor's hammer, found in a barn on Eric's farm. It probably dates from the early days of the settlement, during the period of transition from paganism to Christianity.

*Left* The view from Brattahlid across the waters of Eiriksfjord, which today is frozen from October to May. The landscape the settlers found in Greenland was treeless, and so the buildings were constructed of turf and stones and lined with driftwood.

kilometers along the coast until they reached the shelter of Godthåbsfjord (also its modern name). Here they founded the Western Settlement – which is actually farther north than the Eastern Settlement. The written sources tell us that the Eastern Settlement consisted of over 190 farms, and the Western Settlement of about 90; between them lay a smaller cluster of some 20 farms only, imaginatively termed the Middle Settlement. In recent years extensive surveying and excavation of Norse sites in Greenland have indicated that these figures are far too low. The remains of nearly 450 farms have been identified in the Eastern Settlement alone, many of them thought to be broadly contemporary.

In both major settlement areas the Norse farms were clustered in the more sheltered parts of the inner fjords where climatic conditions were less extreme than on the coast. Climatologists believe that the North Atlantic region as a whole experienced a comparatively mild climate between the 9th and 12th centuries, enabling land that is unproductive today to be used to grow fodder crops so that livestock could be reared and overwintered indoors. Nevertheless, conditions in the Greenland colonies must have been hard, especially in the more northerly Western Settlement. Only in the Eastern Settlement did Norse occupation extend toward the coast, and areas of gently rolling, comparatively low-lying pasture were to be found. Here, at any rate, the statement recorded by the 13th-century writer of the *King's Mirror* that "there are large and fine farms in Greenland" seems to have been accurate.

A study of the animal bones found on Norse settlement sites in Greenland, together with other evidence, shows that as well as sheep (still reared in Greenland) cattle and goats were commonly kept, a fact that seems surprising in view of the climatic restrictions on their farming today. Nevertheless, almost half of all the bones excavated on sites in the Eastern Settlement, and over half of those in the Western

Settlement, are of seals, particularly harp seals. Clearly hunting played a very important part in the Norse economy. Caribou were also killed, and their meat would probably have supplemented lamb in the Norse diet. Expeditions were made on a regular basis to the *Norðrseta*, the hunting grounds of the far north, where the Norse settlers would have been in competition with the indigenous Inuit hunter–gatherers for natural resources.

Most of the sites examined so far in Greenland belong to the Late Norse period. However, excavation of a farm at Narssaq in the Eastern Settlement suggests an occupation date in the primary settlement period. It is a simple structure, similar to those of comparable date in the Faeroe Islands. The most famous Greenland site is at Brattahlid, on a pleasant slope overlooking Eiriksfjord in the Eastern Settlement. Here a building known as "Eric the Red's Farm" can be seen, together with the remains of two other farm groups. However none of these structures can be dated to Eric's day and few traces, if any, of early occupation phases are visible. At the heart of the complex is a magnificent church. This replaced the simple turf structure to the south, which is barely distinguishable today, that has been given the name of "Thjodhild's church", after Eric's wife. She became a convert to Christianity after their son Leif returned to Greenland from Norway charged by King Olaf Tryggvason with the task of introducing the new faith to the colony, and had a small sod church built for herself and a few followers. Eric, however, refused to abandon his pagan beliefs, and Thjodhild refused to live with him thereafter, which – according to the saga writer – "annoyed him greatly". The settlement at Brattahlid was not an isolated one. An extensive survey has revealed the sites of many farms, some with associated churches, along the length of the Qordlortoq valley just to the north, which links Eiriksfjord to Isafjord.

A settlement site at Sandnes in the inner fjord area of the Western Settlement, which was established before the 12th century, has received much attention from archaeologists in recent years. It consists of a group of farm buildings, including two very substantial byres and a smithy, as well as a small church, the latter now submerged by the fjord. It seems clear that Sandnes held territorial power in the inner fjord over a network of other smaller farms. The permafrost conditions of the soil have kept the remains at Sandnes in an excellent state of preservation. The farm buildings were built of turf and stone, as in Iceland, and surviving wooden fragments show that the walls were sometimes boarded internally. The walls remain standing to a considerable height. Wooden artifacts discovered on the site – for example, a sheath used for holding shears found in one of the byres – shed valuable light on the way of life practiced by the hardy farmers of these remote Norse settlements.

## The Vinland settlement

Among the settlers who sailed with Eric the Red's

**Viking Age settlement in Greenland** (*above*)
Greenland's extensive coastline is mostly inhospitable, except where sheltered fjords penetrate a long way inland. The Scandinavian colonizers consequently established three separate areas of settlement considerable distances apart along the western coast. The largest of these, the Eastern Settlement, grew up around Eiriksfjord, where Eric the Red established his family home at Brattahlid. The bishopric of Gardar, founded in the early 12th century, also lay in the Eastern Settlement.

**Viking routes across the North Atlantic** (*right*)
The Vikings gradually expanded westward from Scandinavia to Orkney, Shetland, the Faeroes and Iceland by a process of "island hopping". Greenland was initially sighted when a ship sailing to Iceland was blown off course. Eric the Red subsequently sailed west to confirm the existence of this new land, and colonization soon followed. Bjarni Herjolfsson, from Herjolfsnes in the Eastern Settlement, was probably the first European to sight North America, when his ship was also blown off course, and it was Eric's son Leif who retraced Bjarni's journey to discover Vinland. Thorfinn Karlsefni later established a short-lived colony there.

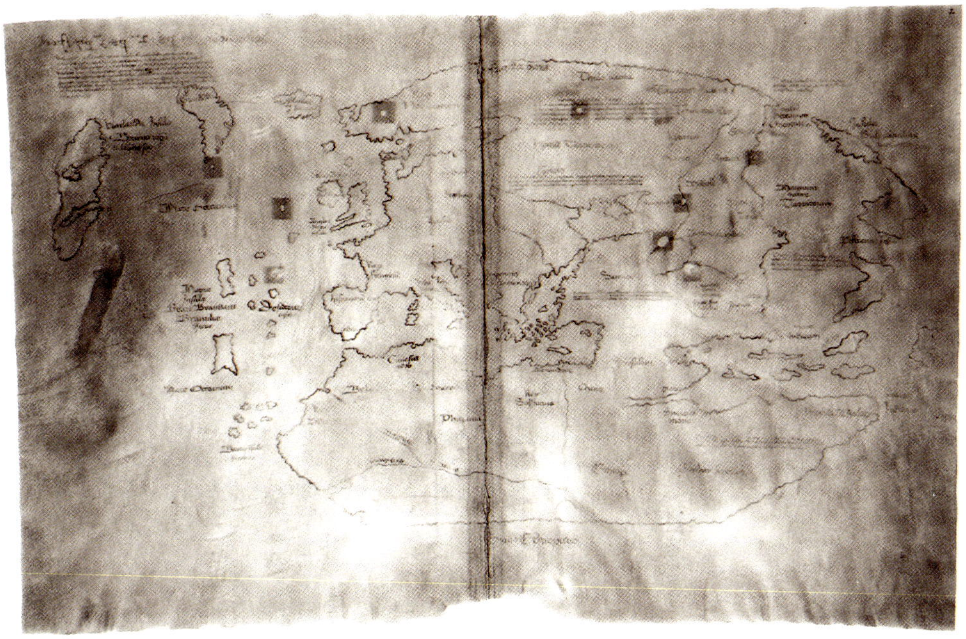

*Above* The Vinland Map is a pen and ink drawing of the world purporting to have been made in the 15th century, though its authenticity has been hotly disputed. It depicts Greenland most accurately as an island and records the discovery of Vinland by Bjarni and Leif, but many now believe this map to be an early 20th-century forgery.

original group of settlers to Greenland in 985 were the parents of one Bjarni Herjolfsson. Later that same year he set out with a cargo from Iceland to join them, but his ship was blown off course and he sailed on westward across the ocean until he came in sight of a flat land covered in trees, to which he gave the name *Markland* ("Forestland"). Bjarni did not land, but turned northward up the coast, passing a mountainous barren land of rocks, *Helluland* ("Slabland"), and then eastward to reach Greenland.

Bjarni was probably the first Norseman to sight North America. It was left to Leif the Lucky, the son of Eric the Red, to make the first landing there some ten to fifteen years later. According to *Eric's Saga*, he set out to retrace Bjarni's journey in reverse. Leaving the Eastern Settlement he sailed up the coast of Greenland, past the Western Settlement, until he reached Disko Island. From there he crossed the Davis Strait to reach *Helluland*, now identified as Baffin Island. Turning south, he found the coast of Labrador (*Markland*), forested as Bjarni had described it, and then sailed on for two further days until he reached a promontory of land to the southwest that he called *Vinland* ("Vineland") after the wild grapes or berries that were found growing there. Leif and his party landed and spent the winter here before returning to Greenland.

It is now generally accepted that the Vikings had reached Newfoundland, off the North American mainland. The sagas tell of more than one attempt to establish a Norse colony here: indeed, the very next year Leif's brother Thorwald led an expedition to Vinland, but was killed by an arrow in a skirmish with a group of Native Americans. Thorfinn Karlsefni is said to have established a settlement of between 60 and 160 people a few years later, but it seems to have lasted only about three years. The continued hostility of the indigenous population, whom the Vikings called *Skrælingar*, a somewhat derogatory term, was undoubtedly a factor in its collapse, but supply routes with the home base in Greenland seem also to have been overstretched.

Until comparatively recently, it seemed that the Vikings had left no evidence of their physical presence in North America. Then in 1965 came the startling discovery of a map, apparently dating from the 15th century, that showed a land called Vinland lying to the

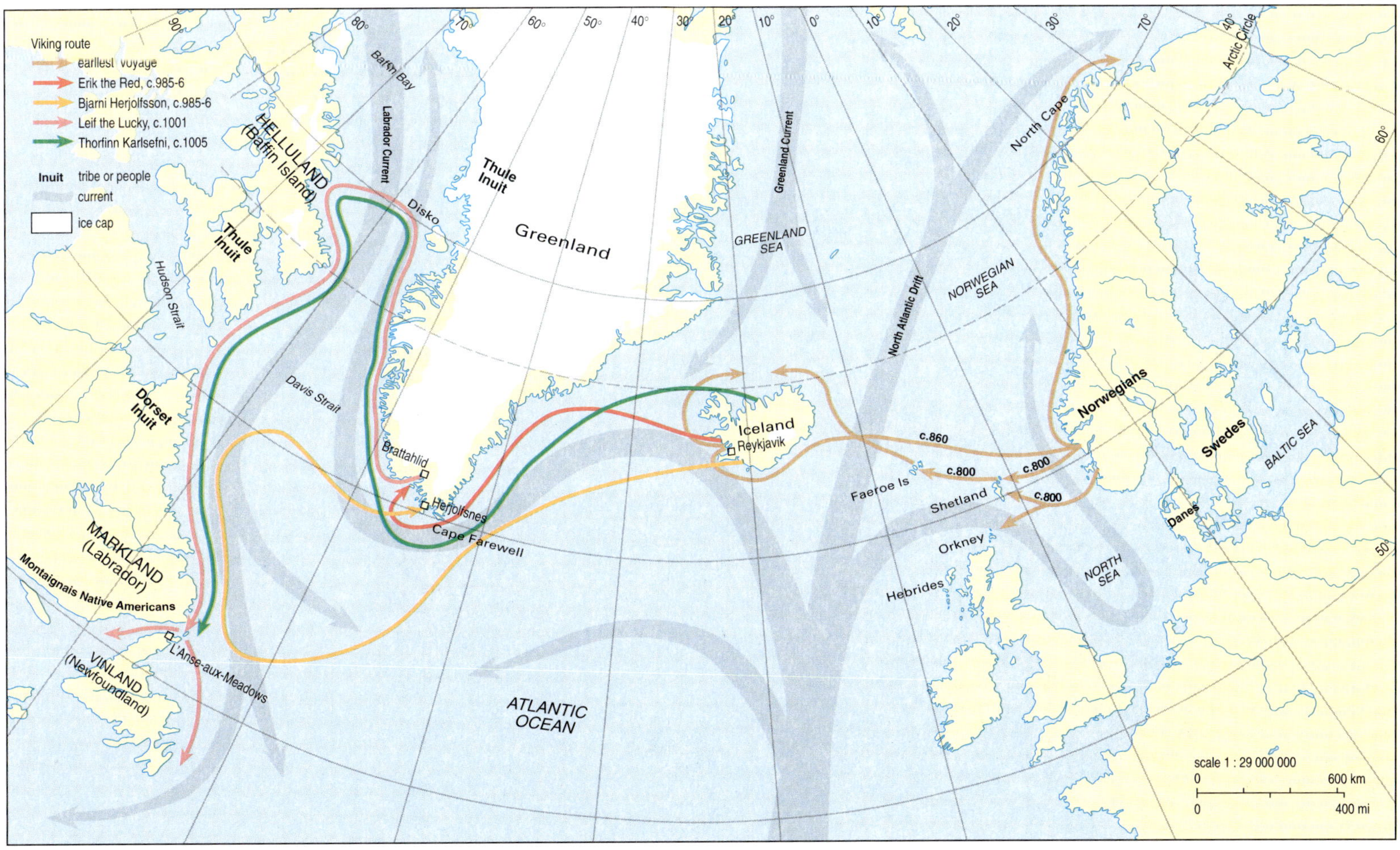

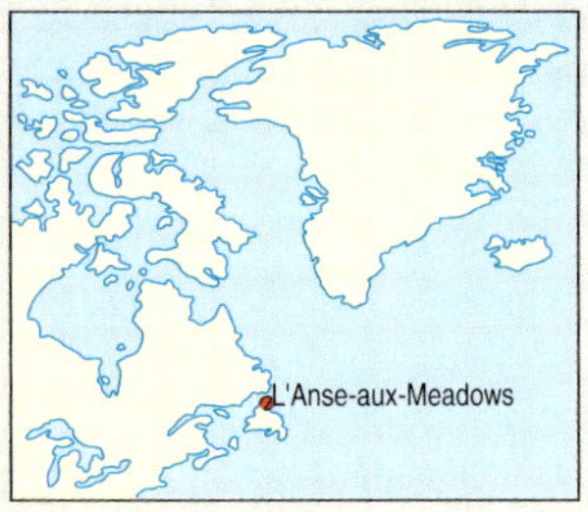


# L'Anse-aux-Meadows

The Norse settlement of L'Anse-aux-Meadows lies on the northernmost tip of Newfoundland; it provides the single proof we have to date of the Viking presence in North America. The story of the site's identification in the early 1960s resembles a modern-day saga. The Norwegian explorer Helge Ingstad, seeking to establish the truth behind the stories of Leif the Lucky's discovery of Vinland, became convinced that the prevailing sailing conditions would have brought ships from Greenland to this part of the Newfoundland coast. Local tradition recorded the memory of a group of buildings at a site in Epaves Bay beside Black Duck Brook. On investigation, the foundations of a number of turf-built houses were uncovered, which unmistakably resembled Norse buildings in Greenland and Iceland.

*Right* A view of the site, facing north over Epaves Bay. The outline of the largest of the Norse houses can be seen within a fenced enclosure to the left of the bus in the right of the picture. The site at L'Anse-aux-Meadows must have seemed welcoming to the Norse sailors after their journey along the barren coast of Helluland (Baffin Island) and the forests of Markland (Labrador). However, hostility from the local Native American peoples may have been one reason why the settlement was short-lived.

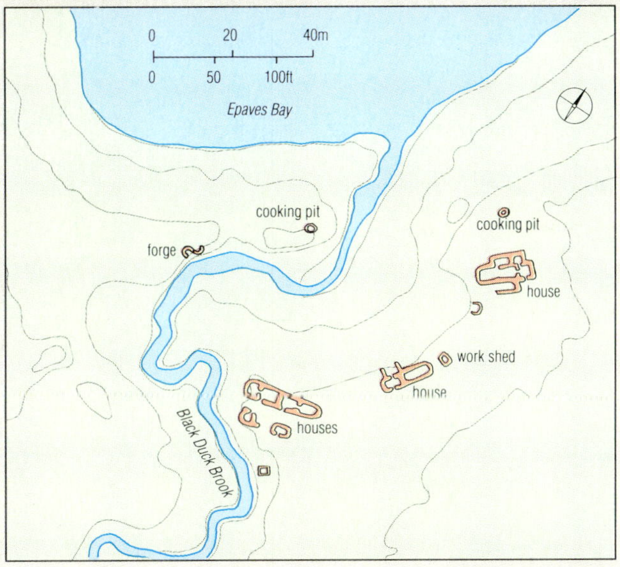


*Left* Some of the buildings at L'Anse-aux-Meadows have been reconstructed close to the settlement site, based on the evidence of the excavations there. Analysis has shown that the turf squares used to build the walls of the houses, and as covering for the roofs, were cut on the site. The wooden lintels and the doors themselves were probably made of driftwood, which must have been plentiful along the shore – the name of Epaves Bay means "the place where flotsam is washed up" Traces of the central hearths and side benches inside the houses completed the identification with Norse buildings elsewhere.

*Above* The Norse at L'Anse-aux-Meadows chose a small marshy bay for their settlement and built their dwelling houses and worksheds on one side of the brook with a smithy on the other. The largest of the houses consists of two halls built side by side, a "doubling-up" arrangement that was typical of Norse buildings in Greenland and would have helped to conserve heat.

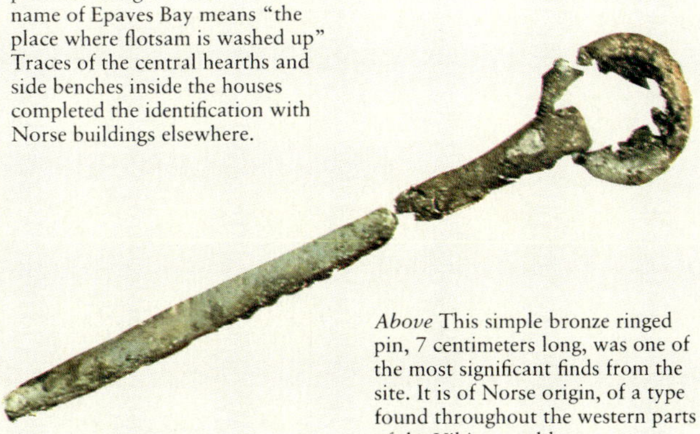

*Above* This simple bronze ringed pin, 7 centimeters long, was one of the most significant finds from the site. It is of Norse origin, of a type found throughout the western parts of the Viking world.

west of the island of Greenland. It was argued that this could only have been drawn from the earlier charts of Norse travelers, and so offered clear proof (if such were needed) that they had reached North America. However, many experts cast doubts on the authenticity of the Vinland Map, arguing that no other contemporary map is known to depict Greenland as an island. Subsequent tests showed that a pigment used in the ink would not have been in use until after the end of the 19th century, and it is now generally held to be a 20th-century forgery.

The excitement and later controversy raised by the Vinland Map deflected attention from the archaeological work then being carried on that provided incontrovertible proof of the Norse presence in Newfoundland. During the 1960s the Norwegian Helge Ingstad, in partnership with his wife, an archaeologist, began to excavate a site at L'Anse-aux-Meadows, on the tip of Newfoundland's northern promontory. Over several seasons' digging, they discovered, facing a shallow bay, a small complex of stone and turf buildings in an arc, lying beside a freshwater stream. Carbon-14 dating showed that the site was occupied in the Viking period, and the overwhelming balance of evidence – not least a number of Norse artifacts, including a bronze ringed pin – pointed to its being a Norse settlement. Iron smelting and smithy work – notably for the production of iron rivets, essential for boat repairs – had been carried on here, and metals were not used by the Native American groups in this area in the late 10th and 11th centuries. The buildings, too, were different in size, style and construction from indigenous ones.

But was this Vinland – the land of wild grapes? It is certainly unlikely that grapes would have been found growing in these northern latitudes, even in the milder climatic conditions of the 10th and 11th centuries, though they may have been in areas not much farther south. There is some argument, however, as to whether "Vinland" refers to vines at all, but to some kind of berry, or perhaps has a different meaning altogether. The discovery in Maine, to the south, of a single silver coin of the Norwegian king Olaf Kyrri (1066–93) does not throw much light on the identification of Vinland either. As with Norse artifacts found in the Arctic regions of North America, it was discovered on a native site, and is suggestive of trading activities rather than local settlement. The most likely suggestion is that L'Anse-aux-Meadows served as the "gateway" to Vinland, but a more precise location for Vinland itself must await the further discovery and authentication of Norse finds in North America.

Whether or not the site at L'Anse-aux-Meadows remains the single proof of actual Norse presence in North America, it is clear that the settlement of Vinland was small in scale and of short duration. Unable to establish good relations with the Native Americans, and with vital supply routes all too easily severed by bad weather, life must have become increasingly insecure for the colonizers living at the very end of the Viking world, and we can easily imagine the relief with which they pulled back to the relative safety and security of Greenland – that is, if their settlements were not wiped out by famine or warfare. The slight possibility remains that some Norse communities may have been absorbed into the native population, but in that case their distinctive material culture would have quickly become diluted, leaving no trace in the archaeological record.

# Viking Navigation

For more than 40,000 years humans have sailed across the world's seas to explore, colonize, trade or raid. The earliest voyages were coastal and between islands, when land was always in sight. In such conditions visual pilotage techniques are used – the seaman checks his position by reference to landmarks such as distinctive cliffs, an estuary or a prominent headland, or in relation to such coastal seamarks as shoals and reefs. By 1000 BC, however, voyages were being undertaken across open sea, out of sight of land. Without magnetic compass or chart, or any other instrument, these early navigators used environmental methods of navigation to find their away across the trackless seas. A form of dead reckoning was used, based on estimates of courses steered and speeds achieved. Directions were estimated relative to the sun and the stars and to the direction of the wind and the sea swell. Speeds were estimated using inherited wisdom and personal experience of how boats behaved in a wide range of circumstances. Furthermore, these early navigators watched carefully for signs of weather changes, for shifts in the wind, and for evidence of land beyond the horizon. These simple empirical methods of ocean navigation were used widely for millennia by many maritime civilizations: by the ancient Chinese, by the Phoenicians and Greeks in the Mediterranean, and by the Vikings. It is generally thought that these non-instrumental techniques prevailed until the introduction of the mariner's magnetic compass in the 12th century AD. However it now seems possible that by the 9th or 10th century AD Arab seamen in the Indian Ocean may have used a simple wooden staff or tablet (*kamal*) to measure the altitude of the Pole Star. As this is related to the latitude of the observer, it was thus possible to use a form of latitude sailing that greatly simplifies the navigational problem.

Some scholars have suggested that the Vikings also used latitude sailing techniques on their Atlantic voyages, but whether they had some simple instrument similar to the Arab *kamal*, or whether they could estimate the altitude of the Pole Star by eye with sufficient accuracy is unknown. In recent years, Captain Søren Thirslund and the Danish archaeologist C. L. Vebæk have proposed that the Vikings may have had a simple sun compass. The sun's apparent path across the heavens from (near) East to (near) West depends on the observer's latitude and on the time of year. The only direction that is fixed, regardless of latitude and of season, is the direction when the sun is at the highest point (zenith) of its daily trajectory at noon: this direction we call South. To estimate directions when the sun is other than due South is not easy, but on voyages of a few days' duration with little change in latitude it can be done with tolerable accuracy, using knowledge of the sun's movements memorized on land before the voyage. Thirslund and Vebæk's suggestion is that the Vikings' sun compass allowed them to make much more accurate estimates of direction, possibly as close as ±5°.

*Right* Evidence of the Vikings' sun compass is based on this broken wooden disk of spruce or larch, dated to c. 1000 AD and excavated in 1946–48 by C. L. Vebæk from a Norse site near Uunartoq fjord in the Eastern Settlement of Greenland. Several years after the find was made Captain C. V. Sølver recognized that two incised lines on the disk's surface corresponded to gnomon curves – the line traced out by the tip of the shadow cast by a gnomon (a short wooden rod or cone, as on a sundial) between sunrise and sunset. The curve varies according to latitude and the season of the year, and the two lines scratched on the wooden half-disk – a straight one and a curved one – appeared to match the sun's path at the equinoxes and at the summer solstice.

*Below* Originally the object would have been a complete circle of wood, c. 7 centimeters in diameter. Notches all the way round the edge marked the 32 points of the compass, and the gnomon projected vertically from the center of the disk. To find which way the ship is heading, the disk is rotated until the gnomon's shadow just touches the appropriate curve, and the bearing is then read off the notches.

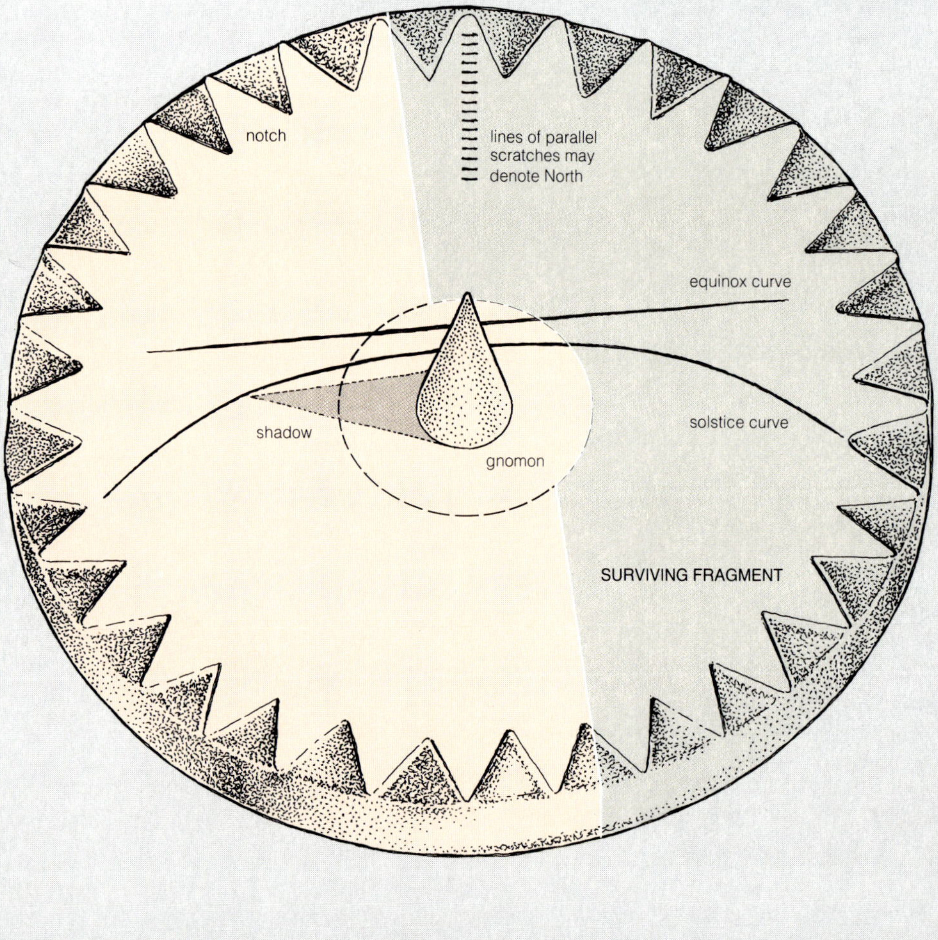

*Right* The gnomon curves for latitude 60° North, close to the route that would have been followed by the Norse navigators. The North-South alignment is found by drawing a line from the gnomon to connect the nearest point of each curve, where the shadow is shortest at midday.

*Far right* The markings on this triangular piece of soapstone found at Vatnahverfi, also in the Eastern Settlement, resemble a gnomon curve. The hole could have held a gnomon, and this object, too, may have been a sun compass.

*Below* The *Saga Siglar* is a modern reconstruction of one of the ships found at Skuldelev. In 1984 it was sailed across the North Atlantic, when a number of successful tests were made using a sun compass similar to the one found at Uunartoq.

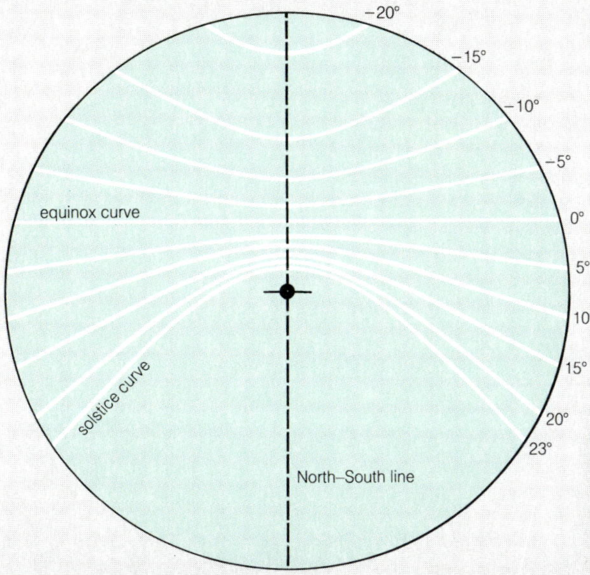

# RUSSIA AND THE EAST

The Viking expansion overseas considered up to now has been confined to the west. The Scandinavians who sailed in this direction were predominantly from Norway and Denmark – naturally enough, given their geographical position and the long-standing westward orientation of their cultural contacts. The Swedish Vikings also traveled great distances during the 9th to 11th centuries, but they naturally looked eastward, where they encountered very different cultures. Beyond the Slavic lands of the southern and eastern Baltic (the area covered by eastern Germany, Poland, Lithuania, Latvia and Estonia today) their journeys took them through the Gulf of Finland to the great Russian river systems of the Volkhov-Lovat-Dnieper and the Volga, south and east to the rich lands of the Byzantine empire and the Abbasid caliphate of the Arabs. From there they were able to connect with the ancient trade routes that stretched as far as India and China.

### The Swedes in the eastern Baltic

The pagan Slavic tribes who lived around the southern and eastern shores of the Baltic were becoming consolidated at this time into larger national groupings in a way that resembled broadly what was happening in Scandinavia. The tribes of the western Slavs – including the Obotrites, Wiltzi and Rugieris in the territory of eastern Germany today, and the Wolins and Pomeranians in western Poland – maintained a number of coastal settlements that were of great importance in the Baltic trading sphere. They would have been well-known to merchants from eastern Scandinavia and farther afield, including the Arabs who sometimes sent embassies and trading missions far to the north. Archaeology has uncovered many of these settlements, and particularly important discoveries have been made at Arkona and Ralswiek on the island of Rügen in the southern Baltic, the capital of the Rugieris, where the remains of a great trading center, a fortress and one of the largest pagan temples in the Slav lands have been found.

Other coastal market centers at Menzlin, Rostock, Mecklenburg, Oldenburg (Germany), and Wolin, Truso and Kołobrzeg (Poland) are of similar character to those of eastern Scandinavia and Gotland. For example, at Wolin, an island at the mouth of the Oder, archaeologists have uncovered the well-preserved remains of a waterside town; the wooden houses and streets surrounded by a rampart with palisade defenses closely resembling those of the contemporary Viking towns at Hedeby and Birka. The buildings contained debris from a wide range of craft-working activities, with particularly fine objects carved in Baltic amber. Wolin was also a center for Slavic cult worship, and an elaborate temple has been excavated, placed by tree-ring dating to around 966. The Scandinavians knew Wolin as *Jómsborg*, and during the 10th century it may have been the base of the semilegendary Viking warrior fraternity known from sagas as the Jomsvikings. It seems likely that Scandinavian merchants were permanently settled in some of these Baltic market centers. A large number of Viking graves have been excavated outside the town at Menzlin, on the Peene river in eastern Germany, and it is possible that an élite group of Scandinavian warriors were permanently settled on one bank of the river from where they may have controlled access to the town.

For the Vikings, the significance of these western Slavic trading centers was that they stood close to the mouths of the Oder and Vistula rivers, the great arteries of trade that gave access, via the Danube, to the Black Sea, and Byzantium (medieval Constantinople and modern Istanbul), and thus to the wealth of the Byzantine empire. The portages along this route were quite difficult to traverse, and many Swedish Vikings, chose to travel to Byzantium by the more easterly route that went through the Gulf of Finland. Along the way they encountered – and perhaps helped to establish – small coastal trading centers controlled by the eastern Slavs at sites such as Druzno in eastern Poland, Kaup on the Kaliningrad coast, Grobin in Latvia, and Tallinn in Estonia. They then sailed their merchant ships up the Neva river to Lake Ladoga and the mouth of the Volkhov river. From here they turned southwards to Novgorod on Lake Ilmen, and thence entered the Lovat-Dnieper river road that led to the Black Sea and Byzantium.

*Right* Crescent-shaped ear-rings were a Slavic rather than a Scandinavian fashion during the Viking Age, though these examples were found in Sweden, as was the crescent-shaped pendant (center). This is of a type produced mainly in western Russia, but possibly also in Poland.

*Below* This silver mount and four openwork tassels were found near the head of a man in a 10th-century grave at Birka, Sweden; they had been attached to a cap that was made at least partly of silk. The geometric granulation on the conical mount is characteristic of silverwork of Kievan-Russian type so that this high-status hat will have been made in the Dnieper region. It has been suggested that such caps were rewards for service in the guard of the rulers of *Rús*.

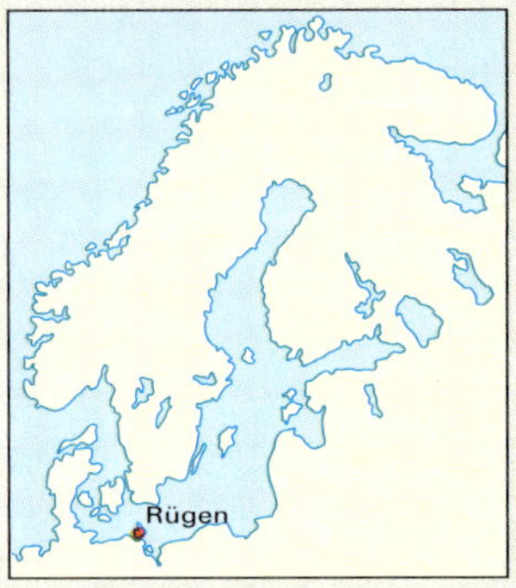


# Rügen

Rügen is a small island a few miles off the coast of eastern Germany lying opposite the southern shores of Sweden and within easy reach of the former Viking settlement at Hedeby. In the Viking Age it was a political center and trading outlet of the Rugieris, a powerful Slav tribe. Excavations have revealed two main settlements on Rügen. A trading center at Ralswiek, situated on Great Jasmund Bay, a large inlet in the north of the island, was occupied from the late 8th century until the 10th. Excavations have uncovered a permanent settlement of about 20 house plots consisting of one main dwelling with ancillary workshops and stores, laid out in a line along the water's edge. Each house plot had its own jetty, with a series of unique shipping docks dug into the shore and strengthened with timber piles. A wide range of craftworking was carried on at Ralswiek, producing finished goods to be traded with foreign merchants – imported objects from all over the Baltic area have been found there. On the nearby beach was a small offering site, perhaps connected with sacrifices for good sailing or trading. Over 400 burial mounds lie on higher ground to the east of the settlement, and many of the grave-goods indicate that a sizable Scandinavian population was living alongside the native Slavs. The second important site, the temple-fortress at Arkona on a northern promontory, was the religious center of the Rugieris. Here lay the temple of the god Svantevit, to whom the Slavs prayed for fertile crops and for success in war. The harvest rites were also associated with a great market, and archaeological finds indicate that merchants from western Europe were present on these occasions from the 9th century onward. Such activities seem to have been strictly seasonal – Arkona does not appear ever to have been continuously occupied.

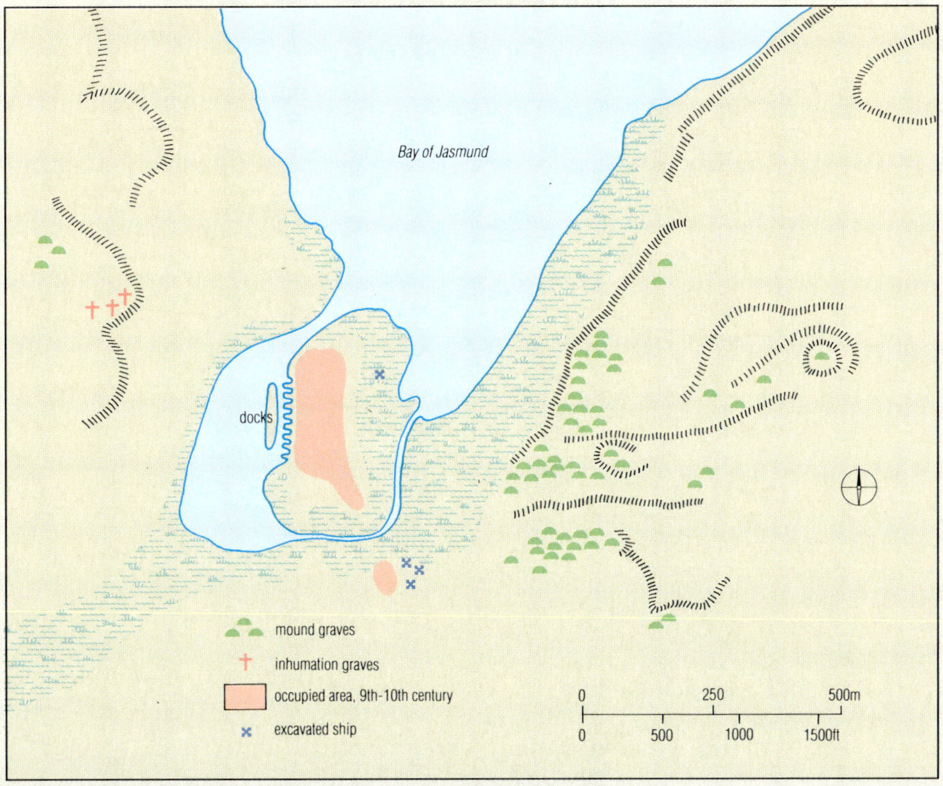


*Left* A shallow creek formed the sheltered harbor of Viking Age Ralswiek (today it is silted up). A sandbank protected the entrance to the docks, which had room for several vessels. The layout of the settlement, with house plots running down to the water's edge, had much in common with Scandinavian towns of the same date.

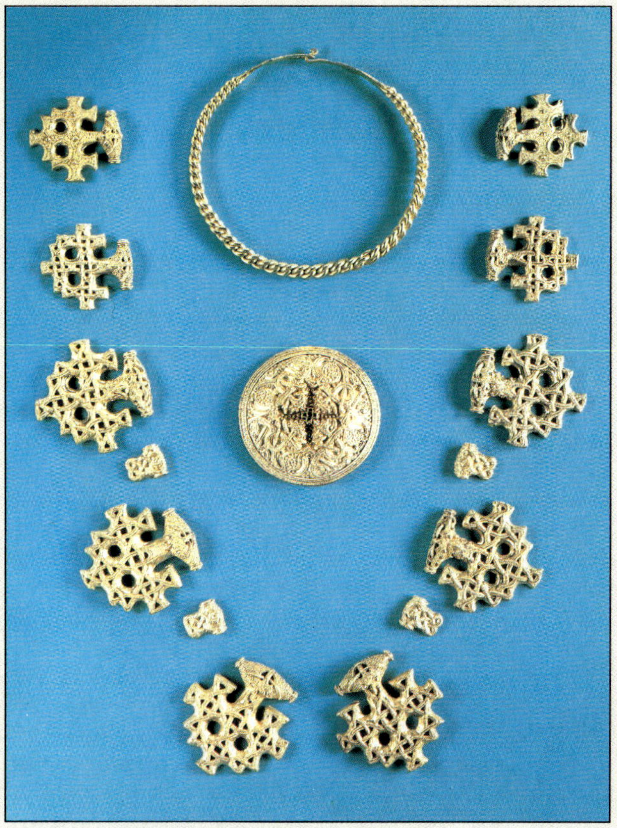

*Right* One of the most spectacular finds from Rügen is this gold hoard from Hiddensee, probably made in Denmark in the late 10th century. The cruciform pendants and filigree spacers decorated with interlace were probably part of a larger necklace. The hoard also contained a circular brooch and a plaited neck-ring. Another hoard, found in a woven basket in a house at Ralswiek, contained 2,270 coins, mostly from 9th-century Arabic and Asian mints.

*Left* The site of the temple-fortress at Arkona remains a dramatic place today, situated on high cliffs battered by the sea. The massive earthen rampart constructed across the narrow promontory on which it lay is still easily visible and was originally surmounted by a covered wooden walkway. Access to the enclosed area was gained by means of a fortified gate topped by a high tower. Much of the interior area of the fortress, including the site of the temple, has been destroyed by the action of the waves.

*Above* Though nothing remains of the temple of Svantevit today, its appearance was probably similar to the Slavic cult building excavated at Gross-Raden in mainland Germany. This reconstruction shows a double-walled building of upright planks topped by carved human heads, surrounded by a fence. This rectangular enclosure is like the one at Arkona described by the Danish historian Saxo Grammaticus about 1200. He mentions the great idol of the god occupying an inner chamber, hung with purple robes and heaped with sacrificial treasure, and also describes the harvest rituals at which a priest offered food and drink to Svantevit, including a special honey-cake the size of a man. Excavations at Arkona have uncovered massive deposits of animal bones that may be the remains of these feasts. The temple precinct housed the stable of a large white horse, believed to be ridden by Svantevit when he waged war against the Rugieris' enemies; the god was served by a special company of 300 riders whose war booty was dedicated at the temple.

## The Russian settlements and the problem of the Rús

At the northern end of this route, on the approaches to lake Ladoga, stood one of the earliest trading centers of eastern Europe, at Staraya (Old) Ladoga. Called *Aldeigjuborg* by the Vikings, Ladoga served as the first port-of-call in the long journey south throughout the history of Scandinavian contact with Russia, and the site grew from a small market center in the 8th century into a large fortified site with a princely residence and a military presence in the 10th. The archaeology of Ladoga and its hinterland provides valuable clues as to the kind of people these early explorers were and the nature of their relations with the native Slav population. The evidence of the cemeteries of varying types that surround the settlement suggests that Scandinavian women as well as men were very likely present at Ladoga, and this certainly implies a more settled and perhaps agricultural existence than appears from the picture that is often painted of the Russian Vikings as an exclusively male class of intrepid warrior-merchants. Excavations of buildings within the town itself show how it expanded in this period, and have much to tell us about the nature of the Vikings' early operations in Russia.

The question of how far the the Vikings influenced the formation of the early Russian state and its towns is one of the most intriguing and controversial aspects of their role in the east. The Scandinavians who ventured and settled in the east were known as *Rús* or *Rhos* to the people they encountered, and there is documentary evidence that they used this name themselves; the meanings or origins of the term are unclear, but its obvious relationship to the name of Russia (that is, "the land of the Rus") is one reason why the debate has been so intense. The word most likely has its roots in the Balt/Finnish word *Ruotsi* meaning "Swedes", but which is derived from the Swedish word *róðr*, meaning a crew of oarsmen. Such a term would be a quite natural way for the early Vikings to describe themselves when meeting new peoples, as their world must at times indeed have seemed limited to that of their own small ships traveling alone into a vast and unknown land.

The debate about the ethnic origins of modern Russia has raged in archaeological and historical studies for decades, and has still not entirely disappeared. However, most scholars today would avoid sweeping generalizations concerning the role of a particular ethnic group, stressing instead the interaction and mutual activities of all the peoples active in the eastern Baltic – Scandinavians, Slavs, Balts and Finns. There is no doubt that Scandinavian contact with the Slavic tribes stimulated cultural change and overseas trading in the area, but few would now argue (as was the case in the past) that the Vikings were actually responsible for the establishment of the early Russian towns and city-states. Rather, the development of the fortified trading centers that grew up in the Viking Age all around the shores of the Baltic from Scandinavia to Russia may be seen as integral to a wider European process of state formation, connected with the centralization of power and the expansion of trading networks and markets. Of all the peoples of the Baltic, however, the Scandinavians were undoubtedly the ones who traveled farthest, and their influence extended to every part of the known world; the permanent presence of Scandinavians in Russia, as revealed by the cemetery evidence at Ladoga, is just one aspect of this larger general process.

From Staraya Ladoga the Vikings sailed south up the Volkhov, passing numerous Slavic settlements on the flood plain, until they reached what they called *Hólmgarðr* – the "settlement on the islands" – situated in the watery landscape at the mouth of Lake Ilmen. When the first Scandinavians reached the area in the early Viking Age there only existed a small settlement on an island south of the modern city of Novgorod, known as Gorodišče. Excavations here have revealed a bustling defended market center that was occupied in the 9th and 10th centuries by a mixed Slavic and Scandinavian population. Its trading connections extended far to the west, whence the craft goods manufactured at the site were transported in return for imports. In the mid 10th century, the settlement expanded to the nearby site of Novgorod (which means "new fortress"), and Gorodišče seems to have continued as a military and administrative center as well as the residence of the princes who ruled Novgorod.

The whole area of islands and lagoons known as the "gates of Novgorod", which controlled the river access to the Byzantine empire and the Abbasid caliphate, became the integrated center of the state that began to evolve from the settlements of the northern Rús. The capital was at Novgorod; satellite settlements such as Gorodišče and the nearby fortified site of Gorodok had specialized roles in the developing political structure. A religious element was also present, from the early Slavic pagan temple of the god Perun on an island near Gorodišče – perhaps the largest and most important such site in the east – to the later network of Christian churches that were built along the shores and islands at the source of the Volkhov river. The wealth and sheer scale of the Novgorod power base has been demonstrated by 60 years of excavations in the city by Russian archaeologists, in some of the richest sites to have been found anywhere in the Viking world.

Novgorod formed the northerly of two major centers of Scandinavian activity on the Russian river-route, the

**Scandinavian influence in the eastern Baltic and Russia**
In the 9th and 10th centuries, the eastern Baltic – peopled by Slavs (Wiltzi, Rugieris, Wolins, Pomeranians and Poles), Balts (Lithuanians, Letts, Kurians, Livians and Ests) and Finns – was the meeting point of many cultures. Scandinavian traders were frequent visitors to the many settlements and market centers along its shores, and seem to have taken up permanent residence in a number of them. As the Vikings moved eastward into Russia, many chose to settle alongside the eastern Slav tribes around Lake Ladoga and along the Volkhov, Lovat and Dnieper rivers, which – together with the Volga – were their main highways to the markets of Byzantium and Asia. The Slavs described these northern travelers as *Rús*. By the late 9th century Novgorod on the Volkhov had grown into the capital of a large territory, the northern *Rús* state, ruled sometimes by Scandinavians and sometimes by Slavs. The *Rús* territory embraced the lands of many different Slavic tribes; the finds excavated in the region reflect this cultural diversity.

*Below* Elizabeth, the daughter of Prince Jaroslav the Wise of Kiev (1016–54), is depicted on the left of this 11th-century wall-painting in the great church of St Sofia in Kiev, built during his reign. She married Harald Hardradi (1015–66), the famous Viking adventurer in the east who served in the Varangian guard of the Byzantine emperor before succeeding to the throne of Norway in 1047.

Saami
Finns
Swedes
Ests
Livians
Kurians
Letts
Lithuanians
Rugieris
Wiltzi
Pomeranians
Wolins
Poles
Merians
Bulgars
Ilmensky Slavs
Krivichians
Radimichians
Vyatichians
Dregovichians
Severyans
Drevlyans
Polyanians
Ulichians
Tivertsy
Magyars
Pechenegs
Khazars
Bulgars
BYZANTINE EMPIRE
BALTIC SEA
BLACK SEA
Sea of Azov
Gulf of Bothnia
Gulf of Finland
Lake Onega
Lake Ladoga
Saimaa
L Peipus
L Ilmen
Åland
Gotland
Öland
Mälaren
Sigtuna
Birka
Helgö
Visby
Tallinn
Riga
Grobin
Kovno
Truso
Rostock
Rügen
Kolobrzeg
Wolin
Staraya Ladoga
Beloozero
Novgorod
Rūs capital 860
Staraya Russa 1070
Izborsk
Pskov
Jaroslavl
Suzdal
Vladimir
Moscow
Murom
Toropets
Polotsk
Vitebsk 1021
Gnezdovo
Smolensk
Pronsk
Logoysk 1078
Minsk 1067
Grodno
Starodub 1079
Pinsk 1097
Turov
Lyubech
Novgorod Severskiy
Kursk
Putivl
Chernigov
Suteska
Vladimir
Lutsk 1085
Kiev
Rūs capital by 900
Pereyaslav
1030
1097
1086
1085
1055
Galich 1097
Odessa
Berezan Island
Tmutorokan
Byzantium
Trebizond
Volkhov
Lovat
Volga
W Dvina
Neman
Vistula
Oder
Bug
Pripet
Dnieper
Dniester
Prut
Danube
Don
Donets
Oka
to England and Normandy
to central Germany
to Bulgar, China, Baghdad and Persia
to Jerusalem, North Africa, Greece and Italy
10°
20°
30°
40°
50°
60°
major Viking Age settlement with date of foundation where known
c.900-1000
c.1000-1150
other Viking Age settlements 9th-11th century
excavated settlement
Finns tribe or people
main trade route
extent of the Rūs state
9th-11th centuries
land gained by 12th century
scale 1 : 12 500 000
0 300 km
0 200 mi

# Staraya Ladoga

Staraya (Old) Ladoga was founded in the 8th century; it served a mixed population of Scandinavians and Slavs, and was the principal market of northern Russia in the early Viking period before the rise of Novgorod and Kiev in the 9th and 10th centuries. Not a true town as such, Ladoga was nevertheless a bustling craft center, and many specialized industries and trades were carried on in its narrow streets. Excavations have uncovered small workshops and house-yards in the central area, which was later enclosed by defenses. After the conversion to Christianity no less than 8 churches and monasteries were constructed in and around the site. The whole settlement is ringed by cemeteries of different kinds, some with cremations under mounds and others with flat inhumations. The varying rituals involved are an indication of the ethnic origin and status of the deceased, and thus it is apparent that each of the cemeteries had a specific character, containing either rich or poor, Scandinavian or Slavic burials. The position of the cemeteries of each type is also important, as some are more prominent than others. Taken with the settlement evidence, the combination of graves and fortifications has been seen by some scholars to indicate a complex network of inter-relationships between the native Slavs and the Scandinavian settlers, with the Ladoga settlement carefully divided into ethnic, political and religious zones of control. If correct, this may shed light on the sophisticated mechanisms behind Viking Age expansion and colonization.

*Below* The plan of the settled areas and excavated sites of Staraya Ladoga, against the topographical background of the Volkhov river and its tributaries, clearly shows the distribution and widely varying character of the cemeteries around the settlement. The division into three "ideological zones" postulated by the Russian archaeologist Lebedev and others translates the distribution of settlement areas and graves into a coherent pattern set out as a deliberate statement of political power and influence.

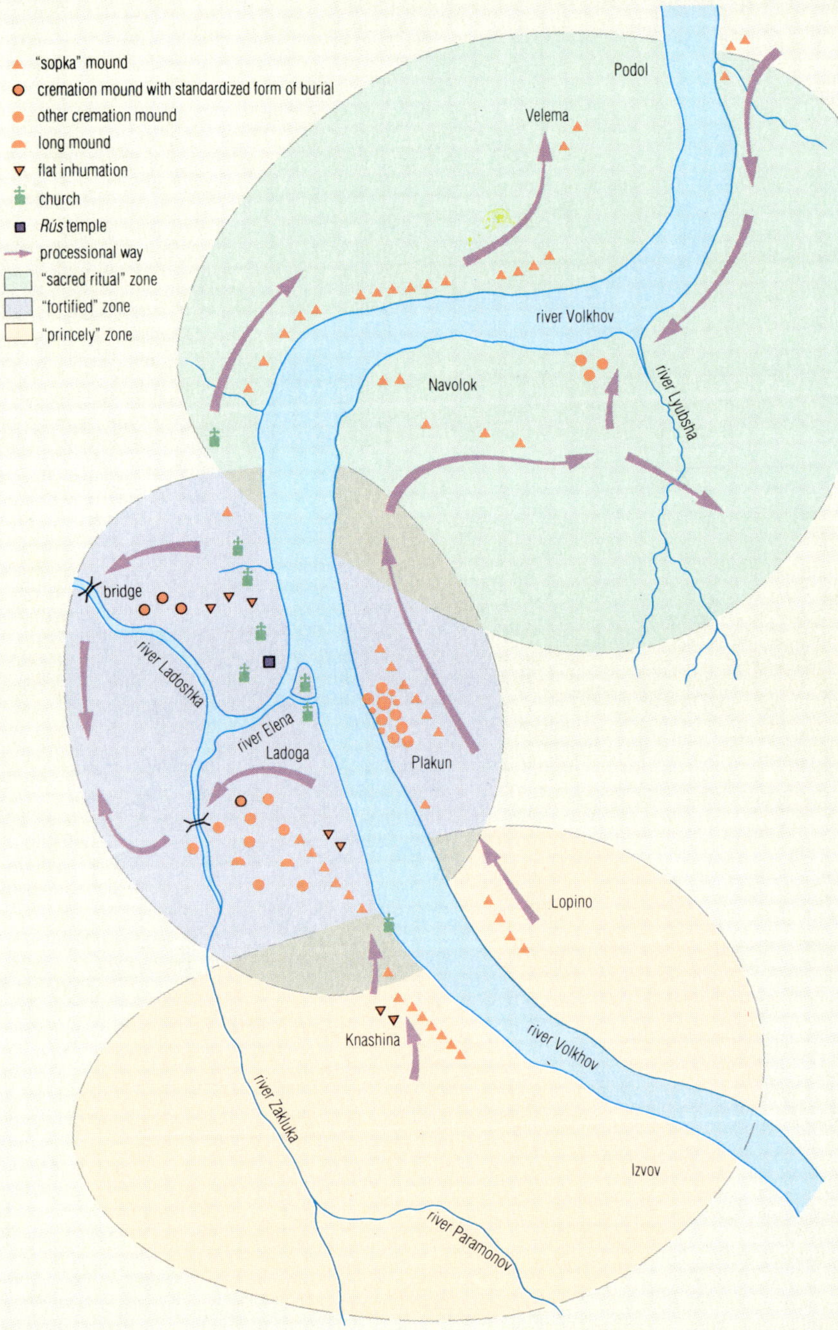


*Right* This bronze object of uncertain function, dating to the 8th century, is one of the finest pieces to have been excavated at Staraya Ladoga. It is only 5.4 centimeters long and may have been a key; alternatively the hollow lower shaft may have fitted on to a small stick for ritual use. The upper part is decorated with the head of a bearded man with long, neatly combed hair; two bird-headed horns meet behind him, and he may represent Odin with his raven servants. The head has been pierced, perhaps for use as a pendant amulet.

The modern site of Staraya Ladoga (*above*) is dominated by the pointed roof of the medieval fortress on the left. The earliest mercantile occupation was located in this area, along the bank of the Volkhov where it is joined by the Ladoshka tributary in the center of the picture. On the right of the Ladoshka is the secondary settlement; it is here that a possible Scandinavian temple has been found on "Varangian street". The so-called aristocratic area of Ladoga lay further to the left, just out of sight. This photograph was taken from the Scandinavian cemetery of Plakun, where the low graves are in marked contrast to the high conical mounds known as *sopki* on Ladoga's peripheries, such as this one (*left*) in the Velema cemetery. These mounds contain Slavic objects buried in a manner that is probably Scandinavian in origin.

*Right* Excavation of the trading center of Ladoga has produced magnificent finds such as this hoard of mid 8th-century smith's tools, so well preserved that the tongs can still be opened and closed. The Odin amulet (*center left*) had been placed on top of the tools inside the box in which they were found, perhaps to protect the valuable contents from thieves.

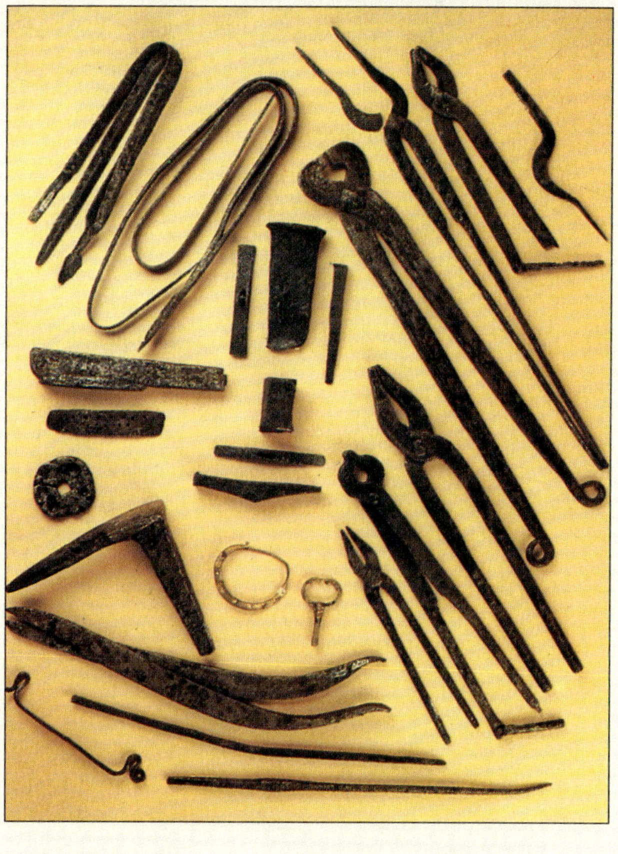

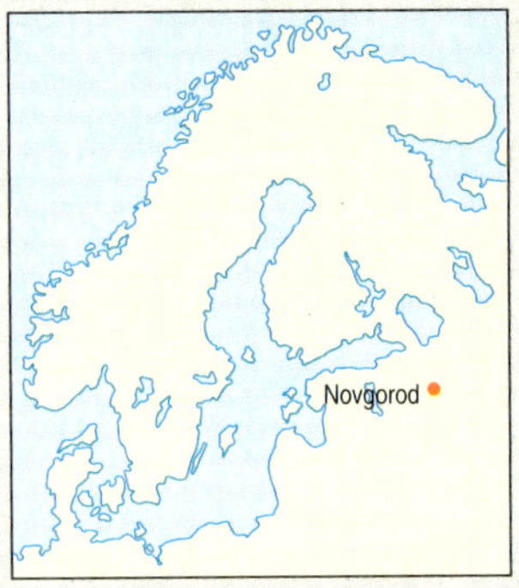


# Novgorod

Settlement in the city of Novgorod, which lies in western Russia just north of Lake Ilmen, began in the 10th century when Scandinavians and Slavs moved there from the defended island of Gorodišče, which lay a few miles to the south. This had been occupied since the early Viking period. The Volkhov river, flowing north to Lake Ladoga, divides Novgorod into two – the Sofia Bank on the west side, and the Merchants' Bank on the east. At the heart of the settlement on the Sofia Bank is the citadel, or kremlin, which was surrounded by a rampart in the 10th century and is still dominated by the cathedral of St Sofia, with its golden domes and towers, which was built in the 11th century: this stone building replaced an earlier wooden structure on the same site. Outside the kremlin, only the Merchants' Bank was defended in the Viking Age.

Though the early medieval city was nominally ruled by a prince, in practice it was governed by a series of popular assemblies (*veche*), one for each of five "ends" or administrative districts into which the town was divided – three on the Sofia Bank, and two on the Merchants' Bank; in the Viking Age, only three "ends" were present. Whether this system of self-government was Scandinavian or Slavic in origin has been hotly debated. The "ends" may also have regulated merchant operations in the town and have been the centers for particular craft activities. Large-scale excavations in the medieval city in waterlogged deposits up to 6 meters thick have uncovered whole neighborhoods of workshops and artisans' dwellings, each enclosed in a small town-yard and laid out along winding, paved streets. Among the numerous artifacts that have been recovered, many of them of wood and leather, is a famous collection of letters written on birch bark: these testify to a considerable degree of literacy among the town's inhabitants. Children's toys, religious idols and masks, furniture, clothes and musical instruments have all been found, contributing to an unrivalled picture of Viking Age urban life.

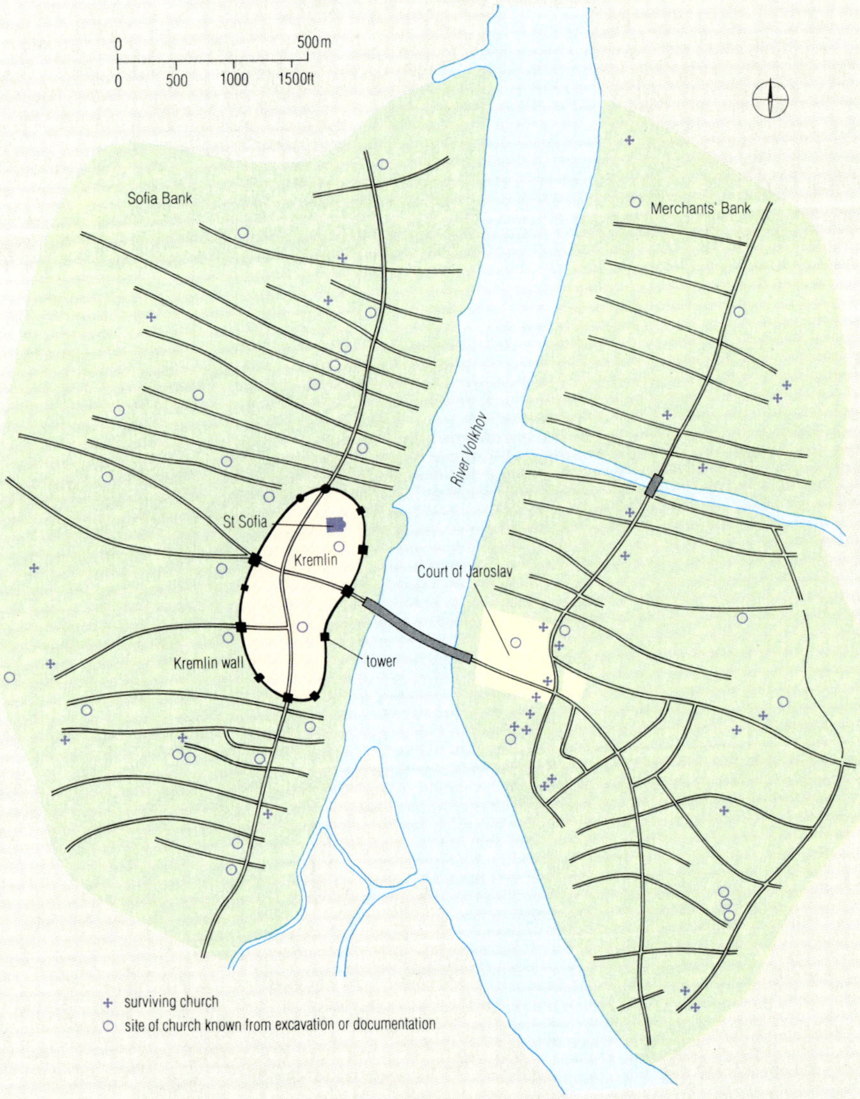

*Left* Early medieval Novgorod, showing the Sofia and Merchants' Banks. The central area of the town around the bridge was controlled by the kremlin and the precincts of the Court of Jaroslav. The street layout shown here is derived from 10th- to 14th-century sources and from excavations: precise dating of the streets is uncertain. The network of churches can be seen to concentrate along the north/south street axis on the Sofia Bank and in the southwest of the Merchants' Bank – the areas dominated by administration and craft activities respectively.

*Above* One of the most striking discoveries of the Novgorod excavations is the network of timber roads found all over the town. Parallel lines of birch and pine were laid out along the route like railroad tracks and then covered with a deck of cross timbers: this formed the surface used by people, animals and vehicles. The roads were repaired often – up to 22 superimposed levels of street contruction have been found in some areas. This fragmentary example comes from the Troitskiy site.

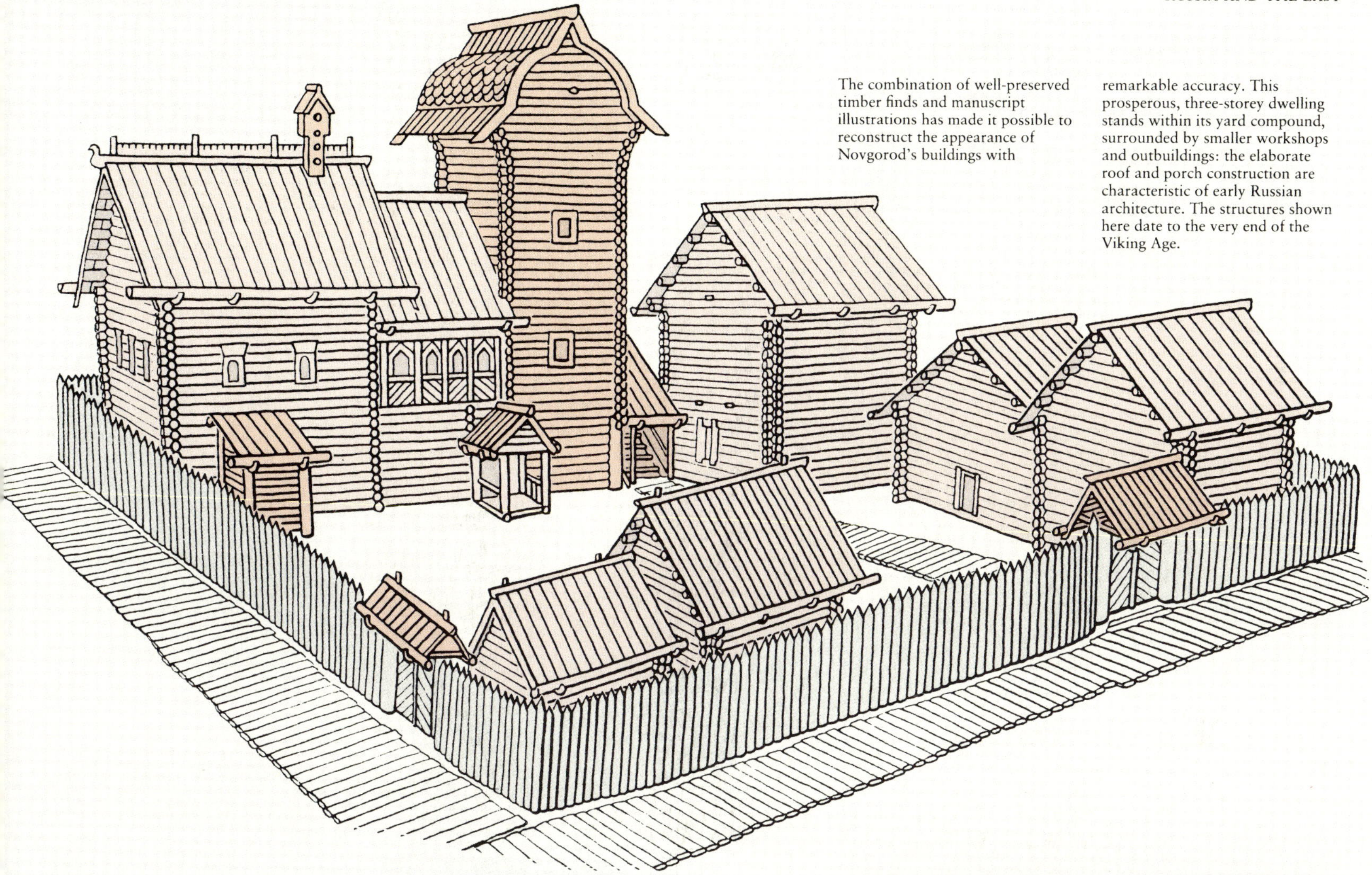

The combination of well-preserved timber finds and manuscript illustrations has made it possible to reconstruct the appearance of Novgorod's buildings with remarkable accuracy. This prosperous, three-storey dwelling stands within its yard compound, surrounded by smaller workshops and outbuildings: the elaborate roof and porch construction are characteristic of early Russian architecture. The structures shown here date to the very end of the Viking Age.

*Left* This typical early Russian church – small and square in plan with a central, onion-domed tower and tall, narrow windows – is one of several that survive on the site of the Court of Jaroslav – the area at the heart of the Merchants' Bank settlement that was used for the popular assembly of the *veche*. Excavations have revealed possible traces of the palace of Jaroslav, named after one of the city's early princes.

*Above* Among the treasures of St Sofia is a massive pair of bronze doors, decorated in relief with small Biblical figures and scenes, and showing many similarities of art-style and design with the nearly contemporary Bayeux tapestry. The doors may have been made for the church of St Olof in Sigtuna – also still standing – and been carried off to Novgorod after a Russian raid on Sweden in the early Middle Ages. An alternative theory places their origin in Magdeburg, Germany.

second being based on Kiev (Ukraine), which the Vikings called *Kœnugarr.* The settlement grew up on the banks of the Dnieper, the river that the Scandinavians reached after sailing south from Novgorod down the Lovat, and carrying their ships across two short portages. The Dnieper connects directly with the Black Sea, and from here the great city of Byzantium on the Bosporus was within easy sailing distance.

Kiev developed in a similar way to Novgorod, and in the 10th century seems to have been ruled by Scandinavians, though with a mixed Slav population. The early 12th-century *Russian Primary Chronicle*, one of our main sources for the early history of the region, states that the Kiev dynasty was founded in the 9th-century by the Scandinavian Rörik and passed to his successors Helgi, Ingvar and the latter's wife Helga. The *Chronicle* records these names in their Slavic forms as Ryurik, Oleg, Igor and Olga. During the 10th and 11th centuries the rulers of Kiev begin to appear with Slavic names such as Svjatoslav, Vladimir and Jaroslav, and this almost certainly reflects a growing blurring of distinctions between the Scandinavian and Slav populations, exactly as seen in the Viking colonies in England and Normandy. From the mid 10th century we find "*Rús*" being used as the usual term for the developing state, though the culture is becoming increasingly Slav-dominated. By the Middle Ages proper, Kiev had replaced Novgorod as the center of the Russian state.

Excavations of Viking Age Kiev have dramatically corroborated the evidence of the written stories concerning its early development. The settlement developed around three hills. One of these, the Starokievskaya, had been the site of an important pagan temple in the pre-Viking period, and by the 9th century had been strongly fortified with timber structures built on its slopes; there was secondary occupation of the other hills. Starokievskaya continued to serve a ritual function as the central cemetery for the growing town. In the later 9th and 10th centuries, traders and artisans settled around the base of the hills (the Podol area) and during the reign of Vladimir (980–1015) the town grew still further, gaining a number of churches including the magnificent Desyatinnaya church, completed in 966, which was built by Byzantine craftworkers and marked the beginning of a truly Russian style of architecture.

Vladimir strengthened the town's defenses with the construction of a strongly-defended citadel (kremlin) on Starokievskaya. Excavations here have revealed the remains of an extensive complex of administrative buildings and ceremonial structures, with residences for court officials, priests and local warrior chieftains. These were surrounded by more humble domestic housing, including structures with sunken floors. Industrial activity seems to have been deliberately confined to the lower town, segregated from the court of the Kievan princes. Kiev expanded still further during the reign of Jaroslav (1015–54), when it acquired even stronger fortifications, and the monumental cathedral of St Sofia, which is still standing, was begun.

Many other settlements within the area of the early *Rús* state show indications of a Scandinavian presence. Chief amongst these is the settlement and cemetery

*Left* The Golden Gate of Kiev was built during the reign of Jaroslav the Wise both as the main entrance to the city and as an integral part of its new fortifications. Originally it stood to a height of 12.5 meters (the same height as the adjoining rampart) but was later raised by the addition of the Church of the Annunciation to the top. The facade was refaced with specially designed bricks when the original structure was restored in 1989.

*Below* After sailing south from Novgorod along the Lovat river, and crossing two short portages, the Scandinavians reached the river Dnieper, which carried them down to the Black Sea and thus to Byzantium. Today, a statue of Prince Vladimir (960–1015), whose dynasty was founded by the Scandinavian Rörik, overlooks the city of Kiev, which was to replace Novgorod as the center of the Russian state by the Middle Ages proper.

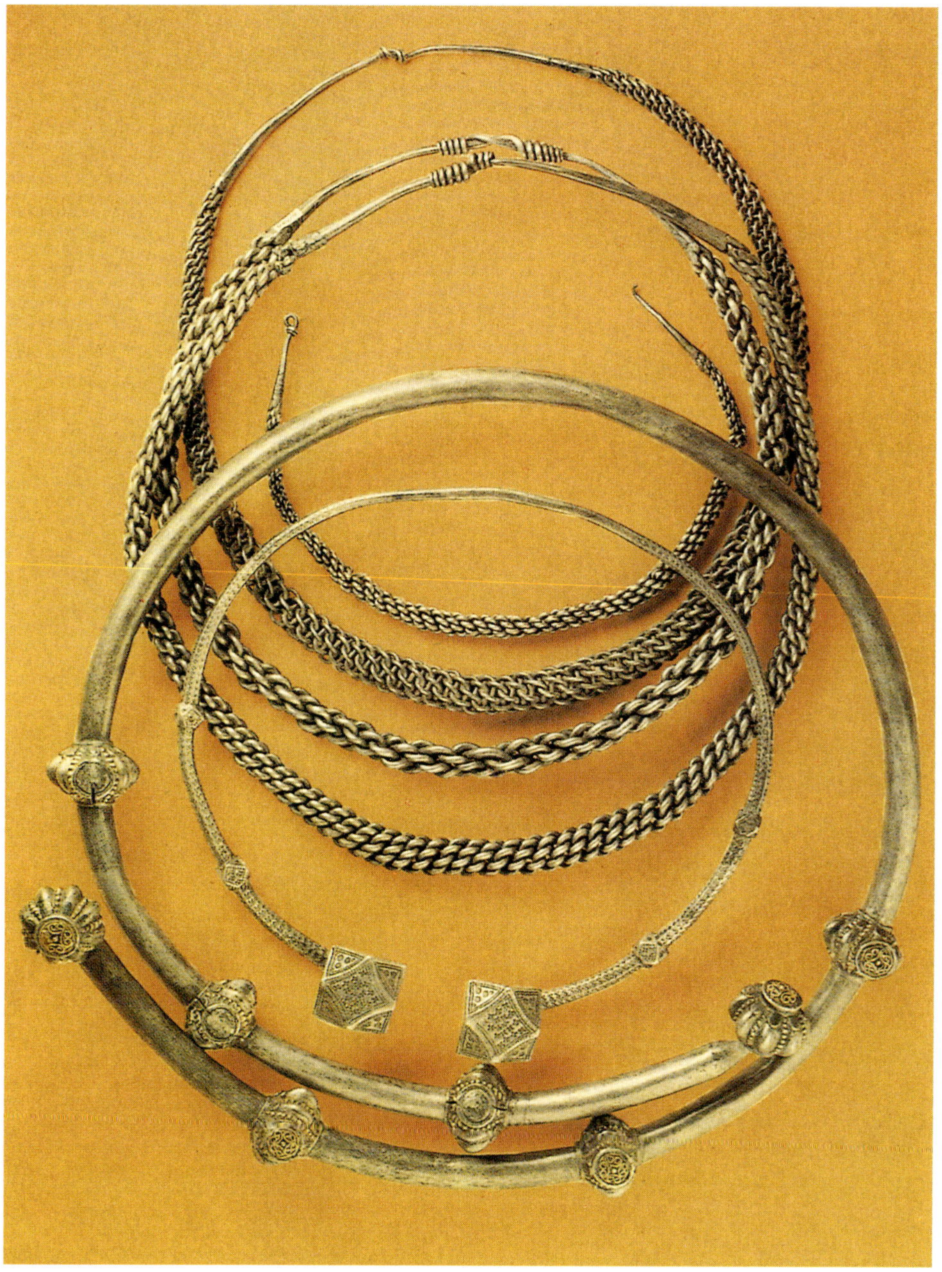

excavated at Gnezdovo, the predecessor of modern Smolensk. This was located halfway along the route from Novgorod to Kiev at the point where the Vikings carried their ships from the Lovat to the Dnieper. Here, Russian archaeologists have recovered many artifacts of Scandinavian type, some of them of great richness and quality, though Slavic objects predominate. Other notable settlements of the *Rús* include Pskov and Izborsk on the Estonian border, which may have been settled from Ladoga in the 10th century. Scandinavian artifacts increase in number in western Russia from the late 9th century into the 10th, but are not found in any quantity farther east, with the exception of the Volga settlements. This distribution provides striking confirmation of the limits of direct Scandinavian activity in the early Russian state.

### The Viking road to *Mikligarðr*

Though their settlements in Russia became one of the most enduring legacies of the Viking Age, the Scandinavians are unlikely to have had colonization in mind when they first set out along the river systems of eastern Europe. Their aim was always to reach Byzantium, the city founded by the emperor Constantine in AD 330. The Roman empire, and the city of Rome itself, had come under increasingly heavy attack from the nomadic barbarian tribes of central Europe in the 5th century and by the later 6th and 7th centuries the focus of power had shifted to the eastern Mediterranean. Byzantium had superseded Rome as the capital of the truncated empire. By the Viking Age it spanned the Bosporus in a massive conurbation that would have been easily the biggest settlement that any Scandinavian had ever seen. The city's great stone defensive walls, its magnificent cathedral and churches, its exotic bazaars and, most of all, the splendid court of the Byzantine emperor, cannot have failed to impress these northern visitors, and they called it simply *Mikligarðr* – "the great city".

Byzantium was attractive to the Scandinavians for several reasons. First and foremost it was a conduit for trade and for the wealth that went with it. Into the city poured goods from the eastern Mediterranean and north Africa, and from the great expanses of Asia. Here the Vikings could obtain silks and embroideries, exotic

*Above* The greatest Viking Age silver hoard from Russia was found at Gnezdovo in 1868. This 10th-century treasure consists mainly of ornaments, most of which are Scandinavian or Slavic in character. Alongside the standard twisted and plaited rod neck-rings is a unique tubular ring with filigree-ornamented knobs.

*Right* This fragment of red taffeta silk, on to which have been stitched yellow silk bands, was excavated at Lund, Sweden. Though a few examples of Chinese silks have been identified at Birka, most of the silks found in Viking Age Scandinavia are believed to have been imported from Byzantium, as is probably the case with this example.

**The Byzantine empire and the Abbasid caliphate**
In the 9th and 10th centuries Islamic rule extended as far west as Spain and as far east as northern India: in the eastern Mediterranean and Asia Minor, only the Byzantine empire stood out against it: Scandinavians fought as mercenaries in the imperial armies as the Greeks sought to extend their empire and counter the Muslim threat to the south and east. After 750, following the overthrow of the Umayyad dynasty by the Abbasids (except in Spain), the center of Islamic power had shifted eastward to Baghdad and many silver mines were opened up in central Asia. It was these rich sources of silver, together with the networks of trade that stretched overland from central Asia to India and China and from Byzantium to the Mediterranean and Africa, that drew the Vikings down the great rivers of Russia to the Caspian and Black Seas.

fruits and wines, spices and fine jewelry. Evidence of this trade has been found in abundance in Scandinavia and throughout the Viking world. For example, textiles from Byzantium have been discovered as far away as England. Analysis of pieces of silk found in 10th-century levels in two different exavation sites, one in York and one in Lincoln, has even shown that they came from the same bale. In exchange for these luxuries, the Vikings traded furs from the northern forests and other commodities, including slaves.

The empire offered other openings for the warriors who had sailed, rowed and hauled their longships all the way across Russia and Ukraine. A continual supply of soldiers was needed for the armies that were either fighting on the empire's borders or maintaining peace within them. The Byzantines recognized the fighting qualities of the Vikings early on, and by the late 10th century the emperor's personal guard was composed entirely of Scandinavian mercenaries, their loyalty bought with silver and a privileged position in the imperial court. It may even have been one of these men, Halfdan, who scratched his name in runes on a balcony in the great church of Hagia Sofia (later a mosque, now a museum) in Istanbul.

The "Varangian guard", as they were called, were famed for their drinking and their terrible battle axes; membership of the guard became a recognized steppingstone in the career of many a famous Viking. One of the best known of these was King Harald Hardradi of Norway (1015–1066), who was a notable commander of the guard and campaigned in Sicily, Italy and Bulgaria for several years. According to the sagas, Harald Hardradi was said to have had an affair with the empress and to have participated in a successful coup on the throne; he would not have been the only Scandinavian to become directly involved in Byzantine politics. On at least two occasions, Scandinavians fought against the empire when Kievan war fleets attacked the walls of Byzantium in the late Viking Age. Once the Russian prince actually nailed his shield to the gates of the city, vividly demonstrating his contempt for the power of the emperor and for the Byzantines who were sheltering within.

The exact meaning of the name "Varangian" (*Varjagi* in Russian sources, *Varangoi* to the Byzantine Greeks) as used of the eastern Vikings is not fully understood. It appears alongside "*Rús*" in the sources, but seems to have had a more warlike association than the latter term. Varangians appear as mercenaries and bodyguards to Russian princes in the 11th and 12th centuries and there have been attempts to trace the word to the Scandinavian *vár*, meaning an oath of allegiance appropriate to professional soldiers. In Staraya Ladoga, a road-name dating from medieval times and still in use today meaning "Varangian street" may indicate that this was a Scandinavian quarter of the settlement. In a dramatic demonstration of the enduring place of the Scandinavians in the popular consciousness of the east, one of the largest aircraft carriers of the former Soviet battle fleet was named "Varangian".

For most of our knowledge about the actual river route taken by the Vikings to the Black Sea we must turn to the Byzantine sources, and in particular to a secret document of the Emperor Constantine Porphyrogenitos outlining the empire's foreign policy strategies in the mid 10th century. This refers to the northern *Rús* as acting as

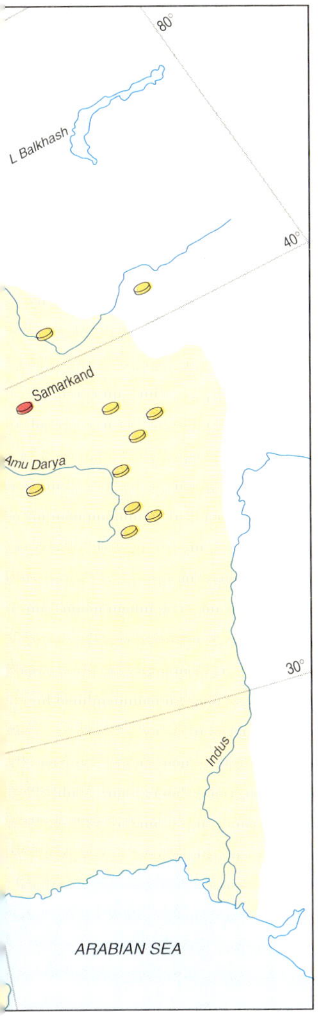


buffers against the aggression of the hostile Slavic tribes. The hazardous journey taken by the Scandinavians down the Dnieper each June after the ice had melted comes vividly to life as we read of them carrying their ships around the series of seven fierce rapids in the river and fighting off the attacks of Slavic bandits. Even in the Greek source, the rapids all have recognizable, descriptive Scandinavian names: *Essupi* (the Gulper), *Baruforos* (Wave-force), *Strukun* (the Courser), *Gelandri* (the Yeller), *Ulvorsi* (Island-foss), *Leanti* (the Laugher). The name given to one of the rapids – *Aïfur* (Ever-noisy) – is found on a Swedish rune-stone from Pilgårds, on Gotland, raised to the memory of a man named Hrafn by his four brothers who had accompanied him on an expedition east. Sweden's runic inscriptions contain a number of references to the river road to Byzantium. It is in tributes to people such as Spialbodi "who met his death in Novgorod" (rune-stone from Sjusta, Uppland) and Rognvald "leader of a troop of men in Greece" (Ed, Uppland) that the Viking push to the east has found some of its most lasting memorials.

### The Volga silver route and the Abbasid caliphate

While some Swedes made the journey south from Staraya Ladoga into Russia and down to the Black Sea, others followed an even more ambitious route directly east to the lands of the Bulgar tribes, the Khazar nomads and finally to the deserts of Arabia and the seat of the Abbasid caliph at Baghdad. After Lake Ladoga these voyagers joined the upper waters of the river Volga, passing through settlements at Beloozero, Jaroslavl, Vladimir and Murom; Scandinavian artifacts have been found at all of these. The Scandinavians may have traveled as family groups rather than as lone merchant expeditions, judging by the numbers of women's graves that have been found along the route; there is also no reason to rule out the possible presence of female merchants. The Volga makes a great bend at Bulgar (close to the site of the modern city of Kazan) as it turns south to the Caspian Sea. This marked the western end of the Silk Road, the overland trade route that ran through Samarkand and Tashkent to China, and here a great market place had developed controlled by the Bulgar tribes. We know that Scandinavian merchants must have encountered the caravans that traveled the Silk Road because Chinese silks have been found in graves at Birka in central Sweden. These finds, together with the figure of Buddha that has been found at the pre-Viking Site at Helgö may even allow us to speculate on the extraordinary possibility that Scandinavians themselves may have journeyed all the way to the Chinese court or the Indian subcontinent.

Bulgar was the first of the markets at which the Scandinavians encountered the massive silver supplies of the Arab world. The Volga trade may have begun as early as the late 8th century with agreements between the Abbasid caliphate and the Khazar tribes of the lower Volga. The Abbasids had swept to power in the Islamic world around 750 by supporting popular revolt against the injustices of the previous ruling family, the Umayyads. After rejecting the old capital of Damascus in Syria as an Umayyad stronghold, the new dynasty eventually established its power base at Baghdad on the Tigris in modern Iraq. By the beginning of the Viking Age the city had grown massively, thriving on the huge silver reserves of the caliphate's dominions. The main mines lay in Afghanistan, discovered in the 9th century, with the richest sources in the Panjshir valley. Other mines were located in central Asia in what are today Uzbekistan, Kirghizia and Tajikistan. The output was

*Right* This worn runic inscription, which was scratched on a marble balustrade in the church of Hagia Sofia in Byzantium, is only partly legible, but the name "Halfdan" has been deciphered. Other runic graffiti have been discovered in the same gallery.

enormous: most of the silver was rendered into coins, and even the relatively unimportant mine at Radrad in Yemen produced enough silver to mint over a million coins a year. The Abbasids grew fabulously wealthy on the silver trade, which reached as far as India, Sri Lanka, China and Persia.

The Vikings seem to have begun to tap the Arab silver sources in the early 9th century, acquiring coins that had been minted a couple of decades earlier. It became their main precious metal, and their appetite for it was enormous. Over 60,000 Arab coins have been found in over 1,000 hoards in Scandinavia alone, with many others in the Viking colonies. It is clear that only a tiny proportion of the silver imported in the form of coins was kept as such; most was melted down and recast as bullion or jewelry. The Vikings bought the silver with similar items to those they traded at Byzantium – furs, slaves, falcons, honey, wax, walrus ivory and strong steel swords.

From the market at Bulgar the Volga river route entered the lands of the Khazar nomads. Their capital was Itil on the shores of the Caspian Sea and they controlled the whole territory through which the southern section of the Volga route passed. The politics of the caliphs were much concerned with negotiating the best outlets for silver through the competing Khazar and Bulgar markets and both the caliphate and the northern merchants were eager to maintain good relations with the Khazars. Khazar influences made their way back to Sweden, where some fashions in jewelry and personal dress reflected eastern taste. This is evident, for example, from many of the objects found in graves at Birka. Some eastern-inspired objects, such as the commonly found twisted and plaited rings, were adopted throughout Scandinavia. From Itil, the Viking sailors could cross the Caspian Sea and continue overland along the caravan route from Gorgan to Baghdad, and the caliph's court. Again, artifacts that can only have originated in the heart of the caliphate have been found in Scandinavia, including particularly fine examples of Arab pottery. Not all Scandinavian voyages to the east were peaceable, however, or made with commerce as the only object in mind. Viking raiders launched several expeditions in the area, including a major attack on Baku and the shores of the Caspian Sea in 912.

The silver trade with the Abbasids gradually declined during the 9th century as the mines became exhausted and the caliphate was torn apart by civil wars, foreign campaigns and the drain of a series of extravagant building projects such as the royal city of Samarra. This stretched for 35 kilometers along the banks of the Tigris and took 46 years to build. By 892, the Abbasid treasury was empty, but around this time massive new silver sources were discovered in Afghanistan and the Arab economy slowly recovered. The client Samanid rulers of Transoxiana, the region including the great trading cities of Bukhara and Samarkand north of the Oxus (Amu Darya) river, soon began to produce huge quantities of coins, which found their way west into Russia and the Viking world. After the beginning of the 10th century, coins from these sources are in fact found farther west than those dating to the first phase of silver production in the 9th century. In Russia alone, several hundred thousand Arab coins have been recovered from hoards. This even more massive export of silver from the caliphate continued almost unabated until around 965 when the Samanid mines, too, seem to have become depleted. Though a trickle of coinage from the east still flowed into Scandinavia in the 980s and 990s, the Vikings had begun to look to European sources for their supply of silver, particularly to new mines in the Harz mountains in central Germany. By 1015 the importation of Arab silver had ceased completely, and the eastern link was broken.

*Above* A heap of assorted silver coins found in Sweden, mostly Arabic and Byzantine, serves as a vivid reminder that silver – above all else – was the magnet that drew the Scandinavians eastward to raid and trade in the Baltic region and down the Russian rivers. In the quest for Arabic silver, mined in enormous quantities at this period, they even reached the Caspian Sea by way of the Volga, though much business was no doubt transacted higher up the river, in the great market at Bulgar.

During the period of the expanding silver trade, the Abbasid caliphate sent many diplomatic and mercantile envoys into the northern lands to negotiate trading terms and to scout for new markets. These ambassadors of Islam were very often men of the highest education and learning, and they have left detailed records of their journeys. Ibn Fadlan's initial impressions of a party of Scandinavian merchants that he met in 922 are well worth quoting for its striking eyewitness testimony, the details of which accord so well with the archaeological evidence of Viking appearance:

*I have seen the* Rús *as they came in on their merchant journeys and encamped on the Volga. I have never seen more perfect physical specimens, tall as date palms, blond and ruddy; they wear neither tunics nor caftans, but the men wear a garment that covers one side of the body and leaves a hand free. Each man has an ax, a sword, and a knife, and keeps each by him at all times...Each woman wears on either breast a box of iron, silver, copper or gold...each box has a ring from which hangs a knife. The women wear neck-rings of gold and silver...their most prized ornaments are green glass beads.*

After describing the offerings made to their pagan gods by these tough-sounding people in the hope of good trading, Ibn Fadlan goes on to quote a Viking adventurer's pragmatic prayer: "I wish that you would send me a merchant with many *dinars* and *dirhems*, who will buy from me whatever I wish and will not dispute anything I say." It is ironic that the most detailed contemporary descriptions we have of the Vikings should come from the periphery of their world. The Arab sources give us unparalleled information about the daily life of the Scandinavians on the move – their dress and fashions, behavior, funeral rituals and warfare – making the Viking expansion to the east one of the most vivid events of the period.

# PART FOUR

# THE END OF THE VIKING WORLD

# THE LATER VIKING AGE AND AFTER

## Scandinavia in the 11th century

The 11th century saw the completion of the Scandinavian kingdoms' transition to nation-states, a process begun in the previous two centuries. Ambitious programs of urban foundation, the establishment of new mints, and the extension of church patronage in the newly converted pagan north played their part in the continued growth of centralized power and kingship. At the same time there was a general expansion of the rural population, with corresponding movement of settlement onto more marginal areas of land and some modification of agricultural practices. All these factors brought material changes to the Scandinavian landscape in the later Viking Age.

## Denmark

As we have seen, urbanization was more advanced in Denmark than in the other Scandinavian countries at the end of the 10th century. A considerable number of towns, roads, bridges and similar works were completed during the reign of Harald Bluetooth in the mid 10th century, and for the most part this process was continued by his son Svein Forkbeard (reigned c.987–1014) and the later 11th-century Danish kings. However, it is clear that Bluetooth's civic engineering programs were considered excessive by many of his subjects, whose taxes had to bear the brunt of their massive costs. It has been suggested that it was the unpopularity of Harald's extravagant projects that led his son to rebel against him, leading to Harald's expulsion from the kingdom and Svein's succession. Certainly Harald's circular fortresses such as Trelleborg and Fyrkat, which may have been administrative centers for tax gathering, went out of use in Svein's time. After Harald's reign, new construction work was no doubt partly funded by silver obtained from a massive renewal of raiding in England – a more popular source of royal revenue than money raised through taxation.

Though the town of Hedeby declined after 1000, its functions were assumed by the nearby settlement of Schleswig, and Ribe flourished under royal patronage, as did Århus, Lund, Odense, Roskilde and Viborg, all founded before or around 1000. Excavations have uncovered the 11th-century streets and buildings of many of these towns, with particularly fine material from Århus, where the remains of cellared buildings have been found, each with benches around the walls and a hearth in one corner. Lund, too, has yielded valuable information. Several levels of carefully laid street surfaces have been preserved in the rich organic soil; some roads were made entirely of leather off-cuts discarded from manufacturing. Many wooden buildings have survived, along with their contents. The finds include such familiar items as childrens' toys, and even a tiny chair with a closable front to restrain a small child and keep it from running about.

The Danish kings were eager in their support of the church as it established itself in the territories newly converted to Christianity, for several reasons. Firstly, they saw the fact of a single faith in the land – as opposed to the highly diverse and variable customs of the old pagan religion – as a useful force for unification in Denmark which, by drawing the populace together, paralleled their attempts to establish a single political state. A second reason may be found in the ideology of kingship: generous patronage of the church was an appropriate attribute for a monarch who wished to be treated as an equal by the kings of mainland Europe. The decrees concerning the support of the church that Cnut the Great (d.1035) made as king of England from 1016 and extended to Denmark when he succeeded to the throne there in 1018 exemplified this pattern. The earliest known example of a stone church in Denmark is one founded in Roskilde by Cnut's sister in 1027. After that, stone became the principal material used for churches, and earlier timber buildings, such as that built at Jelling – perhaps by Harald Bluetooth to house his pagan father's remains – were replaced in stone.

By the later 11th century, the Danish kingdom had a number of bishoprics, necessitating the building of cathedrals. At first craftworkers and masons from

**Scandinavia in the 11th century** By 1000, the Scandinavian countries had achieved a high degree of political cohesion, and the first nation-states were forming. In the course of the century, the centralization and concentration of power in the hands of kings was reflected in the rapid development of true urban centers – planned towns laid out by royal command. New mints were founded and administrative centers and road networks constructed at this time. Christianity had become established throughout Scandinavia in the 11th century, and the new faith was quickly consolidated by the establishment of bishoprics and widespread church-building. By 1100, the three Scandinavian countries were firmly bound into the political and ideological orbit of Christian Europe.

*Above* A coin of the English king, Æthelred II (979–1016) – one of several thousand that have been found in Scandinavia. Many of these are likely to have arrived there in the *Danegelds* paid to the new waves of Danish raiders during the late 10th and early 11th centuries. In some 50 years the English made payments of £250,000 to the Vikings – a valuable source of revenue.

*Below* The baptism of Harald Bluetooth, who is standing in a large cask, is depicted on a 12th-century plaque in Tamdrup church, Jutland – one of a series of seven, made from gilded copper, that illustrate scenes from the life of St Poppo. The saint is credited with having brought about the Danish king's conversion to Christianity by impressing him with his feat of carrying a redhot iron.

England and mainland Europe were employed in their construction. Odense cathedral, for example, built in the 1080s, incorporates features from Germany and Italy as well as England, attributable to the presence of English clerics there. As the country became fully integrated into the Christian cultural sphere of mainland Europe, its urban and rural environments altered in ways that would have made them unrecognizable to a Viking of the later 9th century.

### Norway

In contrast to neighboring Denmark, Norway did not experience urban growth on any scale until well into the 11th century. For reasons not yet fully explained, small seasonal market centers such as Kaupang did not develop in Norway into towns, as they did elsewhere in Scandinavia, and it was not until around the year 1000 that real towns were established at Trondheim or Nidaros (*Niðaross* to the Vikings) in the north and Skien and Oslo in the southeast. Trondheim in particular developed rapidly along the river Nid, and quickly became a royal seat of Norwegian kings. Excavations in the waterlogged deposits beneath the present town have revealed the remains of carefully laid out building plots, houses and yards, together with the waste from the manufacturing that went on inside them. Oslo has produced directly comparable structures dating to the early 1000s.

There seems little doubt that both towns were founded by royal command. Only centralized authority such as the Norwegian kings possessed by this time could have established the protected trade zones that enabled craftworking, other industrial activity and commercial enterprise to flourish. In effect, the entire towns may have been the king's personal property to be let out or rented to specialized communities of artisans and royal officers. The relationship would have been a reciprocal one: in return for protection the king would have exacted his due share of taxes and tolls. The splendor of the royal court was also no doubt enriched by the finest products these urban centers had to offer. At their heart lay the royal residences, surrounded by the halls of the king's retinues and bodyguards. Later in the century, these were joined by mints, churches and cathedrals, all part of the apparatus of power and authority that would have been considered appropriate for a great king. Later towns were founded at Bergen and Stavanger on Norway's west coast, and at Tønsberg near Oslo. All have produced archaeological material from the later 11th century.

As noted earlier, Christianity played an essential role in Norway's progress to nation-state in the late 10th and 11th centuries. The first churches were constructed of wood. No complete structures have survived from this period, but their plans are often preserved as post-holes beneath their 12th and 13th-century stone successors, and it is sometimes possible to identify several phases of rebuilding since the timber buildings were frequently destroyed by fire, or the wooden planks set in the ground rotted and needed replacement. The large numbers of elaborately decorated wooden stave-built churches surviving from the 12th century give us some idea of what these first Norwegian churches were like. The finest, such as Borgund and Urnes, both in western Norway, are among the best-preserved wooden buildings from the whole of medieval Europe. Sometimes timbers from the earlier churches of the later Viking Age are actually incorporated into their structure, and from them we can gain a tantalizing glimpse of how magnificent their carving must have been.

### Sweden

With the exception of Sigtuna, which seems to have assumed the functions of the island town of Birka, probably abandoned in the mid to late 10th century, urbanization was not widely developed in Sweden until the 12th century. Coin inscriptions indicate that Sigtuna was almost certainly a royal foundation; it was laid out in a ribbon development along an arm of Lake Mälaren. Excavations have demonstrated the existence of several churches in the town, along with urban tenements of the kind familiar from late Viking towns in Denmark and Norway.

In a sense, Sigtuna can be seen as an early capital functioning as a royal, ecclesiastical and administrative center for the dynasty that controlled central and eastern Sweden. While the transition of urban settlement from Birka to Sigtuna may in part have been prompted by the falling sea-levels that began to dry out Birka's harbors, there were likely to have been more complex reasons behind the decision to move the largest settlement in Sweden. Occupation could have continued at Birka without much difficulty for longer than it did, but Sigtuna's situation, right at the heart of the developing state, would have offered a more

# Stave Churches

The Viking culture has left many lasting traces of its brief heyday, but a class of particularly unusual monuments has survived in the form of the wooden stave churches that are to be found in Norway and (though to a lesser extent) the other Scandinavian countries. Stave construction was a late development in Viking Age architecture, and began to be used for churches during the 11th century: the technique appears in some domestic buildings slightly earlier. In its simplest form, the stave-building method resembles the construction of a barrel – a row of slightly curved, interlocking vertical timbers is held in place by being clasped between two horizontal grooved timbers along the top and bottom of the wall. This has the effect of raising the wall timbers off the ground, thus protecting them from damp and rot – earlier wooden churches, built of posts fixed in the earth, would have rotted away within a generation of their construction. No stave churches have survived intact from the 11th century, but fragments of their carved timbers have been found preserved in the fabric of their medieval successors and in other buildings: notable examples come from Flatatunga in Iceland and Hemse in Sweden. However, it was in the churches built at the end of the Viking Age and on into the 12th and 13th centuries that stave construction reached its most developed and sophisticated form. Stave churches of this date dot the Norwegian landscape where they stand as remarkable monuments to the architectural and artistic achievements of the early medieval Scandinavians during their absorption into the cultural orbit of Christian Europe.

*Left* The church at Borgund, on the Sogne fjord in western Norway, is without doubt the finest surviving example of a stave church. Its basic structure dates from the 12th century; the magnificent animal-headed finials and multiple roofs were probably added a century later. Such elaborate decoration is typical of the later churches, and sometimes attained an extraordinary sophistication and beauty.

*Below left* The graceful interlacing beasts that frame the keyhole-shaped door of the church at Urnes, not far distant from Borgund, were carved in the 11th century, and have given their name to the Urnes art-style of the late Viking Age.

*Below* The interiors of stave churches were also carved – as here at Borgund – and the intricate construction of the timbers adds an element of simple elegance not popularly associated with the "warlike" Vikings. The extravagant and highly ornate appearance of many stave churches gives us cause to wonder whether Viking Age domestic buildings may also have been covered with rich ornament of this kind.

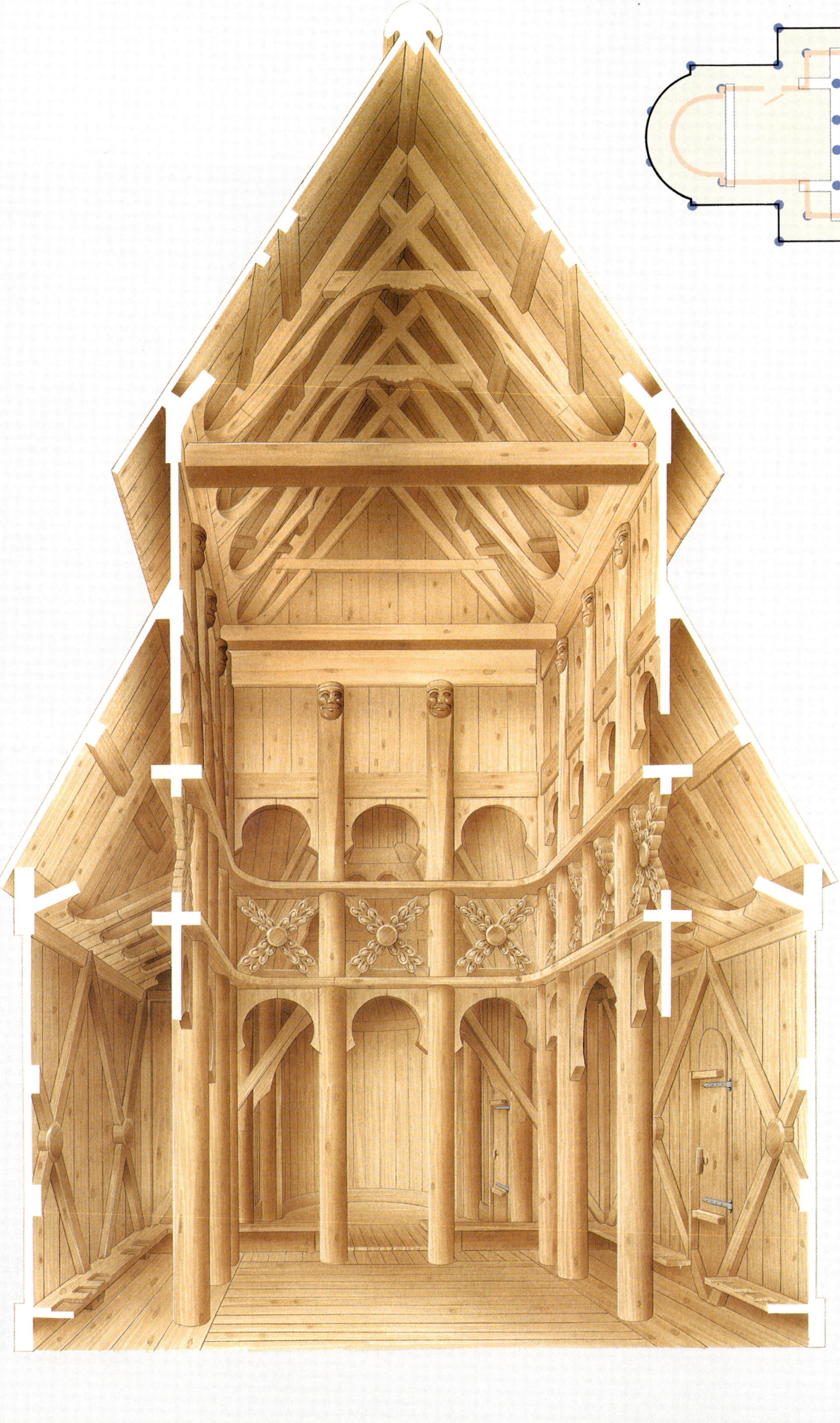

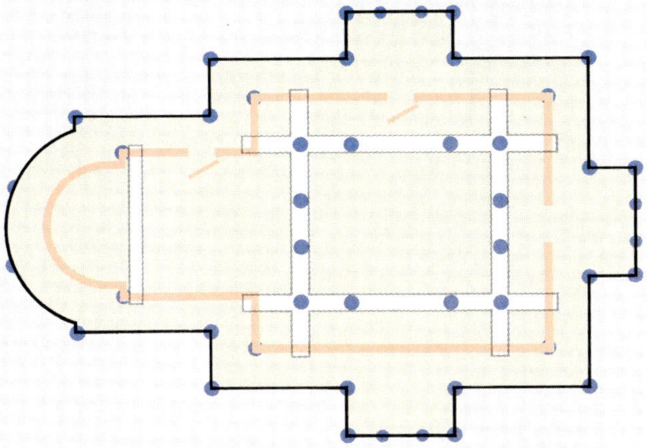

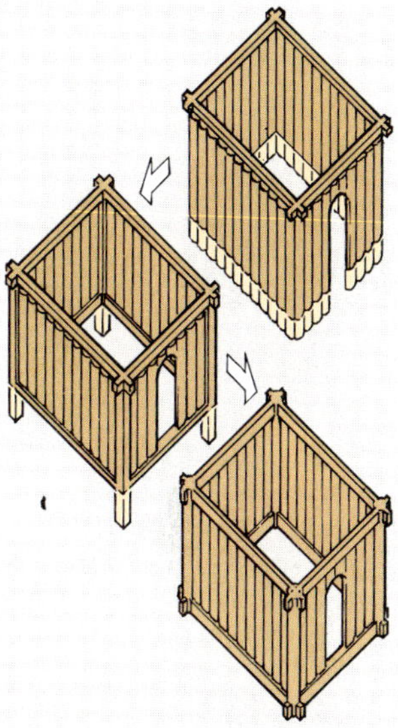

The stave churches of the 11th century were of simple rectangular plan, often with a small square chancel added to the nave and, less frequently, aisles. The later churches embellished this design and were usually centered around four supporting posts set in a square, which reached high up into the building and raised the roof level: Borgund (*shown in cross-section on left*) is a typical example. The central post arrangement was sometimes developed into an arcade and the whole structure was designed as a series of successive squares (*left, and groundplan at top*). Despite these elaborations, the essentials of the stave-construction technique remained constant from the Viking Age well into the medieval period: the development of the method is shown (*above*), from its origins in earth-fast construction, through an intermediate four-post and sill beam stage, to the final form in which the entire structure is raised above the ground.

# Sigtuna

Toward the end of the 10th century, perhaps around 970, the small town of Sigtuna was founded along a northern branch of Lake Mälaren in central Sweden. Like Birka, which it succeeded, it was probably under royal control. From its beginnings, Sigtuna was laid out on a regular plan with a central street following the lakeshore. Long, narrow tenements fronted the street on both sides – possibly more than 100 of them – with the king's residence occupying a site at the heart of the town. From at least 995, King Olof Skötkonung was issuing coins bearing the legend "God's Sigtuna", and the site of the earliest mint in Sweden has been excavated next to the royal residence. Remains of goldsmiths' and other high-status craft workshops have also been found here. Sigtuna was a Christian town, and the probable sites of at least seven churches have been identified, with a number of cemeteries nearby. Many of the archaeological deposits in Sigtuna are waterlogged, and preserve some of the best Viking Age material in Sweden. Excavations near the royal enclosure have revealed four whole tenements, successively rebuilt in ten phases of occupation from the 10th to 13th centuries. The street frontage was occupied by workshops and buildings with dwellings behind – sometimes up to five structures deep on one plot in the 11th century. The wealth of finds testifies to craftworking in metals, textiles, bone and antler and other materials.

*Below* The water level around Sigtuna was 5 meters higher in the late Viking Age than it is today, and occupation layers have been located all along the early shoreline. The spinal axis of the settlement survives today as *Stora gatan* (Main Street); the former site of the royal enclosure at its center lies today beneath Sigtuna museum. The plan also shows the pagan mound burials and Christian cemeteries surrounding the town, and the distribution of churches.

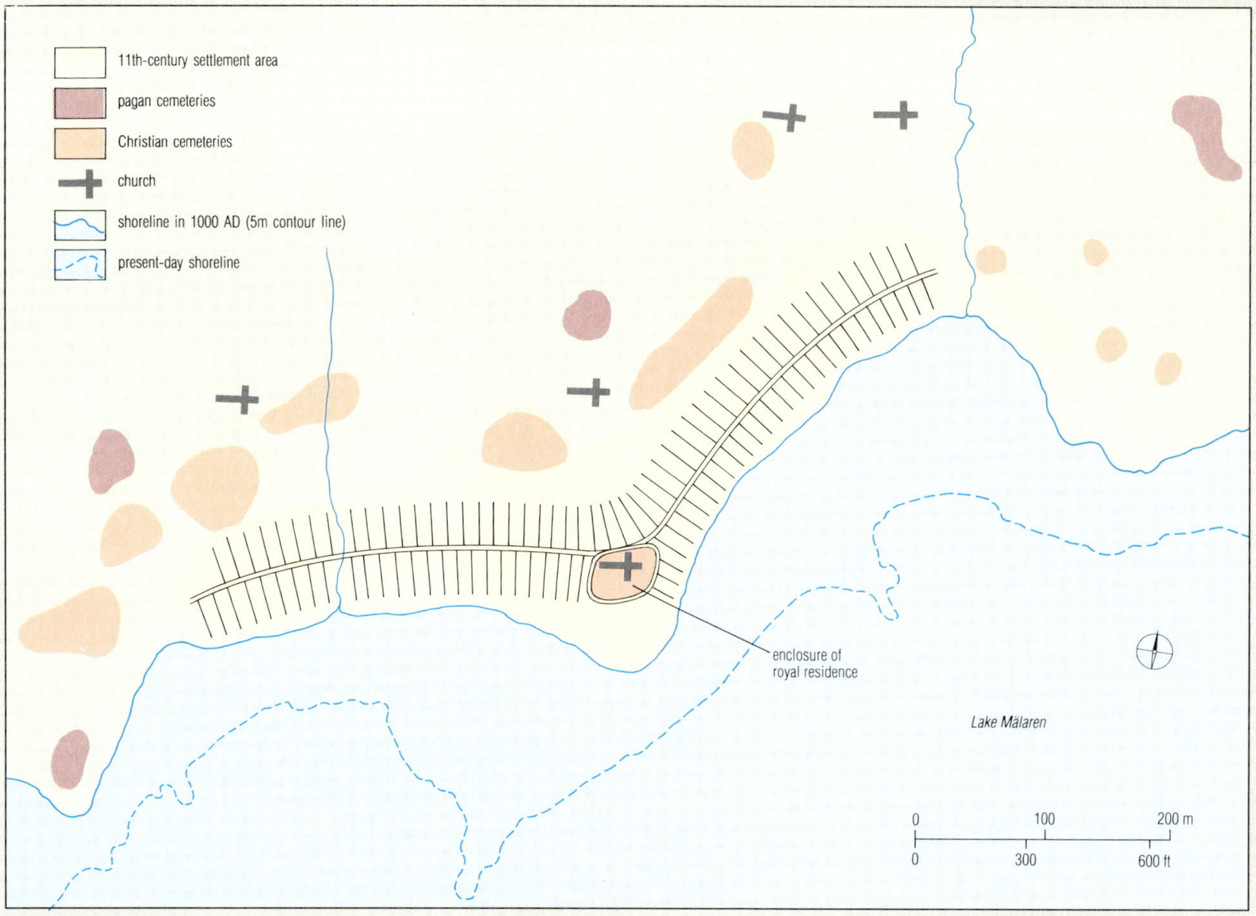

*Left* Sigtuna's foreign contacts can be seen in such finds as this glazed pottery egg, made in Kiev in the early 11th century. Eggs like this seem to have been Christian symbols of the Resurrection, and were distributed from Russia throughout the eastern and southern Baltic.

*Right* Naturalistic portraits are rare in the Viking Age. One of the most famous is this carved head of a warrior, made from elk antler and found in the center of Sigtuna. His conical helmet is decorated with ring-and-dot patterns, and he wears his hair neatly rolled at the back of his neck. The long mustache and carefully trimmed beard were standard elements of male fashion.

*Below* Together with the coin inscriptions, the earliest mention of Sigtuna's name comes from this late 11th-century rune-stone, which tells how a certain Sven brought a female relative to the town.

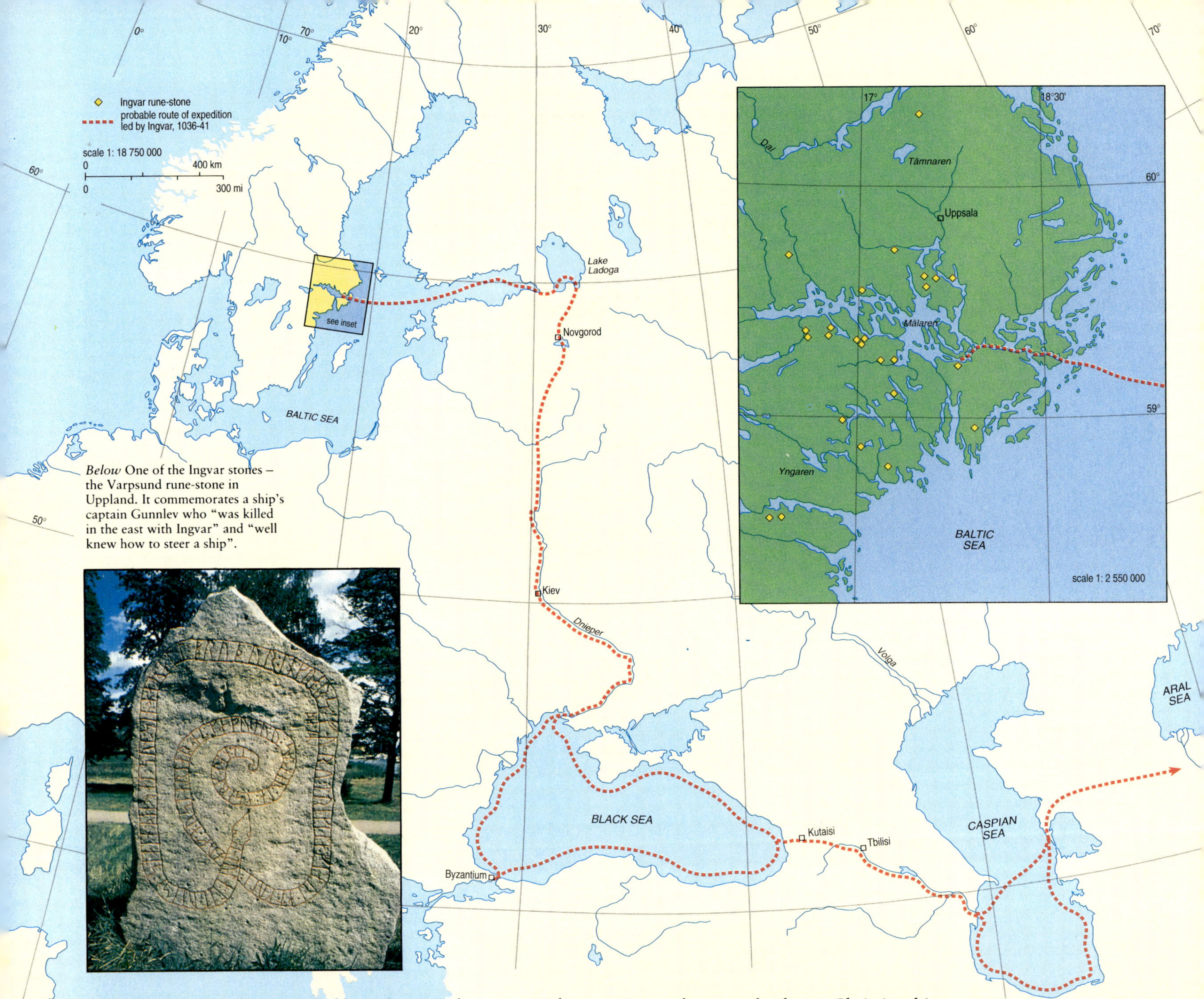


*Below* One of the Ingvar stones – the Varpsund rune-stone in Uppland. It commemorates a ship's captain Gunnlev who "was killed in the east with Ingvar" and "well knew how to steer a ship".

favorable location for a center of royal power than an isolated site in the middle of a lake, more suited to the fragmented political structures of earlier centuries.

Whatever the truth of the matter, Sigtuna is a special case. The many small trading settlements around the Baltic coast, at sites like Löddeköpinge, Köpingsvik, Paviken and Fröjel, did not for the most part develop into major urban centers. Exceptions are Visby on Gotland, which seems to have assumed Paviken's role in the 11th century, and the two towns of the western Swedish lands at Lödöse and Skara.

In many respects, the political and religious organization of Sweden in the later Viking Age is considerably more obscure than in the rest of Scandinavia. As already noted, our documentary sources are few, and are principally concerned with missionary activity; the annals of western Europe pay little heed to events in eastern Scandinavia since they had negligible effect in England or the Frankish empire. We still know relatively little about the growth of Swedish kingship and the process of conversion to Christianity. Ansgar's 9th-century missions to Sweden ended in failure, but in the almost complete absence of written sources for the 10th and 11th centuries we know only that a Christian king, Olof Skötkonung, was ruling in the west of the country around 1000 and had set up Sweden's first bishopric at Skara in 1014. A second, beleaguered bishopric was established at Uppsala in the 1060s.

There is no doubt that paganism was flourishing in the plains of Uppland to the north even at the end of the 11th century. A certain king Svein seems to have led a pagan revival sometime after the reign of Olof, an achievement commemorated in his nickname Blot-Sven (*blót* meaning a pagan sacrifice). The great pagan temple at Uppsala, perhaps the biggest cult center in Scandinavia, described in horrified detail by Adam of Bremen in 1070, did not go out of use until around 1110, and it is likely that private pagan worship continued for generations afterward. The church did not begin to extend its power fully in Sweden, always the wildest and most remote of the Scandinavian lands, until after the Viking Age proper was over. Virtually nothing is known of the early Swedish churches. However, a few decorated wall planks that survive from a handful of sites suggest that they were probably similar to the Norwegian stave-built structures.

**Ingvar's journey to the east**
One of the most ambitious adventures of the entire Viking Age took place between 1036 and 1041 when a young captain named Ingvar led a small fleet of ships from central Sweden and headed east down the great rivers of Russia. What set this voyage apart from other such forays was that Ingvar and his followers seem to have traveled farther than others before or after them – not just to Russia, Byzantium and the Caspian Sea, but perhaps even deep into Asia. An extraordinary series of runic memorial stones in central Sweden records the deaths, far away, of many who took part in the expedition. From the distribution of the stones we can learn much of the area covered by the ship levies that must have provided the crews for Ingvar's fleet, and these raise the possibility that the voyage was in fact an organized military campaign of some kind. Icelandic sagas record that Ingvar's journey ended in disaster, he and his men being wiped out in the eastern wastes.

*Above* A harpist plays, a smith works at his anvil and a farmer plows his fields with a team of oxen. These scenes, in a manuscript written about 1000 in Canterbury, are intended to illustrate stories from the Old Testament, but today provide us with glimpses of life in England during the reign of Æthelred II, at the time when the Viking raids were being renewed with great ferocity.

### The Ingvar stones

Notwithstanding the dearth of conventional documentary material, the hundreds of rune-inscribed stones, most of them dating from the 11th century, that dot the Swedish countryside in far greater numbers than in any other part of Scandinavia are a unique source of evidence. Whether standing as memorials to dead relatives, friends and comrades-in-arms (often telling us as much if not more about those who commissioned the monuments than those they commemorate) or acting as statements of land ownership, deeds of inheritance and legal documents, they contribute to our understanding of the ideas and attitudes current in late Viking Age Sweden and are almost our only contemporary source that comes from Scandinavia itself.

Among the most interesting of the inscriptions are those from a group of about 30 stones from central Sweden that celebrate a number of people who all died together on a great expedition into the east led by a captain called Ingvar. The Ingvar stones, as they are called, mention steersmen, ship's captains and navigators; even Ingvar's brother Harald is commemorated on a stone put up by his grieving mother. Ingvar was about 25 when he led his small fleet east in 1036, and later writers have preserved his nickname – "the Far-Traveled".

Archaeologists have argued for years as to the precise course of Ingvar's voyage, since the stones are not specific and the only written source that mentions the journey, a later medieval saga, is a fabulous story full of monsters and beautiful princesses in which the truth is hard to determine. It is likely, however, that Ingvar followed the route to Byzantium, sailed around the Black Sea and thence made his way overland to the Caspian Sea. He may have gone farther, for it is clear that his journey was thought so extraordinary as to take on an almost mythical quality. The expedition seems to have met with some terrible disaster in the unknown lands of Asia, and few survivors returned to the Mälaren region to tell the tale. The stones erected by the parents and friends of those who died, perhaps put up many years later as the news of the catastrophe filtered back to Sweden, serve both as a fitting tribute to the Viking ideology and as a memorial to a voyage that was the equal and more of the great journeys of the 9th and 10th centuries.

### The final phase of Viking expansion

The emergence of Denmark and Norway as nation-states in the first half of the 11th century set in motion the final phase of Viking expansion against the west as their kings began to flex their political muscles and test their power on a wider European stage. The first step in this process was the renewal of the wars against England. The Viking raids resumed again in 980, after a lapse of nearly 30 years following the English recovery of the Danelaw from its Scandinavian rulers and the ousting of the last Viking king in York in 954.

The raids took the form of a double series of attacks against the southern coast of England and against north Wales. The latter were launched from the Hiberno-Norse colonies in Ireland and around the Irish Sea. They were probably not attempts at conquest, nor even a deliberate program of treasure-hunting as has sometimes been claimed. It is much more likely that the Irish-based Vikings had returned to their practice of opportunistic seasonal looting, which had been temporarily interrupted by the strong leadership provided by the English king Edgar the Peaceable (957–75). This resurgence of activity does perhaps lend some credence to the charge of weak government made against Æthelred II by the *Anglo-Saxon Chronicle*, though there is no doubt that the source paints an excessively gloomy picture of his reign. Æthelred's nickname of "the Unready" is a mistranslation of the Old English *unræd*, which actually means "badly advised".

The attacks against England from the east were clearly motivated by very different ambitions. We do not know how far the Danish kings were involved in the initial raids, but they began to take an active role in the expeditions very soon after the resumption of the attacks in 980. As we have seen, by the later 10th century the supplies of silver from Russia and the Abbasid caliphate had dried up, and the new sources in Germany had only partially replaced them. Political developments within Scandinavia, and the growing centralization of power, had begun to make the business of kingship very expensive – the high costs of

**The renewal of Viking activity in England**
Between 980 and 1009 a new wave of Scandinavian raids shook the English kingdom, disrupting the years of comparative calm and expansion it had enjoyed under Edgar. During this renewed period of fighting, Hiberno-Norse raiders attacked targets in the west of England and Wales, while in the east and south massive fleets from Scandinavia inflicted demoralizing defeats on the English armies of Æthelred II. After 1009 the attacks took a graver turn as in a series of campaigns the royal Danish fleets of Svein Forkbeard and his son Cnut waged all-out war in an attempt to establish themselves territorially in England.

Harald Bluetooth's ambitious programs of civil engineering, road-building and defensive works in Denmark have already been noted, and the royal military retinues also consumed large amounts of the new kingdom's wealth.

If the cost of kingship was rising, so too was the cost of attempting to seize power. The would-be usurpers and royal exiles who had been a prominent feature of Viking politics since the early raids of the 9th century would also have had a mounting need for money. These factors may go some way toward explaining the renewal of raiding in the later 10th and early 11th centuries, for it is clear that those taking part had no interest in land-taking or conquest. The raids had one objective only – the acquisition of as much portable wealth as possible.

During the next ten years the raids intensified quite dramatically. The Viking fleets were large and operated under royal command as highly coordinated forces; in effect, as truly national armies. In addition, a number of fleets led by disaffected royal claimants also took part in the raids. For example, Olaf Tryggvason, who became king of Norway in 995, led a fleet of 93 ships against the southeast of England in 991. The English put up armed resistance to the raids, but by the time of Tryggvason's campaign they had decided to resume the policy of paying *Danegelds* in an attempt to stave off further attacks. This followed their disastrous defeat at the hands of the Danes at the battle of Maldon in Essex (their heroic but doomed defense is celebrated in one of the most famous poems written in Old English). However, the payment of 4,500 kilograms (10,000 lbs) of silver to the Danes seems merely to have had the effect of encouraging them to return in still greater numbers, despite Æthelred's desperate attempts to mobilize the English. In 994 Olaf Tryggvason himself was back, this time in alliance with Svein Forkbeard. Their enterprise was well rewarded with a payment of 7,250 kilograms (16,000 lbs) of silver.

The *Danegelds* continued, paid in escalating sums: 11,800 kilograms (24,000 lbs) of silver in 1002, 16,000 kilograms (36,000 lbs) in 1007 and 22,000 kilograms (48,000 lbs) in 1012. This was an enormous economic drain, and the increasing desperation of the English government can be seen in the terrible order given by Æthelred that all Danes living in England should be killed on St Brice's Day (13 November) 1002; the reality of this command is confirmed by an Oxford charter that refers to Danes seeking sanctuary in a church. The archaeological record appears to confirm the uncertainty of these troubled times. A number of hoards dating to this period have been found in southeast England, suggesting that people were burying their wealth to preserve it from theft, and there is a corresponding increase in the quantity of English silver coinage found in Scandinavian hoards. More than 50,000 coins have been recovered in Gotland alone.

It is clear that a number of the raiders came from Sweden, in contrast to the 9th-century attacks; this development would appear to be linked to the growing centralization of the Russian state, which restricted the Swedes' scope for Viking operations in the east. Several rune-stones from Sweden commemorate men who had died fighting in England, and some mention *Danegelds*. A stone from Yttergärde, for example, tells us that one Ulf was lucky enough to receive three shares: "The first was the one that Tosti paid, then Thorkel paid, then Cnut paid." In addition to looting and extortion, some Scandinavians took a third route to riches, for in 1012 and 1013 a number of Vikings under Thorkel the Tall fought as mercenaries on the English side.

As the Scandinavians grew wealthy on England's silver, their horizons expanded accordingly and the raids took on a further political dimension. Svein Forkbeard clearly began to conceive the idea of a full-scale conquest of England. Such a venture, if successful, would have made him the most powerful king in Scandinavia. He does not seem to have participated personally in the campaigns of 1009–1012, but they were probably conducted on his behalf, and in 1013 he returned to England himself with a massive fleet. The exhausted English were unable to resist the onslaught and in 1013 Svein was accepted as king by the people of the Danelaw; after Æthelred escaped to France this recognition was extended throughout England. However, Æthelred was able to return in 1014, when the *Anglo-Saxon Chronicle* records the "happy event" of Svein's death.

The last two years of Æthelred's reign were spent fighting a losing war with Svein's son Cnut, who had remained in the Danelaw with his army. On Æthelred's death in 1016, his son Edmund put up a fierce resistance to the Vikings, driving them back right

*Below* The causeway between Northey Island and the mainland coast of Essex near Maldon is covered at high tide. It was here, during Olaf Tryggvason's campaign in 991, that a Viking force crossed to confront an English army under the leadership of Byrhtnoth. The massive defeat inflicted on the English was to prove a turning point in Æthelred's reign.

across the south of the country, and earning for himself the nickname Ironside. However, he too died later that same year and the English were left with no choice but to accept Cnut as king. He immediately divided up the country among his commanders. Cnut and his Scandinavian successors were to rule England for almost 30 years.

## The empire of Cnut the Great

On Svein's death, the Danish kingdom had passed to Cnut's brother Harald while Cnut consolidated the position of the Danes in England. When Harald died in 1018, Cnut used English forces to wage a campaign in Denmark to secure the throne for himself. Successful in this goal by 1019, Cnut now ruled a greater territory than any Viking before him, and he set about forging an empire that would dominate the lands around the North Sea. Most of his time was spent in England, perhaps because this enhanced his prestige and standing as a European ruler. To this end, too, and to strengthen his support in England, he married Æthelred's widow and reissued Æthelred's legal code under his own name. The minting of a common coinage for England and Denmark emphasized the merging of the two parts of his kingdom.

From his capital at Winchester in southern England Cnut ruled as the model of a Christian monarch, and made sure everyone knew it by lavishly supporting the monasteries. A page from *The Book of Life* (*Liber Vitae*), which contains "the names of all the brethren and monks as also of the associates and benefactors, living and dead" of the New Minster at Winchester shows Cnut and his wife Emma (Ælfgyfu) presenting a gold altar cross to the abbey. This is a rare portrait of a Viking king. We see Cnut surrounded by angels; the hand of God is pointing out his divine right of kingship, but Cnut has kept one hand on his sword as a reminder of the true source of his power.

Similar patronage was practiced in Denmark. Artistic links clearly existed between the two countries. One of Cnut's most significant introductions to England was the Ringerike style then current in Denmark, which was employed by English artists in new forms such as manuscript illumination. A fragmentary gravestone that was found in St Paul's churchyard in London in the 19th century provides one of the best examples we have, in either England or Denmark, of the style. A magnificent beast, originally painted in red, white and black, strides across the stone, with a ribbon-like snake entwined around its legs. A runic inscription in Old Norse records that "Ginna and Toki had this stone set up."

Cnut was drawn on a number of occasions into fighting wars in Scandinavia and in 1026 was defeated by an allied army of the Norwegian and Swedish kings at the battle of the Holy River in Sweden. In 1028 he took advantage of the quarrels between the Norwegian landowners and King Olaf Haraldsson to foster direct revolt. Once again using English forces to drive the king out, Cnut had himself proclaimed king of Norway at Trondheim: Olaf Haraldsson was killed two years later at the battle of Stiklestad trying to regain his throne. Coins struck in Sigtuna that bear the inscription "Cnut, king of the Swedes" are an indication that his authority was also recognized in Sweden. Cnut was present in Rome in 1027 at the coronation of the emperor Conrad, when he was able to take his place among the rulers of Europe, and on his death in

*Above* Cnut the Great had coins struck in his name on both sides of the North Sea. This penny bears the legend +CNUTREXANGLORUM ("Cnut, King of the English") and shows a crowned bust within a quatrefoil. Cnut set up a network of mints in Denmark, which issued coins based on English originals. Coins struck at Sigtuna, Sweden, that bear his name also follow English types.

*Left* On becoming king of England in 1016, Cnut married Emma of Normandy (called Ælfgyfu by the English), the widow of Æthelred II. Here the royal couple is depicted in the *Liber Vitae* presenting an altar cross to the New Minister in Winchester, blessed by Christ in Majesty. By Cnut, Emma was the mother of Hardacnut, who succeeded for a short time to the Danish and English thrones. Her eldest son by Æthelred was Edward (the Confessor), who became king of England in 1042.

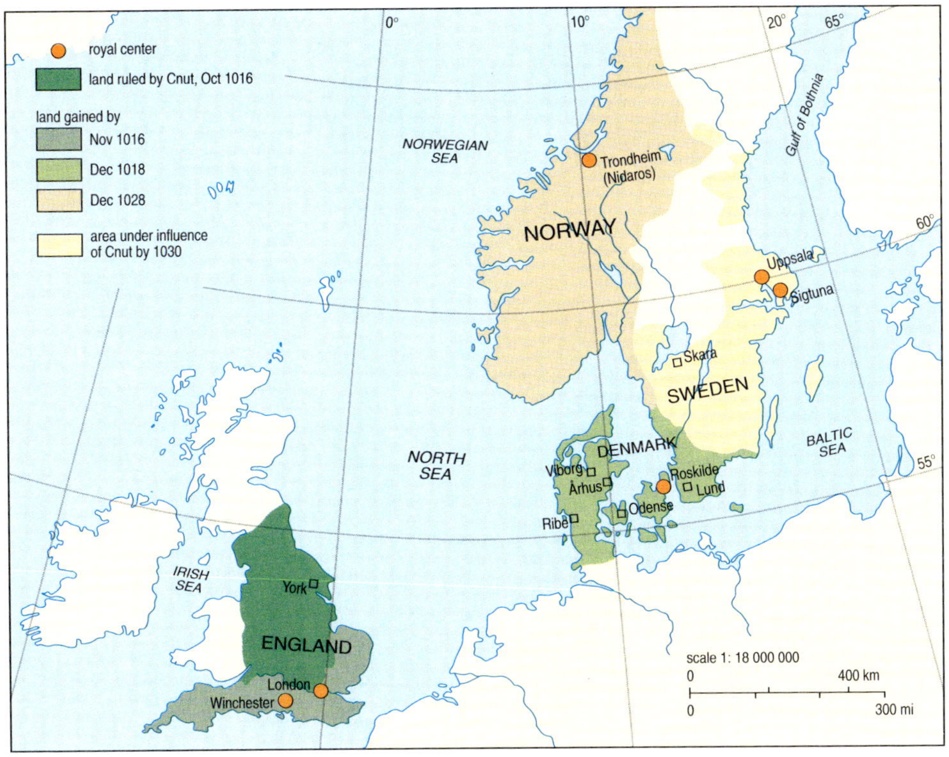


**The empire of Cnut the Great**
In 1016, Cnut was ceded all of central and northern England by King Edmund Ironside. On the latter's death in the same year, Cnut became sole ruler of the country, and thereupon began a process of conquest and diplomacy that was to make him the eventual ruler of a dominion spanning the North Sea. In 1018 he succeeded to the kingdom of Denmark, and his armies conquered Norway in 1028; from around 1030 he also claimed influence over much of Sweden. There is no evidence that Cnut believed himself to be the ruler of an empire as such, though the term is often used today to describe his possessions: he styled himself the ruler of a number of separate peoples. However, on his death he commanded more territory than any Viking before or after him, and well-merited the name of Cnut the Great that later generations of Scandinavians were to give him.

*Left* This stone from St Paul's churchyard in London once formed part of a tomb. The decoration is one of the finest examples of the Ringerike art-style anywhere in the Viking world. Who Ginna and Toki, mentioned in the runic inscription, were is now unknown, but the tomb is believed to have been erected during Cnut's reign.

*Right* The Vikings based in the Loire region of France ravaged Angers in the 9th century when St Aubin was bishop: in this life of the saint, written about 1100, they are depicted in their ship ready to attack. However, these warriors are shown armed in the 11th-century manner, with long mail-shirts and kite-shaped shields of the kind that were used by the Normans at the battle of Hastings and are shown on the Bayeux tapestry. The artist has put the steering-oar on the wrong side of the ship!

1035 was justified in his claim to rule an empire that extended over England, Denmark, Norway and southern Sweden.

As with many such enterprises built on personal ambition, however, Cnut's empire disintegrated on his death. His son, Hardacnut, who succeeded to both the English and the Danish thrones in 1040, did little to halt the decline. On his death at a drinking party in 1042, the English crown reverted to the old royal line when Edward the Confessor, the only surviving son of Æthelred II, was proclaimed king, having returned from 25 years in exile in Normandy.

## Harald Hardradi and the invasion of England

Almost the last episode in the story of direct Scandinavian involvement in England was precipitated by the death of Edward the Confessor in January 1066. It was instigated by Harald Sigurdarson, the king of Norway who had fought his way to power with a savagery that had earned him the nickname Hardradi – "the hard-ruler". Called "the thunder-bolt of the north" by Adam of Bremen, Harald's career was one of the most illustrious enjoyed by any Viking in the 11th century, winning him a reputation that was the equal of that of Cnut; his pursuit of fame as an end in itself is vivid demonstration of the very clear idea that the later Viking kings had of their own mythology.

The half-brother of Olaf Haraldsson, Harald had been present at the battle of Stiklestad at the age of 15, and had fled east to Sweden in the aftermath of Olaf's death. From Sweden Harald journeyed to Russia, where he entered the service of Yaroslav of Kiev, but he soon ventured farther south to Byzantium to join the emperor's Varangian guard. His many adventures fighting in the emperor's service in the east were famous throughout the Viking world, but they came to an end in 1045 when he returned north to make a position for himself in Norway.

The death of Hardacnut in England had left a power vacuum in Scandinavia. During his lifetime Hardacnut had granted sovereignty of his Danish territories to the Norwegian king Magnus, but they were now claimed by Svein, son of Cnut's sister. Harald saw in this situation an opportunity for himself, and formed an alliance with Svein against Magnus. On the latter's death in 1047 Harald succeeded to the Norwegian throne and promptly turned on Svein. During the next 20 years thousands were killed in countless battles as both kings fought a vicious campaign of raids and counter-attacks, characterized by treachery and revenge. Harald's famous banner *Landeyðan* ("the Landwaster") flew over much of Denmark, and even Hedeby was burned. Nevertheless, the war ended in stalemate and in 1064 the two rulers agreed to make peace. By now Harald Hardradi was 50 years old, had fought over most of the known world and had briefly held power in every part of Scandinavia. In 1066 he launched his final adventure – one that was to bring the late Viking Age to a historical close, in spirit if not in fact.

Edward the Confessor of England had died without an heir. Amid some controversy Harold Godwinson, who had been one of Edward's chief councillors, was proclaimed king the next day. The news was greeted eagerly in Norway, since Harald Hardradi saw an opportunity to invade and claim England for himself as the natural successor to Cnut's kingdom. He was encouraged by Harold Godwinson's brother Tostig, the former earl of Northumbria, who had been driven into exile from England the year before, and by the earl of Orkney. Harald Hardradi revealed his great military skills as a tactician by concealing his plans from the English and gathering his forces in secret. In the late summer, Harold Godwinson was taken completely by surprise by the news that a Norwegian fleet of 200 ships had sailed up the Humber estuary to land at Riccall on the river Ouse. It was soon joined by the

*Left* This scene from the Bayeux tapestry shows Duke William in council at Hastings after the Norman landing at Pevensey on 28 September 1066. William – seated between his half-brothers Bishop Odo of Bayeux and Robert, Count of Mortain – is holding his sword with its point uppermost. The tapestry, probably made for Bishop Odo, is a unique record of the events of the Conquest and a valuable source of information about the Norman descendants of the Vikings, including their ships and weapons.

fleets of Tostig and the earl of Orkney, making a combined force of perhaps 300 ships and 9,000 troops. Within a few days of landing, Harald Hardradi's army had destroyed the Northumbrian militias at Gate Fulford. Hostages were taken from the people of nearby York and Harald settled to consolidate his hold on Northumbria before moving south. In mid-September he encamped his army at Stamford Bridge, 22 kilometers from his ships at Riccall and 12 kilometers from York.

Unknown to Harald, Harold Godwinson had begun a desperate forced march north with as many troops as he could muster as soon as he heard of the Norwegians' landing. In only a few days his army was at Tadcaster, just outside York. The Norwegians were still unaware of his presence when on 25 September, after a march of 27 kilometers, the English army fell upon the Norwegians at Stamford Bridge. The first signal of their approach was the glinting of the morning sun on their weapons as they appeared on the horizon: "like the sun on a field of broken ice" was how a later Norse saga described it. At first Harald Hardradi tried to negotiate a truce in the old manner, promising not to fight if he were given the whole of the north. Harold's answer has come down to us: "I will grant you seven feet of English ground, or as much more as you are taller than other men."

The battle was brutal, long and final. It was the biggest engagement on English soil since *Brunanburh* in 937, and the two armies fought the whole day in blazing sun. The Norwegian king called up reinforcements from the ships anchored at Riccall, who ran the distance back in full armor. Despite their efforts, the exhausted Norwegians were annihilated; Harald Hardradi, the last of the great Viking kings, died leading a charge, an arrow in his throat. The English pursued the fleeing Norwegians all night right back to their ships at Riccall. So great was the slaughter that of the original 300 shiploads of invaders, only 24 were needed to carry the wounded back to Norway. The dead were left on the battlefield, their bones remaining a landmark for generations. As the lucky survivors crossed the sea, Harold Godwinson and the English army turned south, in response to the news that Harold had been dreading. Duke William of Normandy had landed at Pevensey on the south coast of England, with a Norman army also intent on conquest.

**William of Normandy and the conquest of England**

While Harald Hardradi had been plotting his invasion in his capital at Trondheim, similar plans had been laid in Duke William's stronghold at Falaise in Normandy. William had been born about 1027, the illegitimate son of Duke Robert, the fourth in direct descent from the Viking Rollo who had been granted Normandy in 911. William's father had died in 1035, and in the absence of a legitimate heir his childhood had been spent amid bitter political fighting that had threatened to tear the duchy apart. On reaching maturity, William had successfully asserted his right to the succession and had stamped his authority on every aspect of Norman society. He campaigned relentlessly against the Capetian kings of France on his borders, reorganizing the army and introducing the deployment of highly trained cavalry units so that by 1066 the Norman war-machine was probably unrivaled in Europe. Like Cnut, William was a staunch patron of the church. He built the magnificent abbey at Jumièges, among many other religious foundations, and at every turn of events was anxious to show himself a loyal servant of the pope in Rome. His half-brother Odo was bishop of Bayeux.

The dynasties of Normandy and England had been related by marriage in the reign of Cnut, and from this alliance William derived a claim to the English throne. He had taken the opportunity to press it even while Edward the Confessor was still alive. In about 1064 Harold Godwinson had visited Normandy, where he had been the guest of Duke William. The circumstances of this meeting are now unclear – the most likely explanation being that Harold was blown off course by a storm on his way to Ireland. There is no doubt, however, that while he was there he was forced to swear allegiance to William and agreed to support him after Edward's death. When William heard that Harold had assumed the throne himself, he was apparently so enraged that he threw his cloak over his face and refused to speak. He immediately gave orders for the construction of a fleet to invade England, and was poised to do so by the beginning of September.

The same wind that had sped the Norwegian army across the North Sea to the Yorkshire coast kept the Norman ships confined to port in Dieppe on the north coast of France. By the time the fleet could set sail on 27 September, Harald Hardradi was already dead at Stamford Bridge. Once across the Channel William's army made an unopposed landing and immediately set about building a fortified base. From here they prepared to meet the English in battle for, unlike the Norwegians, William knew that Harold was coming. The English army marched from York to the south coast, a distance of 400 kilometers, in nine days, unable to stop for reinforcements. The force numbered about 7,000 troops, a large proportion of them peasant militias, and all of them exhausted from the battle of Stamford Bridge fought only a few days before. William had about the same number of troops, but his forces included hundreds of archers and companies of mounted knights.

The two armies met on 14 October at a site on the edge of the modern village of Battle in Sussex, about 14 kilometers from Hastings. The English army was strung out along a ridge overlooking a marshy valley where the Normans were stationed; at the center Harold grouped his bodyguard around the dragon standard of Wessex. At dawn the Normans advanced and were met with fierce resistance. Their horses slipped in the mud, and their infantry were driven back by a rain of spears, rocks and sticks as the English threw anything at them that came to hand. The Breton contingent of William's army broke and fled, taking many of the Norman troops with them. It looked as though Harold had won two great victories in a fortnight. However, as the English levies left the ridge and streamed after them, William rallied his running men and the Norman cavalry turned, cutting down half the English army in the valley floor.

After this it was just a matter of time. As the English retreated back across the ridge, the royal guard around Harold were packed so close together that the bodies could not fall as they were slain, said the Norman chroniclers. First Harold's two brothers were killed, and then Harold himself. Whether he was hit in the eye by an arrow, as the rumor went after the battle, we cannot be sure, but some Normans claimed that William himself rode over the English shield-wall to reach the king. The story of the battle is recounted in many sources, English and Norman, but the most vivid record is depicted on the embroidery known as the Bayeux tapestry. This was commissioned – probably by Odo of Bayeux – from English needleworkers to commemorate the Norman triumph.

After the victory at Hastings, William's army overran the land northward with little resistance. On Christmas Day 1066 he was crowned king of England in Westminster Abbey in London, and thus he achieved, as a fifth-generation Viking, what his ancestors in the north had failed to do for so long. The effects of the Norwegian disaster and the Norman conquest were

*Right* These 12th-century ivory chessmen were carved in western Norway, perhaps in Trondheim, which was an important center for the walrus-ivory trade. They belong to the largest and most important series of such pieces known from the Middle Ages, comprising the remains of four nearly complete sets. Their discovery on the Isle of Lewis, in the Outer Hebrides, highlights the fact that the Western Isles of Scotland were still then politically part of the kingdom of Norway.

wide-ranging. The losses at Stamford Bridge were so severe that no Norwegian king was able to mount any act of largescale aggression for more than a generation. Though a Danish fleet attempted to conquer the north of England in 1069 the Danish armies were similarly exhausted after 17 years of war with Hardradi, and Swedish expansionist ambitions had been neutralized in the same conflict. By 1098 Norway's fortunes had recovered sufficiently for King Magnus Barelegs to launch the last true Viking expedition in the west, raiding around the Hebrides and the Isle of Man, and even fighting the Normans in Wales. But – though Norwegian ships were still harrying the Irish coast as late as the 13th century – to all intents and purposes the Viking tradition in western Europe died with Harald the Hardradi at Stamford Bridge, and was finally laid to rest when his body was brought home to Trondheim by his son in 1067. The arena of power in northern Europe had shifted away from Scandinavia and the North Sea to the countries on either side of the English Channel.

### The Late Norse legacy in Scotland

The Scandinavian presence lasted much longer in northwestern Britain than it did farther south. After the initial period of raiding was ended in the isles of Scotland and the northern mainland of Britain, the Norse settlers put down deep roots that can still be traced today in place-name survivals and elements of the language: indeed, Norn – a regional variation of the Norwegian language – was spoken and understood in Orkney into the last century. Some local building styles, such as the use of birch bark in roof construction, are also evidence of lasting Norse influence.

As we have seen, the earldom of Orkney, Shetland and Caithness came into being at a very early date. The presence of distinctively Norwegian artifacts such as antler combs or soapstone vessels on many sites in Scotland suggests that there was direct contact with Norway's developing towns and manufacturing centers, and there can be little doubt that the Norwegian kings exercised a powerful political influence in their western colonies through the earls. By the time of Earl Thorfinn in the 11th century the earls had become important local leaders with wider territorial ambitions extending westward to the Irish Sea. The *Saga of the Orkney Islanders* notes that in about 1037–39:

*Earl Thorfinn had his hands full with the men of the Hebrides and the Irish, and he felt himself much in need of help in the way of forces...Now early in the spring Earl Thorfinn sent a message to his kinsman Earl Rognvald, asking him to go on a war-cruise with him, and to bring as many men as he could get...Thorfinn and Rognvald harried during the summer round the coasts of the Hebrides and Ireland and far and wide round the coast of the west coast of Scotland. Thorfinn laid the land under him wherever he went.*

It is the *Saga of the Orkney Islanders* that provides the most immediate documentary evidence we have of the Norse occupation of the islands in the 11th century. Though the source needs to be treated with the same caution as the other sagas, being written down after the events they describe, probably in Icelandic centers of learning, the *Saga of the Orkney Islanders* includes details that make it seem very likely that use was made of local informants. Only someone with first-hand knowledge of the hillsides around the Bu at Orphir, for example, could have provided the accurate description it contains of that particular landscape. A collection of runic inscriptions that were carved by Norsemen sheltering in the Neolithic

*Left* Aerial view of Freswick Links on the northeast coast of mainland Scotland where extensive evidence has been found for occupation in the Late Norse period, when large-scale fishing formed an important part of the local economy. The area was one of native Pictish settlement, but there is nothing yet to indicate a Scandinavian presence here in Caithness during the early part of the Viking Age.

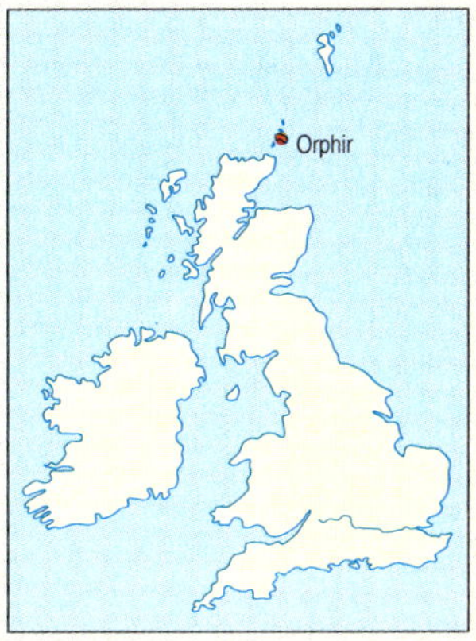


# Orphir

Orphir on Orkney was one of the many high-status settlements held by the earls of Orkney during the Late Norse period. A description is given in the *Saga of the Orkney Islanders* of the residence Earl Paul Hakonsson built there in the 12th century: "There was a great drinking-hall . . . with many huge vats of ale . . . and in front of the hall, just a few paces away, stood a fine church." Though a substantial range of buildings is popularly identified as the earl's hall (or Earl's Bu), it belongs to many different periods. However, part of the 12th-century church is still standing, and excavations have revealed a water mill and a large metal-working site from the Late Norse period.

*Above* An inscribed cattle rib found in a midden at Orphir. The runic inscription reads ". . . this bone was in . . ." More informative are the thousands of cod bones and burnt grains of bere barley found in the midden, which give us a good idea of the diet of Orphir's Norse inhabitants.

*Below* Excavations have uncovered the remains of a horizontal mill close to the site of the buildings popularly identified as Paul Hakonsson's "drinking-hall" and the round church. Farther away lie the mill pond, which may have been dammed in Norse times, and the metal-working site, known as Lavacroon.

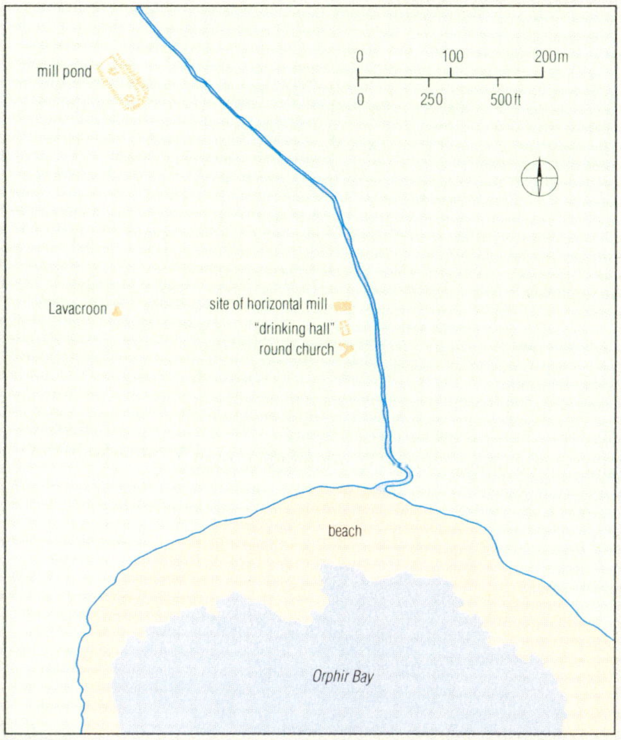


*Below* Orphir's round church is the only circular medieval church in Scotland. Its design may have been based on the Church of the Holy Sepulcher in Jerusalem, following a visit to the Holy Land by Earl Hakon in the 12th century. It was partially demolished when a later church – no longer standing – was built to its west, but a substantial part of the rounded apse is intact.

chambered tomb at Maes Howe in Orkney brings us even closer to the men and women of the past. They tell of travelers and the seizure of treasure from the burial mound, of winter weather and the need for shelter and comfort, of great loves left behind, affording us a human glimpse of these Scandinavian adventurers with a yearning for home fires.

A number of local power centers seem to have developed in the earldom during the 11th and 12th centuries, including Birsay (which Thorfinn made his permanent base) and Orphir on Orkney, Tuquoy on Westray, Westness on Rousay, Jarlshof on Shetland, and Freswick in Caithness. Excavations at these sites have revealed a good deal of evidence about the nature of the Late Norse presence in Scotland. Many of the settlements are quite large and contain a number of buildings serving different economic functions (barns, byres, kitchens, smithies as well as dwelling houses), commonly constructed of coursed stonework. As noted earlier, at many sites – for example at Birsay and Jarlshof – there is evidence of successive periods of occupation, and the buildings from the 11th and 12th centuries often overlie those of earlier Viking or even Pictish settlements. At Birsay, for example, the foundations of several subrectangular structures from a number of periods of occupation are huddled around a small 12th-century church. Sometimes, however – as at Sandwick in Shetland – a site appears to have been occupied for the first time by the Scandinavians in the 11th or 12th century.

Evidence of the way of life of these farmers and fishermen comes to us in a number of ways. A horizontal mill, possibly used for grinding grain, has been excavated at Orphir, and pollen analysis carried out on several sites indicate that bere barley, oats and flax were all grown as crops. Dense banks of fishbones and other debris found in middens excavated at Freswick show that there was largescale fishing.

# Birsay

*Right* The plan of the main site at Birsay shows the complex multiperiod grouping of structures at the cliff edge, with Norse buildings superimposed on earlier Pictish remains, in contrast to the more simple outlines of the Norse houses higher up the slope.

The small tidal island of the Brough of Birsay, which lies at the northwest corner of the mainland of Orkney, has long been identified as a Norse site, for the *Saga of the Orkney Islanders* describes it as a major center of political and ecclesiastical power in the 11th and 12th centuries. Excavation has shown the Brough to have been an important site in the Pictish period also, when it was a manufacturing center producing metalwork of a particularly high quality. Building remains from both periods are most concentrated on the landward, southern side of the island. At the cliff edge, the Norse settlers built directly on top of the Pictish settlement, utilizing stones from its structures, so that it is very difficult to distinguish one building phase from the other. Pictish remains underlie the Norse buildings clustered around the 12th-century church; a fine symbol stone, carved with an eagle and three warriors – reputed to mark the grave of three men – was found here. Higher up the slope the grass-covered stone foundations of several clusters of Norse buildings are clearly visible. For practical purposes of drainage, these were aligned up and down the slope; one settler who opted to build his house across the slope may well have had cause to regret his decision. Isolated Pictish and Norse structures have been identified in the rest of the island, and several Norse burials and buildings have also been uncovered on the mainland facing the island. One of the most important of these, in the center of the modern village of Birsay, is a stone building over 1 meter high in places and measuring at least 12 meters in length.

*Below* Excavation of this simple clay and stone building found by itself on a narrow tongue of land in the south of the Brough proved a challenging task. Since it was built in the 10th century, erosion has helped to make its clifftop location extremely precarious.

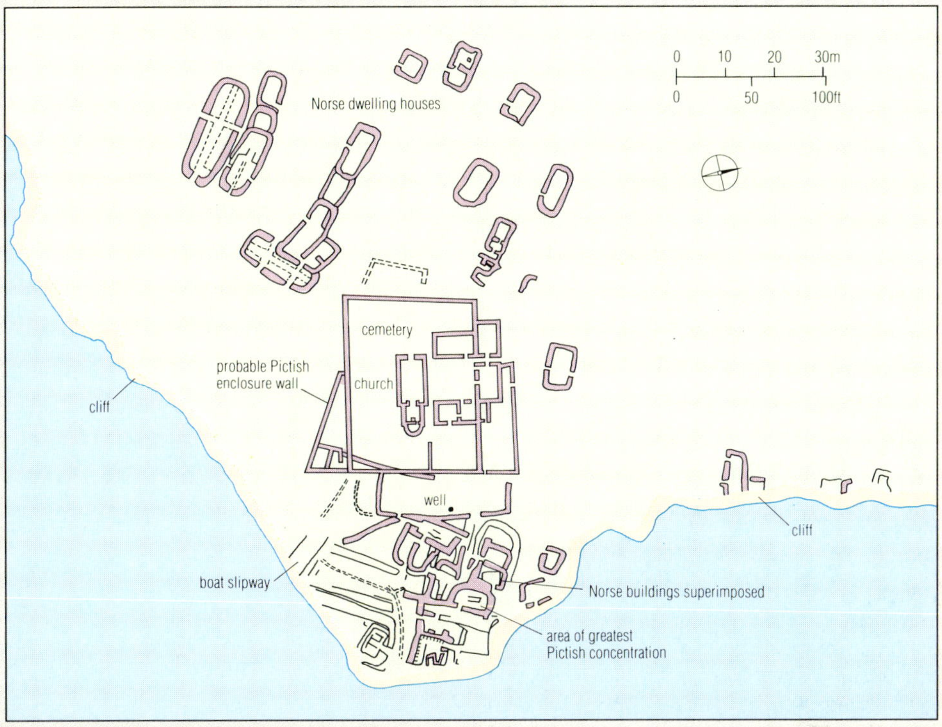


*Below* Very few artifacts have been preserved in the clay soils of the Brough, though traces of soapstone vessels, beads and clay molds have been found. These bone and other pieces are distinctive: a Late Viking comb, a pin, and a seal's tooth with runic characters.

*Bottom* The humpbacked shape of the Brough of Birsay at high tide. It is not certain whether the island was completely detached from the mainland in the Viking period, but it clearly afforded a good natural defensive site.

Fishing weights, a wide variety of knives, spindle whorls and many other tools and articles of daily use found on Late Norse settlements fill out the picture of a hard-working, subsistence economy.

The life of these farming communities must frequently have been disrupted by warfare and feuding. There is evidence in the Late Norse period of a considerable increase in the use of defended settlements (*kastali*) such as Cubbie Roo's Castle (Kolbein Hruga in the *Saga of the Orkney Islanders*) on Wyre. These massive square, stone towers surrounded by deep earthworks are very different from the Iron Age brochs – circular drystone towers – that are more widely found in northern Scotland and the isles, but occupy similarly conspicuous hilltop positions in the landscape.

The wealth and power of the Orkney earls is reflected in the richness of their major ecclesiastical buildings. Considerable controversy surrounds the location of Thorfinn's minster at Birsay, mentioned in the *Saga of the Orkney Islanders*: some people argue that it was on the Brough of Birsay, others that it was in the village of Birsay on the mainland by the modern parish church. Much more solid and substantial are the remains of the round church at Orphir, and St Magnus' cathedral at Kirkwall in Orkney. The resources needed to build these elaborate structures and the distant influences that were brought to bear on their construction suggests that Orkney had by this time become a player on the European stage. While a Scandinavian origin is possible for the round church at Orphir, it has also been suggested that it was inspired by the church of the Holy Sepulcher in Jerusalem. This became a popular model for churches in western Europe after the city was captured from the Arabs by the army of the First Crusade in 1099, and suggests a possible link with the crusading movement.

The cathedral at Kirkwall is a magnificent Romanesque building that mirrors the architectural grandeur of the cathedral at Durham in northeast England, and indeed masons from Durham are known to have been involved in its construction. It is dedicated to St Magnus, the martyred Magnus Erlendsson, who was brought up in Orkney and murdered on Egilsay about 1117. He later became the patron saint of Orkney. The fact that the cathedral church of the Faeroe Islands, at Kirkjubøur, is also dedicated to St Magnus is indication of the enduring strength of the ties between areas of Norse settlement in the west and North Atlantic. Orkney and Shetland remained within the Scandinavian orbit of influence for three centuries more, only becoming part of Scotland in 1468 when they were given away by the king of Denmark (to whom Norway and its possessions had passed in 1397) as the dowry on the marriage of his daughter to James III of Scotland.

### The Kingdom of Man and the Isles

The attacks of Earl Thorfinn along the west coast of Scotland may well have reached as far as the Isle of Man, though there is nothing in the documentary record to confirm this. Very little is known about political organization within Man until 1079 when Godred Crovan established his authority throughout the island at the battle of Skyhill, and founded a dynasty of rulers in Man. He is credited with extending the island's influence northward to the Hebrides, leading to the creation of the kingdom of Man and the Isles. At about this time the diocese of Sodor and Man became established with its cathedral on St Patrick's Isle, the only sheltered harbor on the west coast of Man. When Nidaros (later Trondheim) became an archbishopric in 1152, Sodor and Man fell within its province and accepted its authority, thereby allying itself to the Norwegian rather than the Scottish or English church. Over the years St Patrick's Isle grew into a major ecclesiastical center.

In 1098 King Magnus Barelegs renewed Norway's claims to exercise political power in the Hebrides and Irish Sea by leading an expedition to the west. Though Magnus was ultimately unsuccessful, his warlike progress through the isles is graphically described in a

*Above* Around the year 1150, according to the *Saga of the Orkney Islanders*, "a very able man named Kolbein Hruga farming on Wyre in Orkney ... had a fine stone fort built there, a really solid stronghold". Its remains, known as Cubbie Roo's Castle, are still to be seen there – a stone tower, with domestic outhouses, within a rock-cut ditch – representing the earliest recorded stone castle anywhere in Scotland.

**Northern Britain and Ireland in the Late Norse period** *(right)*
The earldom of Orkney, Shetland and Caithness (the Northern earldom) was under the authority of the kings of Norway in the Late Norse period. Norway also laid nominal claim to the Hebrides, but by the end of the 11th century these had become absorbed into the Kingdom of Man, whose influence also extended into northern Ireland and parts of northwest England. The Hebrides were divided into four groups for administrative purposes, but in 1156 Mull and Islay were taken over by Argyll. By this time the bishops of Man had accepted the authority of the archbishops of Nidaros in Norway. Within a few years the Anglo-Norman invasion of Ireland had brought an end to the Viking kingdom of Dublin and the other Hiberno-Norse towns. As the Norse presence in northwestern Britain and around the Irish Sea was challenged and supplanted by the growing strength of Scotland and England, the Norwegian crown attempted to reassert its authority over Man and the Hebrides, but its overwhelming defeat by the Scots at Largs in 1263 ended its political ambitions in the area. The Northern earldom remained in the Scandinavian orbit until 1468.

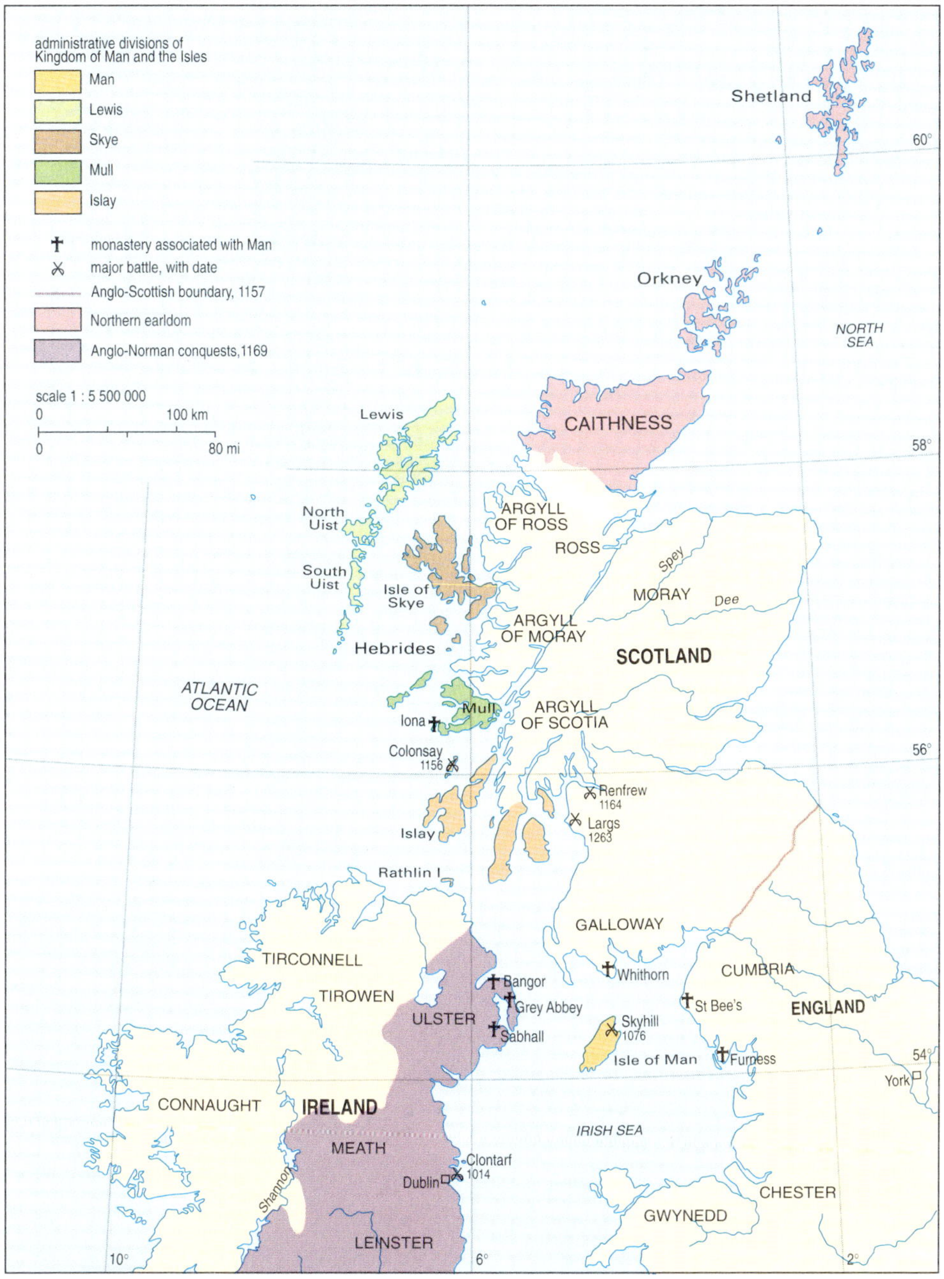


poem by his court-poet Bjorn Cripplehand in a manner that recalls the Viking raids of old:

*The hungry battle-birds were filled*
*In Skye with blood of foemen killed,*
*And wolves on Tiree's lonely shore*
*Dyed red their hairy jaws in gore....*
*On Sanday's plain our shields they spy:*
*From Islay smoke rose heaven-high*
*Whirling up from the flashing blaze*
*The king's men o'er the island raise.*
*South of Kintyre the people fled*
*Scared by our swords in blood dyed red,*
*And our brave champion onward goes*
*To meet in Man the Norsemen's foes.*

In the days of the kingdom of Man the Hebrides were known as *Suðreyjar* (the Sudreys or Southern Isles) to distinguish them from *Norðreyjar* (the Nordreys or Northern Isles) – Orkney and Shetland. For administrative purposes the Sudreys were divided into four groups centered on the islands of Islay, Mull, Skye and Lewis. All the islands sent representatives to the central parliament or Thing, which met (as the first element in its name suggests) at Tynwald on the Isle of Man: these representatives would have been the most powerful members of Norse society. As the wealthiest and most important island, Man sent 16 representatives, and each of the island groups in the Hebrides sent four each, making another 16. However, in 1156, after a descendant of Crovan, Godred II, was defeated in a battle off the small island of Colonsay, the southern groups of Mull and Islay were lost to Somerled, the ruler of the Argyll coast on the Scottish mainland. The number of representatives from the Hebrides was therefore reduced to eight, making 24 in all – still the number of representatives in the lower house of the island's modern parliament, the House of Keys. Directly descended from the Thing, it is a living link with the island's Scandinavian past.

Challenged by the English presence in Ireland from the 12th century and the growing strength of the mainland kingdom of Scotland in the 13th century, Norse influence in the Irish Sea area was coming to an end. Norway's attempt to reimpose its authority over the Hebrides and the surrounding area led to its defeat by the Scots at the battle of Largs in 1263. Three years later Norwegian interests in Man and the Isles were formally purchased by the Scottish crown.

## The Norse in Ireland

In Ireland, the growing weakness of the Dublin Norse was confirmed by the battle of Clontarf in 1014 when their army, allied with Scandinavian forces from Orkney, the Isle of Man, Iceland and Normandy, was decisively defeated by the Irish led by Brian Boru, the king of Munster and the then high king of Ireland. A number of Irishmen from Leinster had fought alongside the Dubliners, fearing the supremacy of Boru's Munster kingdom. Though Boru – who was killed in the fighting – has been hailed by later writers as Ireland's savior from the Norse, his death gave rise to a

*Right* The hilt of an Irish sword found, in its scabbard, in Lough Derg, Co Tipperary: this is Anglo-Scandinavian in form, with its curved pommel and guard and scalloped inner edges to the mounts around its grip, though the nature of their fine inlaid decoration indicates Irish workmanship of about 1100. Irish craftsmen of this period had absorbed influences from the Ringerike and Urnes styles of late Viking art.

# Thingvellir

Thingvellir (meaning "parliament plain") in southwest Iceland is the most famous of the many Thing sites, or places of public assembly, in the Viking world. It was here that the Althing, the national assembly of the Icelanders, met in the open air for two weeks every summer: the site, about 48 kilometers east of Reykjavik, was accessible to all the settlers, though many would have had to make a long journey on horseback to reach it. There was also a system of regional Things that were under the authority of the *goðar*, the local leaders. The *goðar* also had an influential role in the Althing: each *goði* would be expected to argue the cases of the men from his area at the Althing, and in return could call upon their armed support in his feuds with other *goðar*.

The essential function of the Thing in Norse society as the place where all the free men in a region were able to meet, discuss issues and settle grievances is reflected in the way that the system was transported from the Scandinavian homelands to many parts of the Viking world. Eric the Red, outlawed for murder by the Jæren Thing in southwest Norway and then by the Thorsnes Thing in Iceland, established his own Thing close to the settlement he founded at Brattahlid in Greenland. Gardar, a short distance away, also had its own Thing site. In northern Scotland, the names of Dingwall (Sutherland) and Tingwall (Orkney) testify to the former presence of meeting places, and Tynwald, in the Isle of Man, is still the site where the Manx parliament meets, having retained its legal significance for over 1,000 years.

The traditional date given for the founding of the Althing (930), however, enables Iceland to lay claim to having the oldest national assembly in Europe, though it has not enjoyed its powers without a break; it was abolished for a period during the 19th century and later revived in response to the growing nationalist movement in Iceland. In the Viking period, the most momentous decision made by the Althing was that taken in about 1000, when – after a lengthy debate – Christianity was recognized as the official religion in the colony.

*Below* This vivid reconstruction of a meeting of Iceland's Viking Age farmers at the Althing at Thingvellir was painted by the English artist W. G. Collingwood in the early 1870s when he accompanied William Morris, author of a number of long verse romances based on the Norse legends, to Iceland. Collingwood reproduced the topography of the site with painstaking accuracy, and all the details in the picture were based on thorough research, reflecting the state of knowledge then current. The Lawspeaker stands on the rock in the center of the picture.

*Left* The massive lava cliffs of Thingvellir – one of the most spectacular and evocative sites in the Norse world – today, viewed in the opposite direction from that in Collingwood's picture. The rock (*Logberg*, or Law Rock) from which the elected Lawspeaker presided over the proceedings of the assembly is indicated by the white staff.

*Right* This T-shaped bronze crozier head was found at Thingvellir. The decoration is in the Urnes style, and it dates from a few generations after the conversion to Christianity, confirmed by the decision of the Althing in about 1000.

period of dynastic turbulence and political infighting in which the Viking towns placed themselves in the service of first one Irish king and then another. Their usefulness to the Irish lay in their fleets and their control of the seaways. Often they fought against each other. For example, the men of Dublin attacked and burned Waterford in 1087, and an allied force from Dublin, Wexford and Waterford made an unsuccessful assault against Cork a year later.

Despite their growing involvement in the political affairs of the Irish, and a degree of cultural integration (reflected in the use of the Ringerike and Urnes styles by Irish craftsmen) the Scandinavians remained distinct from the Irish population in a number of significant ways. They retained their own language, laws and customs and, furthermore, continued to live and trade in the towns, while the Irish remained unurbanized. After the Scandinavians had become Christian, in the course of the 10th century, they did not adopt the Irish form of ecclesiastical organization, based on the monasteries, but sent priests (initially Irish to judge by their names) to England to be consecrated as bishops for the towns by the archbishop of Canterbury.

In the 12th century the Anglo-Norman rulers of England were beginning to show increasing interest in the affairs of Ireland. They were encouraged by the church authorities who were anxious to extend their influence in Ireland and carry through reform of the Irish church. The walled Viking towns were obvious keypoints from which to launch an invasion, serving as readymade fortresses and enabling supply routes to be maintained with England. In 1169 an Anglo-Norman force led by Richard de Clare (nicknamed Strongbow) seized Waterford, Wexford and Dublin. Led by Ansculf, the last king of Dublin, the Dublin fleet escaped, but was defeated when it returned in 1171, augmented by allies from Man and the Isles – the last time a Norse army fought in Ireland. Later that year the English king Henry II held court in Dublin, handing over the town for colonization by English settlers. The Viking presence in Ireland disappeared, to be replaced in the towns by the English. From then on the history of Ireland lay in an entirely different direction.

### The end of Icelandic independence

For more than 200 years after its foundation the Norse colony on Iceland thrived, proud of its independence from the Norwegian homelands. By 1100 the population was between 70,000 and 80,000, a number not exceeded until the beginning of the 20th century. Government of the country was in the hands of the *goðar*, the local leaders who were responsible for administering the law in their own districts. Through the role they had held in pagan society as religious leaders and guardians of the local temples they were able to retain ownership and control of the local churches. In time, individual *goðar* became very powerful as more and more land was concentrated in fewer hands. The Icelandic sagas relate the many rivalries that sprang up between them, leading to damaging quarrels and feuds. This growing political turmoil allowed the Norwegian kings greater opportunity to intervene in Iceland's affairs.

With the establishment of the archbishopric of Nidaros, the ecclesiastical authorities in Norway increased their efforts to end the independence of the Icelandic church. Ownership of church lands was

removed from the lay *goðar*, and tithes (a church tax) were levied. Iceland's small farmers were already under mounting economic pressure. Overgrazing of pastureland in parts of the island had brought problems of soil erosion and, coupled with the growing severity of the climate, was reducing the amount of land available for farming. Life was becoming increasingly difficult for many in the colony.

The debate and uncertainty over the dating of Mount Hekla's eruptions – once thought to have caused the abandonment of many farms in the densely populated Thjórsá valley at the end of the Viking Age – have already been discussed in a previous chapter in connection with the dating of the Stöng farmhouse. As noted there, recent studies of the valley's tephra deposits suggest that the major eruption that was responsible for making parts of the valley uninhabitable did not take place until the beginning of the 13th century. Recent excavations of settlement sites in the valley have corroborated these findings: in particular, the discovery of distinctive artifacts such as imported pottery and antler combs provide evidence of Late Norse activity in this area. But it is likely that the farmers here were facing increasing poverty, and the demand for tithes may have hastened the demise of many of them, as it did elsewhere in the island.

By 1238 Norwegian bishops occupied all the episcopal sees of Iceland, providing a solid platform of support for the kings of Norway. Icelandic shipping was already in the hands of Norwegian merchants who imported all the goods on which the island depended. Iceland's few remaining *goðar* were unable to resist the strength of Norway's demands any longer, and one by one transferred their allegiance to King Hakon IV (1204–63), thus sealing the fate of the Icelandic republic. Among those who wavered was Snorri Sturluson, one of the most learned of the many Icelandic scholars of the time and the author of the *Prose Edda*, among the greatest of Iceland's medieval works of literature. As a result of his hesitation, he was murdered at Reykholt in 1241. The extinguishing of Icelandic independence was in stark contrast to the initial hopeful founding of the colony.

## The collapse of the Greenland colony

Climatic deterioration had an even more catastrophic effect on the population of Late Norse Greenland than it did in Iceland. We know that the colony in both the Eastern and Western Settlements was active and flourishing well into the 13th century. A diocese was established at Gardar in the Eastern Settlement about 1125, and the great barns and byres that surround the cathedral complex are evidence of the importance of the church in the life of the colony. These stored the tithes – paid in the form of agricultural produce and walrus ivory – that the resident Norwegian bishop levied from his parishioners. The tiny colony on the very edge of the known world was thus incorporated into the organizational structure of the Catholic church. In 1260 Greenland followed the example of Iceland and formally submitted to the Norwegian king, bringing a greater degree of interference into Greenland's affairs, and reinforcing its integral part in Europe's trading and political networks. The central role played by the church is clearly visible in the

*Above* An episcopal seat was established at Gardar, in the Eastern Settlement, following the consecration in Lund of a bishop for Greenland in about 1125. A flagged pathway led to the door of the bishop's residence, which was adjacent to the cathedral, as well as to his byres and barns.

*Left* On the bare top of the island of Kingigtorssuaq, off the west coast of Greenland (at almost 73° North), are the collapsed remains of three small cairns, or piles of rock, erected by three 14th-century Norsemen who also left behind them this runic inscription on a piece of slate no more than 10 centimeters long. It ends with six cryptic runes that have never been satisfactorily interpreted, though it has been suggested that they might indicate the year, which could be 1333.

*Below* This caped hood of woolen cloth with its liripipe, or exaggerated tail, was found wrapped around the feet of a skeleton in the churchyard at Herjolfsnes, in the Eastern Settlement. Its distinctive design shows that the Late Norse Greenlanders were well aware of the 14th-century European fashions in dress – as they continued to be through the 15th century, despite their geographical remoteness and increasing isolation.

archaeological record. Apart from the cathedral complex at Gardar, 17 churches are known in the Eastern Settlement alone. Several of them were obviously finely constructed stone buildings, similar in structure to the churches that were built in Norway at the time.

It is a Norwegian priest serving in Greenland about 1350, Ivar Bardarson – the source of much of our detailed knowledge about affairs in Greenland – who first tells us of the desertion of the Western Settlement at this time. As climatic conditions intensified in severity with the onset of what meteorologists have termed a "Little Ice Age", life had become untenable for the settlers in this far northern outpost, already living on the margins of existence. Excavation of a settlement site at Nipaitsoq in the Western Settlement, where occupation ended about 1350, gives us a vivid picture of the conditions under which it was abandoned: the last occupants had obviously hung on until the last cow and calf, and even the dogs too, had been killed and eaten.

Before the worsening conditions and the increase in pack ice made such journeys dangerous it seems likely that a tenuous presence was maintained in the Arctic

areas between Greenland and North America for some time after the abandonment of the Vinland colony. There certainly seems to have been a gradual expansion from the Western Settlement up the Greenland coast to Disko Island and Upernavik, and the recovery of items such as a number of small wooden figures in "European" dress, found on Baffin Island on a Thule Eskimo site of the 13th century, suggests there was some form of contact across the Davis Strait. This is supported by a scattering of metal objects, including a fragment of mail armor, that have been found in the Canadian Arctic.

It is likely that such objects were acquired when the Inuit came into sporadic contact with the Norse on long-distance hunting trips rather than in the course of regular trading. With the deterioration in the climate these trips would obviously have become fewer and less enterprising. Nevertheless there is evidence that the Norse were still venturing into the *Norðrseta*, the northern hunting grounds of Greenland, as late as the 14th century. A runic inscription found at Kingigtorssuaq, virtually at latitude 73° North, records that three Norsemen were there at the end of April, presumably having overwintered at the site. It may be that desperation had driven them this far north as the struggle for survival forced them into direct competition with Inuit hunter–gatherers, who were themselves moving farther south in search of food resources.

During the "Little Ice Age", Greenland experienced a cooling of at least 2° Celsius. This would have had the effect of extending the southern limit of the Arctic pack ice and increasing the incidence of huge icebergs in the seas around Greenland. As a result of these hazards the European traders who worked the Atlantic waters – by the 14th century they came mainly from English ports rather than those of western Norway or the Baltic – were persuaded to look elsewhere for fur and ivory. The bishops appointed to Gardar became increasingly reluctant to visit their far-flung diocese. Isolated, short of essential supplies of iron, timber and grain, the Greenland colony gradually faded away. We know almost nothing about its last, lingering years, or even when it finally came to an end. A surviving scrap of information tells us that in 1406 a party of Icelanders was blown off course to Greenland and remained there for four years (probably because of pack ice) before returning to Iceland. After this the written record stutters to a close.

Archaeology provides a little more information. A rare insight into the end of the Greenland colony comes from the excavation of the graveyard and buildings of Bjarni Herjolfsson's family farm at Herjolfsnes. Permafrost conditions have preserved the burial clothes of its last inhabitants in an excellent state. Some items are worn and patched, but some of the bodies were wearing the distinctive long, tapering liripipe hoods that were at the height of European fashion in the 14th century. Much can be learnt from comparing the woolen garments of the people buried at Herjolfsnes with the clothing found on a near-contemporary Inuit site at Qilakitsoq. The bodies here were dressed in furs and hide. Thus the archaeological record hints at one of the reasons why the Norse settlement collapsed. It was quite simply a question of the survival of the fittest. Unlike the indigenous Inuit, the Norse inhabitants of Greenland failed to adapt to changing conditions and so the most remote of the settlements in the west was finally extinguished, bringing a lingering end to the world of the Vikings.

# GLOSSARY

**Abbasids** An Arab dynasty of caliphs (rulers) descended from al-Abbas, uncle of the Prophet Muhammad. It supplanted that of the UMAYYADS in AD 749 and was based in Baghdad until 1258 when it was sacked by the Mongols in 1258.
**Althing** The national assembly of Icelanders who met annually, for two weeks, in the open air at Thingvellir.
**Angles** A GERMANIC people from the Danish peninsula of Jutland who, with the Saxons, formed the majority of the settlers who came to Britain in the 5th century AD, following the Roman withdrawal. They gave their name to England, its people and their language.
**Anglo-Saxon** A general term describing the majority of the GERMANIC settlers in Britain, derived from the two main groups who migrated from the European continent – the Angles and the Saxons. It is most often used chronologically, for the period from the first Germanic invasions in the 5th century AD until the Norman Conquest in 1066, but also for the language of the Anglo-Saxons in England (also known as Old English).
**Anglo-Saxon Chronicle** A compilation of annals (or yearly entries of events), begun during the reign of King Alfred the Great (871–99) and continued thereafter, that provides the major historical source for Viking military activity in England.
**Anglo-Scandinavian** A term used following the 9th-century Scandinavian settlement in England of the resultant cultural mixture (eg. Anglo-Scandinavian art).
**Asgard** The stronghold of the gods in NORSE mythology.
***Æsir*** A race of NORSE gods that includes both Odin and Thor.

**bere** (or bear) The original English name for barley, retained for 6- or 4-row barley (the number of vertical rows of grains up the ear), which is coarser and hardier than ordinary 2-row barley and was thus better suited for growing in the north.
**Black Earth** An area of distinctive soil coloration resulting from intensive human settlement activity, as at the Viking town of Birka in Sweden.
**bog sacrifice** Name given to human bodies, animals and artifacts, chiefly weapons, found deliberately deposited in peat bogs and other watery places, most notably in Denmark, but also elsewhere in northwestern Europe.
**bracteate** A disk-shaped pendant of thin metal, resembling a coin or medal.
**broch** A circular tower-like building of dry-stone, found in northern and western Scotland, including the islands, that originated in the mid 1st millennium BC. Most brochs, however, seem to date from around the beginning of the Christian era.
**Bronze Age** The period in the Old World during which bronze (an alloy of copper and tin) provided the main material for the manufacture of tools and weapons. The dates for the Bronze Age vary from area to area, but for Europe in general it conventionally comprises the period from about 2000–700 BC.
***burh*** Any ANGLO-SAXON fortification, but the term is more normally used for the defended settlements built by King Alfred and his successors against the Danes.
**Byzantine empire** The eastern half of the Roman empire, based on Byzantium (later Constantinople, now Istanbul), an ancient Greek settlement on the European side of the Bosporus. It was inaugurated in AD 330 by the Emperor Constantine and survived the collapse of the Western empire until overrun by the Ottoman Turks in 1453. The Eastern Christian empire preserved much of Greek and Roman culture, whilst introducing eastern ideas to the west.

**Carbon-14 (or radiocarbon) dating** Carbon-14 is a radioactive isotope produced in the atmosphere that is continuously being absorbed by all living things, but when a plant or animal dies its intake ceases and the carbon-14 steadily declines according to a known rate. It is possible to measure the remnant carbon-14 in organic matter such as wood and bone and thus calculate how long ago death took place. There are uncertainties involved in making such measurements and thus radiocarbon dates are quoted with a plus-or-minus factor or probable error that limits their use in the medieval period.
**Carolingians** The ruling dynasty that replaced the Merovingians when Pepin II became king of the FRANKS in AD 751. The Carolingian empire, which was the creation of Charlemagne (or Charles the Great), king of the Franks (771–814) and Emperor of the West (800–14), included much of the former territory of the Western Roman empire, stretching from the North Sea to Italy; it was divided into three parts in 843, but soon fell apart. In general cultural terms, "Carolingian" is used for the period c.750–c.900 in western Europe.
**Celt/Celtic** Term used in language studies for a once widespread group of Indo-European languages, including in northwestern Europe both Irish and Scots Gaelic, as well as Welsh, Manx, Cornish and Breton – hence of the peoples speaking these languages, their art and culture.
**crannog** An artificial island for a wooden house built in or beside a lake, in Ireland and Scotland; they have prehistoric origins, but were also in use in the medieval period.
**crozier** The crook or pastoral staff of a bishop or abbot.

***Danegeld*** Tribute paid to the Danish invaders by their victims in western Europe, especially England, to buy off further attacks.
**Danelaw** The name that came to be given to that part of England settled by the Danes in the late 9th century AD, following its partition in the 880s by Alfred and Guthrum, which was thus affected by Danish custom and culture. The maximum area of Danish dominance consisted of the area to the north and east of Watling Street, the Roman road that ran from London to Chester.
**Danevirke** A multiperiod series of earthen ramparts that cut across the base of the Jutland peninsula, forming the southern boundary of Viking Age Denmark (now in Germany). Timbers in its construction have been dated by TREE-RING DATING to about AD 737; recent research suggests they were replacement timbers, and its first building phase may be assumed to have been still earlier. The total length of its various ramparts is about 30 kilometers.
**dendrochronology**: see TREE-RING DATING
***dróttkvætt*** ("court meter") An elaborate verse form much used by the skalds, the professional poets of Viking Age Scandinavia.

***ealdorman*** An ANGLO-SAXON noble or man of high rank who was an administrative official.
**earl** An English title of nobility (*eorl*), derived in the Viking Age from the Old NORSE *jarl*, a royal official or an under-king.
**Edda** The name of two collections of Old NORSE literature: the *Elder* (or *Poetic*) *Edda* consists of early poetry on mythological and heroic themes, some of Viking Age date, whereas the *Prose* (or *Younger*) *Edda* is a handbook for aspiring poets assembled by the Icelandic poet and historian Snorri Sturluson, perhaps in the 1220s.

**filigree** A technique for decorating gold and silver jewelry with fine wires, both plain and beaded, which are soldered to the surface of the ornament – often used in combination with GRANULATION.
**Five Boroughs** The territory of the Five Boroughs (Lincoln, Nottingham, Derby, Leicester and Stamford) comprised the central part of the DANELAW area of England.
**Franks** A GERMANIC tribe originally settled to the east of the Rhine, who expanded west from the later 3rd century AD. The Frankish kingdom was increased in size by Clovis (481–511) to occupy much of Roman Gaul, but reached its greatest extent under Charlemagne (see CAROLINGIANS). They gave their name to Frankia, and thus to France.
**Frisians** The inhabitants of the North Sea coastal plain and islands between the Rhineland and the Elbe (Frisia), who were renowned merchants in the 8th century AD. Their important trading center at Dorestad became a target for Viking raids. Frisia was absorbed into the Frankish kingdom, its conquest being completed by Charlemagne.
**futhark** The runic alphabet, so named from its first six symbols.

**Germanic** The Germanic languages form one branch of Indo-European (see also CELTIC and SLAVIC), comprising two main groups: the Scandinavian languages of northern Europe, and – in western Europe – German, Frisian, Dutch and English. The term is extended to the peoples speaking these languages, and to their art and culture.
**goði** (pl. **goðar**) An Old NORSE word originally meaning a pagan "priest", but as Viking Age priests were secular leaders, it seems also to have been a title of rank.
**granulation** A technique of decorating gold and silver jewelry by soldering small spheres (granules) of metal onto it, often in conjunction with FILIGREE.

**Great Army** The *Anglo-Saxon Chronicle* describes the Danish armies of 865 and 871 as "great"; the latter eventually settled in Northumbria, Mercia and East Anglia (876–80), resulting in the establishment of what became known as the DANELAW.
**"gripping beast"** A stylized animal-motif with gripping paws that was popular in the Oseberg and Borre styles of Viking art; its origins lie in the 8th-century Broa style.

**hacksilver** The fragments of ornaments and ingots that form a major part of many Viking silver HOARDS, having been deliberately cut up in order to be weighed out for the purpose of making payments, before the use of coins as counted money.
**Hiberno-Norse** A term used following the 9th-century Scandinavian settlement in Ireland of the resultant cultural mixture (*Hibernia* being the Latin name for Ireland).
***hnefatafl*** The Old NORSE name for a board-game played throughout Scandinavia during the Viking Age; the rules are not recorded, but it was a form of wargame, requiring skill, for two players.
**hoard** The term used for any collection of objects buried usually at one time, whether as a votive offering (cf. BOG SACRIFICE) or for safety at a time of threat (as was the case with most Viking silver hoards). The deposition dates of hoards containing coins can normally be estimated from them and thus hoards form a particularly useful source of evidence for both commercial and military activity during the Viking Age.
**hogback** A form of house-shaped tombstone, with a curved ridge, which originated in the areas of Scandinavian settlement in northern England in the 10th century.

**inhumation** The practice of burying the dead – as opposed to the cremation or exposure of a corpse.
**interlace** Ornament that consists of twisted and plaited ribbons forming geometric patterns, or of intertwined strands extending from animal and plant motifs.
**Iron Age** The period during which iron formed the main material for making tools and weapons (following on from the BRONZE AGE). In Europe this began during the earlier 1st millennium BC and is generally taken to end with the expansion of the Romans, although outside the empire (as in Scandinavia) the term continues to be used until the MIGRATION PERIOD of the 5th and 6th centuries AD, or even later.

***jarl***: see EARL

**keeill** A small chapel on the Isle of Man. There are over 170; the majority appear to date to the period of the NORSE adoption of Christianity (from the mid 10th century onwards).

***landnám*** The Old NORSE term for land-taking or settlement.
**Lawspeaker** The Scandinavian regional THING (assembly) seems to have been presided over by an office-bearer known as the "lawspeaker". In the case of the ALTHING, Iceland's national assembly, it is known that the Lawspeaker was an elected official who held his paid office for three years in the first instance.
**long-branch** One of the two main versions of the Scandinavian runic alphabet (cf. SHORT-TWIG) used during the Viking Age; sometimes called Danish RUNES.
**longhouse** This term is properly applied to an oblong building incorporating a dwelling and a byre under the same roof, the two halves generally being separated by a cross-passage. The byre was for housing cattle during the winter, while providing warmth for the human inhabitants.
***longphort*** The term used in 9th-century Ireland for the first winter-bases of the Vikings, which took the form of shore forts for the protection of their ships.

**Migration Period** The period of large-scale movement of peoples during the 5th and 6th centuries AD (including the ANGLO-SAXON settlement of England). These are associated with the collapse of the Roman empire, though the GERMANIC migrations had in fact started earlier.

**Neolithic** Meaning the New Stone Age, the term used for the period following the Mesolithic that was marked by the introduction of a farming economy, with the use of ground and polished stone tools, as well as of pottery. It is widely used, but refers to different periods in different areas (beginning c.4000 BC in southern Scandinavia).
***Norðreyar*** The Old NORSE name (meaning the North Isles) applied to the Orkneys and Shetlands – the Northern Isles of Scotland.
***Norðrseta*** (anglicized as Nordsetur) The Northern Encampments, or hunting grounds, to the north of the Western Settlement in Greenland, where the Greenlanders went for seals, caribou and polar bears, and for the ivory tusks of walrus and narwhal.
**Norse** The Viking Age language of Scandinavia is loosely known as Old Norse and so this term has become widely applied, though strictly speaking it refers to Norway. However, differences did exist: West Norse was spoken in Norway (and Iceland), and East Norse in Denmark and Sweden, with further differences developing between the latter during the Viking period.

**ogham** A writing system invented by the Irish about the 4th century AD, but later used also by the PICTS. The letters consist of groups of parallel straight lines cut to and across a base line – in Ireland (and Wales) usually the vertical corner of a stone monument.

***papar*** The name given to the Irish Christian hermits living in Iceland when the Vikings arrived, which survives there in such place-names as Papey, but also on the Faeroe Islands, the Orkneys and Shetlands.
**passage grave** One of the main categories of megalithic tomb (made of large stone slabs) found in prehistoric Europe in which there is a separate entrance passage leading up to the funerary chamber; they are generally covered with round barrows (mounds).
**patrice** A jeweler's die with a raised pattern used to impress either a gold or silver foil before embellishment with FILIGREE, or a clay mold for casting ornamental metalwork.
**pattern-welding** A technique particularly used by swordsmiths for producing blades that were both strong and decorative. Strips of metal of varying hardness and color (sometimes twisted) were welded together and hammered out so as to produce a blade with a patterned appearance. The finest examples have been attributed to FRANKISH workshops.
**penannular** Almost annular (ie. a not fully complete ring); in the Viking Age the term is used of a type of brooch that has a gap in its hoop through which the pin is passed to fix it in place, as also in connection with RING-MONEY.
**Picts** The native inhabitants of Scotland, north of a line between the Forth and the Clyde, who are first mentioned in Roman sources in the late 3rd century AD (as the *Picti*), though they must have been well established before this date. In the mid 9th century they were absorbed by the SCOTS who had migrated from Ireland into western Scotland during the 5th century AD.
**picture-stone** The term used for the unique series of engraved memorial stones (*bildstenar*) that were raised on the Baltic island of Gotland between the 5th and the 11th centuries AD.
**portage** The overland transport of ships between navigable waters.
**posthole** The pit dug into the ground to hold the base of a timber post. After the post has rotted away, the posthole is archaeologically recognizable from the shadow of the rotted wood, surrounded by its associated packing material. A pattern of postholes may provide the only evidence for the size and shape of houses and other wooden structures. The American term for posthole is "postmold".

**Ragnarök** In NORSE mythology, the final day when the gods will be defeated by monsters and giants and the world consumed by fire.
**reliquary** The container in which the relics of a saint or other holy person are kept.
**ring-money** Plain silver arm-rings, PENANNULAR in form, used by weight as a form of currency.
**Romanesque** The term (suggesting a link with the Roman style) used since the 19th century for the style of architecture and art that was at its height during the 12th century.
**runes** The characters of a GERMANIC script consisting of straight lines designed for incising into wood or stone.
**rune-stone** A stone incised with an inscription in RUNES.
***Rús*** The name given to the Scandinavians who ventured and settled in the east – and the origin of Russia (the land of the *Rús*).

**saga** The name given to medieval Icelandic or Scandinavian prose narratives, both fact and fiction, including stories of life in the Viking Age.
**sceat** (pl. *sceattas*) A small silver coin minted in southern England and in Frisia during the 8th century AD, originating in the late 7th.

**Scots** A people (the *Scotti*) from northeast Ireland who established themselves in western Scotland in the 5th century AD, at the expense of the PICTS, forming the kingdom of Dalriada. In the mid 9th century they absorbed the kingdom of the PICTS and hence gave their name to Scotland.
**shieling** A summer pasture to which livestock are driven – and the associated huts or temporary accommodation for seasonal use.
**short-twig** One of the two main versions of the Scandinavian runic alphabet (cf. LONG-BRANCH) in use during the Viking Age; sometimes called Swedo-Norwegian or common RUNES.
**skald** The Old NORSE word for a poet; skalds were professional court poets who composed and recited complex poetry from memory during the Viking Age.
**Slavs** The peoples of central and eastern Europe speaking the Slavic group of Indo-European languages, who emerged in the 1st millennium AD.
**Stamford ware** An ANGLO-SAXON pottery industry centered around Stamford in Lincolnshire that produced well-made glazed ceramics. They were much in demand in the 9th to 13th centuries and were sometimes traded abroad.
**stave church** A church built of wooden staves, consisting of split logs either set directly into the ground or into a wooden sill (horizontal beam).
**stone setting** A setting of stones marking out a grave, known in various shapes, including ships.
***Suðreyjar*** The NORSE name (meaning the South Isles) given to the Hebrides – the Western Isles of Scotland – as seen from Norway. It survives in the name of the bishopric of Sodor and Man.
**Svear** The people of central Sweden who were to give their name to the country. Little is known about their political history in the Viking Age.

**tephra** Solid material ejected during a volcanic eruption.
***tesseræ*** The small pieces of glass (or marble, etc.) of which a mosaic is made.
**Thing** The Old NORSE term for an assembly (see also ALTHING).
**tree-ring dating** (dendrochronology) The age of trees can be calculated by counting their annual growth rings, which vary in size according to the weather. These variations allow correlation of the tree-ring patterns between old trees, dead trees and timber from archaeological sites so that a continuous sequence can be built up. Under ideal conditions of timber preservation, it has become possible to date precisely wooden structures from the Viking Age.
**trepanning** The surgical removal of a small piece of bone from the skull.

**Umayyads** The first dynasty of Arab leaders (caliphs), descended from a Meccan merchant who had submitted to the Prophet Muhammad. The Umayyads seized power in the 7th century AD, but were supplanted by the ABBASIDS in 749.

**Valholl** The great hall in ASGARD of the NORSE god Odin where lived an army of heroes killed in battle, ready to defend the gods at RAGNARÖK.
**valkyrie** The war-maidens of NORSE myth who conducted dead heroes from the battlefield to VALHOLL.
***Vanir*** A group of NORSE gods – the deities of wealth, fertility and physical delight: Niord and his son and daughter Freyr and Freyia.
**Varangian guard** The Scandinavian bodyguard of the later BYZANTINE emperors.
**Vendel Period** A term applied to the 7th and 8th centuries AD in Scandinavia, being the last phase of the IRON AGE before the Viking Age; it takes its name from a site in central Sweden with rich burials.
**Viking** The Old NORSE term often used in general of the peoples of Scandinavia – and of Scandinavian origin – during the Viking Age, but *Víkingr* strictly meant a seaborne raider or pirate.
**Viking Age** The period of Scandinavian history from the 9th to 11th centuries AD that begins with the first Viking raids on western Europe at the end of the 8th century.
**Vinland** The Old NORSE name, *Vínland* (meaning Wineland), given to the region of North America where the Norsemen are said to have found grapes and wheat growing wild.

**wattle-and-daub** Intertwined boughs (wattle) plastered with clay or mud (daub) used as walling material.
**whorl** A circular object with a central perforation used to weight the end of a spindle and act as a fly wheel, giving momentum to its rotation while spinning thread.

# BIBLIOGRAPHY

The first section of this list consists of general works, in English, covering most aspects of the Viking Age in Scandinavia and overseas. Many of these books have extensive bibliographies that will guide the reader to such works in other languages, as well as to specialist studies. (It is worth noting that it is common for academic publications in the Scandinavian languages to be accompanied by summaries in English or German.) Subsequent sections consist of selected suggestions for further reading on particular themes and individual topics; this has also been restricted, for the most part, to works in English.


**The Vikings: general works**

B. Almgren et al, *The Viking*, Gothenburg, 1967.
H. Arbman, *The Vikings*, London, 1961, rev. 1962; Boulder, 1961.
P. G. Foote and D. M. Wilson, *The Viking Achievement*, London, 1970, rev. 1980; New York, 1970.
J. Graham-Campbell, *Viking Artefacts: A Select Catalogue*, London, 1980.
J. Graham-Campbell, *The Viking World*, London, 1980, rev. 1989; New Haven, New York, 1980.
J. Graham-Campbell and D. Kidd, *The Vikings*, London, New York, 1980.
J. Jesch, *Women in the Viking Age*, Woodbridge, 1991.
G. Jones, *A History of the Vikings*, Oxford, New York, 1968, rev. 1984.
M. Magnusson, *Vikings!*, London, 1980.
P. Pulsiano and K. Wolf (eds), *Medieval Scandinavia: An Encyclopedia*, Hamden, 1992.
E. Roesdahl, *The Vikings*, London, 1991, rev. 1992.
E. Roesdahl and D. M. Wilson (eds), *From Viking to Crusader: Scandinavia and Europe 800–1200*, Copenhagen, 1992.
P. H. Sawyer, *The Age of the Vikings*, London, 1962, rev. 1971.
P. H. Sawyer, *Kings and Vikings: Scandinavia and Europe AD 700–1100*, London, New York, 1982.
D. M. Wilson, *The Vikings and their Origins*, London, 1970, rev. 1980.
D. M. Wilson (ed), *The Northern World: The History and Heritage of Northern Europe AD 400–1100*, London, 1980.

**The Scandinavian Background: Chapters One and Two**

K. Borg et al (eds), *Eketorp: Fortification and Settlement on Öland/Sweden*, Stockholm, 1976.
J. G. D. Clark, *The Earlier Stone Age Settlement of Scandinavia*, Cambridge, 1975.
H. R. Ellis Davidson, *Pagan Scandinavia*, London, 1967.
P. V. Glob, *The Bog People: Iron-Age Man Preserved*, London, 1969.
A. Hagen, *Norway*, London, 1967.
L. Hedeager, *Iron-Age Societies: from Tribe to State in Northern Europe 500 BC to AD 700*, Oxford, Cambridge MA, 1992.
W. Holmqvist, *Germanic Art during the First Millennium AD*, Stockholm, 1955.
J. Jensen, *The Prehistory of Denmark*, London, New York, 1982.
E. Kivikoski, *Finland*, London, New York, 1967.
K. Kristiansen (ed), *Settlement and Economy in later Scandinavian Prehistory*, Oxford, 1984.
J. P. Lamm and H.-Å. Nordström, *Vendel Period Studies*, Stockholm, 1983.
A. Lundström (ed), *Thirteen Studies on Helgö*, Stockholm, 1988.
T. Sjøvold, *The Iron Age Settlement of Arctic Norway*, vol. 1, Tromsø, 1962.
M. Stenberger, *Sweden*, London, New York, 1963.
M. Stenberger and O. Klindt-Jensen, *Vallhagar: A Migration Period Settlement on Gotland, Sweden*, Stockholm, 1955.

**Daily Life and State Formation in Viking Age Scandinavia: Chapters Three, Four and Eleven**

P. Anker, *The Art of Scandinavia*, vol. 1, London, New York, 1970.
J. Brøndsted, "Danish inhumation graves of the Viking Age", *Acta Archaeologica* 7, Copenhagen, 1936.
A. Bugge, *Norwegian Stave-churches*, Oslo, 1953.
G. Bugge, *Stave-churches in Norway*, Oslo, 1983.
O. Crumlin-Pedersen (ed), *Aspects of Maritime Scandinavia AD 200–1200*, Roskilde, 1990.
O. Crumlin-Pedersen and M. Winner (eds), *Sailing into the Past*, Roskilde, 1986.
A.-S. Gräslund, *Birka IV: The Burial Customs. A Study of the Graves on Björkö*, Stockholm, 1980.
K. Krogh, "The royal Viking-age monuments of Jelling in the light of recent archaeological investigations: a preliminary report", *Acta Archaeologica* 53, Copenhagen, 1982.
E. Nylén and J. P. Lamm, *Stones, Ships and Symbols: The Picture Stones of Gotland from the Viking Age and Before*, Stockholm, 1988.
O. Olsen and O. Crumlin-Pedersen, *Five Viking Ships from Roskilde Fjord*, Copenhagen, 1978.
T. Ramskou, "Viking age cremation graves in Denmark", *Acta Archaeologica* 21, Copenhagen, 1950.
K. Randsborg, *The Viking Age in Denmark*, London, 1980.
E. Roesdahl, "Aggersborg in the Viking Age", *Proceedings of the Eighth Viking Congress* (ed H. Bekker-Nielsen *et al.*), Odense, 1981.
E. Roesdahl, *Viking Age Denmark*, London, 1982.
E. Roesdahl, "The Danish geometrical Viking fortresses in their context", *Anglo-Norman Studies* 9, 1987.
E. Roesdahl, "Prestige, display and monuments in Viking Age Scandinavia", *Les Mondes Normands (VIIIe – XIIe s.)* (ed H. Galinié), Caen, 1989.
E. Roesdahl, "Princely burial in Scandinavia at the time of the Conversion", *Voyage to the Other World. The Legacy of Sutton Hoo* (eds C. B. Kendall and P. S. Wells), Minneapolis, 1992.
P. Sawyer, *The Making of Sweden*, Alingsås, 1988.
T. Sjøvold, *The Iron Age Settlement of Arctic Norway*, vol. 2, Tromsø, 1974.
K. Skaare, *Coins and Coinage in Viking-Age Norway*, Oslo, 1976.

**Towns, Trade and Crafts: Chapter Five**

B. Ambrosiani and H. Clarke (eds), *Investigations into the Black Earth*, vol 1 (= *Birka Studies* 1), Stockholm, 1992.
K. Ambrosiani, *Viking Age Combs, Comb Making and Comb Makers in the Light of Finds from Birka and Ribe*, Stockholm, 1981.
P. Anker, *The Art of Scandinavia*, vol. 1, London, New York, 1970.
G. Arwidsson and G. Berg, *The Mästermyr Find: A Viking Age Tool Chest from Gotland*, Stockholm, 1983.
H. Clarke (ed.), *Iron and Man in Prehistoric Sweden*, Stockholm, 1979.
H. Clarke and B. Ambrosiani, *Towns in the Viking Age*, Leicester, 1991.
W. Duczko, *Birka V: The Filigree and Granulation Work of the Viking Period*, Stockholm, 1985.
E. Fridstrøm, "The Viking Age woodcarvers: their tools and techniques", *Universitetets Oldsaksamlings Skrifter* 5, Oslo, 1985.
B. Hårdh, "Trade and money in Scandinavia in the Viking Age", *Meddelanden från Lunds Universitets Historiska Museum*, 1977–78.
A. E. Herteig et al, *Archaeological Contributions to the Early History of Urban Communities in Norway*, Oslo, 1975.
S. Jensen, *The Vikings of Ribe*, Ribe, 1991.
S. O. Lindquist (ed), *Society and Trade in the Baltic during the Viking Age*, Visby, 1985.
N. Lund (ed), *Two Voyagers at the Court of King Alfred*, York, 1984.
H. B. Madsen, "Metalcasting: techniques, production and workshops", *Ribe Excavations 1970–76* (ed M. Bencard), Esbjerg, 1984.
D. M. Wilson and O. Klindt-Jensen, *Viking Art*, London, Ithaca, 1966; Minneapolis, rev. 1980.

**Learning and Religion: Chapter Six**

W. H. Auden and P. B. Taylor (trans), *Norse Poems*, London, 1981.
C. J. Clover and J. Lindow, *Old-Norse Icelandic Literature: A Critical Guide*, Ithaca, 1985.
H. R. Ellis-Davidson, *Gods and Myths of Northern Europe*, London 1964, New York, 1965.
H. R. Ellis-Davidson, *Scandinavian Mythology*, Feltham, 1969.
A. Faulkes (trans), *Snorri Sturluson: Edda*, London, Melbourne, 1987.
E. Haugen, *The Scandinavian Languages: An Introduction to their History*, London, 1976.
L. M. Hollander (trans), *Heimskringla: History of the Kings of Norway*, Austin, 1964.
S. B. F. Jansson, *Runes in Sweden*, Stockholm, 1987.
J. Kristjánsson, *Eddas and Sagas*, Reykjavik, 1988.
E. Moltke, *Runes and their Origin: Denmark and Elsewhere*, Copenhagen, 1985.
L. Musset, *Introduction à la runologie*, Paris, 1965, rev. 1976.
R. I. Page, *Runes*, London, 1987.
R. I. Page, *Norse Myths*, London, 1990.
B. Sawyer *et al* (eds), *The Christianization of Scandinavia*, Alingsås, 1987.
G. Steinsland and P. Meulengracht Sørensen, *Viking Age Man*, Oslo, 1992.
E. O. G. Turville-Petre, *Myth and Religion of the North: The Religion of Ancient Scandinavia*, London, 1964, Westport, 1975.
E. O. G. Turville-Petre, *Scaldic Poetry*, Oxford, New York, 1976.

**The Viking Age in England and Western Europe: Chapters Seven and Eleven**

R. N. Bailey, *Viking Age Sculpture in Northern England*, London, 1980.
D. Bates, *Normandy before 1066*, London, 1982.
J. Campbell (ed), *The Anglo-Saxons*, London, 1982. G. Fellows-Jensen, "Scandinavian place-names and Viking settlement in Normandy: a review", *Namn och Bygd* 76, Uppsala, 1988.
G. Fellows-Jensen, "Anglo-Saxons and Vikings in the British Isles: the place-name evidence", *Angli e Sassoni al de qua e al di là del mare* (= *Settimane di Studio* 32), Spoleto, 1986.

G. Fellows-Jensen, "Scandinavian influence on the place-names of England", *Language Contact in the British Isles* (eds P. S. Ureland and G. Broderick), Tübingen, 1991.
S. H. Fuglesang, "The relationship between Scandinavian and English art from the late eighth to the mid-twelfth century", *Sources of Anglo-Saxon Culture* (ed P. E. Szarmach), Kalamazoo MI, 1986.
J. Graham-Campbell, "The archaeology of the Danelaw: an introduction", *Les Mondes Normands (VIIIe – XIIe s.)* (ed H. Galinié), Caen, 1989.
R. A. Hall, *The Viking Dig: The Excavations in York*, York, 1984.
R. A. Hall, *Viking Age Archaeology in Britain and Ireland*, Princes Risborough, 1990.
D. Hill, *An Atlas of Anglo-Saxon England*, London, 1981, rev. 1984.
J. T. Lang, "The hogback: a Viking colonial monument", *Anglo-Saxon Studies in Art and Archaeology* 3, Oxford, 1984.
R. McKitterick, *The Frankish Kingdoms under the Carolingians, 751–987*, London, 1983.
N. S. Price, *The Vikings in Brittany* (= *Saga-Book* 22:6), London, 1989.
J. Renaud, *Les Vikings et la Normandie*, Rennes, 1989.
E. Roesdahl *et al* (eds), *The Vikings in England*, London, 1981.
J. D. Richards, *Viking Age England*, London, 1991.
F. R. Stenton, *Anglo-Saxon England*, London, New York, rev. 1971.
D. Whitelock (ed), *English Historical Documents, c. 500–1042*, vol. 1, London, 1955, rev. 1971.
D. M. Wilson (ed), *The Archaeology of Anglo-Saxon England*, London, 1976.
D. M. Wilson, *The Bayeux Tapestry*, London, 1985.

**The Viking Age and Late Norse Period in the Celtic World: Chapters Eight and Eleven**

B. Almqvist and D. Greene (eds), *Proceedings of the Seventh Viking Congress: Dublin*, Dublin, 1976.
C. E. Batey, *Freswick Links, Caithness: A Re-appraisal of the Late Norse Site in its Context*, Oxford, 1987.
C. E. Batey *et al* (eds), *The Viking Age in Caithness, Orkney and the North Atlantic*, Edinburgh, 1993.
G. Bersu and D. M. Wilson, *Three Viking Graves on the Isle of Man*, London, 1966.
J. Bradley, "The interpretation of Scandinavian settlement in Ireland", *Settlement and Society in Medieval Ireland: Studies presented to F. X. Martin o.s.a.* (ed J. Bradley), Kilkenny, 1988.
B. Crawford, *Scandinavian Scotland*, Leicester, 1987.
C. L. Curle, *Pictish and Norse Finds from the Brough of Birsay 1934–74*, Edinburgh, 1982.
W. Davies, *Wales in the Early Middle Ages*, Leicester, 1982.
C. E. Fell *et al* (eds), *The Viking Age in the Isle of Man*, London, 1983.
A. Fenton and H. Pálsson (eds), *The Northern and Western Isles in the Viking World: Survival, Continuity and Change*, Edinburgh, 1984.
D. Greene, "The evidence of language and place-names in Ireland", *The Vikings* (eds T. Andersson and K. I. Sandred), Uppsala, 1978.
J. R. C. Hamilton, *Excavations at Jarlshof, Shetland*, Edinburgh, 1956.
R. H. Kinvig, *The Isle of Man. A Social, Cultural and Political History*, rev. 1975.
H. R. Loyn, *The Vikings in Wales*, London, 1976.
C. D. Morris, "The Vikings in the British Isles: some aspects of their settlement and economy", *The Vikings* (ed R. T. Farrell), Chichester, 1982.
C. D. Morris, "Viking Orkney: a survey", *The Prehistory of Orkney* (ed C. Renfrew), Edinburgh, 1985.
W. H. F. Nicolaisen, *Scottish Place Names*, London, 1976.
D. Ó Corráin, *Ireland before the Normans*, Dublin, 1972.
H. Pálsson and P. Edwards (trans), *Orkneyinga Saga*, London, 1978.
A. Ritchie, *The Picts*, Edinburgh, 1989.
A. Ritchie, *Viking Scotland*, London, 1993.
P. Wallace, "The economy and commerce of Viking Age Dublin", *Untersuchungen zu Handel und Verkehr der vor- und frügeschichtlichen Zeit* 4 (eds K. Düvel *et al*), Göttingen, 1987.
P. Wallace, *The Viking Age Buildings of Dublin*, Dublin, 1993.
D. M. Wilson, *The Viking Age in the Isle of Man*, Odense, 1974.
D. M. Wilson, "Scandinavian settlement in the North and West of the British Isles: an archaeological point-of-view", *Transactions of the Royal Historical Society*, 5th series, 26, London, 1976.

**The Viking Age and Late Norse Period in the North Atlantic: Chapters Nine and Eleven**

C. E. Batey *et al* (eds), *The Viking Age in Caithness, Orkney and the North Atlantic*, Edinburgh, 1993.
G. F. Bigelow (ed), *The Norse in the North Atlantic* (= *Acta Archaeologica* 61), Copenhagen, 1990.
S. Dahl, "The Norse settlement of the Faroe Islands", *Medieval Archaeology* 14, London, 1970.
A. S. Ingstad, *The Discovery of a Norse Settlement in America: Excavations at L'Anse aux Meadows, Newfoundland, 1961–1968*, Oslo, 1977, rev. 1985 (as *The Norse Discovery of America*, vol. 1).
H. Ingstad, *The Norse Discovery of America*, vol. 2, Oslo, 1985.
G. Jones, *The Norse Atlantic Saga*, Oxford, New York, 1964, rev. 1986.
K. Krogh, *Viking Greenland*, Copenhagen, 1967.
M. Magnusson, *Iceland Saga*, London, 1987.
M. Magnusson and H. Pálsson (trans), *The Vinland Sagas*, London, New York, 1965.
C. D. Morris and D. J. Rackham (eds), *Settlement and Subsistence in the North Atlantic*, Glasgow, 1992.
V. Ö. Vilhjálmsson, "De ældste gårde på Island. Arkæologisk analyse af byggetraditioner og bosættelsesmønstre i landnamstidens Island", *Aarbøger for Nordisk Oldkyndighed og Historie*, forthcoming.
E. Wahlgren, *The Vikings and America*, London, 1986.
B. L. Wallace, "The Vikings in North America: myth and reality", *Social Approaches to Viking Studies* (ed R. Samson), Glasgow, 1991.

**The Viking Age in Russia and the East: Chapter Ten**

M. Brisbane (ed), *The Archaeology of Novgorod, Russia*, Woodbridge, 1992.
K. Hannestad *et al* (eds), *Varangian Problems* (= *Scando-Slavica*, Supplementum I), Copenhagen, 1970.
J. Herrmann, "The Northern Slavs", *The Northern World* (ed D. M. Wilson), London, 1980.
J. Herrmann (ed), *Wikinger und Slawen*, Berlin, 1982.
O. M. Ionnisyan, "Archaeological evidence for the development and urbanization of Kiev from the 8th to the 14th centuries", *From the Baltic to the Black Seas: Studies in Medieval Archaeology* (eds D. Austin and L. Alcock), London, 1990.
I. Jansson, "Communications between Scandinavia and Eastern Europe in the Viking Age", *Untersuchungen zu Handel und Verkehr der vor- und frügeschichtlichen Zeit* 4 (eds K. Düvel et al), Göttingen, 1987.
M. Müller-Wille (ed), *Oldenburg, Wolin, Staraja Ladoga, Novgorod, Kiev: Handelsverbindungen im südlichen und östlichen Ostseeraum während des frühen Mittelalters* (= *Bericht der Römisch-Germanischen Kommission* 69), Mainz, 1989.
T. S. Noonan, "The Vikings and Russia: some new directions and approaches to an old problem", *Social Approaches to Viking Studies* (ed R. Samson), Glasgow, 1991.
A. Stalsberg, "Scandinavian relations with north-western Russia during the Viking Age: the archaeological evidence", *Journal of Baltic Studies* 13:3, 1982.
R. Zeitler (ed), *Les Pays du Nord et Byzance*, Uppsala, 1981.

# LIST OF ILLUSTRATIONS

Abbreviations t = top, tl = top left, tr = top right, c = center, b = bottom etc.

**Key**
IoA Institute of Archaeology, London University; NMC National Museum of Denmark, Copenhagen; NMC2 National Museum of Denmark, Greenland Secretariat; RIKS Riksantikvarieämbetet, Stockholm; SHM Statens Historisk Museum, Stockholm; TS Ted Spiegel; UOO Universitetets Oldsaksamling, Oslo; WFA Werner Forman Archive, London; YAT York Archaeological Trust

*Endpapers*: reconstruction of Oseberg tapestry: UOO

All site plans drawn by John Brennan

Map acknowledgements: Primary source for map on page 167, A.C. Larsen, *Vikingetidsgårde i Nordatlanten*, Specialeafnandling til Magisterkonferens 1992, Institute of Prehistoric and Classical Archaeology, University of Copenhagen, unpublished, 1993. Primary source for map on page 173, V. orn Vilhjalmsson, *De aeldste garde pa Island*, Arkaeologisk analyse af byggetraditioner og bosaettelsesmonstre i landnamstidens Island, unpublished, 1993.

# GAZETTEER

An entry includes a descriptive term if it is a physical feature and the modern country name eg Jura (*isl*), (*UK*). An entry followed by an asterisk indicates a territorial unit eg a province, kingdom or region.

# INDEX

Figures in *italics* refer to map and illustration captions.

# S



# T



# U

# V



# W



# Y